Transitional Justice

ONE WEEK LOAN

# TRANSITIONAL ——— ——— JUSTICE

Ruti G. Teitel

**OXFORD**
UNIVERSITY PRESS

# OXFORD
## UNIVERSITY PRESS

Oxford   New York

Auckland   Bangkok   Buenos Aires   Cape Town   Chennai
Dar es Salaam   Delhi   Hong Kong   Istanbul   Karachi   Kolkata
Kuala Lumpur   Madrid   Melbourne   Mexico City   Mumbai   Nairobi
São Paulo   Shanghai   Singapore   Taipei   Tokyo   Toronto

and an associated company in Berlin

Library of Congress Cataloging-in-Publication Data
Teitel, Ruti G.
Transitional justice / Ruti G. Teitel.
p.   cm.
Includes index.
ISBN 978-0-19-510064-8; 978-0-19-515126-8 (pbk.)
1. Political crimes and offenses.   2. Justice and politics.
3. Ex post facto laws.   4. Constitutional law.   5. Social change.
6. Newly independent states.   7. World politics—1989–   I. Title.
K5250.T45   1999
320′.01′1—DC21      98-55948

Portions of the introduction of this book, shorter versions of chapters 1 and 6,
and an excerpt of chapter 2 were previously published as "Transitional
Jurisprudence: The Role of Law in Political Transformation" in
*Yale Law Journal* 106 (1997), 2009–2080, reprinted by permission of the
Yale Law Journal Company and Fred B. Rothman & Company.

Printed in the United States of America
on acid-free paper

For my parents

# Preface

$\mathcal{T}$his book project was inspired by the heady wave of liberalization at the end of the twentieth century. In the early 1980s, a debate emerged regarding the implications of "transitional justice" for states' liberalizing prospects. The question of "punishment or impunity," whether there is an obligation to punish in democratic transitions, was the subject of a policy meeting convened in 1990 at the Council on Foreign Relations in New York, for which I was invited to prepare the background discussion paper.[1] At the time, I concluded that, despite the moral argument for punishment in the abstract, various alternatives to punishment could express the normative message of political transformation and the rule of law, with the aim of furthering democracy.

With the collapse of the Soviet Union and the fall of the Berlin Wall, the question of transitional justice took on renewed urgency. Those of us who had been involved in the debates concerning the Latin American transitions participated in debates convened in East and Central Europe. There the debate over punishment broadened to include the implications of the sweeping decommunization measures pervasive in the region. In 1992, I received a grant from the U.S. Institute of Peace to begin this comparative project and to advise governments on the issues of justice in transitions. Participating in several conferences in the region helped shape the issues: "Political Justice and Transition to the Rule of Law in East Central Europe," sponsored by the University of Chicago and by the Central European University in Prague in 1991, and the Salzburg Conference titled "Justice in Times of Transition" in 1992, convened by the Foundation for a Civil Society. In 1993, at a conference, "Restitution in Eastern Europe," convened by the Central European University, I presented ideas that were later elaborated on in the chapter on reparatory justice. My ideas concerning the role of historical inquiry were shaped by a conference I helped organize at the Central European University, Budapest, in the fall of 1992, and elaborated on in a paper delivered at a conference convened in 1994 at Yale Law School titled "Deliberative Democracy and Human Rights." Further comparative aspects were explored at the Seventeenth Annual German Studies Association, where I presented "Justice in Transition in Unified Germany." Study of the postwar precedents was nurtured in numerous symposia I helped to convene over the years at Boston College Law School, under the auspices of the Holocaust–Human Rights Research Project, as well as at New York Law School.

I spent my sabbatical as Senior Schell Fellow at Yale Law School, where I taught a seminar on the book and benefited from discussions both inside and outside class.

Various portions of this book were presented at Yale Law School's Faculty Workshop, as well as workshops at Boston College Law School, Cardozo Law School, Columbia University Law School, University of Connecticut Law School, Cornell Law School, New York Law School, and University of Michigan Law School. Portions of the concluding chapter were presented at the New York University Political Theory Workshop. Portions of the constitutional justice chapter were discussed at the Georgetown University Law School Biennial Constitutional Law Discussion Group (1995). At the American Philosophical Association's Eastern Division meeting (1996), I was a participant on a panel entitled "Justice, Amnesties, and Truth-Tellings." Some of the issues in the criminal justice chapter were presented in an endowed lecture I was invited to give at the University of Frankfurt (January 1998). Portions of the criminal justice chapter concerning East Europe were presented at the American Association of International Law annual meeting (April 1998). Portions concerning criminal justice and clemency were presented at a workshop at the University of Edinburgh (June 1998).

Many colleagues and friends have been helpful in giving valuable comments, advice, and encouragement in this book project. First, my thanks to my editors at Oxford. My gratitude to Jack Balkin, Robert Burt, Paul Dubinsky, Stephen Ellmann, Owen Fiss, John Ferejohn, George Fletcher, Richard Friedman, Ryan Goodman, Robert Gordon, Derek Jinks, Paul Kahn, Harold Koh, Bill Lapiana, Larry Lessig, Klaus Lüderssen, Tim Lytton, Jack Rakove, Andrzej Rapacynski, Michel Rosenfeld, András Sajó, Marcelo Sancinetti, Peter Schuck, Tony Sebok, Richard Sherwin, Suzanne Stone, Ariel Teitel, and two anonymous reviewers. Special thanks to Zoe Hilden and Jonathan Stein for their very helpful advice and editorial suggestions. I am most grateful for the support of Dean Harry Wellington at my home institution, New York Law School, and Dean Anthony Kronman at Yale Law School. My thanks to a number of constitutional court justices for their generosity in contributing to my research: Vojtech Cepl, Lech Garlicki, Dieter Grimm, Richard Goldstone, and Laszlo Solyum. I am grateful to the students of human rights in transitional regimes at New York and Yale Law Schools for helpful discussion of many of the ideas here. I am indebted to Camille Broussard of the New York Law School Library and to research assistants at both New York and Yale Law Schools, including Dana Wolpert, Sabrina Bagdasarian, Federica Bisone, Jayni Edelstein, Jonathan Holub, Jessica LaMarche, Karen Owen, and Naveen Rahman, for help in the research of this book.

For their contribution to the researching of this book, I am grateful to Neil Kritz of the U.S. Institute of Peace, Dwight Semler and Ania Budziak of the University of Chicago's Center for Constitutionalism in East Europe, Holly Cartner of Human Rights Watch, Robert Weiner of the Lawyers Committee for Human Rights and Ariel Dulitsky of the Center for Justice and International Law. I am most grateful to Brenda Davis Lebron for word-processing assistance and to Belinda Cooper and Leszek Mitrus for translation assistance.

Financial support for the researching of this book was provided by the Ernst Stiefel Fund at New York Law School, a U.S. Institute of Peace grant awarded in 1992–1993 and by the Orville H. Schell, Jr., Center for International Human Rights at Yale Law School for 1995 and 1996.

Last, I am indebted to the late Owen M. Kupferschmid. Our many conversations about postwar justice and his loving encouragement inspired the beginnings of this project.

As this book was written over these last years, it recapitulates the breathtaking events of the end of the twentieth century. Yet, even as the writing draws to a close, the transitions continue; for example, South Africa's transition out of apartheid is still ongoing, and there are breakthroughs in Northern Ireland and elsewhere. These developments imply an inevitable incompleteness to the book. They also attest to the subject's relevance and vitality, at once humbling and a source of inspiration.

*New York City*                                                          R. G. T.
*December 1999*

# Contents

# Transitional Justice

# Introduction

*I*n recent decades, societies all over the world—throughout Latin America, East Europe, the former Soviet Union, Africa—have overthrown military dictatorships and totalitarian regimes for freedom and democracy. In these times of massive political movement from illiberal rule, one burning question recurs. How should societies deal with their evil pasts? This question leads to others that explore the question of the relation of the treatment of the state's past to its future. How is the social understanding behind a new regime committed to the rule of law created? Which legal acts have transformative significance? What, if any, is the relation between a state's response to its repressive past and its prospects for creating a liberal order? What is law's potential for ushering in liberalization?[1]

The question of the conception of justice in periods of political transition has not yet been fully addressed. Debates about "transitional justice" are generally framed by the normative proposition that various legal responses should be evaluated on the basis of their prospects for democracy.[2] In the prevailing debates about the relation of law and justice to liberalization, there are two generally competing ideas, the realists versus the idealists on the relation that law bears to democratic development. Either political change is thought necessarily to precede the establishment of the rule of law or, conversely, certain legal steps are deemed necessarily to precede political transition. The privileging of one developmental sequence or another derives either from disciplinary bias or from the generalization of particular national experiences to universal norms. So it is that in political theory the dominant account of how liberalizing transition occurs comprises a sequence in which political change comes first. On this account, a state's transitional responses are explained largely in terms of the relevant political and institutional constraints. Justice seeking in these periods is fully epiphenomenal and best explained in terms of the balance of power. Law is a mere product of political change. Political realists generally conflate the question of why a given state action is taken with that of

3

what response is possible.[3] Such theorizing clarifies why transitional justice is a vital issue in some countries but not in others.[4] The prevailing balance of power, structuring the "path" of the transition, is thought in turn to explain the legal response. However, to say that regimes will "do what they can" does not well explain the great diversity of transitional legal phenomena. Indeed, to contend that, as in the realist account, states do what is possible simply conflates the descriptive account with its normative conclusions.[5] The connections between a state's response to the transition and its prospects for liberalization remain largely unjustified.

From the idealist perspective, by contrast, the question of transitional justice generally falls back on universalist conceptions of justice.[6] Ideas of full retributive or corrective justice regarding the past are considered necessary precursors to liberal change. While, in the abstract, certain legal ideals may be thought necessary to liberal transition, such theorizing does not account well for the relation of law and political change. Ultimately, this approach misses what is distinctive about justice in times of transition.

The realist/idealist antinomy on justice in transition, like liberal/critical theorizing, divides on the relation of law and politics. Whereas in liberal theorizing, dominant in international law and politics,[7] law is commonly conceived as following idealist conceptions largely unaffected by political context,[8] critical legal theorizing, like the realist approach, emphasizes law's close relation to politics.[9] Again, neither liberal nor critical theorizing about the nature and role of law in ordinary times accounts well for law's role in periods of political change, missing the particular significance of justice claims in periods of radical political change and failing to explain the relation between normative responses to past injustice and a state's prospects for liberal transformation.

This book moves beyond prevailing theorizing to explore the role of the law in periods of radical political transformation. It suggests these legal responses play an extraordinary, constitutive role in such periods. *Transitional Justice* adopts a largely inductive method, and, exploring an array of legal responses, it describes a distinctive conception of law and justice in the context of political transformation. *Transitional Justice* begins by rejecting the notion that the move toward a more liberal democratic political system implies a universal or ideal norm. Instead, this book offers an alternative way of thinking about the relation of law to political transformation. Important phenomena here discussed relate to the contemporary wave of political change, including the transitions from Communist rule in East and Central Europe and the former Soviet Union, as well as from repressive military rule in Latin America and Africa. When relevant, the book draws on historical illustrations, from ancient times to the Enlightenment, from the French and American Revolutions through this century's postwar periods up to the contemporary moment.

The interpretive inquiry proceeds on a number of levels. On one level, I attempt to provide a better account of transitional practices. Study of the law's response in periods of political change offers a positive understanding of the nature of accountability for past wrongs. On another level, I explore the normative relation of legal responses to repressive rule, related conceptions of justice, and our intuitions about the construction of the liberal state.

The problem of transitional justice arises within the distinctive context of transition—a shift in political orders. By focusing its inquiry on the stage of "transition," this book chooses to shift the terms of the debate away from the vocabulary of "revolution" often deployed by theorists to an analysis of the role of law in political change.[10] Rather than an undefined last stage of revolution, the conception of transition advanced here is both more capacious and more defined. What is demarcated is a postrevolutionary period of political change; thus, the problem of transitional justice arises within a bounded period, spanning two regimes.[11]

Of course, the above characterization continues to beg the question of transition to what? What rule of recognition governs transitions? Within political science, there is substantial debate about the meaning not only of "transition" but also of its limiting stage, "consolidation," as well as, ultimately, "democracy" itself. Within one school of thought, "transition" is demarcated by objective political criteria, chiefly procedural in nature. Thus, for some time, the criteria for the transition to democracy have focused on elections and related procedures. For example, Samuel Huntington's formulation, following Joseph Schumpeter, defines twentieth-century democratization to occur when the "most powerful collective decision makers are selected through fair, honest and periodic elections."[12] For others, the transition ends when all the politically significant groups accept the rule of law. Beyond this school are others that embrace a more teleological view of democracy. Nevertheless, the teleological approach has been challenged for incorporating a bias toward Western-style democracies.[13]

In the contemporary period, the use of the term *transition* has come to mean change in a liberalizing direction, which is true concededly of the transitions discussed here. The liberalizing trend is well illustrated historically, earlier in the century in the democratic transitions of West Germany, Italy, Austria, France, Japan, Spain, Portugal, and Greece.[14] To date, political scientists have not incorporated this positive normative direction expressly in their definition of the term. This book explores the significance that the contemporary understanding of transition has a normative component in the move from less to more democratic regimes. It is this phenomenology of liberalizing transition that is the subject of this book.

The aim here is to shift the focus away from the traditional political criteria associated with liberalizing change to take account of other practices, particularly the nature and role of legal phenomena. The constructivist approach proposed by this book suggests a move away from defining transitions purely in terms of democratic procedures, such as electoral processes, toward a broader inquiry into other practices signifying acceptance of liberal democracy and the rule-of-law. The inquiry undertaken examines the normative understandings, beyond majority rule, associated with liberalizing rule-of-law systems in political flux.[15] The phenomenology of transition points to a close tie in the normative shifts in understandings of justice and law's role in the construction of the transition. Not all transformations exhibit the same degree of "normative shift." Indeed, one might conceptualize transitions along a transformative continuum in their relation to the predecessor regime and value system varying in degree from "radical" to "conservative" change.

Understanding the particular problem occasioned by the search for justice in the transitional context requires entering a distinctive discourse organized in terms of the profound dilemmas endemic to these extraordinary periods. The threshold dilemma arises from the context of justice in political transformation: Law is caught between the past and the future, between backward-looking and forward-looking, between retrospective and prospective, between the individual and the collective. Accordingly, transitional justice is that justice associated with this context and political circumstances. Transitions imply paradigm shifts in the conception of justice; thus, law's function is deeply and inherently paradoxical. In its ordinary social function, law provides order and stability, but in extraordinary periods of political upheaval, law maintains order even as it enables transformation. Accordingly, in transition, the ordinary intuitions and predicates about law simply do not apply. In dynamic periods of political flux, legal responses generate a sui generis paradigm of transformative law.

The thesis of this book is that the conception of justice in periods of political change is extraordinary and constructivist: It is alternately constituted by, and constitutive of, the transition. The conception of justice that emerges is contextualized and partial: What is deemed just is contingent and informed by prior injustice. Responses to repressive rule inform the meaning of adherence to the rule of law. As a state undergoes political change, legacies of injustice have a bearing on what is deemed transformative. To some extent, the emergence of these legal responses instantiates transition. As the discussion proceeds, it will become evident that the law's role in periods of political change is complex. Ultimately, this book makes two sorts of claims: one, about the nature of law in periods of substantial political change and, the other, about law's role in constituting the transition. For, contrary to the prevailing idealist accounts, law here is shaped by the political circumstances, but, also challenging the prevailing realist accounts, law here is not mere product but itself structures the transition. The association of these responses with periods of political change advances the construction of societal understanding that transition is in progress.

The role of law in periods of political change is explored by looking at its various forms: punishment, historical inquiry, reparations, purges, and constitution making. In the prevailing transitional justice debates, the punishment of the ancien régime is frequently advocated as necessary in the transition to democracy; yet, exploration of the legal phenomenology in periods of political shift suggests that though these are generally thought to be discrete categories of the law, there are affinities. Illuminated is law's operative role in the construction of transition. These practices offer a way both to delegitimate the past political regime and to legitimate its successor by structuring the political opposition within the democratizing order.

Each chapter of the book explores how various legal responses in periods of substantial political change enable the construction of normative shift. Adjudications of the rule of law construct understandings of what is fair and just. Criminal, administrative, and historical investigations establish past wrongdoing. Reparatory projects vindicate rights generated by past wrongs to victims as well as to the broader society. Transitional constitutionalism and administrative justice reconstruct the parameters of the changing political order in a liberalizing direction. The analysis proposed here focuses on law's phenomenology in periods of political change, termed "transitional jurisprudence."

Chapter 1 concerns the rule of law in transition. In established democracies, adherence to the rule of law depends on the application of principles constraining the purposes and application of the law, but this is not its primary role in transitional times. In periods of radical political change, the law is unsettled, and the rule of law is not well explained as a source of ideal norms in the abstract. Within the context of a transitional jurisprudence, the rule of law can be better understood as a normative value scheme that is historically and politically contingent and elaborated in response to past political repression often perpetuated under the law. Thus, the transitional rule of law comprises distinctive values particular to such periods. While the rule of law ordinarily implies prospectivity in the law, transitional law is both settled and unsettled; it is both backward- and forward-looking, as it disclaims past illiberal values and reclaims liberal norms. Although the rule of law and constitutionalism both concern the norms that seek to guide lawmaking in democracy, these understandings are seriously challenged during transitional periods. Despite prevailing theorizing, neither the concepts of the rule of law nor constitution making are well understood as sources of idealized foundational norms. A transitional jurisprudence helps to elucidate the variation in the ideas of the rule of law across legal cultures and over time, as it also shows the rule-of-law concepts varying as a measure and in relation to past legacies of its abrogation.

Chapter 2 concerns criminal justice in transition. Successor trials are commonly thought to play the leading foundational role in the transformation to a more liberal political order. Only trials are thought to draw a bright line demarcating the normative shift from illegitimate to legitimate rule. Nevertheless, the exercise of the state's punishment power in the circumstances of radical political change raises profound dilemmas. Transitional practices show trials to be few and far between, particularly in the contemporary period. The low incidence of successor trials reveals the dilemmas in dealing with often systemic and pervasive wrongdoing by way of the criminal law. So it is that in the transitional context, conventional understandings of individual responsibility are frequently inapplicable, spurring development of new legal forms. The emergence of partial sanctions falls outside conventional legal categories. These developments offer a deeper understanding of the relation that remedies bear to wrongs and, in particular, the distinctive wrong of state persecution. The transitional sanction illuminates the relation between the concepts of democratic accountability and individual rights in their contribution to the construction of a liberal politics.

The third chapter explores the workings of historical justice. Following periods of repressive rule, transitional societies commonly create historical accountings. Historical inquiry and narrative play an important transitional role linking past to present. Transitional accountings incorporate a state's repressive legacy and by their very account draw a line that both redefines a past and reconstructs a state's political identity. Transitional historical justice illuminates the constructive relation between truth regimes and political regimes, clarifying the dynamic relation of knowledge to political power.

Chapter 4 turns to justice in its reparatory dimension. The focus of transitional reparatory justice is the repair of prior wrongs. Perhaps the most common transitional form, reparatory justice's pervasiveness reflects its multiple roles and complex functions in periods of radical political change. Reparatory measures appear most definitional of the liberalizing move, as these responses instantiate recognition of individual rights. The equal protection of individual rights is fundamental to the liberal state; therefore, this remedy plays an important constructive role in periods seeking to reestablish the rule of law. In the dual economic and political transitions that characterize the contemporary wave of political change, reparations play explicitly political roles mediating the change by enabling the creation of new stakes in the political community in the midst of transition. Transitional reparatory measures depart from their conventional compensatory role to perform functional and symbolic roles particular to the state's political transformation.

Chapter 5 explores administrative justice and the uses of public law to redefine the parameters of political membership, participation, and leadership that constitute the political community. While political purges and disabilities are concededly common after revolutions, the question is whether any principles guide such measures in political transitions. More than any other transitional response, explicitly political collective measures pose a challenge to the construction of the rule of law in the liberalizing regime. Administrative justice illuminates law's distinctive potential for restructuring the relation of the individual to the political community in the transition. These public law measures define new boundary conditions on a sweeping and explicitly political basis. Through administrative justice, public law is used to respond to the past regime, as well as to reshape the successor political order. This response exemplifies transitional jurisprudence in its most radical form.

Chapter 6 explores transitional constitutionalism. Transitional constitutionalism serves conventional constitutionalism's constitutive purposes, but it also serves transformative purposes. While our intuitions are to conceive constitutions as forward-looking and foundational texts; in periods of radical political change, constitutions are instead dynamic mediating texts, simultaneously backward- and forward-looking, comprehending varying constitutional modalities and degrees of entrenchment. Transitional constitutionalism, criminal justice, and the rule of law share affinities in the contingent relation that the norms protected bear to prior rule, as well as to the new political order.

The concluding chapter brings together and analyzes the various ways in which new democracies respond to legacies of injustice. Patterns across legal forms[16] inform a paradigm of "transitional jurisprudence." The analysis proposes that law's role here is constructivist, and that transitional jurisprudence emerges as a distinct paradigmatic form of law responsive to and constructive of the extraordinary circumstances of periods of substantial political change.[17] In transitional jurisprudence, the conception of justice is partial, contextual, and situated between at least two legal and political orders. Legal norms are decidedly multiple, the idea of justice always a compromise. Transitional jurisprudence centers on the law's paradigmatic use in the normative construction of the new political regime. Eschewing general prescriptive principles from legal and political theorizing, the dynamic relation of law and political change contended for here challenges the reigning rhetoric regarding the course of political development. This study of law's role in political change suggests criteria beyond the fairness of elections, stability of institutions, or economic development by which to evaluate new democracies.[18] Legal responses are both performative and symbolic of transition.

This book offers the language of a new jurisprudence rooted in prior political injustice. Conceiving of jurisprudence as transitional helps to elucidate the nature and role of law during periods of radical political change. Transitional jurisprudence also has implications that transcend these extraordinary periods. Offering another way of conceptualizing law should have ramifications affecting our intuitions about the nature and function of law more generally. The problem of justice during periods of political transformation has a potentially profound impact on the resulting societal shift in norms and the groundwork for transformed constitutional and legal regimes. Unresolved problems of transitional justice often have lasting implications over a state's lifetime. This book offers a new perspective by which we can understand the significance of the enduring political controversies that presently divide our societies. Ultimately, the recent changes of Latin America, East and Central Europe, the former Soviet Union, Africa, as well as the historical European transitions, offer us an opportunity to reflect on what is a liberal democratic response to the illiberal state, as well as, more broadly, on the potential of law in a transformative politics.

## CHAPTER ONE

# The Rule of Law
# in Transition

*T*his chapter explores the various legal responses to illiberal rule and
the guiding rule-of-law principles in these times. The attempt to adhere to the rule of law during periods of political upheaval creates a dilemma.
There is a tension between the rule of law in transition as backward-looking
and forward-looking, as settled versus dynamic. In this dilemma, *the rule of
law is ultimately contingent;* rather than merely grounding legal order, it
serves to mediate the normative shift in values that characterizes these extraordinary periods. In democracies, our intuition is that the rule of law means
adherence to known rules, as opposed to arbitrary governmental action.[1] Yet
revolution implies disorder and legal instability. The threshold dilemma of
transitional justice is the problem of the rule of law in periods of radical political change. By their very definitions, these are often times of massive paradigm shifts in understandings of justice. Societies are struggling with how to
transform their political, legal, and economic systems. If ordinarily the rule of
law means regularity, stability, and adherence to settled law, to what extent are
periods of transformation compatible with commitment to the rule of law? In
such periods, what does the rule of law mean?

The dilemma of the meaning of the rule of law transcends the moment of
political transformation and goes to the heart of the basis for a liberal state.
Even in ordinary periods, stable democracies struggle with questions about the
meaning of adherence to the rule of law. Versions of this transitional rule-of-
law dilemma are manifest in problems of successor justice, constitutional beginnings, and constitutional change.[2] The rule-of-law dilemma tends to arise
in politically controversial areas, where the value of legal change is in tension
with the value of adherence to the principle of settled legal precedent. In ordinary periods, the problem of adherence to legal continuity is seen in the challenge posed by political and social change over the passage of time. Accordingly, the ideal of the rule of law as legal continuity is captured in the principle
of stare decisis, a predicate of adjudication in the Anglo-American legal sys-

tem. "[T]he very concept of the rule of law underlying our own Constitution requires such continuity over time that a respect for precedent is, by definition, indispensable."[3] In transformative periods, however, the value of legal continuity is severely tested. The question of the normative limits on legitimate political and legal change for regimes in the midst of transformation is frequently framed in terms of a series of antinomies. The law as written is compared to the law as right, positive law to natural law, procedural to substantive justice, and so forth.

My aim is to resituate the rule-of-law dilemma by exploring societal experiences that arise in the context of political transformation. My interest is not in idealized theorizing about the rule of law in general. Rather, the attempt is to understand the meaning of the rule of law for societies undergoing massive political change. This chapter approaches the rule-of-law dilemma in an inductive manner by resituating the question as it actually arises in its legal and political contexts. It explores a number of historical postwar cases, as well as precedents arising in the more contemporary transitions. Although the rule-of-law dilemma arises commonly in the criminal context, the issues raise broader questions about the ways in which societies in periods of intense political change reason about the relation of law, politics, and justice. As shall become evident, these adjudications reveal central ideas about the extraordinary conception of the rule of law and of values of justice and fairness in periods of political change.

## The Rule-of-Law Dilemma: The Postwar Transition

In periods of substantial political change, a dilemma arises over adherence to the rule of law that relates to the problem of successor justice. To what extent does bringing the ancien régime to trial imply an inherent conflict between predecessor and successor visions of justice? In light of this conflict, is such criminal justice compatible with the rule of law? The dilemma raised by successor criminal justice leads to broader questions about the theory of the nature and role of law in the transformation to the liberal state.

The transitional dilemma is present in changes throughout political history. It is illustrated in the eighteenth-century shifts from monarchies to republics but has arisen more recently in the post–World War II trials. In the postwar period, the problem was the subject of a well-known Anglo–American jurisprudential debate between Lon Fuller and H.L.A. Hart, who took as their point of departure the problem of justice after the collapse of the Nazi regime.[4] Such postwar theorizing demonstrates that in times of significant political change, conventional understandings of the rule of law are thrown into relief.[5] Although the transitional context has generated scholarly theorizing about the meaning of the rule of law, that theorizing does not distinguish understandings of the rule of law in ordinary and transitional times. Moreover, the theoretical work that emerges from these debates frequently falls back on grand, idealized models of the rule of law. Such accounts fail to recognize the exceptional issues involved in the domain of transitional jurisprudence. Recognition of a domain of transitional jurisprudence, however, raises again the issue of the relation of the rule of law in transitions to that in ordinary periods.

The Hart-Fuller debate on the nature of law focuses on a series of cases involving the prosecutions of Nazi collaborators in postwar Germany. The central issue for the postwar German courts was whether to accept defenses that relied on Nazi law.[6] A related issue was whether a successor regime could bring a collaborator to justice and, if so, whether that would mean invalidating the predecessor laws in effect at the time the acts were committed. In the "Problem of the Grudge Informer," the issue raised is set out in a hypothetical somewhat abstracted from the postwar situation: The so-called Purple Shirt regime has been overthrown and replaced by a democratic constitutional government, and the question is whether to punish those who had collaborated in the prior regime.[7] Hart, an advocate of legal positivism,[8] argued that adherence to the rule of law included recognition of the antecedent law as valid. Prior written law, even when immoral, should retain legal force and be followed by the successor courts until such time as it is replaced. In the positivist position advocated by Hart, the claim is that the principle of the rule of law governing transitional decision making should proceed—just as it would in ordinary times—with full continuity of the written law.

In Fuller's view, the rule of law meant breaking with the prior Nazi legal regime. As such, Nazi collaborators were to be prosecuted under the new legal regime: In the "dilemma confronted by Germany in seeking to rebuild her shattered legal institutions . . . Germany had to restore both respect for law and respect for justice . . . [P]ainful antinomies were encountered in attempting to restore both at once." Whereas the rule-of-law dichotomy was framed in terms of procedural versus substantive ideas of justice, Fuller tries to elide these competing conceptions by proposing a procedural view of substantive justice.[9] According to the German judiciary, there is a dichotomy within the rule of law between the procedural legal right and the moral right. In "severe cases," the moral right takes precedence. Accordingly, formalist concepts of the law, such as adherence to putative prior law, could be overridden by such notions of moral right. The natural law position espoused by the German judiciary suggests that transitional justice necessitates departing from prior putative law. For Fuller, however, it would not imply such a break, because past "law" would not qualify as such for failure to comply with various procedural conditions.[10]

The above debate failed to focus, however, on the distinctive problem of law in the transitional context. In the postwar period, this dilemma arose as to the extent of legal continuity with the Nazi regime: To what extent did the rule of law necessitate legal continuity? A transitional perspective on the postwar debate would clarify what is signified by the rule of law. That is, the content of the rule of law is justified in terms of distinctive conceptions of the nature of injustice of the prior repressive regime. The nature of this injustice affects consideration of the various alternatives, such as full continuity with the prior legal regime, discontinuity, selective discontinuities, and moving outside the law altogether. For positivists, full continuity with the prior legal regime is justified by the need to restore belief in the procedural regularity that was deemed missing in the prior repressive regime; the meta-rule-of-law value is due process, understood as regularity in procedures and adherence to settled law. The natural law claim for legal discontinuity is also justified by the nature of the prior legal regime but according to the conceptualization of past tyranny. On the natural law view of the rule of law, Fuller's approach appears more nuanced, as it attempts to offer a procedural understanding of substantive justice values. Given the predecessor regime's immorality, the rule of law needs to be grounded in something beyond adherence to preexisting law.[11]

To what extent is adherence to the laws of a prior repressive regime consistent with the rule of law? Conversely, if successor justice implied prosecuting behavior that was lawful under the prior regime, to what extent might legal discontinuity instead be mandated by the rule of law? The transitional context fuses these multiple questions of the legality of the two regimes and their relation to each other.

In the postwar debate, both natural law and positivist positions took as their point of departure certain presumptions about the nature of the prior legal regime under illiberal rule.[12] Both positions draw justificatory force from the role of law in the prior regime; nevertheless, they differ on what constitutes a transformative principle of legality. The positivist argument attempts to divorce questions of the legitimacy of law under the predecessor and successor regimes. The response to past tyranny is thought not to lie in the domain of the law at all but instead in the domain of politics. If there is any independent content given to the rule of law, it is that it ought not serve transient political purposes. The positivist argument for judicial adherence to settled law, however, relies on certain assumptions about the nature of legality under the predecessor totalitarian regime.[13] The justification for adhering to prior law in the transitional moment is that under prior repressive rule, adjudication failed to adhere to settled law. On the positivist view, transformative adjudication that seeks to "undo" the effect of notions of legality supporting tyrannical rule would imply adherence to prior settled law.

The natural law position highlights the transformative role of law in the shift to a more liberal regime. On this view, putative law under tyrannical rule lacked morality and hence did not constitute a valid legal regime. To some extent, in this normative legal theory, collapsing law and morality, the transitional problem of the relation between legal regimes disappears. Insofar as adjudication followed such putative law, it, too, was immoral in supporting illiberal rule. Thus, the cases of the informers are characterized as "perversions in the administration of justice."[14] From the natural law perspective, the role of law in transition is to respond to evil perpetuated under the past administration of justice. Because of the role of judicial review in sustaining the repression (this topic was discussed in the Hart-Fuller debate),[15] adjudication as in ordinary times would not convey the rule of law. This theory of transformative law promotes the normative view that the role of law is to transform the prevailing meaning of legality.[16]

In the postwar debate, the questions arose in the extraordinary political context following totalitarian rule. Yet, the conclusions abstract from the context and generalize as if describing essential, universal attributes of the rule of law, failing to recognize how the problem is particular to the transitional context. Resituating the problem should illuminate our understanding of the rule of law. I now turn from the postwar debate to more contemporary instances of political change illustrating law's transformative potential. Those instances exemplify the tension between idealized conceptions of the rule of law and the contingencies of the extraordinary political context. Struggling with the dilemma of how to adhere to some commitment to the rule of law in such periods leads to alternative constructions that mediate conceptions of transitional rule of law.

### Shifting Visions of Legality: Post-Communist Transitions

The "velvet" revolutions' rough underside has been revealed in courts of law, where debates about the content of the political transformation continue to simmer. A number of controversies over successor criminal justice exemplify the transitional rule-of-law dilemma. Here, I focus on two: In the first case, a Hungarian law allowed prosecutions for offenses related to the brutal Soviet suppression of the country's uprising in 1956;[17] in the other, unified Germany prosecuted border guards for shooting civilians who were attempting to make unlawful border crossings along the Berlin Wall. The cases involve weighty symbols of freedom and repression: 1956 is considered the founding year of Hungary's revolution, whereas the Berlin Wall and its collapse are the region's central symbols of Soviet domination and demise. The cases illustrate the dilemmas implied in the attempt to effect substantial political change through and within the law. Although the two cases seemingly suggest diverging resolutions of the rule-of-law dilemma, they also reveal common understandings.

After the political changes of 1991, Hungary's Parliament passed a law permitting the prosecution of crimes committed by the predecessor regime in putting down the popular 1956 uprising. Despite the passage of time since these crimes were committed, the law would have lifted statutes of limitations for treason and other serious crimes,[18] effectively reviving these offenses. Similar legislation reviving the time bars elapsing during the Communist regime was also enacted elsewhere in the region, as in the Czech Republic.[19] The problem of statute-of-limitations laws commonly arises after long occupations when societies attempt to prosecute crimes committed under predecessor regimes. Thus, in the postwar transitions in Western Europe, the rule-of-law problem posed by the passing of statutes of limitations did not arise in the immediate postwar period but only later in the 1960s.[20] The controversy over the statute-of-limitations law raised a broader question: To what extent is a successor regime bound by a prior regime's law?

Hungary's Constitutional Court described the dilemma in terms of familiar antinomies: the rule of law understood as predictability versus the rule of law understood as substantive justice. So framed, the choices seemed irreconcilable; yet, ultimately the statute-of-limitations law and the proposed 1956-era prosecutions were held unconstitutional. The principle of the rule of law required prospectivity in lawmaking, even if it meant the worst criminal offenses of the prior regime would go unpunished. The opinion begins with a statement of the court's characterization of the dilemma it confronted: "The Constitutional Court is the repository of the paradox of the 'revolution of the rule of law.'" [21] Why a paradox? "Rule of law," the court said, means "predictability and foreseeability."[22] "From the principle of predictability and foreseeability, the criminal law's prohibition of the use of retroactive legislation, especially ex post facto . . . directly follows. . . . Only by following the formalized legal procedure can there be valid law."[23]

The dominant vision of the rule of law for the Constitutional Court was "security."[24] "Certainty of the law demands . . . the protection of rights previously conferred." The proposed law, which would have opened the way to ancien régime prosecutions, was classically ex post and, as such, threatened individual rights to repose. In its discussion of the meaning of security, the court analogized the right of repose at issue to personal property rights. Although protection of personal property rights could generally be overridden by competing state interests, such interests, the court maintained, ought not override an individual's criminal process rights to repose. By protecting the rule-of-law value of "security" from invasion by the state, the Constitutional Court sent an important message that property rights would be protected in the transition.

In ordinary times, the idea of the rule of law as security in the protection of individual rights is frequently considered to be a threshold, minimal understanding of the rule of law basic to liberal democracy. Yet, in the economic and legal transitions of East and Central Europe, this understanding represented a profound transformation. If the totalitarian legal system abolished or ignored the line between the individual and the state, the line drawn by Hungary's Constitutional Court posited a new constraint on the state: an individual right of security. Insistence on the protection of individual rights, said to be previously acquired, was constructed in the transition. This ruling sent an important message that the new regime would be more liberal than its predecessor.

Compare a second case. In its second round of successor cases in this century, Germany's judiciary once again confronted the transitional rule-of-law dilemma when East German border guards were put on trial for Berlin Wall shootings that occurred before Unification. The question before the court was whether to recognize defenses that relied on the predecessor regime's law. The Berlin trial court framed the dilemma in terms of the tension between "formal law" and "justice" and rejected former East German law because "not everything is right that is formally right." Comparing the Communist laws to those of the Nazi period, the court relied on postwar precedents holding that evil legislation lacked the status of law: "Especially the time of the National Socialist regime in Germany taught that . . . in extreme cases the opportunity must be given for one to value the principle of material justice more highly than the principle of legal certainty." Procedurally, legal rights were distinct from moral rights. Characterized as "extreme cases," the border guards cases were analogized to those of the postwar collaborators and accordingly guided by the same adjudicative principle.

The transitional courts of East and Central Europe, despite facing different legal issues, confront a problem common to successor regimes: What are the rule-of-law implications of prosecuting for actions that were "legal" under the prior regime? As the earlier postwar debate suggests, this question raises (at least) two questions, one about the legitimacy of law in both predecessor and successor periods and another about the relation between the two. The juxtaposition is always between the rule of law as settled norms versus the rule of law as transformative. In the contemporary cases, as in the postwar debate, what emerges are new transitional understandings of the rule of law. Considered together, the two decisions present an interesting puzzle. For the Berlin court, the controlling rule-of-law value was what was "morally" right, whereas for the Hungarian court, the controlling rule-of-law value was protection of preexisting "legal" rights. In one case, the rule of law requires security understood as prospectivity, with the consequence of forbearance in the criminal law. In the other view, justice is understood as equal enforcement of the law. Can the two approaches be reconciled?

Probing the language of the successor cases exposes a conception of the rule of law peculiar to the transitional moment. Judicial rhetoric conceptualizes the problem in terms of multiple competing rule-of-law values in seemingly intractable conflict: one value deemed relative, and the other essential. The transitional judiciaries in these cases characterized the dilemma they confronted as involving a balancing of two senses of the rule of law: the rule of law as it is ordinarily understood versus a transformative understanding. Which of these values will dominate the transitional balance will depend on distinctive historical and political legacies. Accordingly, after totalitarianism, the dominant vision of the rule of law in Hungary is to draw a bright line of positive security on which individuals can rely and which is beyond the reach of state power. In unified Germany, the transitional rule of law is defined within a preexisting jurisprudence, which continues to respond to legality under Fascism. When the German judiciary ruled that the border guards cases constituted "extreme cases" it analogized Communist rule to that of National Socialism. In this way, the legal response to World War II injustice continued to guide contemporary adjudication in the transitions out of Communist rule. As in the postwar period, the post-Communist Berlin court invoked overriding principles of natural law. After Nazi rule, under which a repressive security apparatus functioned outside the law and the legal machinery was itself used to persecute, the dominant sense of the rule of law was of equal protection in the administration of justice. These are transformative understandings.

Despite idealist theorizing to the contrary, the transitional precedents suggest that no one rule-of-law value is essential in the movement toward construction of a more liberal political system. Transcendent notions of rule-of-law values in transitional societies are highly contingent, depending, in part, on the states' distinctive political and legal legacies and, in particular, on the role of law in the predecessor regime. There has been a lively scholarly debate on this question and recent comparative work concerning the role of adjudication under oppressive rule in Germany under Nazi control, Latin America under military rule, and South Africa under apartheid rule. Despite substantial theorizing about the potential role of various adjudicative principles under tyrannical rule, to the extent that there has been empirical study of the judiciary's role in repressive periods, neither positivist nor natural law adjudicative principles correlate with greater rule of law in such periods. In varying contexts, scholars come to disparate conclusions, suggesting that variations in interpretive strategies, whether of positivist or natural law, do not in and of themselves explain the judiciary's role under repressive rule. Thus, some claim Nazi judges' free-ranging principle of interpretation led to support of repressive rule, while others emphasize the positivist jurisprudence understood as the separation of law and morality.[25] The meaning of the rule of law is highly contingent in relation to the social meaning of injustice in the region and its response.

This transitional perspective on the rule of law offered here sheds light as well on the puzzling gulf between American and Continental philosophers over the putative associations of various legal philosophies with repression or, conversely, with liberal rule. That positivism is associated with repression and with liberalism—on opposite sides of the ocean—clarifies its contingency as a transitional response to its use by evil judges. Thus, in the United States, positivism is frequently associated with the jurisprudence that upheld the slavery regime, whereas in Germany, it is not positivism but the natural law interpretation that is associated with the Reich judiciary.[26] Whereas the conventional understanding of the conception of tyranny is the lack of the rule of law as arbitrariness, the transitional rule of law in the modern cases illuminates a distinctive normative response to contemporary tyranny. From its inception in the ancient understanding termed "isonomy," the ideal of the rule of law emerges in response to tyranny. In ancient times, isonomy is forged in response to tyranny understood as arbitrary and partial enforcement of the law. Because prior tyranny is associated with lawmaking that is both arbitrary and unequal, the ancient understanding of the rule of law comprehended both values of security in the law and equal enforceability of the law. As in ancient times, the contemporary ideal of the rule of law is forged in the context of the move from repressive to more liberalizing rule.[27] Where persecution is systematically perpetuated under legal imprimatur, where tyranny is systematic persecution,[28] the transitional legal response is the attempt to undo these abuses under the law.

## Transitional Constructions of Legality

The discussion above leads to a more differentiated understanding of the rule of law, and it illuminates an understanding of legality that is distinctly transitional. These understandings of the rule of law bridge the discontinuity from illiberal to liberal rule; as such, one might consider these values and processes to mediate the transition. The discussion focuses on three such mediating concepts that follow. These are the social construction of the rule of law, the role of international law in transcending domestic legal understandings, and, finally, the core rule-of-law value: to transcend the passing politics of the times.

### The Role of Social Construction

One mediating concept of the transitional rule of law is its social construction. What matters in establishing the rule of law is legal culture, not abstract or universal ideas of justice.[29] The socially constructed understanding of the transitional rule of law is evident in the post-Communist adjudications. In the border guards cases discussed above, the prevailing social understanding of law was used to justify the rejection of prior legal defenses. The validity of prior law depended on the social practices of the time, such as the norm's publication and transparency.[30] "In the then-GDR, too, justice and humanity were illustrated and represented as ideals. In this respect, generally sufficient conceptions of the basis of a natural lawfulness were set out."[31] The border policy, which was generally secret and covered up whenever foreigners were in the country, lacked the transparency ordinarily associated with law. The Berlin court found not only that the border policy did not comport with the prevailing social understanding of law but also that the prior understanding of law was consonant with that of the West. The guards stood at a geographical and juridical border. This treatment signaled an illegitimacy of regulation of the border in its legal culture. A similar concern animated Hungary's Constitutional Court when it emphasized the rule-of-law value of security as continuity in the law. In the transitional context of political upheaval, the judiciary constructed the understanding of legal continuity. The perception of rule of law is created by that court's own adherence to procedure.

What makes law positive? Prevailing theorizing about the rule of law posits that among the conditions for law is that it be known.[32] Is knowledge of law equated with publication? In transitional periods, there is commonly a large gap between the law as written and as perceived. What makes law positive is the popular perception in the public sphere. This understanding broadens, indeed democratizes, sources of legality with societal involvement in the constitution of legal culture. Indeed, in the contemporary media age, at any one time there may well be multiple sources of law, as well as numerous forms of publication that overshadow the written law.[33] Social understanding in the public sphere is a rule of recognition by which the legal systems of illiberal regimes are evaluated, an understanding of law that stands independent of the sovereign's decrees and, as such, is less affected by political upheaval. Guided by this mediating principle of transitional legality, the legitimacy of the predecessor regime's law would depend on popular understandings of legality in the ambient culture.

Understanding the rule of law as socially constructed offers a principle for evaluating legality in periods of movement between dictatorships and democracies. Recognition of a legitimacy gap between the law as written and as socially perceived offers a useful way to explain law's construction under illiberal rule. Indeed, as public belief in prevailing political systems wanes, one might expect this gap to widen, leading to the transition.

## The Role of International Law

Another mediating concept of the transitional rule of law is international law. International law posits institutions and processes that transcend domestic law and politics. In periods of political flux, international law offers an alternative construction of law that, despite substantial political change, is continuous and enduring. Local courts rely on these international understandings. The potential of this understanding of international law gained force in the postwar period. A jurisprudential debate arose, particularly in the United States, over whether postwar trials convened at Nuremberg and Tokyo were in keeping with the rule of law. International law served as a mediating concept to mitigate the dilemma of the rule of law raised by successor justice in transitional times and to justify the legality of the Nuremberg trials against concerns over retroactivity.[34] In the contemporary moment, international law is frequently invoked as a way to bridge shifting understandings of legality. In the post-Communist cases discussed above, the controversy over the attempt to revive old political prosecutions was ultimately resolved by turning to concepts of international law. For example, in its review of a law proposing to reopen political cases related to the 1956 uprising, the Constitutional Court of Hungary reasoned that reopening such cases was discontinuous with prior law. Such discontinuity, the Constitutional Court said, threatened the understanding of legality in the successor period; there was no principled way to break selectively with prior law. "The legitimacy of the different (political) systems during the past half century is irrelevant . . . ; from the viewpoint of the constitutionality of laws it does not comprise a meaningful category."[35] In a second round of judicial review, the court upheld a new statute authorizing 1956 prosecutions based on offenses constituting "war crimes" and "crimes against humanity" under international law.[36] The rule of law required continuity. Such continuity was considered to exist in international legal norms, such as the postwar Geneva Convention Relative to the Protection of Civilian Persons in Time of War,[37] which norms overrode domestic law. A similar decision was taken in Poland invalidating the extension of statutes of limitations, other than for those offenses considered violations to international human rights.[38] The notion that international law took precedence over domestic law was by no means clear, as Hungary's Constitution was silent on the relative priorities of domestic and international law. The Constitutional Court nevertheless indicated that it would interpret the constitution guided by international norms, declaring that "generally recognized rules of international law took precedence." Some constitutions explicitly provide for such priority ranking.[39] Throughout the region, international law would become the basis for judicial interpretation of punishment policies, because these norms were thought to transcend the past regimes' politicized law. In Germany's border guards cases, the judgment explicitly rests on international law.[40]

In periods of political flux, international law offers a useful mediating concept. The framing of the rule-of-law dilemma easily shifts from the antinomies of positivism and natural law. Grounded in positive law, but incorporating values of justice associated with natural law, international law mediates the rule-of-law dilemma. Positive international law norms are defined in conventions, treaties, and customs.[41] Moreover, in its circumscription of the most heinous abuses, international law offers a source of normative transcendence. An illustration is the concept of crimes against humanity, discussed further in the chapter on criminal justice, suggesting conceptually opposite and yet related values, in the universalized normative response to persecution epitomizing evil in varying cultural contexts.[42] Whereas international law preserves that ordinary understanding of the rule of law as settled law, it also enables transformation. In so doing, it mediates the transition. International law principles serve to reconcile the threshold dilemma of law in periods of political transformation.

### The Rule of Law as Limit on Politics

The defining feature of the rule of law in periods of political change is that it preserves some degree of continuity in the legal form, while it enables normative change. The previous politicized nature of law and adjudication partially justifies nonadherence during the transition. This understanding of the rule of law as antipolitics is a common theme throughout the contemporary transitional controversies discussed above. The border guards trials were characterized as "extreme cases," justifying departure from ordinary rule-of-law considerations.[43] The German court elevated what was morally right over the political. Other cases in the region suggest similar judicial interpretations of the rule of law. Hungary's invalidation of the 1956 prosecutions law presented a limit on politicized anti-Communist policies. In elevating a law that would have extended the time for prosecution of crimes committed under prior rule, the Czech Constitutional Court upheld it on the basis that it would serve the goal of undoing past politicized punishment policy and administration of justice. The law would suspend the time limitations for forty-one years (the time between February 25, 1948, and December 29, 1989) for acts previously not prosecuted or punished for "political reasons."[44] If under repressive rule the administration of justice was conducted purely as an exercise of political will,[45] this understanding is most clearly disavowed when the successor regime adopts the overriding rule-of-law value that most clearly expresses a principled normative vision independent of transitory politics.

The construction of the transitional rule of law as independent of politics shares certain affinities with the understanding of the rule of law applicable in ordinary times. Yet, controversies over transitional justice in highly politicized contexts present hard cases for adherence to the rule of law. Despite radical political change, the aim is rule of law not primarily motivated by politics. Transitional jurisprudence reveals a shining vision of the rule of law as antipolitics.

## The Transitional Judiciary

In periods of political transformation, the problem of legality is distinct from the problem of the theory of law as it arises in established democracies in ordinary times. There is a working out of core questions about the legitimacy of the new regime, including the nature and role of the transitional judiciary. The choice of the principles of adjudication implies a related question about where, as an institutional matter, the work of transformation should lie: judiciary or legislature? This is the question to which I now turn.

The transitional justice dilemma arises during periods of substantial political change. When a legal system is in flux, the challenge to ordinary understandings of the rule of law is surely at its greatest. The challenge was less severe of the postwar transitions than of the contemporary movements from Communist rule, periods of simultaneous economic, political, and legal transformation. In these periods, newly founded constitutional courts have borne the institutional burden of establishing new understandings of the rule of law. The burden of transformation to a rule-of-law system has to some extent devolved on the judiciary, chiefly the new constitutional courts. A similar transformative response can be seen in other recent transitions, such as in South Africa. South Africa's transitional constitution creates its new Constitutional Court.[46] One might question whether continuity with the prior regime is a determination properly for the transitional judge or a political question properly subject for broader public debate. When this question arose in the contemporary post-Communist transitions, the judiciary assumed the decision-making responsibility. The issue began as a political question in unified Germany, but in its consideration of the question of the validity of German Democratic Republic (GDR) law in the border guards cases, the Berlin court elided the political agreement of the two Germanys. The Unification Treaty contemplated continuity in former GDR criminal law, providing that East Germany's criminal code should be applied to criminal acts committed before reunification. However, the court rejected the border guards' defenses grounded in GDR law.[47] In so doing, the court demonstrated its independence from the legislature and its political agenda. However, that transformative response to the political was less necessary in unified Germany than elsewhere in the region because of the nature of the transitions. Similarly, when Hungary's Constitutional Court overturned the 1956 prosecutions law, it sent a clear message of judicial independence to the country's political branches.[48] These decisions reveal a core understanding of rule of law forged by a transitional judiciary striving for some independence from politics.

Political theorists often distinguish liberal from illiberal regimes by their constitutions; the role of transitional constitutionalism is discussed more fully in chapter 6. Yet, the inquiry undertaken here suggests that what distinguishes liberal political systems depends less on the specifics of any one institutional arrangement and more on the degree to which there is a sense of meaningful enforcement and understanding of the rule of law. Although the Communist-era constitutions enumerated rights, these were largely rights on paper that were rarely enforced. So it was that, after Communism, the mere passage of new rights charters would not produce a sense of transformation in the rule of law. Responding to this distinctive legacy of injustice are the dozen constitutional courts to enforce the new constitutions.[49] This role for the judiciary is the "critical" legal response that affirmatively signals a transformative turn toward the constitutional systems of liberal democracies.

The constitutional courts assist in the transformation to rule-of-law systems in a number of ways. First, the courts emerge out of systems of centralized state power; as new forums specially created in the period of political change and transformation, their very establishment defines a break from past political arrangements. Second, access to constitutional courts through litigation enables a form of participation in the fledgling democracy. Over time, access to the courts could enable popular input into constitutional interpretation, developing a societal understanding of limited government and individual rights protection. Popular access to courts for individual rights enforcement is a potent symbol of a new governmental openness.[50] Third, to the extent the constitutional courts have explicit mandates to engage in judicial review they are the guardians of the new constitutional order. In much of the region, broad jurisdictional rules allow abstract judicial review and access to review by political actors, such as the president of the country, or by minority factions of the legislature.[51] The courts in the region are active in interpreting new constitutional norms under preexisting constitutions, under general mandates to uphold the rule of law. An example is the Hungarian Constitutional Court's review of the law concerning the state's prosecutions policy previously discussed.[52] The constitutional courts have the potential to delineate state power and to redefine individual rights, thus creating a rights culture. Through transformative adjudication, the transitional judiciary deploys activist principles of judicial review toward normative change and a more liberal rule-of-law system.

Transformative adjudicatory practices raise a crucial question: Insofar as the transitional judiciary bears the burden of the transformation of the rule of law, to what extent are such practices compatible with the role of the judiciary in established democracies? In democracies in ordinary times, activist judicial decision making is generally considered illegitimate, largely for two reasons. First, retroactivity in judicial decision making challenges the rule of law as settled law.[53] Second, judicial decision making is thought to interfere with democracy; unlike legislative decision making, judicial decision making lacks the legitimacy associated with democratic processes.[54] The question is whether these objections relevant to ordinary times apply to adjudication in transitional times.

Our intuitions about the appropriate site of lawmaking depend on implicit assumptions about democracy and democratic accountability that ought not be automatically applied to illiberal regimes nor to regimes moving away from such rule. In established democracies in ordinary times, our intuitions are that transformative lawmaking should occur by legislation rather than by adjudication. The judiciary is constrained from creating law, for such lawmaking is considered a departure from the general predicate of democracy, majoritarian lawmaking.[55] In transitional times, the problem of illegality is far more prevalent; indeed, it is often pervasive. Periods of political transformation are frequently accompanied by radical legal change. The most recent wave of political change correlating with economic transformation (in the post-Communist changes) implied major reforms of preexisting law. The conventional concern of the absence of democratic accountability posed by judicial lawmaking seems less apt in periods of political flux. In such periods, the transitional legislature frequently is not freely elected and, further, lacks the experience and legitimacy of the legislature operating in ordinary times.[56]

Another reason the judiciary is not ordinarily seen as the proper lawmaking body is its ostensible lack of institutional competence and capacity. This concern was raised, for example, in the postwar debate over the establishment of the rule of law. In the positivist position, the burden of legal transformation was thought properly to fall on the legislature, while the natural law position assumed a transformative role for adjudication. Yet, the postwar debate did not sufficiently take account of the transitional context. As periods of political change are also periods of legal flux, controversies in such times are often characterized by a lack of relevant law.[57] Moreover, controversies in such extraordinary periods often necessitate speedy considerations. Whereas in ordinary times, making law in a case-by-case fashion may well appear too slow and too variable, in transitional times, judicial decision making is often relatively faster than the legislative process, which may be slowed down by a compromised past or political inexperience. Moreover, in the context of political flux, the judiciary may well be comparatively more competent for nuanced, case-by-case resolution of transitional controversies.[58] Indeed, judicial decision making allows for substantial change and is characterized here as the ambivalent directionality of the law in such periods. The question of what institution is most competent and legitimate is contingent and will depend on the particulars of predecessor legacies of injustice in that country.

Finally, transformative adjudication is self-regarding. By changing adjudicatory principles and practices, institutions compromised by their decision making under prior rule can transform themselves. In high-profile cases, a compromised judiciary can transform itself by changing its principle of adjudication. This self-regarding institutional mechanism is particularly pertinent when the judiciary supported prior repressive rule.[59] Yet, even where the judiciary is not the successor to a compromised institution, there are other beneficial implications of transformative adjudication.

Theories of adjudication associated with understandings of the rule of law in ordinary times are inapposite to transitional periods. Our ordinary intuitions about the nature and the role of adjudication relate to presumptions about the relative competence and capacities of judiciaries and legislatures in ordinary times that simply do not hold in unstable periods. The cases discussed above demonstrate an extraordinary role for courts exercising principles of transformative adjudication. In periods of political change, the very concerns for democracy and legitimacy that ordinarily constrain activist adjudication may well support such adjudication as an alternative to an even greater politicization of the law.

## Transformative Adjudicative Practices: Some Conclusions

This chapter began by positing that there is a special dilemma in the adherence to the rule of law in periods of political change. The ordinary understanding of the rule of law as adherence to settled law is in tension with transformative understandings of the rule of law. I now consider what normative rule-of-law principles are associated with adjudication in periods of political change.

In these extraordinary periods, as discussed above, rule-of-law norms do not constitute universals. The tensions posed by adherence to the rule of law in these periods are reconciled through a number of mediating concepts. Legality in such periods is socially constructed; in some part, it is judge-made. Exploration of precedents in such periods suggests that the understandings of the rule of law are constructed within a transitional context. By cabining politicized uses of the law, this rule-of-law principle guides interim legal decisionmaking on the road to democracy.

Recognizing a principle of transformative adjudication during periods of political transition has significant implications for prevailing legal theory about the rule of law. First, recognition of such a principle throws into relief the extent to which prevailing legal theory has failed to take account of the significance of the varying normative understandings of the rule of law manifested in transitional times. Further, the transitional rule of law implies an implicit critique of the dominant theories regarding the nature and role of law. In liberal political theory, a long-standing precept of the rule of law is that lawmaking through adjudication is conceived as somehow neutral and autonomous from politics.[60] These liberal understandings are challenged by accounting for circumstances associated with the role for transformative law, in which the rule of law is defined in constructive relation to past politics.

The principle of transformative adjudication perhaps poses a more serious challenge to critical theorizing of law. Critical legal theorizing has been criticized for going too far in collapsing law and politics. As such, this theoretical approach has often lacked explanatory power for why, or in what circumstances, law has any distinctive claim on society. Although critical legal theorizing has laid claims to a diminished rule of law as a general matter,[61] the above discussion suggests that this is most true in extraordinary political circumstances of transition. Transitional rule of law clarifies a role for hyperpoliticized adjudication. From the perspective of critical legal theory, the challenge posed by the transformative adjudicatory practices discussed here is the challenge posed by the boundedness of law's political action.[62] The jurisprudence of these periods shapes the transition. Normative understandings of the role of law vary dramatically with the transition's political circumstances. Within transitional democracies, there is a place and a role for bounded political judgment. Legal processes enable measured rationalized change.

Beyond adjudication, normative change constructive of a new legality is also effected through other forms of law. Thus, the role of criminal sanctions ordinarily limited to punishing individual wrongdoing is greater during transitions, as such legal responses challenge past state criminality and therefore go to the core illegitimacy of past rule. These legal responses serve to condemn and delimit abuses of past state power. In the next chapter, I turn to the uses of criminal justice in transformative periods.

## CHAPTER TWO

# Criminal Justice

*I*n the public imagination, transitional justice is commonly linked with punishment and the trials of ancien régimes. The enduring symbols of the English and French Revolutions from monarchic to republican rule are the trials of Kings Charles I and Louis XVI. A half century after the events, the leading monument to the Nazis' World War II defeat remains the Nuremberg trials. The triumph of democracy over military rule in Southern Europe's transitions is represented in Greece's trials of its colonels. Argentina's junta trial marked the end of decades of repressive rule throughout Latin America. The contemporary wave of transitions from military rule, throughout Latin America and Africa, as well as from Communist rule in Central Europe and the former Soviet bloc, has revived the debate over whether to punish.

Punishment dominates our understandings of transitional justice. This harshest form of law is emblematic of accountability and the rule of law; yet, its impact far transcends its incidence. Review of transitional periods reveals that successor criminal justice raises profoundly agonizing questions for the affected societies, so that its exercise is often eschewed. The debate over transitional criminal justice is marked by profound dilemmas: Whether to punish or to amnesty? Whether punishment is a backward-looking exercise in retribution or an expression of the renewal of the rule of law? Who properly bears responsibility for past repression? To what extent is responsibility for repression appropriate to the individual, as opposed to the collective, the regime, and even the entire society?

The central dilemma intrinsic to transition is how to move from illiberal rule and to what extent this shift is guided by conventional notions of the rule of law and individual responsibility associated with established democracies. A core tension emerges here in the use of law to advance transformation, as opposed to its role in adherence to conventional legality. To what extent is transitional criminal justice conceptualized and adjudicated as extraordinary in the relevant societies or guided by the ordinary rule of law of established democracies? This core dilemma implies many others. What is the relevant legal order? Military or civilian? International or national? And, no matter what the relevant legal order, to what extent ought understandings of criminal responsibility be projected backward? Is the entire justice project hopelessly ex post? Who should be held to account, and, for what offense? These dilemmas of transition organize this chapter. These are the dilemmas successor societies struggle with; ultimately, as discussed below, they commonly strike a transitional compromise of the "limited criminal sanction," which is, more than anything, a symbolic form of punishment.

## The Foundational Argument for Criminal Justice in Transition

Why punish? The leading argument for punishment in periods of political flux is consequentialist and forward-looking: It is contended that, in societies with evil legacies moving out of repressive rule, successor trials play a significant foundational role in laying the basis of a new liberal order. At these times in a variant of the conventional "utilitarian" justification for punishment, the basis for punishment is its contribution to the social good.[1] But unlike the conventional arguments for punishment in ordinary times that either tend to focus on the perpetrator or on the consequences of punishment for the society, as deterrent, for example, the arguments for punishment in transition take another form. Rather than an argument for punishment in the affirmative, the argument is generally made in a counterfactual way—what result if no punishment? To what extent are broader rule-of-law values jeopardized without punishment? Here is where the particular political circumstances of the transition play a role. While the argument from "impunity," that is, arguing from the consequences of the failure to punish, is also made in ordinary times,[2] it is apparently stronger in transition, because in the conditions of prior lawlessness, expectations are greater of the impact of even isolated acts of accountability on rule of law. For these are extraordinary circumstances of past injustices, often state sponsored. It is against this backdrop that the argument from impunity takes on new meaning. In this context, the exercise of criminal justice is thought to best undo past state justice and to advance the normative transformation of these times to a rule-of-law system. Repressive regimes are often defined by criminal behavior, such as torture, arbitrary detention, disappearances, extrajudicial executions, all substantially state sponsored; even when past evil is perpetrated by private actors, the state is often, nevertheless, still implicated, whether in policies of persecution, by acts of omission in failing to protect its citizens, or, finally, in the cover-up of criminal acts and impunity. While the circumstances of transition, primarily the involvement of the state in criminal wrongdoing, make a most compelling argument for punishment over impunity, the paradox is that the very transitional circumstances of the ancien régime's implication in wrongdoing also raises significant dilemmas challenging the uses of the criminal law as effective response to state wrongdoing.

To enforce norms of the rule of law in the context of wrongdoing at the level of the state in the international realm is punishment's historic role. The foundational argument for successor trials has a rich historical pedigree going back to the Middle Ages, drawing from international legal norms relating justice to unlawful political violence. Trials have long been used to express international legal norms regarding injustice in war. The attribution of criminal responsibility to prior political leadership for waging unlawful war, or other similar bad state rule, is the thread running through the ancient successor trials of the tyrants of the city-states described by Aristotle and the trials of Kings Charles I and Louis XVI, to the trials in the contemporary period: the Nuremberg trials, the Tokyo war crimes trials, Greece's trial of the military colonels, and Argentina's trial of its military commanders.

Historically, successor trials rely on a concept of tyranny grounded in treason; of the unjust war as the lost war.[3] This early understanding of the relation of law to justice yields to another formulation at Nuremberg, where trials were used to express a much broader normative message going beyond the judgment of a defeated foreign régime, to distinguish "just" from "unjust" violence. In the contemporary moment, successor criminal justice is generalized beyond its postwar uses to other transitions in which its central normative force appears to be condemnatory of past political violence. The delegitimation of ancien régime violence goes beyond the purview of the postwar trial. Trials of the political leadership are used to construct the very meaning of state injustice. Punishment is largely defended on the grounds that it advances the society's political identity in the transition as a democratic rule of law-abiding state. Contemporary theorizing largely justifies punishment in transition for its potential role in constructing a newly democratic political order.[4] Successor trials are said to be politically useful in drawing a line between regimes, advancing the political goals of the transition by delegitimating the predecessor regime, and legitimating its successor. The trials of Kings Charles I and Louis XVI, as well as the Nuremberg trials, are said to be foundational political acts. As Michael Walzer writes, "Revolutionaries must settle with the old regime: that means they must find some ritual process through which the ideology it embodies . . . can be publicly repudiated."[5] Of the trial of King Louis XVI, Walzer contends that "public regicide is an absolutely decisive way of breaking with the myths of the old regime, and it is for this very reason, the founding act of the new."[6] The king's trial was politically definitive, because it established that he was not above the law.[7] Through the successor trial, the law instantiated equality under the law, thereby performing the essential normative shift implied in the movement from monarchic to republican rule. Successor trials were defended on similar grounds by the late Judith Shklar: "Trials may actually serve liberal ends, where they promote legalistic values in such a way as to contribute to constitutional politics and to a decent legal system."[8] In Otto Kirchheimer's words, trials enable "the construction of a permanent, unmistakable wall between the new beginnings and the old tyranny."[9]

In much prevailing political theorizing, successor trials are thought to have the potential of playing a distinct role in drawing the line between old tyrannies and new beginnings. Criminal justice offers normative legalism that helps to bridge periods of diminished rule of law. Trials offer a way to express both public condemnation of past violence and the legitimation of the rule of law necessary to the consolidation of future democracy. Successor criminal justice is generally justified by forward-looking consequentialist purposes relating to the establishment of the rule of law and to the consolidation of democracy.[10] This version of the consequentialist argument particular to transitions is characterized here as the "democracy" justification of punishment largely on the basis of the purposes of the transition. Criminal proceedings are well suited to affirm the core liberal message of the primacy of individual rights and responsibilities.

Nevertheless, successor trials' role in such periods is less foundational than it is transitional. Using criminal justice to draw the line between regimes raises profound dilemmas chiefly relating to the implied relation of law to politics. While trials in these political contexts are intended to serve political purposes—relating to the extraordinary message of transitional justice to lay the foundation of the political transition, to disavow predecessor political norms, and to construct a new legal order—these very features are in tension with conventional understandings of the rule of law. The core dilemma relates to the central feature of transition: the political context of the normative shift. This core dilemma raised by the political shift from illiberal to liberal rule is inextricably enmeshed in the problem of retroactivity in the relevant norms during the change of regime and the exercise of the successor regime's new normative rules as applied to the past regime's behavior. As the dilemma's full ramifications are played out, its consequences are deeply paradoxical: For trials to realize their constructive potential, they need to be prosecuted in keeping with the full legality associated with working democracies during ordinary times, and when they are not conducted in a visibly fair way, the very same trials can backfire, risking the wrong message of political justice and threatening a fledgling liberal state. Accordingly, successor trials walk a remarkably thin line between the fulfillment of the potential for a renewed adherence to the rule of law and the risk of perpetuating political justice. The apparent intractability of the dilemmas raised by the uses of the criminal law for transitional rule-of-law purposes clarifies why successor societies frequently forgo its use and why it has given rise to the development of a more "limited" form of the criminal sanction.

The transitional normative message is most clearly expressed through the international legal order, as its strengths are a normative machinery with the capacity to comprehend extraordinary political violence deployed outside the ordinary legal order. As such, it is well suited to express the transitional message of normative shift. Paradoxically, its strength is also its weakness, for its extraordinary nature clearly, at least to some extent, falls outside conventional legality and, therefore, ultimately does not sufficiently adhere to ordinary understandings of the rule of law to affirm democratizing transformation.

### The Legacy of Nuremberg

Since World War II, the vision of successor justice is dominated by the legacy of Nuremberg. The significance of the Nuremberg trials is best understood, in its full historical and political contexts, by returning to post–World War I transitional justice and its failed national trials policy.[11] Justice policy at Versailles throws into clear relief the justice policy at Nuremberg and clarifies why national trials were considered to be hopelessly political and doomed. The failure of that earlier postwar national justice is said to explain only the subsequent resurgence of German aggression; the failure of accountability is itself considered to cause the failure of liberalization. War-related guilt borne by the country as a whole was deemed to prevent a transition to lasting democracy. The view of national justice as hopelessly political represents prior postwar policy, with apparent repercussions for the century.

So it was that at Nuremberg the obverse of the postwar response became the norm. As after World War I, the mechanism for accountability is the trial, and the primary offense continues to be aggression. Nevertheless, the similarities end there. Nuremberg's significant differences are that accountability remained in Allied hands; jurisdiction was not national but international. And, rather than punishing the country, the aim was ascribing individual responsibility. Yet, as we shall see, the reality of the Nuremberg trials diverged from its intended mandate.

Nuremberg's legacy is complicated by the evident gap between the scholarly idealization of this singular precedent and its historical reality. A half century later, the trials' reverberations are still being felt. How justice was done at Nuremberg, including its profound irregularities, has become virtually synonymous with successor justice. A legal anomaly at the time, the Nuremberg trials remain a largely anomalous precedent, given the record of successor practices in this century. Yet, one way to better understand Nuremberg's precedential significance is to distinguish between various understandings of the precedent, for example, between Nuremberg as the proceedings, in the convening of the International Military Tribunal and the international criminal justice proceedings, and its doctrinal aspects, that is, the Nuremberg judgments. Beginning with the precedential aspect of the convening of these proceedings, it is here that the precedent is on the shakiest ground. In the fifty years since Nuremberg, while there is often talk about the desirability of such a tribunal, heightened during wartime, it has rarely culminated in trials, although, as we come to the century's end, momentum has been building for the establishment of a permanent international criminal court.[12]

The weight of the precedent is not in the proceedings but, rather, in the way it has shaped the pervasive understanding of transitional criminal justice. In the last half century, Nuremberg has shaped the dominant scholarly understanding of successor justice with the shift in approach, from national to international processes, as well as from the collective to the individual. Successor criminal justice—Nuremberg style—implied a wholly novel and international judicial forum, multinational criminal procedure, as well as offenses such as the "crime against humanity." The approach to successor justice is thoroughly international in its relevant offenses, bases for jurisdiction, and legal principles.

A historiographical look reveals the precedent's substantial impact in the scholarly literature, in particular, in how accountability is largely conceptualized in terms of international law. Review of the bibliographies concerning accountability for grave state crimes reveals that literature about international law responses to atrocities since World War II, particularly in the English language, has grown rapidly, while the comparative study of national experiences is, by contrast, virtually ignored.[13] Historically, one reason for the weight of scholarship relating to postwar successor justice is that it reflected the parallel developments of international law. The postwar period witnessed an unprecedented successful multilateral cooperation in the International Military Tribunal at Nuremberg, the establishment of the United Nations, as well as the passage of numerous conventions and resolutions regarding international crimes. The depth of the atrocities of the National Socialists and their collaborators spurred a previously unattainable international consensus. The optimism and momentum of the newfound consensus about international crimes, as well as the international cooperation of the trials, made credible the hope of creating a body of international criminal law regarding state persecution that would be enforced by some manner of international tribunal. Legal literature reflects these advances in international legal structures and pronouncements. A burgeoning international law literature regarding the responses to state persecution incorporated the themes and vocabulary of an emerging international criminal law: the way the crimes were defined, the significance of the International Military Tribunal, the expansion of jurisdiction over certain acts, and, perhaps the most significant notion, the emergence of national rights and duties within a new international community. All became major areas of study that continue to the present.

Nevertheless, the historical justification for framing the successor justice question in international law terms has largely dissipated. Postwar hopes for developing an international criminal law today remain largely unfulfilled. The early enthusiasm for international law's advances is now tempered by sober reflection on the relative inefficiency of international mechanisms for responding to atrocity. International penal law remains in its infancy: There is still no international criminal code. And, despite repeated calls for an international criminal court or even the creation of criminal jurisdiction in the International Court of Justice, the forum has yet to be created. In very recent developments, a consensus has emerged in the international community supportive in principle of a standing international criminal court before the end of the century.[14] Yet, granting an international body jurisdiction over criminal offenses other than genocide remains a sticking point with countries that are staunchly opposed, such as the United States. Even in international law controversies of a noncriminal nature in which international jurisdiction has been premised on consent, it is fair to say that there has been a race to the bottom.[15] Accordingly, international crimes that have been defined have not always been accompanied with universal jurisdiction. With standing in the International

Court of Justice exclusively for states and with incentives for states to remain impervious to suit, the present international legal structure has not helped in the enforcement of the convention protecting against genocide and other international law guarantees. The literature calling for increased international norms and enforcement mechanisms extends well beyond the parameters of the postwar consensus and the international legal system.[16] The gap between international law's definitions of crimes and its mechanisms for enforcement remains a yawning chasm. Nevertheless, despite its extraordinary nature, international law offers a normative vocabulary that somehow mediates many of the dilemmas of transitional justice.

## Transitional Dilemmas and the Nuremberg Paradigm Shift

The paradigm of justice established at Nuremberg and its vocabulary of international law, despite its shortcomings, continue to frame the successor justice debate. Within the international legal system, the dilemmas of successor justice fall away. The view of national justice as hopelessly political derives from the earlier history of post–World War I policy, with apparent repercussions for the century. In the abstract, the dilemmas of successor justice are seemingly best resolved by turning to an autonomous legal system. While within the national legal scheme, the question of justice seems inextricably political, from an international law perspective, the question of justice is somehow divorced from national politics.[17] Even where international justice is utterly ad hoc, as for example regarding atrocities in the Balkans conflicts, somehow it is, nevertheless, considered less political than the alternatives in the region. International law is thought to lift justice out of its politicized national context.

### International Law and the Dilemma
### of Retroactive Justice

The core transitional dilemma is how to conceptualize justice in the context of a massive normative shift. This problem is mitigated within international law, for international law offers a degree of continuity in law and, in particular, in standards of accountability. Thus, the postwar entrenchment of international legal norms is considered to afford a jurisdictional basis that goes beyond the limits of domestic criminal law. International law seemingly offers a way to circumvent the retrospectivity problem that is endemic to transitional justice. International standards and forums uphold the rule of law, while satisfying core fairness and impartiality concerns. The precedential and binding value of international legal action is frequently deemed superior to efforts undertaken on a state-by-state basis. Differences in domestic law mean certain crimes will be punishable in some countries and not in others. Further, truly heinous crimes, such as atrocities, do not easily fit in national law, because such crimes are conceptualized in fundamentally different ways than are offenses under national law. Certain crimes, such as torture, either fit awkwardly or are often not recognized in national law, though the move toward the incorporation of international law standards into domestic law may somewhat obviate this problem.

International criminal law offers an intelligible way to conceptualize the somewhat paradoxical possibility of the responsibility of an evil regime under the law. So it is that international criminal law builds a historical analogy of postwar justice that dominates the Nuremberg trials. It is definitional of justice at Nuremberg, with the arch offense, the waging of war. And, according to its charter, the trials' purpose was to prosecute the major war criminals for offenses—all in some way related to the war. And the trials' forum is an international military tribunal, and the leading offense, aggression. Even "crimes against humanity," atrocities committed against civilians, were prosecuted at Nuremberg, only if related to the war. This prudential restraint observed by the tribunal perpetrated the historical view of state injustice as that perpetrated by a foreign power. This narrow line circumscribing the Nuremberg prosecutions would have ramifications constraining the precedent's potential for transitional justice.

### The Dilemma of State Crimes but Individual Responsibility

Transitional criminal justice raises a core dilemma of how to ascribe criminal accountability for offenses that often implicate the state in repression policy. International jurisprudence offers a standard in the Nuremberg principles. Formulated after the trial at the request of the United Nations General Assembly, the "Nuremberg Principles" comprise the distillation of the Nuremberg judgment and constitute a pivotal turning point in the conceptualization of responsibility for state crime. For the first time, the tribunal and the follow-up trials clearly established that responsibility for atrocities under international law could be attributed to individuals: "Any person who commits an act which constitutes a crime under international law is responsible therefore and liable to punishment."[18] Further, in rejecting traditional defenses to individual responsibility for atrocities, Nuremberg dramatically expanded the potential individual criminal liability for state wrongs. While, traditionally, heads of state enjoyed sovereign immunity under the Nuremberg Principles, public officials could no longer avail themselves of a "head of state" defense based on their official positions but, instead, could be held criminally responsible.[19] Although under traditional military rules applicable in a command structure, "due obedience" to orders is a defense, under the Nuremberg Principles, persons acting under orders could be held responsible.[20] In eliminating the "act of state" and "superior orders" defenses, the Nuremberg Principles pierce the veil of diffused responsibility characterizing the wrongdoing perpetrated under totalitarian regimes. Under the law of war, the principle of command responsibility affords a basis for attribution of responsibility to superiors for wrongdoing. This basis is reinforced by the Nuremberg Principles lifting the defense of immunity from the heads of state. The extreme in status-based prosecutions after

Nuremberg is illustrated in the Tokyo war crimes trials for atrocities committed in the Philippines, where the principle of command responsibility was broadly enforced. In the Tokyo trials, General Tomoyuki Yamashita was held criminally responsible for atrocities committed by his troops, convicted, and executed—all without any showing of personal involvement or even knowledge of the acts committed by his subordinates. Nevertheless, the courts hearing his case said that "he should have known" of the violations of the law of war in the area under his command.[21] From the vantage point of subsequent history, *Yamashita*'s negligence standard for command responsibility would be sui generis, an extreme in the conception of official responsibility for the persecution perpetrated by subordinates. In the subsequent *High Command* and *Hostage* trials against high-ranking German army officers, the *Yamashita* standard was rejected, and the courts insisted on knowledge and individual participation or acquiescence in the criminal acts or criminal neglect: "Criminality does not attach to every individual in this chain of command. . . . There must be a personal dereliction."[22]

Vietnam revived scholarly interest on the question of leadership responsibility for grave state crimes, and it made very clear the high political stakes involved in a permissive principle of command responsibility.[23] Cases concerning the Mylai atrocities led to the narrowing of the principle of command responsibility. There had to be some connection between the atrocities occurring in the area under the commander's control and some sense of personal fault on the commander's part.[24] This version of the principle of command responsibility is now enshrined in the international legal conventions: Failure to take measures to avert particular harm is proscribed. Explicitly rejecting the *Yamashita* "should have known" standard, under article 86 of the postwar Geneva Conventions, "knowledge" triggers a duty to take "all feasible measures" to prevent or repress the breach.[25]

International humanitarian law offers a normative framework and language for thinking about successor justice.[26] Regime wrongdoing can be conceptualized and accommodated under the rubric of the law of war. Thus, the principle of individual responsibility at Nuremberg is complex, seen in the evolution of the principle of command responsibility, as well as in the way the principle itself mediates individual and collective responsibility. It is also seen in the International Military Tribunal's reliance on principles, such as the law of conspiracy, whereby individuals were prosecuted purely on the basis of their membership in particular groups.[27] Nevertheless, it is difficult to adjust international law and its military analogy to incorporate a full account of successor justice. For the international paradigm implies a status-based approach to successor criminal justice, which largely relates individual political status to context within the regime. Yet, a broad status-based liability standard, as exemplified in the *Yamashita* case, suggests that holding commanders accountable for the acts of their subordinates can backfire. When such prosecutions rely on official status as a basis for criminal liability, they threaten the principle of individual responsibility.

After Nuremberg, our understanding of successor liability was never the same. For the Nuremberg Principles wrought a radical expansion of potential individual criminal liability—at both ends of the power hierarchy. Postwar jurisprudence signified a radical expansion in potential individual criminal liability with no clear stopping point. The absence of a recognized stopping point was conceded even at the time. While prosecutions commenced with the major war criminals, nothing in the Nuremberg Charter limited ascribing responsibility to the Nazi regime's top echelon. On the contrary, the charter explicitly contemplated that holding the leaders accountable was just the beginning and that there would be all sorts of follow-up trials.[28] During the postwar transformation in the understanding of individual responsibility for grave state crimes, the following dilemma emerges: While the principles generated at Nuremberg radically expanded the potential individual criminal liability, they do not offer a basis for deciding who, among all of those potentially liable, to bring to trial.

The post-Nuremberg liability explosion has massive ramifications that have not yet been fully absorbed. Among political analysts and legal scholars, Nuremberg is understood to have effected profound changes in the understanding of individual criminal responsibility under international law, but there is no appreciation of how the changes pose dilemmas of liability. The massive contemporary expansion in potential criminal liability raises real dilemmas for successor regimes deliberating over whom to bring to trial and for what crimes. Indeed, the problem is evident in the scholarship regarding punishment in transition,[29] going to the reasons that transcend the particulars of a country's political contexts and, rather, go to contemporary developments in the conceptualization of legal responsibility. To the extent that there is even a workable guiding principle, it is the implied one of proportionality. The priority is to target those "most responsible for the worst crimes," starting with those at the highest level of responsibility for the most egregious crimes.[30] Yet, as is more fully discussed below, proportionality in the abstract does not fully address the dilemmas raised by the attempt to respond to pervasive crimes of repressive rule within the criminal law. Indeed, as transitional practices discussed below suggest, the punishment priority is not a universal ideal but, rather, contingent on the particular society's political circumstances, as well as on the extent of its normative shift.

## Playing out the Nuremberg Precedent in National Courts

Though deploying military principles of responsibility may be sensible in a postwar context, and transitions often follow war, they also occur in other ways, and the Nuremberg standards do not easily guide this successor justice. Nevertheless, the appeal of the international criminal justice framework extends beyond postwar trials to other modes of successor justice.

Transitional justice is caught between the analogies of war and peace and, relatedly, between international humanitarian and domestic law. The military analogy is evident when successor trials policy begins with prosecution of the prior regime's leadership. Grounding criminal responsibility on political status extends the logic of the analogy to war crimes to abuses perpetrated under dictatorship and other repressive rule. Our intuitions after nondemocratic rule may well be that it is fair to ascribe responsibility to the top political leadership, yet the grounding of transitional justice in the extraordinary international law paradigm and the law of war seems at odds with our intuitions about criminal justice. The question raised is whether responsibility for wrongs perpetrated under repressive regimes can be fairly attributed to a state's top political echelon. To what extent is the political authority arrogated by dictators, or a repressive regime in and of itself a basis for criminal liability? Grounding criminal liability on the basis of the offender's official status would generally be at odds with our intuitions about the operation of the criminal law in democracies and poses a profound challenge to the rule of law.

Successor trials grounded in international law's reliance on the law of war are few and far between. Thus, Latin America's transitions out of military rule are a rare contemporary example. In Argentina, it was the defeat in the Falkland's war that brought the army to collapse and enabled the transition from military junta to democracy, culminating in the prosecution of junta leaders for "gross negligence" in the waging of war.[31]

In another contemporary example, after the Soviet collapse, the transitions in that region are haunted by a pervasive sense of occupation, analogous to postwar defeat. So it is that the revolutions in Hungary and the former Czechoslovakia begin in commemorations of the resistance to the Soviet and Nazi invasions. There were critical questions of transitional justice in the region: Whose dictatorship? Whose justice? After the Communist collapse, the pivotal question of successor justice is to what extent the repression could be viewed fully in terms of the long-standing postwar paradigm—as that of a foreign occupier. Ultimately, the question framed shifts from that of national responsibility to that of individual responsibility. So it is that the former leadership was called to task for collaboration in the Soviet invasions of their countries. Successor trials are conceived around defining juncture points, drawing the line between freedom and repression, resistance and collaboration. This is the line that is being drawn and redrawn in the trials in the region.

The critical juncture point in the former Czechoslovakia was 1968. In the first wave of prosecutions after the "velvet" revolution, former party leaders were brought to trial for treason in collaborating, framed in terms of abuses of public power in the crushing of the Prague spring.[32] Four years later, a new law declaring communism "unlawful" and "illegitimate" laid a basis for further prosecutions.[33] The law defined as an offense, the "joining of forces with a foreign power," such as assisting in the country's occupation after 1968. Thus, the former secretary of the Central Committee of the Communist Party, Vasil Bilák, was charged with treason for inviting the armies of the Warsaw Pact countries into Czechoslovakia in 1968. Ultimately, however, these prosecutions largely culminated only in investigations of the period.[34]

In Poland, the question dominating the Polish parliamentary commission's investigation of the country's former leader, General Wojciech Jaruzelski,[35] was whether the former regime's 1981 imposition of martial law crushing the Solidarity movement was the result of Soviet pressure or a sign of an all-too-willing Polish collaboration. If Jaruzelski's decision to impose martial law resulted from an agreement with a foreign government, it could have become the basis for a treason trial.[36] Other prosecution proceedings were limited to those constituting "war crimes," pursuant to the analogy to international law.

Successor justice in Hungary was formally grounded on the basis of treason defined as collaboration with the Soviets and, in particular, in the bloody suppression of the 1956 uprising.[37] Constitutional review of Hungary's treason law addressed core transitional dilemmas raised by using criminal law to condemn what had been previously condoned under the prior regime. When Hungary's Constitutional Court held newly enacted treason legislation unconstitutional because it suffered from retroactivity,[38] a follow-up law that limited prosecutable offenses to "war crimes"[39] enabled the prosecutions to go forward based on an analogy to postwar trials. When the Communist Party leadership was put on trial in Romania in trials otherwise lacking in the rule of law, it was for war crimes under international law. "Genocide" charges were brought in military courts against the top leadership for attempting to put down a popular uprising in 1989, though convictions were ultimately obtained on lesser charges. "Crimes-against-humanity" charges were invoked also against former Communist officials in Albania in the transition.

A concerted effort is now underway to expand and normalize postwar understandings of state persecution. This effort is evident, for example, in developments in international humanitarian law in which understanding of the offense of wartime persecution extends beyond the international response to actions within the state.[40] It is also seen in the jurisdiction of the ad hoc international war crimes tribunal regarding the former Yugoslavia, as well as in that jurisdiction of the proposed international criminal court. In these contemporary instances, a dynamic understanding of "crimes against humanity" moves beyond a predicated nexus to armed conflict to become virtually synonymous with persecution.[41]

International law's perceived advantage in creating criminal accountability, in particular, international humanitarian law combined with the real advances of the immediate postwar period, has rendered international criminal law the dominant language of successor justice. Though its strength is not evident in a record of international trials, its profound normative force is evident in the emerging understanding that state persecution transcends national law to imply international accountability. The recognition of a shared language gives rise to a form of accountability, in the identification and exposure of persecution across national borders.[42] When states fail to protect, the leading response of the international human rights community to state persecution is in documenting and reporting grave abuses. In recent years, significant developments have occurred in the strengthening of international mechanisms designed to investigate and publicize claims of atrocities. Worldwide accountability occurs primarily through the exposure and public censure of state persecution. Thus, if and when it is established, the role of a permanent international criminal tribunal may well be as an ongoing investigatory and indicting body. The greatest legacy of the Nuremberg precedent is that the question of state accountability would never again be confined within national borders but instead, would be a matter of international import.

## Transitional Justice and the National Legal Order in Comparative Prespective

Despite the appeal of the international scheme, as a general matter, most regimes in transition attempt to normalize the succession by integrating their responses within the existing legal system. The questions then become how successor justice might account for the change in political regimes and, in particular, how to accommodate the central feature of transition, the normative shift implied by the change in political regimes. Transitional responses in national law vary in their ability to accommodate political transformation, because these juridical processes are convened within a prevailing legality. Often, the attempt to obtain accountability for predecessor wrongdoing stretches domestic law systems to their limits. These responses to extraordinary political violence test core rule-of-law principles of security and general applicability of the law.

A record of national trials follows waves of political transition. Before World War I, there were trials for atrocities committed against Armenians within the Ottoman Empire.[43] After World War I, the agreement at Versailles was for Germany to conduct its own national trials; these would be very limited in number. Following World War II, the actions of the National Socialists and their collaborators prompted massive attempts at accountability. Despite the dominance of the international paradigm in the scholarly literature, the legal responses to National Socialism and its collaborators were, in the main, domestic in nature. Prosecutions of those implicated in World War II–related atrocities still constitute the largest body of precedent of criminal accountability at the national level. These national trials span close to five decades, encompassing common law, civil and socialist legal systems, and extending to almost every country where the crimes were committed and beyond.[44] Moreover, throughout Europe, the domestic law impact of the postwar transitions is still being felt. In Germany, World War II–related prosecutions have been ongoing, from the 1950s to the contemporary period.[45] In France, the late 1980s' trial of Klaus Barbie was followed by other cases brought against high-level French collaborators, such as Paul Touvier and Maurice Papon.[46] Holland continues to prosecute its collaborators. Australia and Canada saw prosecutions of World War II collaborators residing in these countries in the late 1980s.[47] In the United Kingdom, the War Crimes Act of 1991 was passed to enable prosecuting of suspected wartime collaborators residing throughout the United Kingdom.

In the twentieth century's second wave of transitions, in southern Europe, instances of successor trials are those of the Greek and Portuguese juntas.[48] In the third wave of political transition in Latin America and Africa, Argentina put its military commanders, as well as other army officers on trial; and in the Central African Republic, despot Emperor Jean-Bedel Bokassa was brought to trial. In the transitions out of Communist rule, there have been scattered trials of the top leadership in Romania and Bulgaria, and in the former Czechoslovakia, trials of high- and mid-level party officials. In Germany, there have been trials at all levels, generally relating to the shootings at the Berlin Wall.[49] The collapse of Yugoslavia sparked Bosnian conflicts and atrocities and was followed by trials. After the collapse of its Marxist regime, Ethiopia put on trial the top echelon of the prior regime.[50] Since its political transition, Rwanda has been in the midst of genocide trials.[51]

### State Crimes but Individual Justice

Transitional criminal justice raises the dilemma of trying to apply the principle of individual responsibility to grave crimes committed under illiberal rule. After repression, the central problem is that the state ought to respond where it is responsible through a prior regime implicated in prior wrongdoing. How can the state mediate the normative shift between regimes in these paradoxical, compromised circumstances of justice that involve the likelihood of state implication in past wrongs? In these conditions, what is the relation of individual and state responsibility?

In shifts after repressive rule, the pervasiveness of persecution in undemocratic societies often defies principled attempts to secure retribution. The ensuing critical question that arises in attributing criminal accountability is, What should the priority be? Should it be the political leadership that masterminded the repression or those at the very bottom of the political echelon who personally committed the brutal acts? Should a successor punishment policy prosecute all wrongdoers, or might selective prosecutions be fair? And, if a selective prosecution policy is adopted, on what basis should such policy be adopted?

Where ought a prosecution policy begin? The normative claim that punishment advances the rule of law does not necessarily justify punishing all offenders. Indeed, the aims of defending democracy and affirming the rule of law can well be served by exemplary prosecutions. As a practical matter, it would seem that some selectivity is inevitable, given the large numbers generally implicated in modern state persecution, scarcity of judicial resources in transitional societies, and the high political and other costs of successor trials. Given these constraints, selective or exemplary trials, it would seem, can advance a sense of justice.[52] But the line is a thin one. An exemplary prosecutions policy runs the risk of undermining the very democracy purposes of the trials, advancing instead a rank message of political justice. Selective prosecutions policy can threaten the rule of law.

Who is properly accountable for the atrocities of repressive societies?

How should criminal accountability be ascribed between those who gave orders to persecute and those who followed? What principle can do this work? Ordinarily, our sense of what makes for criminal responsibility is that there should be a degree of fault, a relation between the harm and individual wrongdoing.[53] Nevertheless, our intuitions regarding criminal liability do not well account for the peculiar nature of transitional dilemmas. For prosecuting crimes perpetrated in the context of repressive rule implies a special case of systemic wrongdoing and, therefore, of related governmental liability, such as the violation of special duties, of public officials' responsibility for their subordinates, and, more basically, of the state's core duty of protection of its citizens.[54]

Historically, those considered most responsible for past wrongdoing in transition have been in the top political leadership. Contemporary successor trials demonstrate the difficulty of holding the political leadership accountable for the worst abuses of repressive rule. Thus, for example, in the successor trials following the Communist collapse, the attempt to bring the prior leadership to account meant prosecuting offenses perpetrated either at the very beginning of repressive rule or during the regime's last gasps. Returning to offenses committed in the course of the Communist takeover meant going back about half a century. Bringing trials after the passage of time implies difficulty in gaining jurisdiction and procedural irregularities that threaten the very ability of successor trials to reestablish the rule of law. Under most systems of law, whether common law, continental law, or Socialist law, liability is circumscribed on the basis of time in statutes of limitations; therefore, bringing trials after time necessitates tampering with the prevailing law. For the most egregious crimes—those constituting genocide or persecution under international law—international legal norms have been incorporated into national law, precisely to mediate the problems of reconciling the extraordinary dilemmas of transitional justice within domestic legal systems. Thus, for example, in Hungary, where a thirty-year limitations law prevented the trials of those responsible for the violent suppression of the 1956 uprising, the attempt to lift the law after the fact was deemed unconstitutionally ex post facto. Nevertheless, an exception was made for the most serious crimes—war crimes under international law—which were deemed to have ongoing normative force. A similar accomodation was made in Poland.[55] The dilemma of the norm change was exemplified in unified Germany's prosecutions for offenses relating to the East's border policy. Challenges based on prevailing legality, such as on the basis of retroactivity, were superseded by alternative norms drawn from international law (elaborated on in the prior chapter discussing the rule of law). Similar limitations barred the trial of the former Romanian interior minister, and head of the secret police, for violent crimes committed in 1954.[56] In the 1990s, Poland's former security officers, including the head of the Ministry of Public Security, were brought to trial for crimes committed between 1946 and 1952 involving the torture and deaths of political prisoners; because of the passage of time, prosecutions of these Stalin-era crimes necessitated parliamentary lifting of the applicable statutes of limitations.[57] Ultimately, the accommodation would be limited, as in Hungary, to war crimes prosecutable under international law after the passage of time. Similar tampering with the prior limitations law in the Czech Republic was sustained by its Constitutional Court.[58] In sustaining the law allowing the change, the court said its choices were the difficult ones of either approving or condemning the legality of the prior Communist regime. To reconcile the apparent dilemma, adherence to the past statute of limitations and past legality was considered by the court to be merely "procedural," letting the prosecutions go forward in the name of political transformation.

Perhaps the extreme case of attempting to accommodate the criminal response to the context of prior totalitarian repression is that of Germany's prosecution of its former East German Stasi security police chief, Erich Mielke. The attempt to bring this senior official to justice led all the way back to 1931, when he murdered two policemen in the last days of the Weimar Republic—sixty-one-year-old offenses.[59] Yet, prosecuting Mielke for offenses committed under the predecessor regime, long before his assuming Communist leadership, hardly relates to the abuses perpetrated under his rule. This transitional precedent exemplifies the difficulty of accounting for repression within ordinary understandings of criminal justice.

Bringing to justice the top echelon for the most heinous crimes has otherwise devolved on the violence attending last-ditch efforts to sustain Communist rule. Thus, for example, in Romania, aides to Nicolae Ceauşescu were convicted for their roles in the attempted suppression of the 1989 anti-Communist uprising.[60] In the Czech Republic, charges were brought against the head of the Communist Party, the Prague former security chief, and the former interior minister and his deputy general for the brutal repression of demonstrations in 1988 and 1989.[61] In Russia, one of the few criminal proceedings initiated was against the perpetrators of the August 1991 putsch.[62] Yet, these trials seem strangely besides the point. Prosecuting offenses committed in the predecessor regime's last gasps can hardly express a critical normative message against totalitarian rule.

Criminal accountability has otherwise devolved on the basis of "bad rule," which after the fall of Communism has generally meant economic crime. In the transitions from command economies to free market systems, economic crime prosecutions have a unique transformative force. Just as the trials of the eighteenth-century transitions out of monarchic rule attacked the institution of monarchical rule, so, too, the successor trials in the twentieth-century transitions have been used to delegitimate Communism. Post-Communist economic crime trials condemn the predecessor regime's values regarding the normative relation of the economy and the state. Prosecutions against the former leadership were initiated for all sorts of economic crimes: Bulgaria's was the most ambitious, with embezzlement charges brought against the country's longtime ruler, Todor Zhivhov.[63] In the only other trial of a Communist head of state, Albania's former president, Ramiz Alia, was prosecuted for abuse of power and embezzlement for misappropriating state property.[64] In Germany, the head of East Germany's labor federation was prosecuted for stealing union money and convicted of "fraud against socialist property."[65] In the Czech Republic, former Communist leaders were subject to criminal investigations relating to tax evasion.[66] Economic offenses have centered on the theft of "communal property," though such property and the related crimes largely no longer exist in the post-Communist regimes.

Another example is the Moscow trial of its Communist Party.[67] Although there are precedents for criminalizing organizations, such as at Nuremberg, there the organizational convictions served as predicates for subsequent individual charges.[68] Individual prosecutions were based on criminal membership. "Bernays' brain-child," named after the lawyer who masterminded the procedure, was developed in order to surmount the practical and evidentiary obstacles to the potential prosecutions of several thousand members of the German SS for atrocities committed. In its unconventional use of the criminal process, the Moscow trial tests the boundaries of the criminal law for transitional justice. To the extent party practices could be shown to be corrupt and unlawful, the attempt was to put communism out of the bounds of legitimate political choice. Similar trials of the antecedent regime were initiated in Ethiopia in its post-Marxist transition.[69]

When prosecutions target offenses relating to the past economic system that have lost their force with the change in economic regime, they illustrate the mirror image of the retroactivity problem endemic to successor justice, in so far as they lack legal prospectivity. While successor trials frequently raise the ex post facto problem of prosecuting new offenses in the former Communist bloc, failing to adhere to principles protecting prospectivity or guarding against similarly conventional legality.

Though transitional regimes often attempt to bring the prior leadership to account, the dilemma is that the most serious offenses perpetrated under the prior regime often cannot be attributed to the prior regime's leadership. Indeed, it is often difficult to make out enough of a connection between the political leadership and the worst offenses of repressive rule, so that in successor trials, the leadership is often brought to trial for offenses that are seemingly besides the point. When a criminal justice policy targets the prior leadership to prosecute offenses that fall short of the most grave, for example, when the elements of political responsibility and gravity of offense become attenuated, successor trials are most vulnerable to the perception of political justice. Such prosecutions are in tension with our intuitions about adherence to the rule of law.

In other successor trials held at the national level, justice has not been brought to bear necessarily against its highest echelon but instead against those responsible for perpetrating the worst offenses in the former regime. This punishment policy can lead all the way down to the lowest rung of the security state, to the police and guards who personally committed brutalities. A prominent example of such trials was Greece's 1975 "torturers trials."[70] A more contemporary example is unified Germany's trials of its border guards. These cases suggest that it is difficult to pursue successor justice from the perspective of an ordinary crime framework. Though such prosecution policy may well have the virtue of identifying and condemning the serious offenses of the prior rule, they raise a significant rule-of-law dilemma. For while they enforce the value of general and equal applicability of the law, they also simultaneously test the limits of this rule-of-law value. Equality under the law is instantiated; in prosecuting anyone implicated in past wrongs, there is an attendant, somewhat paradoxical, arbitrariness in such prosecution policy, which is a central dilemma in the uses of the criminal law to construct democratic transition.

## The Problem of Responsibility in the Transition

The successor trials discussed above suggest that it is difficult to conceptualize and apply ordinary understandings of criminal wrongdoing under domestic law in the aftermath of repressive regimes, for successor criminal justice raises a quandary about who is the proper subject of the punishment policy. What is the right standard of accountability in shifts between regimes characterized by command control to those associated with greater individual agency? Should penal law model itself after understandings of responsibility prevalent in totalitarian and authoritarian regimes, or should law's role be transformative, modeling itself after understandings of responsibility characteristic of liberal states? And to what extent does the criminal law itself play a role in the political shift? In the late twentieth century, the direction has been toward an ever-increasing expansion in potential criminal liability: After Nuremberg, both leaders and soldiers are potentially responsible for state wrongdoing. How to conceptualize responsibility along a power echelon? To what extent ought both leaders and subordinates be held responsible for the same criminal act? Does the attribution of criminal responsibility to the one imply lesser criminal responsibility to the other; might prosecuting superiors absolve subordinates, or vice versa? As a practical matter, at the level of proof, there is often an undeniable relation in the liability of leaders and their subordinates. Command responsibility can be proved top-down often depending on evidence of unlawful policy set at the top or, conversely, if low-level officers resort to due-obedience defenses, proven "bottom-up" by establishing evidence of crime at the lower levels.

This problematic aspect of transitional justice is illustrated both in historical postwar as well as contemporary successor trials, such as Argentina's trials of its military and unified Germany's trials relating to the shootings at the Berlin Wall. Historically, the question of the relativity of liability for the wrongs perpetrated under repressive rule arose in Germany's national trials for World War II–related atrocities. These cases squarely raised the problem of how to characterize criminal responsibility along a power continuum. For example, in a case concerning the brutal massacre of four thousand near the Lithuanian border, the Ulm County Court struggled with how to characterize defendants' responsibility. Adolf Hitler and his immediate circle were held to be the "chief perpetrators" of the relevant annihilation measures, while the defendants in the case were considered to be merely acting as "accomplices"—contributing to the deeds of the "chief perpetrators." In these cases, the national courts followed an apparently "zero-sum" approach to the notion of criminal responsibility, ultimately limiting the total liability for prior wrongdoing.[71]

The problem of the relativity of liability in transition is epitomized by unified Germany's prosecutions for the shooting deaths at the Berlin Wall. For nearly a half century, the Berlin Wall was the leading international symbol of Communist oppression. The site of repeated escape efforts to freedom and state-ordered shootings, the wall expressed the totality of the Communists' viselike hold, and its fall also symbolized the massive political changes in the region. After its collapse, the question became how to ascribe criminal responsibility when repression was engineered by the country's political leadership but executed by its guards.

Prosecutions of the Berlin Wall shootings are distinguished by their lopsided verdicts as many low-level guards were brought to trial, while there has been comparatively little or no accountability at the top. In the leading case, two guards were convicted for a shooting death at the border, though they claimed to be merely following orders.[72] These convictions sounded a ringing reaffirmation of the Nuremberg principle that the defense of due obedience must yield to the principle of individual responsibility; nevertheless, vindication of the principle rang somewhat hollow in the general dearth of similar accountability at the top. Although former East German leader Erich Honecker and five other senior officials were indicted for masterminding the "shoot-to-kill" policy at the border, most of the proceedings were dropped.[73] Of those few convicted, the sentences received were minimal. When the lead architects of a country's "shoot-to-kill" policy evade accountability, the principle of individual responsibility appears to be vulnerable. Consider why this might be so. The border guards cases suggest that there is an intimate relationship between commander and subordinate responsibility for crimes perpetrated under systemically repressive rule. The dilemma of individual responsibility is resolved by the similar charging of so-called armchair perpetrators and hitmen apportioning liability all around and diffusing responsibility for the crimes of totalitarian rule.

The above dilemma arising in post-totalitarian periods is also evident in other transitions. After military rule, how do we conceptualize the legal responsibility of commanders and their subordinates for the brutalities of the police state? When one person orders another to commit a crime, who is the "perpetrator?" This was the central question in Argentina's successor trials of its military junta. The "coauthorship" theory put forward by the lower courts considered superior responsibility to be fully compatible with subordinate responsibility for the same offense under a German doctrine termed "control of the act," whereby criminal responsibility attaches to both the indirect and direct perpetrators. Thus, the junta was held responsible for its role in the planning and ordering of torture and disappearances as "indirect perpetrators," while others implicated in the offenses were held responsible as "direct perpetrators."[74] However, on appeal, the "coauthorship" theory was modified by the country's Supreme Court, which in a divided opinion sought to apply ordinarily applicable notions of criminal responsibility to the crimes of the repressive apparatus. "The simultaneous existence of both levels of criminal responsibility is unfounded," the high court held, because if a person is responsible for performing a crime, he has "control of the act," leaving no room for "indirect perpetrator" liability in the commanders. Accordingly, the commanders were considered, instead, "accomplices" to persecution.[75] Strangely, this characterization of criminal responsibility apparently converted the principals of state repression into its agents. The junta precedent elided what is significant about high ranking official complicity in persecution. Moreover, the ramifications of this view of responsibility were profound. Though there were few penal consequences of the charges for the ex-commandents, their prosecutions as "indirect authors" seemingly opened the door to the limiting of liability in the security apparatus' lower ranks, and ultimately led to the prosecution policy's undoing. Recognition of commander responsibility as perpetrators of repressive policy set from the top encouraged the invocation of "due obedience" in the so-called subordinates, and the apparent circumscription of individual responsibility. After relentless military resistance to the prosecutions, the due-obedience defense was revived as a way to cap the potential number of trials, exempting only "atrocious" acts that went beyond the terms of orders given. In the end, these trials were halted as well. The failure of the successor trials program in Argentina illustrates the risky consequences of the attempt to pursue punishment in the context of the contemporary expansion in understandings of responsibility, and yet nevertheless in transitional circumstances. Lacking any obvious limiting principle, much of the country's army was exposed to potential prosecution, a specter causing great instability, which, ultimately culminated in systemwide pardons and amnesties.[76]

After military rule, Argentina's prosecution policy was vulnerable for beginning with the ruling junta but stopping at the lower echelon. Conversely, after Communism, Germany's prosecution policy was vulnerable for largely failing to bring to justice those at the higher echelons. Both experiences of successor justice reveal the difficulty of using criminal justice after authoritarian and totalitarian rule to construct a normative message of liberalizing change. Pursuit of individual responsibility for offenses committed pursuant to systemic repression implies profound dilemmas of responsibility. The question is where responsibility ought to be attributed following systemic repression. The successor practices discussed suggest that these systemic crimes defy ordinary understandings of criminal responsibility and relevant guiding principles. Systemic wrongdoing spans the power continuum of leaders and followers, challenging the criminal sanction. Ultimately, the appropriate level of responsibility is captured by offenses that incorporate the mediating role of policy that characterizes contemporary repression.

## The Limited Criminal Sanction

Transitional practices over the last half century suggest there are recurring problems of justice as a result of the paradigmatic norm shift characterizing transition. These compromised conditions of justice imply limitations on, and forbearance from, the exercise of the punishment power in transitions. Despite the dramatic expansion in criminal liability in the abstract, enforcement lags far behind. Successor practices reveal a pattern of criminal investigations and prosecutions often with little or no penalty. Whereas ordinarily punishment is conceptualized as a unitary practice comprehending both the establishment and punishment of wrongdoing, in the transitional criminal sanction, the elements of establishing and sanctioning have become somewhat detached from one another. The ensuing partial criminal process here termed the "limited" sanction is what distinguishes criminal justice in transition.

The "limited criminal sanction" comprises prosecution processes that do not necessarily culminate in full punishment. In the limited sanction, the phases of ascertaining guilt and of ascribing penalty are differentiated. Depending on just how limited the sanctioning process, investigations may or may not lead to indictments, adjudication, and conviction. Moreover, convictions are commonly followed by light or no punishment. Thus, in transitional periods, the criminal sanction may be limited to an investigation establishing wrongdoing. The notion of a verdict on the offense as opposed to the accused, is a feature that exists in some civil law countries.[77] Thus, in Germany the judiciary bears an independent duty of the *Aufklaerungspflicht*, "investigation or clarification," of wrongdoing, separate from the ascription of guilt of the accused.[78] But the limited criminal sanction takes this one giant step further, in a form of criminal justice peculiar to transitional circumstances.

The limiting of the criminal sanction in transition is illustrated throughout history: in post–World War I trials,[79] in World War II cases, and in the postmilitary trials of southern Europe, as well as by the contemporary successor criminal justice in Latin America and Africa, and, most recently, in the wave of political change in Central Europe, following the Soviet collapse. Post–World War II successor justice well illustrates the limited criminal sanction, though this is an oft-repressed side of the understanding of postwar justice. After the International Military Tribunal and in the midst of the Allied Control Council No. 10 follow-up trials began the reversal of the prevailing punishment policy. Between 1946 and 1958, a process of reviews and clemency culminated in the mass commutation of sentences for German war criminals. Many convicted in the Control Council No. 10 trials by occupation authorities were hardly punished under a clemency program supervised by U.S. High Commissioner John McCloy.[80] A similar sequence unfolded in Germany's national trials. Out of the more than one thousand cases tried between 1955 and 1969, fewer than one hundred of those convicted received life sentences, and fewer than three hundred received limited terms.[81]

Years later, a similar sequence unfolded in the Southern European transitions. Thus, Greece's trials of its military police culminated in suspended or commutable sentences. The government's position was that the trials and convictions had done the work of justice and that, by contrast, in the "final phase, a high sense of political responsibility must prevail."[82] A similar pattern appeared in the transitions out of military rule in Latin America. Soon after the

1980s, Argentine junta trials began the limits on the follow-up trials and the pardons.[83] While at the transition's start, the punishment power loomed over the military, it was progressively chiseled away—first in presidential pardons and then through legislative acts limiting jurisdiction and granting blanket amnesties. Ultimately, presidential pardons extended to everyone convicted of atrocities, even the high-ranking junta leaders. Amnesties became the norm throughout the rest of the continent, for example, in Chile, Nicaragua, and El Salvador, the ramifications of which are discussed later in this chapter.

The story repeats itself in successor punishment after the Communist collapse. Ten years after the revolution and all over the region, there is evidence of the transitional limited criminal sanction. In Germany's border guards trials, suspension of sentences is the norm,[84] which is also true of the few prosecutions in the Czech Republic. In Romania, former Communist leaders and police jailed in connection with the December 1989 massacres were released over a two-year period, either on health grounds or as a result of presidential pardons. In Bulgaria, the primary attempts at punishment fizzled out; Todor Zhivkov failed to serve time for embezzlement, while others in the regime were pardoned. In Albania, an amnesty law immunized many of the prior regime leaders sentenced for abuse of power, including the country's last Communist president. Throughout the approximate five years of transition in the region, the course of developments evinces a limiting of the final phase of punishment policy. As was true historically, there is a de facto limiting of the criminal sanction.

The same phenomenon is seen elsewhere. Thus, in postdictatorship South Korea, presidential leaders convicted for corruption were pardoned after serving only short prison terms. In Chile, despite a law exempting its military from prosecution, the exemption was conditioned on officers' cooperation in criminal investigations relating to past wrongdoing under military rule.[85] Penalties were dropped up front and on condition of confession to wrongdoing. Similarly, in postapartheid South Africa, the amnestying of crimes deemed political nevertheless leaves a window open for investigations into past wrongs allowing a limited prosecutorial process.[86]

Other contemporary legal responses, such as the ad hoc international tribunals set up to adjudicate genocide and war crimes, reflect similar developments. The international criminal tribunals convened to adjudicate atrocities committed in the former Yugoslavia and Rwanda evince just this understanding of the limited sanction.[87] The pursuit of justice in a fragile peace has significant consequences for the effective application of the criminal law, that is, for the possibility of adversarial trial and punishment, accordingly resulting in the limitation of the criminal sanction in these circumstances. Thus, for example, the general absence of custody over the accused, and of control over the evidence and the constraints relating to war crimes prosecutions has meant that the International Tribunal often has had little choice but to investigate and indict—and go no further. So it is that the international proceedings have given rise to their own version: a hybrid procedure between indictment and conviction that exemplifies the limited sanction. In the so-called superindictment proceeding provided for under tribunal rules, all

the underlying evidence is marshaled and publicly read;[88] and the indictment confirmed, despite the absence of the accused, publicly establishing
the truth of the events in controversy and condemning them. This process enables establishing the underlying wrongs, as well as issuing formal, public
judgment.

## Limited Criminal Justice and the Construction of Transition

Consider the limited criminal sanction's significance for political transition.
Why, despite the aftermath of the successor trials above discussed, is it none-
theless the common perception that at the Nuremberg Tribunal, in Greece's
Military Court, and in Buenos Aires Federal Court, justice has been done?
Despite the absence of full or lasting punishment, the transitional criminal
sanction appears to constitute a symbol of the rule of law.

   Our intuitions about punishment are to justify it in terms of purposes relating to the particular offense and punishment of individual perpetrators,
while the limited criminal sanction is largely justified for purposes extending
beyond the particular crime, to the transitional circumstances. While our intuitions are that the nature and role of the criminal sanction are fixed and that
stability is often thought to be a core rule-of-law value, the transitional sanction instead exposes criminal justice's dynamic role in advancing normative
change. Punishment practices in these periods advance transitional purposes
of transformation. In the limited criminal sanction, law mediates the transition. Its purposes are backward- and forward-looking, retrospective and prospective, discontinuous and continuous. Separation from the predecessor
regime is advanced by punishment practices; prosecuting predecessor wrongs
renders them past. Even when responsibility for past wrongdoing is not fully
ascribed, the establishing of past wrongs, nevertheless, advances important
punishment-related purposes, such as the clarification of past crimes in controversy.[89] The limited sanction enables the investigation and condemnation
of past wrongdoing; criminal processes are deployed to investigate, establish,
and denounce wrongdoing with significance beyond a particular controversy's
perpetrators and victims to the broader society in the grips of political upheaval. The clarifying function of the transitional criminal investigation, its
"epistemic" purpose, goes back to an early-sixteenth-century meaning of "prosecution," signifying to know precisely, to delve in detail into a matter.[90] The
formal criminal investigation enables fact-finding about wrongdoing that is
controversial in the state, conducted in the criminal process at a high standard
of knowledge and through formal public proceedings. In periods of political
flux, offenses perpetrated under prior rule have a public dimension often implying state policy, so that the criminal investigation enables a riven country to
construct a shared past through a collective public ritual. And, though the account obtained through a trial record or criminal investigation may appear
limited in comparison to a more thoroughgoing historical account, such a
record can be advantageous in transitional periods. Transitional criminal jus-

tice enables a highly controlled and bounded form of investigation of the past. Through the process of bringing charges, the state's successor regime effectively controls the direction of the historical investigation, shedding light on discrete periods of the country's political past. Even in limited form, the transitional criminal sanction advances the purposes of establishing and denouncing past wrongdoing.

The transitional limited sanction offers pragmatic resolution of the core dilemma of transition, namely, the problem of attributing individual responsibility for systemic wrongs perpetrated under prior repressive rule. The emergence of the limited sanction suggests a more fluid way to think about what punishment does, clarifying wrongs, without necessary attribution of blame or the infliction of penalties. Whereas in prevailing penal theory, retributive justifications relate to punishment generally conceived as a unitary practice, the sanction in transition prompts rethinking the theorizing of punishment and its justification as more closely related to various discrete stages of the criminal process. The transitional sanction suggests an alternative sense of the retributivist idea.[91] Though the transitional sanction is characterized by being limited, the experiences discussed suggest that core retributive purposes are vindicable by diminished—even symbolic—punishment. Core retributive aims advanced by the limited criminal process are recognition and stigmatization of past wrongdoing. Condemnation of past wrongs has transformative dimensions. Wrongdoing that is publicly individuated, in and of itself, isolates the perpetrator and liberates the collective in a measured process of transformation. Simple exposure of wrongs stigmatizes and can disqualify the affected persons from entire realms of the public or private spheres, positions of political leadership, or comparable authority in the successor regime. Such exposure affirmatively constructs past wrongs in the public sphere and relegates them to a predecessor regime. In extraordinary circumstances of radical political change, some of the purposes advanced by the conventional criminal process are advanced in its more limited form. These partial exclusions also constitute civil sanctions, discussed later in chapter 5.

The advent of the limited sanction tells us something of how criminal responsibility is conceptualized in the transitional context. Although our intuitions are to justify punishment in terms of behavior plausibly that of a responsible agent,[92] in transition, the question is whether there is any theory of individual responsibility that can span the move from a repressive to a more liberal regime. The transitional limited sanction is that mediating form. The absence of plenary punishment suggests more complex understandings of criminal responsibility in the application of the principle of individual responsibility in a context of criminal liability associated with systemic crimes in shifts out of repressive rule. Recognition of the limits to individual responsibility comes in the mitigation of the penalty phase of the process. The general acceptance of diminished penalties in these times suggests an implied recognition of a diminished sense of blameworthiness and related criminal responsibility associated with periods of nondemocratic rule, with attendant ramifications for the application of principles of legal responsibility in the transition. Finally, when the institutions and processes of criminal justice lack the legitimacy ordinarily associated with the rule of law, the partial criminal form nonetheless shows that attributes of the rule of law are working. The limited sanction constitutes a practical resolution of the transitional dilemmas posed by the uses of the criminal law to effect the normative shift associated with liberalizing rule.

## The Transitional Amnesty

The practices discussed here point to forbearance in the criminal law's response to past state evil. Indeed, the limiting of the criminal process is further seen in the common amnestying of past state crimes: the transitional amnesty. Indeed, contemporary political shifts suggest at least at a descriptive level a correspondence between transitions and amnesties. For the dilemma of whether to impose criminal justice does not arise in a vacuum but after wars, internal strife, dictatorships, or other repressive rule, and at these times, transitions often result from negotiations, and, in this context, criminal justice often becomes a bargaining chip, with the agreement to amnesty the predicate for liberalizing the political order. From the start then, amnesty appears to play a part in advancing the political transformation.

### The Dilemma of Peace or Justice

Consider whether the pursuit of peace and reconciliation is compatible with the pursuit of justice. How to reconcile the goal of securing the peace with that of justice?[93] The dilemma of peace or justice assumes numerous manifestations in transition, whether associated with wars, other forms of internal conflict, or regime change. Perhaps the clearest example of the tension posed in securing peace and justice is presented either during or just after war; during hostilities, there is often a patent conflict between securing the peace and doing justice, as the threat of criminal accountability looms over the smooth progress of peace negotiations. The dilemma is evinced in the historical debates during World War II over the convening of the Nuremberg Tribunal. It was evinced again more starkly in contemporary debates over the prosecution of war crimes relating to the hostilities in the former Yugoslavia.[94] The Balkans conflict vividly demonstrates the dilemmas that arise in the simultaneous pursuit of peace and justice. Hence, the problem of the apparently paradoxical efforts to bring the leadership to justice were complicated by the fact that some of those subject to prosecution were partners in the peace negotiations under the overarching United Nations authority. The question became all the more pressing with the issuing of international indictments against the Bosnian Serb leader, Radovan Karadžić, and their military commander, Ratko Mladić, despite the sought-for cooperation in ongoing peace negotiations. On the one hand, justice could not be seen to yield to politics, hence the indictments; nevertheless, had the peace negotiations culminated in amnesties, there would have been the inevitable perception of politicization. The example brings into focus the pros and cons of criminal justice in transition. If war criminals are not legitimate parties to peace agreements, to what extent should criminal justice even be attempted during wartime? Whereas continuing peace negotiations with alleged or indicted war criminals in the midst of a justice project could well be viewed as a form of political appeasement, conversely, commencing judicial proceedings in these circumstances could backfire and have a harmful impact on the project of justice, signaling the lowering of human rights standards.

There is, nevertheless, a role for justice during hostilities, though it may not be fully actualizable. Mere deliberations over justice may serve important purposes of deterrence in a particular conflict: thus, for example, France's convening of trials of German soldiers during the pendency of World War I;[95] similarly, the threats of punishment issued during World War II. Once the Allies became aware of the atrocities but before hostilities ended, the Moscow Declaration warned that the Allies would "pursue the guilty to the uttermost ends of the earth and deliver them to their accusers."[96] To what extent did the declaration's warning serve some deterrence purpose? This question is vital in the more contemporary punishment threats issued in the Balkans, although it would be difficult to prove, since massacres, such as those at Srebrenica took place, despite the threat of punishment.

When hostilities come to a close, other features of the dilemma of peace and justice come to the fore. Notoriously in "victor's justice," postwar trials often necessitate balancing interests in peace and justice. The conflict between these interests is illustrated in the charges formulated in postwar trials, such as at Nuremberg, where individuals were held accountable for the offense of "aggressive war." The dominant conception of criminal offenses at Nuremberg in stark terms of war and peace underscores the proceedings' joint aims of doing justice and securing the peace.[97] Yet, beyond criminal justice's uses to bring on the peace are the far more common illustrations of the forbearance in the criminal power in order to further political transition.

### Democracy's Amnesties

Both historical and contemporary experiences point to a close relation between amnesties and liberalizing transformation. Transitional amnesties appear often to be the precursors to, or coincident with, liberalizing political change. An ancient illustration appears in the account in the Athenian Constitution of the reconciliation following Athens's defeat in the Peloponnesian War. Transitional oligarchic rule and the subsequent restoration of democracy (though not, to be sure, democracy of modern times) raised the question of whether and to what extent to punish the prior despotic regime. This ancient instance of reconciliation took place in accordance with the following agreement: "[N]o one was to recall the past misdeeds of anyone except the Thirty, the Ten, the Eleven and the governors of the Piraeus, and not even of these if they successfully submitted to an *examination*." In this classical account, the move from war and tyrannical rule to democracy is predicated on a broad but not universal amnesty. There were important limits to the amnesty: "Trials for homicide should be held in accordance with *tradition* in cases where a man had himself performed the act of killing or wounding."[98] In exempting cases involving possible revenge, motivated by personal reasons or religious duty, the amnesty's parameters are circumscribed to those involving political purposes. As will be seen, the terms of this ancient amnesty foreshadow those up to the contemporary moment—for the transitional amnesty, like transitional punishment, is intended to respond to and to repudiate past regimes' politics.

In modern times, perhaps the leading case of transitional amnesty is post-Franco Spain. After Fascist rule, Spain eschewed successor trials altogether and, nevertheless, successfully consolidated democratic rule; therefore, Spain's amnesty policy has become paradigmatic of amnesty's potential in political transition.[99] "Letting bygones be bygones" captures the tenor of the Spanish amnesty; after a long (forty years) period of authoritarian rule, the amnesty was truly an agreement to forget a distant past. It was broad and all encompassing, reaching state and nonstate actors, repressive dictatorship and civil war.

As in the earlier European transitions, throughout the Americas in the 1980s, the spirit of amnesty blew strong. Throughout the region, in Chile, Uruguay, El Salvador, Haiti, and Guatemala amnesties relating to prior repressive military rule were precursors to political change, peace, and reconciliation. The Latin amnesties illustrate their role in negotiated transitions.[100] The promise of amnesties for past wrongs appeared to broker the political impasse and enable liberalizing change.[101] Thus, for example, in the negotiated transitions in Uruguay, Haiti, El Salvador and Guatemala, an important bargaining chip in the negotiations was the promise to amnesty human rights abuses during military rule. The power to prosecute was bargained away in exchange for the peace. The agreement reached with the junta was in exchange for a general amnesty. Following the agreement, debates ensued regarding the scope of the amnesty to be legislated.[102] In the Salvadoran peace negotiations process conducted under United Nations aegis, though the amnesty was not an explicit part of the peace accords, a week after the accords were signed on January 16, 1992, the Law on National Reconciliation was enacted. The timing of the subsequent legislative amnesty suggested an amnesty agreed to *sub silentio* in the peace process.[103] A similar agreement enabled the transition in Uruguay, where the course of the amnesty was deliberated over several stages. The Naval Club Pact, amnestying those responsible for rights abuses, was agreed to by the country's political representatives in the negotiations over the terms for transition to civilian rule. The agreement was subsequently ratified by Uruguay's legislature in its Law of National Pacification, enacted in 1986. Finally, four years later, a much more sweeping Law Nullifying the State's Claim to Punish Certain Crimes was put to popular referendum.[104] These "pacted" amnesties, themselves fruits of the transitional negotiations, tell us something about the interests at stake in the pursuit of criminal justice. In the negotiated transitions, both the military representatives and political opposition involved in the past conflict tend to have a strong self-interest in securing immunity from justice. Elsewhere in the region, other forms of clemency went hand in hand with the transition. Despite initial trials of the junta in Argentina, a series of legislative acts put a stop to prosecutions.[105]

Transitional amnesty bargains are often struck to stabilize and consolidate the transition. Yet, what this implies, perhaps paradoxically, is that amnesties are made conditional on other political interests of the society in the transition, and, therefore it appears that the predicates for punishment's waiver are often not dissimilar from those for its exercise. Amnesties, particularly where conditional and granted on an individual basis, can operate like punishment. Punishment's waiver, like its threat, can be an effective form of transitional political regulation. Thus, for example, after the American Civil War, amnesties were made conditional on the Confederacy's continued loyalty to the Union.[106] In South Africa, agreements to end apartheid rule were conditioned on amnesty for "political" offenses relating to the past rule.[107] The Promotion of National Unity and Reconciliation Bill conditions the granting of amnesties on confessions to the underlying acts. Their explicit purpose is assertedly societal unity. The trade-off reveals the political and instrumental character of transitional amnesties and their asserted relation to societal reconciliation and, relatedly, to the restoration of the rule of law. In periods of flux, criminal justice determinations are manifestly part of a larger political calculus. This trade-off of the balancing of perpetrators' political rights in exchange for support of the newly constituted union and for the aim of political stability mirrors punishment's more conventional goals of assuring ongoing rule of law. So it is that amnesties can advance the normative project of the political transition.

### Justice, Mercy, Politics, and the Rule of Law

Punishment or impunity? Returning to the debate with which this chapter begins, amnesties' substantial role in transitions as a descriptive matter leads to the broader question of clemency's relation to the rule of law and, in particular, in the circumstances of transition. "Clemency" has a broad meaning, which includes amnesty and pardon. Though some distinguish these two terms because of their impact, or occurrence pre- or post-conviction, they are often used interchangeably. Transitional amnesties pose a perplexing challenge to the claim with which this chapter begins, that punishment is necessarily connected to democratic consolidation. In the strong form of the foundational argument for punishment in transition, good revolutions do not culminate in amnesties, because insofar as a society fails to bring perpetrators of past wrongs to account, it continues the "impunity" practices of past regimes, subverting its liberation processes.[108] The impunity is apparently ongoing, seamless in the transition between regimes, unless vitiated by acts of punishment. This form of justice is said to be essential to the restoration of the rule of law. According to this argument, transitional amnesties amount to a "selling out" of justice to transient political interests, to the detriment of democratic prospects.

But there is also the converse argument: that it is restraint in the punishment power that heralds the return to the rule of law.[109] Here, the normative claim appears entirely conflated with the descriptive: The observation that amnesty practices are often de facto associated with transitions is somehow turned into a normative statement about the relation of exercises of mercy to the liberal rule of law.

When the question of amnesty is debated as if it is primarily an issue of transition, the tenor of the challenges to the transitional amnesties assumes that suspension of the prosecutorial power offends a core predicate of the rule of law associated with established democracies; yet, restraint in the exercise of the criminal justice power is hardly limited to the transitional moment. What is obscured is where the transitional amnesty stands in light of our intuitions about clemency more generally. What are the relevant standards? Whose power to amnesty? By what principle? What rights and duties are implicated? These questions are the baseline against which to evaluate the transitional amnesty.

Consider the international law argument for punishment, whereby the duty to punish is thought to derive from various conventional and customary norms.[110] Nevertheless, international law's remedial scheme, which is structured in terms of individual rights, in no way constructs punishment as an enforceable right such that it would impose an obligation on states. And, even if the argument is based on analogues to established democracies, punishment's exercise, as is discussed below, is nevertheless currently subject to some discretion in most legal systems. Within the international legal system, the conventions themselves have been interpreted as satisfied by alternative remedies. In a landmark decision reviewing a case of impunity in Latin America, the Inter-American Court ruled that the duty to protect citizens from persecution could be nonetheless satisfied after the fact through a number of alternative remedial measures, such as investigations and reparations.[111] However, in other decisions evaluating the Argentine and Uruguayan amnesty laws, the Inter-American Commission on Human Rights held that amnesties for grave human rights actions violated numerous state duties under the American Convention on Human Rights to protect and ensure human rights, as well as the victims' rights to seek justice.[112]

Beyond the international law argument for an obligation to punish are the traditional arguments marshaled in the legal systems of established democracies. Yet, as discussed below, these arguments also do not make out an obligation to punish in transition but do offer a helpful baseline from which to evaluate the transitional amnesty. As becomes clear, even in ordinary times, the rule of law is not predicated on a fully enforced criminal justice, and the reasons for forbearance are often, as in transitional times, political. The retributive argument for punishment is made not in terms of future benefits for the society but, rather, in terms of the moral considerations inherent to the implicated acts. A well-known account in the writing of Immanuel Kant hypothesizes about a society on a desert island about to disband, which is deliberating over the question of whether to punish and contends that it is its obligation to punish "every last murderer" so that "everyone will . . . receive what his actions are worth and so that the . . . blood guilt will not be fixed on the people."[113] Even the disbanding society is obligated to apportion individual punishment, to lift moral responsibility from the rest of the society. The Kantian claim for punishment within a "disbanding" society tests the justification for punishment in a context that lacks the forward-looking utilitarian purposes implied where there is social continuity, with particular resonance for punishment in transitional circumstances. From a retributive perspective, failure to punish means the society bears ongoing collective responsibility, with consequences for the legitimacy of its institutions of judgment. Criminal justice plays a role not only in delineating individual and collective responsibility but relatedly in defining legitimate institutions of judgment; as such, it draws an important line between regimes. Individuating wrongdoing lifts collective responsibility from the prior regime and relegitimates state authority.

While the retributive argument makes a compelling claim for an obligation to punish, it does not well explain our intuitions about punishment's role in the legal system, whether in ordinary or transitional times.[114] Threshold understandings of punishment's relation to the rule of law vary widely in legal cultures. In civil law systems, the principle of legality contemplates close to full enforcement. However, in common-law countries, the presumption of legality is altogether different: The baseline norm is an underenforced prosecutorial power, and discretion is a predicate of the fairness of the system.[115]

Accordingly, clemency in ordinary times offers a point of departure for evaluation of transitional amnesties. Clemency in ordinary times shares affinities with the transitional amnesty in its political provenance and exercise. In working democracies, pardons or amnesties (such as legislative or tax amnesties) are generally associated with the transfer of political power in ordinary administration shifts. This suggests an analogy between ordinary changes in administration and shifts between political regimes in transitions; and points to the analogy between the amnesty power and punishment. Amnesty, like punishment, is a practice that signals sovereignty—showing where political power lies. Accordingly, punishment's waiver, like its exercise, defines the political transition. Clemency's significant political nature and role are recognized and even defined by the institutional separation of power, for example, the separation of the pardon from the judicial power. In ordinary times, political actors have substantial discretion over the pardon power. Thus, for example, in the American constitutional scheme, the pardon power deriving from the king's historical pardon power is vested in the executive.[116] That the pardon power is vested not in the judiciary but in the executive, where it is exercised on a case-by-case basis and predicated on discretion, underscores its political nature. Separation of punishment and clemency powers is hardly peculiar to the Anglo-American system. In the Latin American constitutional scheme, differentiation of the pardon power is even more pronounced. In the American system, prosecutorial and clemency powers both are vested in the executive and deemed to imply policy concerns; in the Latin system, the prosecutorial power is vested in the judiciary, while the pardon power is vested in the executive.[117] This extraordinary differentiation of the punishment and pardon powers emphasizes clemency's political function. Established democracies' institutional arrangements reveal the attempt to differentiate processes of justice and mercy. While justice is the province of the judiciary and subject to principled constitutional standards and justifications, mercy is the province of the political branches exercised freely to advance political aims,[118] and explicitly justified in transitional terms, such as on the basis of peace and reconciliation.[119]

Even though clemency appears to be built into ordinary notions of the rule of law, there are also significant differences in its exercise in periods of heightened political change. There is a higher incidence of amnesties, as well as limitations on the exercise of the criminal sanction. After repressive rule, transitional amnesties present the structural problem of relating to offenses that concededly imply a threshold level of state complicity. The question that arises is thus the fairness of the state's exercise of the punishment/amnesty power even for a successor regime. A variant of this problem surfaced in the eighteenth-century writings of John Locke and Kant against clemency because of abuses in the monarchic pardoning power. Whereas in the state of nature, the right to punishment (and its waiver) is considered to reside originally in the community, the social contract shifts the community's right to the sovereign. In established democracies, the clemency power is generally vested in the sovereign, but in times of political crisis, the right appears to revert to the citizenry.[120] So it is that following the French Revolution, for example, the pardon power was suspended, as it was associated with the king's arbitrary and illegitimate exercise. And, in another example, the limited pardon powers of the American executive[121] vividly illustrate the transitionality in the constitutional definition of the amnesty power and the extent to which its parameters derive from prior historical experience in the exercise of the power.

Legacies regarding past repression help shape the state's authority over punishment and clemency powers. Indeed, the above suggests that the lack of legitimacy in institutions affect the conditions for the exercise of both punishment and clemency in transition. The pervasiveness of transitional amnesties suggests that whatever institutional continuity in prior illegitimate rule carries over to the successor regime undermines the successor regime's authority to sit in judgment. The successor regime's exercise of punitive power is often perceived as a continuation of the political justice characterizing illiberal rule. Whenever regime change has not gone hand in hand with reform of the judiciary, successor punishment is compromised by "tu quoque," or unclean hands. The exceptional nature of successor trials throws into relief the compromised circumstances of justice in transition relating to the distinctive features of state complicity in the relevant crime, as well as the general absence of legitimate institutions of judgment. Recognizing that these are the conditions of justice may help to explain the prevalence of the Latin amnesties, for in this region, the judiciary was heavily compromised by its implication in the prior repression, and little or no institutional reform followed the transitions. In these circumstances, the institutions of judgment lack legitimacy, with potentially dire consequences for the legitimacy of successor punishment. In this context, acts of clemency may well have greater legitimacy, particularly so when they emanate from newly elected political actors, such as the executive or the legislature. So it is that the pervasiveness of amnesties in transitional circumstances tells us something important about the rule-of-law conditions that are predicates to punishment's legitimate exercise.

The intimate relation between punishment and amnesty is evident in that transitional amnesties' parameters comprehending crimes deemed political constitute the limits of the legitimate exercise of punishment in periods of upheaval. The political transition is the defining principle of the amnesty. Thus, El Salvador's amnesty law defines the covered crimes as "acts which include political crimes or any crime with political ramifications or common crimes committed by no less than twenty people."[122] South Africa's Promotion of National Unity and Reconciliation Bill similarly defines the relevant offenses subject to amnesty as "acts associated with political objectives." Transitional amnesties along political lines raise a risk analogous to that indicated at the beginning of this chapter—the spectre of political justice. Just as punishment policy risks becoming part of a cycle of blame and a form of political justice, clemency policy exercised on political grounds is its mirror image.

. Both punishment and amnesties can play constructive roles in defining the political transition. But there are also rule-of-law constraints on transitional amnesty practices, important limiting principles on the clemency power's legitimate exercise. Some of these constraints go to the amnesty procedure and to a minimal rule of law. Accordingly, the so-called auto-amnesties present one such limit, those self-dealt by the predecessor regime, such as those of the Argentine military, are generally considered illegitimate and invalidated in the transition.[123] Further, both punishment and amnesty must follow regular procedures and be legitimated by public deliberative processes. "Democratic" amnesties, those deliberated over and supported by some popular consensus, reflect the attempt to legitimize the exercise of clemency in transition. The classical prototype of the democratic amnesty goes back to ancient Athens, where clemency was voted on by the people, [124] in the "adeia" procedure necessitating the support of 6,000 citizens. Following the Athenian Civil War, the amnesty of 403 B.C. was passed by majority vote and affected virtually everyone who had participated in the war. Transitional amnesties are often negotiated by representatives of the ancien régime with the opposition. Although amnesty pacts may well inhere in bargaining and nonlegislative processes, they are generally subsequently ratified in progressively more participatory justificatory processes over the course of the transition. In contemporary transitions, as in ancient Athens, plebiscites and the exercise of direct sovereignty lend transitional amnesties' popular legitimacy.

Through democratic processes, amnesties obtain a measure of political accountability; the political processes accompanying legislative amnesties, enable broad deliberation concerning the nature and significance of the past wrongdoing for the state. An example is Uruguay's amnesty referendum processes, as well as South Africa's parliamentary deliberations.[125] The amnesty deliberations phase itself advances some of the transitional penal purposes, for these debates often imply legislative hearings and findings relating to past wrongdoing. The democratic provenance of many of the transitional amnesties can mean that they are frequently more transparent and deliberated over than conventional punishment. Thus, even punishment's waiver can advance transitional aims, such as the clarification and condemnation of past regime wrongs.

Transitional amnesties are structured in other ways by the rule of law. Beyond the procedural constraints discussed above, whether in the exercise and restraint of punishment policy, there is a parallel commitment to equal protection under the law. Constitutional equal protection principles impose parameters on concededly political amnesties. Equal protection implies like treatment of similar cases and also excludes reliance on certain unjustifiable bases, such as race, religion, or other similar classification; so that it is uncontroversial that race, religion, or ethnicity ought not be a basis for clemency's grant or denial.[126] Constitutional equal protection concerns pose further profound constraints on the politicization of criminal justice. Thus, while politics is a permissible categorical basis for clemency, there are limits regarding amnesties grant on the basis of political viewpoint, leading to their expansion beyond partisan politics. While the bipartisan grant may well be vulnerable for expanding the amnesty, it also advances the rule of law and legitimacy in the exercise of clemency.

In the foundational argument for punishment in transition, amnesties are said to prolong delay in the restoration of the rule of law. Yet, as discussed above, even in stable democracies, the criminal justice power is underenforced. Of course, in established democracies, clemency practices occur in the context of a more general adherence to the rule of law; whereas transitional amnesties generally occur after periods of widespread lawlessness. Nevertheless, transitional amnesties ought to be evaluated in light of this outstanding rule-of-law context of the transitional circumstances of justice, associated with generally compromised institutions of judgment. Transitional amnesties have their greatest legitimacy when they result from democratic processes, such as direct referenda. Adoption of amnesty policies do not necessarily mean forgetting the underlying past wrongs, as these are often made conditional upon individual case-by-case investigations equivalent to those of a punitive process. What emerges is the systemic role played by both punishment and amnesty practices in the construction of political transition. Ultimately, amnesties and punishment are but two sides of the same coin: legal rites that visibly and forcefully demonstrate the change in sovereignty that makes for political transition.[127] Transitional punishment and amnesty practices each play defining roles in the construction of these political periods. Both punishment and amnesty help define the regime shift, as by establishing past wrongs they help construct the political legacy. These transitional practices play the role of defining political time: the discontinuity of transition—its before and after—as well as their related role in defining the continuity of transition.

## Limits to Clemency in the Liberal State: The Crime against Humanity

A limit on political restraints on the punishment power in the liberalizing state is the "crime against humanity," for this offense of political persecution lacks any of the conventional jurisdictional parameters. The adjudication of the crime against humanity limits and condemns the state's past political persecution, a limit that appears to be largely immune to national politics. As such, the adjudication of this offense has acquired the force of a reigning symbol of the liberal rule of law. It is apparent in the contemporary move to entrench transitional punishment responses in the permanent International Criminal Court. Invocation of the crime against humanity is constructive of core constitutional norms that lie at the heart of the rule-of-law state. For here is what distinguishes the liberalizing regime from that which is illiberal. Here, transitional justice's normative potential is at its greatest.

The crime against humanity comprehends the extreme form of persecution, transcending national borders to offend the international community. Codified for the first time after World War II in the Nuremberg Charter, the crime against humanity comprises grave offenses, such as murder, deportation, and torture, historically proscribed wherever committed in wartime against civilians, as well as "persecution on political, racial, and religious grounds."[128] Going beyond prior war crimes proceedings, Nuremberg took jurisdiction over persecution committed by a state against its *own* citizens. Such abuses were considered offenses that transcended the confines of national law to violate the laws of all nations and, as such, were prosecutable by an international tribunal. Nevertheless, despite the consensus on the assumption of international jurisdiction as a matter of law and in light of their comparative novelty at the time and the attendant concern for retroactivity, crimes against humanity prosecutions were, in effect, limited to those related to the war. So, despite its being formally an independent charge, the crime against humanity was assimilated to other war crimes and to the parameters of waging war.[129]

The central meaning of the crime against humanity as the "offense against mankind" is exemplified and instantiated wherever the response to state atrocities spills over national borders to the international arena. Its history predates the modern postwar proceedings. International remonstrances occurred, for example, in response to the Greco-Turkish warfare of 1827; and in the early 1900s, "in the name of humanity," against persecution in Romania and Russia. Following World War I, a commission was convened regarding the methods of the waging of war, which declared unlawful violations of the "established laws and customs of war and the elementary laws of humanity" and "warned that" all persons belonging to enemy countries who have been guilty of offenses against the laws and customs of war, or the laws of humanity are liable to criminal prosecution."[130] In 1917, the charges threatened were similar to those later proscribed in the post–World War II instruments: murder, torture, and racial persecution of minorities by their own government. At the time of the drafting of the London Charter and Control Council Law No. 10, the United

Nations War Crimes Commission defined the term *crimes against humanity* as "systematic mass action," as

> crimes which either by their magnitude and savagery or by their great number or by the fact that a similar pattern is applied at different times and places, endanger the international community or shock the conscience of mankind, warrant intervention by states other than that on whose territory the crimes have been committed, or whose subjects have become their victims.

As a historical matter, the jurisprudence evinces the delimiting of state power on the basis of individual rights.

The crime against humanity poses the purest, most idealized illustration of law's potential to effect normative transition. Law is at its most significant when that's all there is, when jurisdiction over the offense is taken outside the affected territory and absent other political change. The idea is exemplified whenever states respond to atrocities in ways that transcend national borders; therefore, the very form of the response instantiates the core norm of a transcendent justice. Over the years, adjudication of the crime against humanity has come to forge the very meaning of the contemporary response to modern persecution. The core feature of political persecution is that it transcends ordinary crime in eliciting international response. In its modern form, the crime against humanity extends beyond the state's attack against enemy foreigners to abuses perpetrated against its own citizens, whereby citizens are rendered enemies in their own land, thus destabilizing the international order even during peacetime. The applicable jurisdictional principles transcend the traditional parameters of territoriality, and the passage of time. The crime against humanity is conceived as an offense to all humanity, and hence prosecutable by all nations, giving rise to the related jurisdictional principle of "universality." Whereas criminal offenses must be known and written into law, lest they violate basic principles against retroactivity, the crime against humanity is considered an offense "among civilized nations" and therefore punishable with, or without, prior legislation. This extraordinary exemption of crimes against humanity from the ban on retroactive legislation has been ratified as part of the European Convention for the Protection of Human Rights and Fundamental Freedoms. Article 7(2) exempts prosecutions of crimes against humanity from retroactivity constraints: "This Article shall not prejudice the trial and punishment of any person for any act or admission which, at the time it was committed, was criminal according to the general principles of law recognized by civilized nations."[131] The principle of universality as it relates to crimes against humanity is epitomized by the prosecution of Adolf Eichmann for crimes committed in Europe during the second World War II. Though the trial was held decades after the events in the state of Israel, it violated neither retroactivity nor territoriality principles.[132] If, under the traditional jurisdictional principle of territoriality, the wronged community is considered contiguous to the site of the crime, it is in the nature of the crime against humanity that the relevant wronged community is all nations, and the relevant offense perpetrated against humanity. Similar understandings of universality underlie contemporary crime-against-humanity proceedings.[133] In more contemporary World War II–related trials, such as those convened by Canada, jurisdiction is afforded for those crimes that "would have been prosecutable in Canada" at the time of commission.[134] More recently, prosecutions in Spain of crimes against humanity committed under military rule in Argentina and Chile rely on similar understandings of universality.[135] Deploying the concept of universal jurisdiction involves a projecting backward, a constructive prospectivity. This construct is a recurring one in the notion of transitional legality, as it reconciles the dilemma of the normative shift while it adheres to more conventional rule-of-law principles of stability and continuity in the law.

Given the political conditions of persecution, its adjudication usually takes one of two forms: either the offenses are prosecuted in other states, jurisdictions with more liberal political conditions, as discussed above, or in the place where the crimes occurred but only after the passage of time. In either context, prosecution of these offenses, while affected by political circumstances, is hardly driven by them, demonstrating the persistence of the law's responses to grave offenses, and its normative force.

## The Paradox of the Passage of Time

Consider the phenomenon of the timeless prosecutions of crimes against humanity. These cases connect regimes, running a political thread in space—and through time—perpetuating a sense of ongoing responsibility for past wrongs that is ultimately constructive of the state's enduring political identity. For crimes against humanity are apparently unconstrained by generally applicable jurisdictional principles, such as time limits. There are gaps of close to half a century between both the Nazi and Communist reigns of terror and their successor prosecutions, colliding with our ordinary intuitions about criminal justice's operation.[136] More than half a century after the events, World War II–related trials persist throughout Europe, Canada, and Australia. The pursuit of criminal justice ordinarily declines with the passage of time, reflected in most legal systems' time limits even for the most grave crimes. Only a minority of countries following Anglo-American law fail to limit the prosecution of the most serious crimes over the passage of time.

The debate over whether crimes against humanity should be constrained by the time limits ordinarily applicable to other offenses was waged in the context of postwar proceedings, when in 1965, according to then-prevailing law, twenty-year limits on war-related charges would have set in. In Germany, despite Parliamentary attempts to stop World War II-related trials, the statutes were tolled twice, under the rationale that previously (during the occupation) Germany's courts had lacked sovereignty to prosecute. Finally, in 1979, the underlying substantive question could no longer be put off: To what extent should crimes against humanity be treated like ordinary crimes and, therefore, prescribable after time, or were these somehow extraordinary offenses that stood outside the ordinary jurisdictional parameters? After heated debate, the resolution was to limit virtually all war-related prosecutions, except for those involving "base murder," that is, murder committed with a racial or sadistic intent[137] involving persecutory motive, such as that implicated in crimes like those against humanity. At the international level, the dilemma was resolved in the enactment of the United Nations Convention on the Non-Applicability of Statutory Limitations to War Crimes and Crimes against Humanity.[138] Special jurisdictional standards applicable to crimes against humanity would also be incorporated into national law. Thus, for example, in France, the "crime against humanity" is the only offense exempted from the country's stringent statute of limitations.[139]

Our intuitions are that the political will for punishment diminishes with time. Yet, the reverse is true of the prosecution of the crime against humanity. Its significance does not lessen over time. Consider why this is so. The nature of political persecution, in particular, the complicity of the state in this offense, has implications for the paradoxical effects of the passage of time. Systemic persecution challenges evidentiary and jurisdictional assumptions regarding the role of the passage of time. When the state is itself implicated in wrongdoing, significant aspects of the offense are often covered up and simply not publicly known at the time of the commission of the acts, only emerging with the passage of time: not only perpetrators' identities but, even more significantly, the very facts and character of the offense itself. Moreover, the state's implication in these offenses, as well as in the cover-up, increases the likelihood of the inherent politicization of punishment policy. In the World War II–related prosecutions, the political will to prosecute surged, waned, and flowed again with the passage of time. While just after the war, there was considerable Allied interest in justice, the cold war and attendant shift in the political winds eviscerated the impetus to justice. The passage of time implies regime change that in turn enables justice. Thus, for example, the transition to democracy in the 1980s in Bolivia enabled the extradition to France and subsequent prosecution of Nazi henchman Klaus Barbie, more than four decades after his wartime atrocities.[140] Regime change often spurs evidentiary change, such as newfound access to governmental archives and other sources of evidence regarding the predecessor regime enabling justice after time. So, for example, political change in the former Communist bloc meant newfound access to the KGB and Communist Party files and a flow of information enabling prosecutions. Finally, new evidence appears after time purely by chance. Thus, for example, a serendipitous series of events spurred Germany's national trials, when in the mid-1950s, in the small town of Ulm, the Nazi-related past of a party in a noncriminal case surfaced by chance.[141] This discovery set in motion the chain of events culminating in Germany's ongoing World War II–related trials program.

In a contemporary example, two decades after junta rule in Argentina, the public confession of a member of the navy to the crimes against humanity of disappearances reopened the events of the period. The so-called "Scilingo Effect"[142] spurred a new round of investigations into disappearances and the rearrest of junta leaders.

The strange persistence of crimes against humanity prosecutions suggests the passage of time operates here in utterly paradoxical fashion and contrary to our ordinary intuitions. Generations after and despite the passage of time, successor regimes continue to prosecute old regime wrongs, though this is often associated with few sanctions. The persistence of crimes against humanity jurisprudence is not well explained by the traditional arguments for criminal justice. As perpetrators and victims age, retributive purposes pale. Convened years after the implicated controversy, these proceedings hardly advance traditional penal purposes of deterrence or reform. Moreover, even the forward-looking purposes of justice, such as the aim of democracy building, become attenuated after time as many of the political changes have run their course. Nevertheless, the debates over whether to continue to punish crimes against humanity despite the passage of time recognize their profound gravity at the apex of a hierarchy of offenses. At the United Nations Debate on the Convention on the Non-Applicability of Statutory Limitations to War Crimes and Crimes against Humanity, the lifting of time limitations was justified on the basis of the extraordinary "atrocity" of these crimes.[143] In Germany's debates over its statutes of limitations, extensions were similarily justified on a normative basis, on the grounds of the crime's gravity. In other subsequent debates over prosecutions, the preservation of victims' dignity, with clemency's implications for their equal protection rights under law, becomes an oft-asserted purpose.[144] The sense that it is "now or never" and that victims' equal protection rights continue to remain at stake is seen in their energetic role in the war-related justice at the era's end. This was exemplified in the long postponed World War II trials of Klaus Barbie, Paul Touvier, and Maurice Papon in France. The same is true in England, where victims' groups brought to the government's attention the presence of alleged Nazi war criminals in the United Kingdom.[145] Victims' roles in transitional justice vary dramatically among legal cultures. Continental law contemplates victims' prosecutions, in which victims function as private attorneys general, exemplified by the *partie civile* procedure in France and the *querellante* procedure in Latin America. In Anglo-American law, however, private parties' participation in the criminal process is often thought to conflict with separation-of-power principles and to threaten the rule of law.[146]

The law's response here operates in a heightened symbolic way, expressing a message affirming the rule-of-law state.[147] Over the years, developments in international law have expanded the crime against humanity definition further, to that of modern persecution, imposing a limiting constraint on state sovereignty, that is carried over even into the traditional governmental discretion over punishment. The conceptualization of persecution begins with a largely "objective" view defined in terms of the attributive status of protected classes of victims, so that, historically, the crime against humanity is defined in terms of civilians' wartime-related protected status and offenses implicating ethnic, religious, and racial persecution. The contemporary conceptualization is broader, as it extends beyond the treatment of aliens to abuses perpetrated against fellow citizens even in peacetime, thus, protecting against racial, ethnic, religious, and politically motivated persecution. Thus, in the 1987 prosecution of Klaus

Barbie, the Nazi chief in occupied Lyons, for ordering deportations to death camps, the critical issue was whether armed members of the resistance, victims not clearly of protected civilian status, would nevertheless be protected within the rubric of the crime against humanity. Ultimately, the relevant question, the French high court held, was not the victim's status but the accused's intent. What distinguishes the crime against humanity is persecutory purpose.[148] Persecution was defined by the court as being as committed in a systematic manner in the name of a "[s]tate practicing a policy of ideological supremacy."[149] In another contemporary example, the protective doctrine of the ad hoc international war crimes tribunals reaches well beyond the postwar period, transcending the line between civilians and combatants, war and peace. The ongoing evolution in the transitional jurisprudence of the crime against humanity goes beyond attributive status—to persecutory motive.[150]

The contemporary understanding of inhumane acts ultimately focuses on state policy and, as such, goes some way toward explaining why, despite the passage of time, crimes against humanity are nevertheless deemed to merit ongoing punishment. Though not explicitly predicated on state sponsorship, persecution constitutes a crime of such a scale that, even when not overtly state promoted, the offenses are nevertheless perpetrated against a backdrop of governmental policy. In its most recent elaboration, in the codification for the permanent International Criminal Court, the crime against humanity is defined in terms of its nexus to "widespread or systematic attack against any civilian population."[151] Persecution policy implies collective liability, with ongoing consequences for the state's political identity over time. Persecution transcends the affected individual victims and perpetrators with implications for the society as a whole.

When it is the state that is complicit in persecution, fundamental notions of criminal justice are turned on their head; state complicity, cover-up, and other obstructions affect the very possibility of justice. The crime against humanity exposes the impact of the state's role in past wrongs as a significant element of the circumstances of justice compromised in transitional times. Indeed, this factor goes a long way toward explaining why there is an apparent intractable tension when successor regimes fail to respond to injustice, itself constituting something of the nonideal circumstances of transitional justice. In the succession of regimes, the problem has led to the construction of the somewhat self-referential (i.e., regime-related) understanding of ongoing criminal responsibility termed "impunity." This notion of an ongoing violation (in the absence of punishment) reconceptualizes the relevant offense. Further, the logic justifies lifting ordinary time limits on prosecution for crimes against humanity, just as analogous reasoning in ordinary criminal law justifies the lifting of time limits applicable to offenses like embezzlement or conspiracy whenever they implicate public officials, for state involvement has obvious attendant consequences limiting the possibility of justice. The problem is widely compounded in persecutory regimes where the ostensible custodians of justice become its violators.

When the state is complicit in persecution, threshold notions of equality and security under the law are put into jeopardy. Accordingly, the transitional response's significance transcends the individual case to express a normative message of equal protection that is basic to the rule of law. Prosecuting crimes against humanity helps to construct the transitional normative shift by condemning past repression even as it affirms the present restoration of security and equal protection.

The normative implications of this legal response transcend the transition. Prosecutions of crimes against humanity illuminate the ongoing significance of the state's response to persecution over time. At the end of the twentieth century, persecution as a matter of systematic policy is incontrovertibly the paradigm of contemporary tyranny. In the crime-against-humanity jurisprudence, law's strongest sanction mounts a critical response to past repressive policy. Where past persecution was perpetrated under the imprimatur of law, its prosecution constructs a normative break and shift toward a new legality. Criminal justice is deployed to reinvent the differences between illiberal and liberal regimes. Enforcement of the crime against humanity instantiates rights protections relating to the contemporary distinctions between authoritarian and liberal rule. Successor criminal justice may help to explain the significance of other contemporary trials. Thus, for example, in American constitutional jurisprudence, state-sponsored discrimination is accorded the highest constitutional scrutiny. The importance of prosecution of race-related crimes, even after time, is well understood in the American historical context of long-standing state-condoned racial discrimination, raising a problem of unresolved transitional justice. Even when racist offenses are privately sponsored, they revive past state-sponsored persecution and raise the possibility of ongoing collective responsibility, with potentially shattering social consequences unless there is a transformative response.[152]

## Transitional Criminal Justice: Some Conclusions

Transitional criminal justice does not simply advance the conventional purposes of punishment in the rule-of-law state. The role of criminal justice in transitional times, as the above experiences suggest, transcends that of conventional punishment. It goes beyond the concerns ordinarily internal to criminal justice, such as deterrence, which is already implicit in and advanced by the very political reforms attending the transition, where change in the state's institutional structures affects the calculus of consequences of any prospective behavior. Nevertheless, transitional justice advances other purposes that are particular to the political change, such as advancing the reconstruction of the rule of law in the transition. And it is with respect to this purpose that transitional criminal justice raises profound dilemmas regarding law's role in periods of political flux: chiefly, how to reconcile normative change with adherence to conventional legality. The dilemma is reconciled in the transitional practices discussed above by the limiting of the punishment to partial, symbolic processes, a highly controlled basis for change. The transitional sanction plays a complex role in political transformation: Law, here, is constructive of transition, condemnatory of wrongs—even as it renders them past—while affirming the rule of law. Thus, transitions vary in the extent to which they promote substantial norm transformation. If the prior regime was sustained by persecutory policy rationalized within a legal system, it is this policy rationale that is challenged by critical legal responses. Going beyond conventional criminal law's role of affirming and protecting entrenched preexisting values,[153] what distinguishes transitional criminal measures is their attempt to instantiate and reinforce normative change. This attempt is plainly seen in the transitional responses' particular focus varying from country to country to "undo" rationalized past political violence through procedures of inquiry and indictment, rituals of collective knowledge that enable isolation and disavowal of past wrongs.[154] These critical responses to past persecution clarify that the policy is manmade, and hence reformable. With isolating knowledge of past wrongdoing and individuating responsibility comes the notion of the possibility of liberalizing change. In this way, the transitional criminal sanction liberates the successor regime from the weight of states' evil legacies. Through ritualized legal processes of appropriation and disappropriation, of avowal and disavowal, of symbolic loss and gain, societies move in a liberal direction, through processes that allow transformation and the possibility of redemptive return.[155]

Criminal justice in some form, transitional practices suggest, is a ritual of liberalizing states, as it is through these practices that norms are publicly instantiated. Through known, fixed processes, a line is drawn, liberating a past, that allows the society to move forward. Though punishment is conventionally considered largely retributive, in transition, its purposes are corrective, going beyond the individual perpetrator to the broader society. This purpose is seen in the primacy of systemic political offenses, for example, in the persistence of prosecutions of crimes against humanity—the offense of persecutory politics, constituting a critical response to illiberal rule through the criminal law. Moreover, whereas ordinarily punishment is thought to divide society, in transition, wherever punishment is exercised it is done so in a limited fashion to allow the possibility of return to a liberal state. As such, criminal processes have affinities with other noncriminal responses, discussed in other chapters, that constitute transitional justice.

In transitional justice, rule-of-law dilemmas are heightened because of the extraordinary conditions and circumstances of radical political change. But these periods are not fully discontinuous but, instead, vividly display in exaggerated form, problems that are ordinarily less transparent in more established justice systems, and, as such, transitional jurisprudence may illuminate our understanding about the criminal justice politics more generally. Most significant, the above experiences illuminate the criminal law's potential not merely as an instrument of stability but also as one of social change.

## CHAPTER THREE

# Historical Justice

*T*his chapter explores the historical response to evil legacies and the question of what role historical accountability plays in liberal transition. Transitions appear—almost by definition—to imply periods of historical discontinuity. Wars, revolutions, and repressive rule represent gaps in the life of the state that threaten its historical continuity. The questions that arise are: as a descriptive matter, how do societies treat these periods of apparent historical glitch? To what extent is the response to past evil rule historical? And, normatively, in what sense is historical accountability a corrective, ushering in liberalization?

A popular view among contemporary political analysts is that a historical inquiry and record that assimilates the evil past is necessary to restore the collective in periods of radical political change. The claim is that establishing the "truth" about the state's past wrongs, like successor constitutions or trials, can serve to lay the foundation of the new political order:

> [S]uccessor government[s] [have] an obligation to investigate and establish
> the facts so that the truth be known and be made part of the nation's history.
> . . . There must be both knowledge and acknowledgment: the events need to
> be officially recognized and publicly revealed. Truth-telling . . . responds to
> the demand of justice for the victims [and] facilitates national reconciliation.[1]

Like the normative claims for constitutions and trials in transition, the normative claim for an official historical account is that it enables the shift to a more liberal order. Collective history making regarding the repressive past is said to lay the necessary basis for the new democratic order. The claim is that this process is essential to liberalizing transition: The transitional history directed at a better future envisions a dialectical, progressive process. In the spirit of an earlier age, this hearkens back to the Enlightenment view of history—of Immanuel Kant, or Karl Marx, whereby history itself is universalizing and redemptive. On this view, history is teacher and judge, and historical truth in and of itself is justice. It is this view of the liberalizing potential of history that inspires the popular contemporary argument for historical accountability in transitions. Yet, the assumption that "truth" and "history" are one and the same[2] evinces a belief in the possibility of an autonomous objective history of the past belying the significance of the present political context in shaping the historical inquiry. However, modern theorizing about historical knowledge considerably challenges this conception.[3] When history takes its "interpretative turn,"[4] there is no single, clear, and determinate understanding or "lesson" to draw from the past but, instead, recognition of the degree to which historical understanding depends on political and social contingency.

The questions then are: What is the particular role of historical inquiry and representation in transition? What is a transitional history? And what, moreover, is a liberalizing transitional history? What might the practices of transitional societies reveal about the normative claim regarding historical inquiry's role in advancing liberalization? How, if at all, does the pursuit of a collective past advance a more liberal future?

What constitutes history in such periods, as the discussion below suggests, is contingent not only on the regions' historical and political legacies but also on the context that is peculiar to transition. The idealized view of transitional histories as "foundations," that is, as beginnings, elides the preexisting historical account. Historical accounts generated in transitional times are not somehow autonomous but build on antecedent, national narratives. The background of ongoing collective memory defines a society. Thus, the transitional truths are socially constructed within processes of collective memory. As societal practices in these periods reflect, the historical accountings are less foundational than transitional.

Transitions are vivid instances of conscious historical production. In these times it is historical production in a heightened political context and driven by political purposes. Politics has its epistemic implications. The intimate relation between the imposition of power and the control of knowledge is well explored in the works of Friedrich Nietzsche and Michel Foucault.[5] Nevertheless, even modern intuitions resist explicitly politicized historical inquiry, as it poses a challenge to the ideal view of a philosophy of history characterized as largely independent of political concerns. Historical inquiry in transitional periods, therefore, poses a sharp challenge. The politicized nature of history often associated with repressive rule is exposed by the responses in transition. Though particular historical accounts have always been associated with certain political regimes, the uses of knowledge in politics are generally obfuscated by those in power. Historical narratives are always present; all regimes are associated with and constructed by a "truth" regime.[6] Changes in political regimes, accordingly, mean attendant changes in truth regimes.

Collective memory is a process of reconstructing the representation of the past in the light of the present.[7] Yet, the reconstruction process takes a distinctive form in periods of transition. In transformative periods, the relation of the construction of collective history to politics is simultaneously discontinuous and intertwined. For the construction of history in periods of political transformation is predicated on drawing a line of discontinuity, even as there is also adherence to some historical and political continuity. Transitional histories have their own narratives, but also link up and reappropiate strands of longer state history. Striking a balance between discontinuity and continuity, as we shall see, defines the practice of transitional history making, rendering it a delicate enterprise, yet endowing it with real transformative potential.

An understanding of how liberalizing politics influences the construction of history in moments of substantial political transformation ultimately can contribute to a better understanding of the role of history in ordinary times. The question of historical accountings in periods of radical political flux is an instance of a broader question of how societies construct shared truths. Epistemic consensus in a society is ordinarily considered to be created by the mechanisms of cultural transmission; truth's meaning in societies presumes threshold shared understandings.[8] Yet, in transitions, these threshold understandings are often fragile or missing altogether. What happens when a polity breaks down as it does in periods of repressive rule? Where is the authority in transition? The problem posed in periods of radical political change is that the usual bearings regarding shared judgment are missing. These are periods when shared notions of political truth and history are largely absent. In transition, the very foci of shared judgment that form the basis for a new social consensus are expected to emerge through the historical accountings.

How do societies go about constructing their pasts in a way that is collectively understood as shared and true? How do they establish what happened during much-contested periods of state history often involving massive state crimes? Below, the processes entailed in the construction of transitional histories are explored. Whereas contemporary theorizing emphasizes the relation of interpretive principles to their political and social context, transitional histories expose the relation of the given historical accounts to their legal forms and practices. What makes for transitional historical accountability is generated by forms and practices within a legal system. Transitional histories reveal how certain legal forms and practices enable historical productions and transformed truths, shedding new light on our intuitions about the role of history in liberalizing political change.

The country experiences discussed in this chapter illuminate the varieties of historical accountability: how societies struggle with the question of how to construct a collective account in radical political change, the many ways transitional societies create public histories, and the role of the law in these constructions. Collective memory is created in frameworks and through symbols and rituals. In transition, the oft-shared frameworks—political, religious, social—are threatened; so it is the law, its framework, and processes that in great part shape collective memory. In transitions, the pivotal role in shaping social memory is played by the law. Transitional historical narratives are produced through varying legal measures, such as the trials of the ancien régimes, or bureaucratic bodies convened for these purposes, and still other legal responses that imply marshaling a factual predicate. Finally, yet other independent accounts derive from private journalists' or historians' initiatives, though even these often draw on the law for their authority and as a constraint.

Historical accounts in periods of political transformation take diverse forms. The sources and forms that the transitional truths take vary: trials, truth commissions, official histories. The analysis here illuminates what may well be ever-present but which is vivified in periods of transition: "Each society has its regime of truth, its 'general politics' of truth; that is, the types of discourse which it accepts and makes function as true."[9] The variety of truth regimes, truth's contingency, is dramatically exemplified in the transitional context. The substance of the transitional truth regime depends on the nature of the predecessor's truth regime and the extent to which there is critical transformation. Transitional histories' justificatory epistemes define the direction of political transformation. It is through the framework of law, the language, procedures and vocabulary of justice, that this reconstruction is advanced. Below are explored instances of the construction of collective memory in transition.

## Law's History: Historical Justice and the Criminal Trial

Trials play the arch long-standing role in transitional history making. History operates as "judge" in the processes of criminal justice. So it is that in the contemporary debates over transitional justice, the issue is often framed as "punishment versus amnesty." Punishment is identified with collective memory, and punishment's waiver with collective amnesia.[10]

Consider the role of punishment in the pursuit of historical justice. Trials are long-standing ceremonial forms of collective history making. But beyond this, trials are the primary way of processing events in controversy.[11] The ordinary criminal trial's purposes are both to adjudicate individual responsibility and to establish the truth about an event in controversy. Though the importance of the truth's purpose to the criminal trial varies among legal systems and cultures,[12] in transitions, the trial's role of settling historical controversies can not be gainsaid. As transitions are periods of political and relatedly historical conflict, after a regime's change, successor trials are commonly held out as the primary means to establish a measure of historical justice. Also, successor trials are frequently used to establish historical accounts in political transitions; indeed, this is often their primary purpose. Through the trial, the pursuit of historical truth is embedded in a framework of accountability and in the pursuit of justice. In some respect, the use of trials to pursue a historical inquiry about events in controversy follows our intuitions about punishment's epistemic function. Yet, transitional histories through the criminal trial transcend our intuitions of trials' ordinary role in criminal accountability and yet are structured by the trial's frame of vision. In this context, the accounting for the past affects and constructs a distinct view of historical justice. The transitional history cannot help but shape a particular account of a state's controversial past.

In the criminal trial's historical accounting, truth is produced along with justice and thus plays a role in the process of delegitimating the predecessor regime and, relatedly, in establishing the legitimacy of the successor regime. While military or political collapse may well succeed in bringing down repressive leadership, unless the repressive regime is not only defeated but also publicly discredited, its political ideology may well endure. Thus, the eighteenth-century debates over whether to bring King Louis XVI to justice were seen by Thomas Paine as an opportunity to establish the "truth" of the evil of monarchic rule: "When he the king is looked upon . . . as an accused man whose trial may lead all nations in the world to know and detest the disastrous system of monarchy and the plots and intrigues of their own courts, he ought to be tried."[13] Other leading successor trials, whether of the major war criminals at Nuremberg or of Argentina's military junta, are today largely remembered not for their condemnation of particular individuals but, rather, for their role in creating a lasting record of state tyranny.

Successor criminal processes enable manifold historical representations of past evil legacies. Trials enable vivid representations of collective history through the recreation and dramatization of the criminal past in the trial proceedings. Further, this historical account is generally commemorated in a written transcript, often published. In the contemporary moment, the representational possibilities have been dramatically increased through the mass media and televised court proceedings, infusing popular culture. The written and other records of the trial and judgment are enduring representations.

How does the criminal form construct the truth?[14] There is no one answer, because various aspects of the truth production result from varying features of the criminal process. For example, the criminal trial enables the establishment of a historical record at the highest legal standard of certainty; in Anglo-American jurisprudence, it is "truth beyond a reasonable doubt."[15] The leading example remains that of the Nuremberg trials and judgment. The evidence of atrocities at Nuremberg, mostly drawn from Germany's own files, included 10,000 documents of decision making. There was a distinct preference for documentation as proof, for testimony was perceived to be political. In Chief Prosecutor Robert Jackson's words, "We will not ask you to convict these men on the testimony of their foes." *The Trials of War Criminals Before the Nuremberg Military Tribunals* constitutes a permanent record of Nazi persecution policy, still relied on by historians and others.[16] In a more contemporary example, the 1983 trial of Argentina's military junta enabled a public airing of the country's past. The trials of the military junta, since Argentina's legal system follows the largely nonadversarial, European-derived, nonpublic system of criminal procedures, were the first such trials in the country's history to be conducted in a similarly public fashion. Through the junta trials, for the first time since the collapse of military rule, the terrible events of the military repression were aired openly to the public and to the media over an extended period. The truth of what happened was established by the testimony of victims and corroborated by international nongovernmental organizations, human rights groups, and foreign governments—all attesting to the brutality of the prior regime.[17] Another successor trial, of former Central African Emperor Jean-Bedel Bokassa, was similarly notable for its representation of the past dictatorship. After a decade of repressive rule, Bokassa was overthrown by the French and put on trial for atrocities, including political massacres and even cannibalism. Through television and radio reports broadcast nationwide, the lengthy Bokassa trial created a vivid oral narrative of the brutality of his dictatorship.[18] Ultimately, and despite a subsequent amnesty, nationwide reporting of the trial proceedings sought to ensure that the offenses of the Bokassa regime would not be relegated to oblivion. The force of trials in shaping collective memory is seen in the extent to which it is these records that frame long-lasting social constructions of knowledge in these periods.

The force of criminal justice in historical construction is perhaps best illustrated in the connection between World War II–related criminal proceedings and accounts of the period. Postwar historiography points to the ongoing import of prominent trials in framing and preserving historical understandings. The force of legal representations in the construction of the scholarly and popular historical understandings of wartime atrocities is evident in the course of historical understandings over time. Legal and historical understandings regarding the nature of persecution developed in similar directions, pointing to the force of law in historical construction in transitional periods. The initial historical understanding of the Nazi persecution coincides with legal understandings of responsibility constructed at the postwar trials. Understandings of responsibility for wartime persecution began by concentrating on the individual at the top echelons of power. (It then would move toward a view of responsibility as more diffuse and pervasive.) Accordingly, at Nuremberg, the greatest crime is deemed the waging of "aggressive war"; and those put on trial are its military leaders. As the first trials targeted the top German military echelon, so, too, the then-prevailing historical school characterized responsibility for wartime persecution as extending from the top-down. The "intentionalist" school interpreted Nazi policy as Hitler-dominated; therefore, responsibility for wartime atrocities was attributed to the top Nazi echelon.

With time came a more nuanced legal understanding of responsibility, which went hand in hand with changes in the historical understanding. After Nuremberg, the Allied Control Council No. 10 trials witnessed a construction of accountability that shifted the burden of responsibility for war crimes from the top military rung to Germany's civilian elite. Historical interpretations in this period moved from the "intentionalist school," which viewed responsibility as concentrated (chiefly in one person) to the "functionalist school," which viewed responsibility as pervasive and diffused throughout all sectors of German society as throughout other countries.[19] Lower-level trials correspond to the change in understanding of responsibility. The convening of the *Eichmann* trial coincides with Raul Hilberg's *The Destruction of the European Jews* (1961). In subsequent decades, the net of prosecutions has expanded to include collaborators as well as those at lower echelons of power. Wartime collaborators were tried in the countries of what had been occupied Europe, notably the Netherlands and France. Leading examples of such prosecutions are the trials in France of Klaus Barbie in 1987 and of Paul Touvier and Maurice

Papon in the 1990s. Legal proceedings taking place in the United States, England, Scotland, and Australia arose out of these states' granting of safe haven to persecutors at the war's end.[20]

Whereas trials are often thought inapt for adequate historical representation because criminal justice appears to offer a narrow individual accountability,[21] and accounting for modern persecution clearly transcends the individual case, contemporary transitional justice mediates antinomies of the individual and the collective through constructs in the law of motive and policy. In these instances, the interaction of legal and historical constructions of responsibility supports a complex view of wrongdoing as perpetrated by individuals within a changing society. These legal developments coincide with an increase in theorizing about the increasingly dense obligations of humanitarian intervention, again raising ultimate questions about moral and legal responsibility for atrocities. Whether this is a case of law shaping history or of history shaping law, what is evident is the overall dynamic—that juridical and historical understandings have moved in similar directions over time. At the century's end, there is a mounting sense that responsibility for modern persecution derives from individual agency against a background of systemic policy. The historical understanding keeps changing in the light of present frameworks. Thus, the historical legacy of the postwar trials and its precedential meaning is also ever-changing. The view that Germany's trials were intended to establish individual responsibility for war crimes has given way to a more complex understanding of human rights abuses.

In the modern rule-of-law state, trials are traditional ceremonies affording a ritual to publicly contextualize and share past experience of wrongdoing. In transitions, trials play an even more significant role as they are well suited to the representation of histories in controversy, common in periods of radical flux. Yet, these rituals involving contested histories of the individual case often break down in the face of the massive systemic atrocities that characterize the repression of the modern state.

## The Dilemma of Political Justice

Instances of successor trials show that in their transitional form, trials are able to frame broad understandings of responsibility. Thus, though trials are commonly thought to emphasize individual agency in wrongdoing, transitional trials' accounts mediate between understandings of individual and collective responsibility. Despite successor trials' promise for establishing a historical record of states' evil legacies, the trial's uses for such purposes also presents a challenge to the rule of law. Troubling dilemmas arise whenever a punishment policy is undertaken chiefly to establish a historical record, whenever the primary purposes of transitional punishment are external to those ordinarily associated with the criminal justice system. Contemporary illustrations are the uses of post-Communist trials, such as those concerning 1956 Hungary, to shed light on previously obscured historical junctures. The trials run the risk of being perceived as political justice. Public history making through the criminal law raises the specter of sacrificing individual rights to the societal interest in establishing a historical record. An extreme case would be the trial of an innocent person to make a historical point. Such overt political uses of trials would simply amount to a "show trial." When emerging democracies turn to trials for historical justice, they risk its politicization—and the appearance that nothing has changed.

Even when trials are intended to advance liberalizing change and adhere scrupulously to due process, once set in motion, their impact is often not easily controlled. The direction of the historical rendition through the trial can not be known in advance, since at least in the adversarial legal system the proceedings involve explicitly competing historical accounts: Historical trials may backfire and, rather than express the normative liberalizing messages, end up subverting their democracy-building purpose. A notorious example is the case of Adolf Eichmann in Jerusalem. In bringing Eichmann to trial in 1961, the Israeli government intended to make vividly present the history of the Holocaust for the first Israeli-born generation. Despite the state's attempt to create a vivid historical account of Eichmann's responsibility, the trial could not help but trigger other, more controversial historical interpretations, such as that of supposed collaborator responsibility attributable to sectors of the organized Jewish community, recounted by Hannah Arendt in *Eichmann in Jerusalem: A Report on the Banality of Evil.*[22] Similarly, in 1988, when France brought Klaus Barbie, the "Butcher of Lyons," to trial, the public expectation was that the trial would enable a revisiting of the history of occupied France. And, indeed, much of the trial did enable a dramatization of wartime history. Private parties, including more than thirty victims and resistance and communist groups, joined the prosecution and used the trial as a vehicle to tell their version of the occupation. So-called general witnesses testified not to particular incidents in controversy, as in an ordinary trial but, rather, to their interpretations of war-related history, giving rise to the perception that the trial's aim was primarily to help unify France's divided political identity. Ultimately, the trial did have an impact on French wartime historical understanding but, as with the *Eichmann* trial, not necessarily that which was intended. Barbie's defense to charges of crimes against humanity was to countercharge France with war crimes in Algiers, leading some to say that what began as a trial about collaboration in Nazi persecution culminated in the worst sort of comparative genocide. Even the private-party testimony seemed to support a universalist view of wartime persecution popular among the French left. Ultimately, the historical account elaborated in the *Barbie* trial appeared to subvert the state's broader political purposes in favor of a narrower partisan message.[23]

These instances reveal the potential for politicization in the use of trials to construct transitional historical understanding. The problem is responding to crimes perpetrated in a political context through juridical means that are explicitly designed to establish one official account in a sea of contested histories. This limitation has tended to work against the use of trials for historical production. As previously discussed, the typical response is a somewhat limited criminal process that fails to fully individuate responsibility but that, nevertheless, establishes a public record. The "limited" criminal sanction advances investigation and documentation purposes, as it implies a formal criminal investigation by a presumably neutral judiciary at the highest legal of evidentiary standards in the law. Even when there is little or no attribution of individual responsibility, the limited sanction can, nevertheless, advance a historical record and the construction of public shareable knowledge about past repression. The limited sanction advances the criminal law's epistemic purposes. Moreover, where constructed in the juridical context, knowledge can be liberating: when the trials symbolically isolate individual wrongdoing, the larger society is redeemed.

## Disappearance and Representation

Repressive periods are commonly seen as gaps in a state's historical time; the sense of such a break was most pronounced in Latin America following military rule and the continent-wide policy of disappearance. Transitions in the Americas followed decades of military dictatorship and brutal repression, involving widespread abductions, detention, torture, and disappearances, all carried out in the name of "national security" and in absolute secrecy. Revelations about the past that emerged in the transition reveal the depths of a state's criminality whose very hallmark is "impunity." Though Latin American disappearances appear to redefine impunity, the disappearance policies—for example, of Argentina—built on the World War II Fascist "night and fog" policy of detaining and secreting away victims "without a trace," implemented by the National Socialists to destroy their political enemies and to instill terror in the population.

   Consider what it means if the victim's body in a crime disappears—perhaps the crime never happened? Disappearances meant the ultimate evidence of the crime, the victim's body, was missing.[24] Michel Foucault conceived of "the body [as] . . . directly involved in a political field; power relations have an immediate hold upon it; they invest it, mark it, train it, torture it."[25] Adding to these forms of social control, the repression in 1970s Latin America revealed a singularly coercive state power—to make the body disappear, making citizens vanish, rendering them *desaparecidos*. During Argentina's military rule, more than 10,000 persons were abducted, detained, and tortured, vanishing without a trace. Like the secrecy of the abduction and detention, the victim's ultimate disappearance is endemic to the "impunity crime." Every step of the military's process—kidnapping, detention, and torture, culminating in murder—is denied by the disappearances. As long as citizens remain disappeared, the military has triumphed, preserving its power hold. The disappearance of the citizen displays a perversely cruel and absolute sovereignty.

   When freedom returned, in a striking response, in the undoing associated with transition, the disappeared victims became the symbols of the dictatorship. The disappeared were the hapless victims; disappeared, too, was the body politic that had seemingly vanished in the vise of military repression; and disappeared was the state that had ceased to be. It was in the nature of the disappearance that the crime was indeterminate. Should the state fail to explain the victims' fates and whereabouts, was the wrong potentially ongoing and never ending? Thus, it was the disappearances that squarely raised the question of ongoing liability for the successor regime. At stake was an agonizing choice between justice and impunity, between punishing the military or seemingly endlessly reliving the past. Would the fragile balance of power and inability to punish the military mean depriving victims and survivors of any criminal investigation of their cases? Would failure to punish be tantamount to not even knowing the wrongs committed under the prior regime and to the state's continuing complicity in the perpetration of the disappearance policy?

The agonizing question confronted by countries moving away from brutal rule was how to deal with the historical gap implied by the state impunity that characterizes repressive rule in modern times. How to respond to the gap created by disappearance policy? How to establish what happened to the massive numbers of disappeared and dead characteristic of administrative murder and the modern security apparatus, and how to report such atrocities? The limited use of trials suggested that the sheer magnitude of the wrongs defies the capacity of the criminal justice system. By the same token, the popular response to the disappearances indicates the development of a new form: the bureaucratic response to bureaucratic murder.

How to establish the crime of "impunity"? How to prove what happened under repressive rule, when disappearances meant vanished victims, terrorized witnesses, and complete governmental cover-up? The problem of proof leads to the advent of the so-called truth commissions.[26] The scope of a truth commission's investigation lends itself to establishing the facts of bureaucratic mass murder, with its overwhelming scale of violence, of incidents often numbering in the tens of thousands. The commission of inquiry thus emerges as the leading mechanism elaborated to cope with the evil of the modern repressive state, since bureaucratic murder calls for its institutional counterpart, a response that can capture massive and systemic persecution policy.

When the survivors and representatives of the disappeared demanded that the successor regime disclose the truth about what happened under junta rule, their demand spurred the creation of a commission of inquiry. The mandate of the National Commission on the Disappeared (CONADEP) was to establish the truth about the fate of the disappeared and the repression, leaving open the question of what remedies might follow. Though victims' groups had petitioned for a governmental commission, the CONADEP was a political compromise, only semigovernmental. Lacking criminal powers, the commission was more a fact-finding than an investigatory body; its mandate was to report what happened under military rule. After nine months, a voluminous report identified the disappeared, who were presumed dead, and documented the systematic nature of junta repression. Though the report named the disappeared, controversially, it failed to name the perpetrators. Responsibility was attributed, however, to the various branches of the military junta, and this attribution of responsibility later became the basis of criminal proceedings brought against the military commanders.[27]

Truth commissions as a response to past military persecution spread quickly to other countries. Wherever states made delicate transitions out of brutal military rule and eschewed the prior regime's punishment, the burning question was whether past wrongs would simply be forgotten. The truth commission emerged as impunity's antidote and amnesty's analogue. Throughout the Americas—in Argentina, Chile, El Salvador, Honduras, Haiti, and Guatemala—wherever the violence was massive in relation to the population, making dim the possibility of criminal retribution, the truth commission became a central mechanism of political transition.[28] As it sought to implement liberalizing political change in Chile, the successor regime's response to prior repressive military rule was the historical inquiry of the National Commission on Truth and Reconciliation.[29] The investigation, confined to establishing the facts about those lost in the military's disappearance policy, concluded that the policy affected thousands of citizens. When the bloody civil war ended in El Salvador, after about a decade, with 75,000 killed and thousands displaced, the final peace accords stipulated the creation of an international "truth commission" to investigate past abuses. Emerging after protracted conflict, and a creation of the peace accords, the commission's mandate was to document "serious abuses" committed by both pro- and anti-government forces throughout the prolonged civil war.[30] For the first time since the post–World War II transitions, impartial investigation of a nation's abuses would be carried out by an outside international body. Similarly, the truce in Guatemala, following a thirty-six-year war, which had resulted in the deaths and disappearance of hundreds of thousands of people, was established on the promise of establishing the truth.[31] The Commission on Historical Clarification found sustained racial persecution and even genocide. In Honduras, after more than a decade of disappearances, a Commission for the Protection of Human Rights was established in 1992 to investigate. The commission's 1994 report made findings of close to two hundred cases of disappearances and named several members of the army high command as perpetrators.[32] In Haiti, the National Commission on Truth and Justice was created in 1995 to establish the truth about the most serious violations of human rights perpetrated between 1991 and 1994 domestically and abroad and to help in the reconciliation of all Haitians.[33]

As in the Americas, in Africa, after repressive rule, in the context of fragile fledgling democracies, commissions were created in Uganda, Chad, and post-apartheid South Africa.[34] Uganda created an investigatory commission in 1986, after more than two decades of brutality under the despotic Idi Amin and Milton Obote regimes, which took the lives of close to one million people. Affinities in historical and criminal accountability appear in the truth commissions' meticulous investigation and documentation of contested incidents, as well as in the extent to which the reports attribute individual responsibility. Thus, in Chad, after the 1990 overthrow of the Habré regime, under the advice of international organizations, a commission of inquiry was appointed to investigate and report on the atrocities committed during prior rule. It concluded that about 40,000 people had been tortured and executed by the Habré security apparatus. The documentary report approximated the recording and stigmatizing impact of the criminal sanction: Individual offenders were identified, and perpetrators' photographs were even included in the report.[35]

The turn to administrative inquiries in lieu of punishment was also true of postapartheid South Africa. South Africa's Truth and Reconciliation Commission's inquiries into apartheid were agreed to pursuant to the determination to pursue a nonretributive policy. Amnesties were to be exchanged for cooperation in the truth commission processes.[36] The multivolume report of the Commission on Truth and Reconcilation addresses "the commission of gross violations of human rights on all sides of the conflict," as well as the larger history and institutional and social structures of the apartheid system. In a highly divided society, the truth was to establish a basis for reconciliation.

When political impetus for an official investigation was lacking, the construction of collective memory and the investigation and documentation of past repression were taken up by the civil society's nongovernmental organizations, such as churches. The community that suffered perhaps the greatest number of unsolved disappearances on the continent was the Mayan community of Guatemala. Before the end of the three-decade-old war, the task of investigation was taken up by a church organization, the REHMI Oficina de Derechos Humanos del Arzobispado (Archbishop Office of Human Rights, or ODHA). Its unofficial report, with the mandate to pursue the "restoration of historical memory" based on victims' confessions, was to be integrated in the official report that appeared likely as a result of the settling of the war.[37] These unofficial findings of racial persecutions would rock the country, only to be subsequently confirmed by the official report, "The Memory of Silence." Likewise, elsewhere on the continent in countries where military rule ended without clear political transition, as in Brazil, or following difficult negotiations, as in Uruguay, governmental investigation was out of the question. In Brazil, investigating past wrongs was left to courageous clergy members, who wrote a report entitled *Never Again,* based on files secretly removed from military control. To this day, the clergy report remains a rare record of the 1970s Brazilian military repression and has been disseminated throughout the country.[38] Though Brazil and Uruguay's truth-tellings were unofficial, they emulate official accounts on the continent, such as Argentina's, conveying how even private reporting will be perceived as social truth so long as it follows the authoritative transitional form. Both the Brazil and Uruguay reports appropriate the features of the official governmental report. Entitled *Nunca Más,* or *Never Again,* both reports expressly follow Argentina's first such report: in title, organization, scope of mandate to investigate what happened during prior rule, and sources of evidence, deriving from official governmental sources. In this way, even unofficial reports can be said to construct an "official" truth. Brazil's report, drawn entirely from the government's own files, though not a trial record, amounted to a de facto confession of state wrongdoing, indeed, one extracted by Brazil's leading clergy members. And, because the Uruguayan repression was characterized by unlawful incarceration and torture (rather than executions), there were survivors, so that former prisoners had the potential of giving testimony as direct evidence in the historical record.[39] By their very names—*Nunca Más* in Spanish is translated as "Never Again"—the Latin American truth reports offer the promise of deterrence of future criminal wrongdoing, generally considered the province of punishment.[40] Deterrence of prospective wrongdoing is commonly a primary justification for punishment; yet, in transitions such rule of law concerns are thought to be advanced by alternative means—administrative inquiries. The popularity of such investigations in countries forgoing criminal justice points to continuities in the criminal and administrative forms in transition.

## A Truth Commissioned: The Epistemology of the Official Truth

Consider what the transitional inquiries might tell us about how the official truth is produced. The advent of the truth commission—not quite a traditional trial, but a quasi-official investigation—challenges our intuitions about the nature and form of historical justice. As is elaborated further on, the epistemology of the transitional truth is closely tied to the truth commission's administrative structure, powers, and processes. Public knowledge about the past is produced through elaborate processes of representation by perpetrators, victims, and the broader society, grounding the historical inquiry with a basis for social consensus. It is a truth that is publicly arrived at and legitimated in nonadversarial processes that link up historical judgment with potential consensus. The truth commission mandates emerged as principled compromises on the transitional justice issue of "punishment or impunity." Like prosecution, the semigovernmental commissions are delegated powers by the executive, ordinarily the source of prosecutorial power. While some truth commissions have broader investigative powers, such as subpoena power—for example, South Africa's Commission for Truth and Reconciliation—none has full judicial powers. The construction of a plausible public truth depends on other ratifying processes outside the government and emanating from the people. Transitional truth that is socially acceptable is produced within a newly democratic structure drawing from two sorts of narrators: the people and a representative elite. Truth commissioners tend to be prominent citizens chosen for their integrity, a moral elite. Moreover, as a body, the commission is also expected to be politically balanced and neutral. The question of neutrality is particularly important in transitions following civil war; thus, for example, the problem of political neutrality posed in post–civil war El Salvador led to a commission comprised of non-Salvadorans, foreigners outside the polarized state. The same was largely true of Guatemala's Historical Clarification Commission. The recurring image is of the truth as somehow impartial, and therefore foreign.[41]

What constitutes "the official story"? If the commissioners offer the moral authority of voices of political dispassion and neutrality, victims conversely offer the moral authority of the impassioned voices, of those who suffered state horror firsthand and up close. The victims of prior oppression are the historical inquiry's primary source of evidence, the stewards of the nation's newfound history. Truth commissions depend on victims' testimony, and it is fulsome, as unlike a trial, lacking in challenging confrontation or cross-examination. Those who previously suffered most at the hands of the state become its most credible witnesses and authoritative voices. When the victims' testimony is narrated by the commissioners' quasi-state authors, it becomes a shareable truth, a national story, and the basis of transitional consensus.

Social knowledge of the past is constructed through public processes. These proceedings generate a democratizing truth that helps construct a sense of societal consensus. The processes are also performative: they assume a profoundly critical and transformative aesthetic—a ritual that inverts the prior repression's knowledge policy. While impunity reigned under repressive rule and the military regimes were known for their cover-ups, by contrast, successor regimes are known for their due process. The right to a hearing, a traditional part of governmental administrative procedures, publicly affirms rights to political participation and individual dignity. The administrative inquiry depends on citizens' participation—encouraged by the state through strong incentives, such as victims' reparations and perpetrators' immunity. South Africa offers an example of incentive structure implicit in the administrative commission's dependence on testimonies and confessions conditioned on reparations and amnesties. Further, beyond these incentives, the process of testifying is itself thought to be cathartic. If the predecessor regime failed to protect its citizens from violations of their security, under liberalizing rule, the opportunity for a governmental hearing goes some way to restoring a small part of the prior dignitary harm. The impact of victims' testimony is heightened when the truth commissions' hearings are held at public sites of prior persecution. This public process also goes some way to legitimating the new regime. Those previously tortured and silenced now speak openly about their experiences under the repression.[42] Survivors' stories are compared and patterns of systematic abuses revealed. Together with other evidence, these stories make up the official truth. Testimony of victims and other witnesses is deftly reconstructed by commissioners into a unified story of state repression. The official truth reports constitute a distinctive form of narrative, and so it is not surprising that the chairs of the truth commissions are often leading authors, such as Ernesto Sábato, the chair of Argentina's landmark CONADEP.

Transitional truth inquiries are mandated to establish "what happened" under prior evil rule. Truth commission practices suggest adherence to a principle of documentation. The truth reports follow the literal style of official documentation. Consider by what standard of certainty the "official truth" is known. American law emphasizes standards of proof as the defining characteristic distinguishing criminal and civil fact-finding. Yet, this notion of varying standards of proof and accounts seems odd from the vantage point of truth in other legal cultures. Thus, the truth in continental systems, by contrast, is a commonly unitary understanding transcending the particular legal proceeding.[43] The transitional truth commissions' hybrids of civil and criminal inquiry have attempted to forge a similar unitary approach to the "truth." Most commissions elide the question of the appropriate evidentiary standard. When the question was addressed by El Salvador's truth commission, it drew on the two-source rule, the evidentiary standard generally employed by historians and journalists. The minimum evidentiary standard, "sufficient evidence," corresponded to a preponderance of the evidence, necessitating more than one source.[44]

The truth reports are not generalized accounts but detailed documentary records. The reports are a sea of details: they document the disappearance by the street where the abduction occurred, the name of the detention center, the nicknames of the torturers, the names of co-inmates, and the names of the witnesses who testified.[45] Every detail is recounted in bare fashion without literary license. In plain, matter-of-fact language, the unbelievable is made believable. The greater the detail, the stronger the counterweight to prior state silence. The more precise the documentation, the less is left to interpretation and even to denial. What is seen throughout transitional histories is that the official truth must be known with precision. To know precisely is to close the gap on past events that by their very horror and state sponsorship would otherwise be disbelieved and forgotten. The official truth of state atrocities must, therefore, be established by meticulous documentation, and the paradigm of official representation of the state atrocity is the literal account. Rituals of accountability invert the practices of disappearances, dispelling the policies of "night and fog." The literal account responds to and limits the possibility of competing narratives. The "report" has become the dominant way to chronicle stories of human rights abuses and atrocities. What style there is might best be described as juridical.[46]

## The Politics of Memory: Linking Historical to Political Regimes

> My dreams are like your vigils.
> Jorge Luis Borges, *A Personal Anthology*

Making the truth "official" presumes a degree of democratic consensus; yet, in transition, democratic processes are often not fully consolidated, with implications for the authority and legitimacy of transitional production of knowledge. In transitional truth-telling, accordingly, there is a concerted attempt to make historical and political accountability converge. Transitional truth regimes are not autonomous but, rather, inextricably related to particular processes of creating knowledge, as well as to prior historical narratives. Consensus on the history produced is predicated on the truth's dissemination and acceptance in the public sphere. From where does the official truth derive its power? Legal processes of presentment and ratification display the stuff of authority and its legitimation in newly democratized processes. Once completed, truth reports are presented back to the governmental actor delegating the commission its powers, generally the country's executive.[47] This dissemination was the sequence in Chile; for example, following the Rettig Commission's presentment to the president, the report was presented to the country.[48] An analogous process occurred in the Salvadoran international commission's presentment to the United Nations.[49]

Public rituals of accountability are often accompanied by governmental apology. Thus, for example, in postmilitary Chile, the president publicly presented the truth commission report's key findings to the country, in a large sports stadium. The very same stadium had been the site of state arrests and torture, illustrating once again that the critical rituals are inversions—cooptations of the predecessor rituals of repression—which in the reenactment are infused with new meaning. In his presentment, President Patricio Aylwin declared the disappearances "executions" by "agents of the State," formally recognized state accountability and called for a societal apology.[50] President Aylwin "assume[d] the representation of the nation in order to, in its name, acknowledge accountability to the relatives of the victims."[51] The transitional apology offered a public rehabilitation to victims, whose reputations had been attacked under the prior regime, which had defamed them as "enemies of the state." These representations had societal consequences more profound than those associated with ordinary defamation, underscoring affinities in historical and reparatory justice. While by the executive apology the president assumed representative responsibility to victims on the nation's behalf, he also affirmed the need for "gestures of recognition of the suffering" throughout the nation.

Public representation of the truth, through executive presentment, offers nuanced expressions of transitional political accountability and a striking illustration of the dilemma of successor responsibility in the transition. When the new truth regime is presented and the successor regime's representative apologizes to the people on the nation's behalf for acts committed under the predecessor regime, what is implied is a certain continuity of the state and of the rule of law. The transitional apology allows for the continuity of state responsibility, even as it also affords discontinuity—a letting go of the past. Of course, official apologies play a role in acknowledgment of governmental wrongdoing. Executive apologies enable formal governmental acknowledgment of wrongdoing, particularly in the sphere of international relations.[52] While this has been common practice at the level of states, transitional experiences show the extension of these practices internally of successor governments vis-à-vis their citizens. As the culmination of the truth-telling, transitional apologies do added work, related to constructing the shift in political regimes.

If the truth commissions' mandate is to establish what happened during past rule, fulfilling this mandate goes beyond amassing the facts. For what is at stake is a contested national history. Accordingly, truth commissions, like successor trials, are a forum of public historical accountability regarding contested traumatic events, for transitions imply a displacement, or substitution, of truth regimes. In the shifts out of military rule, the pivotal contested truth goes to the very characterization of the violence of prior rule. In the standard military account, the violence perpetrated was "war," the disappeared were "guerillas," and repression was justified as the "war against subversion." It is to these representations that transitional truth reports explicitly respond, substituting successors' truth for the account of the prior regimes.[53] Transforming predecessor representations of state action is enabled through the devices of what might be termed "categorization" and "emplotment" in the new successor narratives. Categorization and emplotment are devices deployed in transitional narratives to recast and restructure the state's legitimating stories that justified its past. Constructing past state action as illegitimate requires reporting facts in ways highlighting the relevant distinctions, through the use of parallel or juxtaposed categories, in and against the context of the past repressive rule. For example, Chile's report is structured by categories of state action, distinguishing between victims of "political violence" and "human rights violations."[54] Representations of perpetrators' and victims' status and actions constitute the elements for reconstructing the prior representations of the wrongdoing. What happened under previous rule is represented in changed categories of violence. Beyond the newfound facts is the renegotiation of the representational language of political violence: "armed conflict," "insurrection," "political terrorism," "crimes against humanity," and "genocide." Historical transformation occurs through the explicit re-presentation involving re-categorization of the facts in controversy—in particular, the nature of and the justification for the predecessor's political violence. Thus, for example, in the transitions out of military rule, the critical truths are those that strike at the heart of the national security state and its doctrine. Successor reports offer critical responses to predecessor military regimes' claims in asserting that governmental brutalities were not justified by national security doctrine in the so-called wars against subversion, that those killed were not political terrorists but ordinary citizens, and that disappearances were not justified by reasons of security. When Argentina's *Nunca Más* report concludes by soberly observing that fully one-fifth of the disappeared were students,[55] victims categorized as "unarmed civilians," these representations constitute a critical revisionism forcing change, or transition, in the truth regimes. Such representations strike at the heart of the prior regime's justification of political violence. For this reason, successor reports are largely devoted to identifying and categorizing victims systematically, with grave implications for the prior regime. Establishing that victims were unarmed civilians, and not combatants, both refutes the predecessor truth regime of the military's claim of a war against terrorism and accordingly establishes that what happened under prior rule was systematic state-sponsored persecution.

But the attempt to redraw the line of justifiable political violence is a delicate enterprise, the risks of politicization many, and the line quite thin, particularly so when the attempt is to distinguish between political and human rights violence and when by way of juxtaposition within the same inquiry and report that attempt means the risk of juridical and moral equivalence. The truth regime that supports peace, the rule of law, and the political aims of the successor is not always historically just and hence may be unstable and short lived. It is a truth for a particular politics.

This tension implicit in guarding historical transition, while in entrenching a transformed understanding of past violence, is seen in the post–civil war transitions, in which historical accountability takes a distinct form: Settlements, negotiated after civil war–like conflicts, rely on historical accountings to advance the concededly political purposes of reconciliation. Bringing these conflicts to an end often depends on express commitments to bilateral historical investigations, involving bipartisan representations of violence. Accordingly, post–civil war commissions are often charged with mandates to create a unitary historical account jointly representing both sides in the civil war. The political agreement is to a historical representation of shared responsibility, though the role of the state is dominant. It is these accounts that make most clear the relation the truth regime bears to the political regime.

There are numerous illustrations of recent negotiated agreements ending conflict throughout Central America and Africa. Civil wars in El Salvador and Guatemala ended with agreements to a bilateral inquiry into regime and opposition violence culminating in a unitary report.[56] Following civil war, the truth commission's conciliatory purposes were central to transition. In contemporary post–civil war transitions, a twofold official inquiry report comprehending military and opposition violence offers a form of historically based reconciliation. Thus, in El Salvador's truth report, the account of the country's civil war is characterized in terms of "serious acts of violence" structured formally in parallel sections, entitled: "Violence against Opponents by Agents of the State," and "Violence against Opponents by the Frente Farabundo Marti para La Liberación Nacional." The balancing of state and opposition violence is effected through the use of paradigm or exemplary cases. Guatemala's Report of the Commission for Historical Clarification refers to the country's past as "fraternal confrontation" perpetrated by the state security forces and the insurgency.[57] Given the toll of the civil wars in countries like El Salvador and Guatemala, the truth commissions' mandate for reconciliation depended on limited investigation of exemplary cases—within both camps. Thus, two kinds of violence, state and opposition, are juxtaposed through parallel categories, parallel titles, exemplary cases, all comprehended within the covers of one truth report.[58] A balanced history is told, a narrative commissioned in support of a political agreement.

A similar agreement became law in South Africa. Under the overarching rubric of apartheid, the South African truth commission's mandate was to investigate the prior regime's offenses, together with those of nonstate actors.[59] A question of moral equivalence is raised by South Africa's Report of the Truth and Reconciliation Commission. The focus of volume 2 is on perpetrators. While the report begins with the exposition of the role of the state, immediately juxtaposed against this part is a discussion of the "Liberation Movements" and their role in abuses. Moreover, an even more complex equivalence occurs in the truth processes. Perpetrators and victims are generally characterized as equals; perpetrators are analogized to victims and, hence, on a par:

> The wicked and the innocent have often both been victims. . . . The families of those unlawfully tortured, maimed or traumatised become more em-

powered to discover the truth, the perpetrators become exposed to opportunities to obtain relief from the burden of a guilt. The country begins the long
and necessary process of healing the wounds of the past. . . ."[60]

The ethical and political implications of this sort of transitional narrative
are exemplified in Hannah Arendt's "Report" of the major Nazi trial in Israel.[61]
Arendt's so-called trial report is an instance of relentless normative argument
through juxtaposition, most saliently, of Adolf Eichmann's responsibility as
perpetrator against that of his victims. Indeed, it is this juxtaposition within
the same account, of Eichmann's bureaucratic role against that of his victims
that is thought supportive of Arendt's central claim of the "banality" of evil.

The risk of the politicization of transitional historical justice is illustrated
in the transitional truth reports. Whenever peace agreements precommit to
conjoining the investigation of state—with other—violence, a commission's
agreement to a particular account seemingly runs the risk of being history's
version of a "show" trial. The question that arises is, to what extent does the
preceding political agreement constrain the independence and even predeter-
mine the historical inquiry? Political representations run along a spectrum
of continuity and discontinuity, with attendant implications for the perception
of the possibility of liberalizing change. When the two sorts of violence are
conjoined, the representation is one of continuity, of a seeming relativization
of state wrongdoing, of the equation of the official repressive apparatus with
the political opposition. The joint process of investigating and reporting the
dual violence of government and opposition leads to the juxtaposition of the
acts of state and nonstate actors in parallel categories and introduces a controversial comparison: Apposition of both sorts of violence in one document,
through the uses of parallel categories and exemplary cases, apparently constructs symmetric representations and even an equation of evils—a moral
equivalence.

The transitional narratives can be structured or "emplotted" in a variety of
ways so as to tell multiple stories. For example, the question is partly how broad
should be the historical lens brought to bear on the relevant inquiry. Against a
historical context that is longstanding, rather than immediate, the story told is
one of cyclical violence. When the historical accounting is organized in ways
that revive preexisting historical categories and judgments, the nature and
causes of the violence appear overdetermined and not to admit of change.[62]

The transitional commissions can also constitute other normative truth
regimes that are radically transformative. When the successor regime's truth
report presents the prior repression in categories that explicitly respond to the
prior regime's own accounts, this representation advances a "critical" response. Transformative successor counteraccounts depend on the deployment
of juridical categories responding to those of the predecessor truth regimes.
The response to and refutation of the predecessor account of the repression
provides a form of historical accountability. Such historical accountability is
enabled by principles of documentation, representation, and entrenchment of
a successor account. Transforming the prior categorization, the reports seek to
expose the nature of the state's wrongdoing. What the truth commissions'

painstaking documentation achieves—seemingly against all odds—is an authoritative counteraccount. Affinities emerge between historical and criminal
justice: Just as a trial concludes with the determination of the veracity of one
version of a contested event, so, too, the transitional truth inquiries culminate
with a similar determination.

## Truth or Justice: Truth as Prelude to Justice?

Consider the role of historical narratives produced in periods of political transformation. To what extent are the transitional truth-tellings a form of justice?
Or are they a prelude or an alternative to justice? To what extent is historical
accountability a goal in itself in transition, as opposed to a means to another
end? To what extent is the construction of truth performative, and to what extent instrumental? A key performative function of the construction of transitional truth is the display of "reconciliation," as truth commission hearings
bring victims and perpetrators together, through their testimonies, to participate in the state's processes. Beyond victims' testimony, commissions rely on
perpetrators' confessions. Indeed, this is particularly true when the goal is reconciliation. In bringing perpetrators and victims together to talk about their
experiences, the truth commission inquiries constitute a reenactment and a
shared testimonial about the past. When victims and perpetrators testify,
there is a self-purging and the possibility of personal change regarding the past
experience. Nevertheless, despite these processes' cathartic function, there is
the latent potential of conflict between victims' and perpetrators' needs and
the interests of the state. Throughout transitions, victims have challenged
amnesty laws for greater control and vindication of their "rights" to knowledge. Leading examples are the Mothers of the Plaza de Mayo in Argentina
and the Biko family in South Africa.[63]

Beyond this potential conflict, truth sets in motion other consequences.
Changes in interpretation offer justification for other political changes. Once
a new truth regime is established, it has further consequences as it sets the
standard for defining other claims. Accordingly, historical accountability sets
off a dynamic in the transition. When there is a newly constructed response, it
alters the political and legal landscape. Thus, "truth" is not an autonomous response; reconstructing critical facts is inextricably tied up in other societal
practices. When the "truth" becomes known, when certain critical knowledge
is publicly recognized, the shared knowledge often sets in motion other legal
responses, such as sanctions against perpetrators, reparations for victims, and
institutional changes.

In some countries, exploration of the past began under a mandate to explore an open-ended inquiry. Truth is seen by some as a precursor phase that
leads to other legal processes, such as prosecution, whereas others see the
truth inquiries as a fully independent alternative to other responses. Thus, for
example, *Nunca Más*, Argentina's report, was just the first stage in the country's project of dealing with its past. Whereas, generally speaking, "truth com-

missions" do not reveal the names of individual offenders,[64] in Argentina, wherever there was a suspicion of wrongdoing, the commission turned its list of names over to the courts, and the allegations would pave the way to individual trials. Revelations of past wrongdoing had further consequences, leading to convictions. The transitional role of official investigations as a first-step predicate to other remedies is analogous to ordinary times. Thus, for example, in Canada and Australia, historical inquiries to investigate those states' World War II–related role culminated in criminal prosecutions. In their aftermath, events rarely stand still. Unless the truth inquiry is controlled a priori, it leads in diverse directions, to trials, other sanctions, victims' remedies, and structural changes.

Truth or justice? Again, truth inquiries have in some countries been considered not a prelude but an alternative to punishment.[65] In contexts in which punishment is not available or politically advisable, historical investigation processes have been advocated as alternatives to punishment. Thus, for example, in Chile, El Salvador, Guatemala, and South Africa, where retributive justice was eschewed, these tightly controlled inquiries, constrained from the start by government-asserted purposes of reconciliation appeared to serve some of the avowed state interests in pseudo-punishment. In the language of the Chilean Truth and Reconciliation Report, the truth itself constitutes a "moral conviction."

There is often thought to be a trade-off between truth and justice. Yet, as the earlier discussion of criminal justice reflects, construction of public knowledge regarding repressive pasts takes varying forms, so that the choices between criminal and historical inquiries turn out hardly to present a choice between truth and justice. The question, instead, is what sort of "truth"?

The defining feature of truth regimes in transition relates to the extent of the successor societies' tolerance for multiple representations of the "truth." When transition is effected on the promise of the future reconciliation of a factionalized society, the attempt is to cohere around a shared historical account. Historical consensus is tightly linked to building political consensus. Thus, there is often an attempt to constrain other competing historical accounts, and incentives are offered for victims and perpetrators to participate in the official historical processes. Apologies offered and amnesties promised are used to control counteraccounts that might subvert the official account, which is illustrated in the contemporary inquiry in South Africa. Constraints that are put on alternative accounts of the past constitute a form of "gag rule."[66] Other sorts of gag rules regarding controversial state pasts appear in the transitional constitutions of these periods, discussed later in this chapter.

Truth is not synonymous with justice; neither is it independent of justice. Instead, it is better understood as a virtue of justice. So it is that there are affinities between historical and other transitional forms of accountability, all constructing various forms of collectively shared knowledge regarding the past. Transitional histories advance epistemic and expressive purposes associated with the criminal sanction. A further affinity between historical and criminal accountability is the attribution of individual responsibility for past wrongdoing. These affinities were evident in South Africa's postapartheid Commission for Truth and Reconciliation, where historical testimonial processes were predicated on individual, case-by-case amnesties. As in a criminal scheme, the individual confessions bore the hallmarks of punishment, as there were individualized inquiries establishing wrongdoing, with findings made public in formal ritualized processes. Exposure of perpetrators' offenses itself is an informal form of punishment, of "shaming," subjecting perpetrators to social censure and ostracism. This form of sanction risks the possibility of limitless condemnation, ultimately threatening the rule of law.[67]

Another connection between historical and other forms of justice is that establishing past wrongdoing gives victims a form of reparation, as well as delineates a line between regimes. Telling the victim's story sets the record "straight" on prior false allegations of political criminality, as, for example, in Latin American regimes, where many of the disappeared had been previously accused of subversion. A similar rehabilitation of reputation played an important role in Eastern Europe and Russia. Rehabilitation of political prisoners from the Stalin era, numbering in the thousands, continues to be an important, ongoing function of human rights organizations there, primarily in the work of Memorial, the organization established in the late 1980s to shed light on the political repression. Setting the record straight for victims occurs in a number of ways, through overturning of individual convictions, passage of legislation, presentment of truth reports in apologies, and publication of counteraccounts. What emerges is the pervasive corrective aim distinguishing transitional historical justice. Whether in making victims whole or in restoring peace and reconciliation to a divided society, the truth's purpose in these cases is a story of eternal return.

Historical justice's virtues display affinities with other forms of transitional justice in liberalization in its essentially corrective aim, evident in that many of the truth reports go on to make recommendations of a structural nature. For example, when El Salvador's truth commission reported that responsibility for grave human rights abuses lay in the country's military high command, it went on to recommend purges of that body.[68] When repressive rule in many of the Latin American reports is attributed to the absence of an independent judiciary, strengthened judicial institutions are frequently recommended in the reports, as is deep change in the legal culture, particularly concerning human rights.[69] The transitional pursuit of accountability often metamorphosizes into a more permanent institution, for example, Uganda's truth commission, which led to a permanent human rights office to investigate abuses under the freely elected successor regime.[70] Something similar happened in Chile, whose Truth and Reconciliation Commission led to the establishment of the National Chilean Corporation of Reparation and Reconciliation, which also deals with new cases.[71]

Finally, dissemination of the truth reports in successor societies attempts to transform public opinion regarding state tyranny. Truth reports generally reveal a high level of past societal acceptance of state terror. Societal acquiescence, particularly in the elite, reflects that rights abuses were an acceptable cost of increased control over the opposition; and, in part, it was this attitude that enabled the military's repressive hold in the region.[72] If punishment expresses what behavior a society is unwilling to tolerate, then many postmilitary societies lack consensus about the unacceptability and, more specifically, the criminality of the behavior of the dictatorship. Truth reports' critical interpretation of the predecessor regime, as through prosecutions, can break the silence characterizing prior repressive rule.Societal tolerance for state repression may lessen over time.

Given the role of the truth commissions and attendant reports in transforming societal attitudes toward state repression, how then does this transformation enable historical justice in the sense of accountability? How does the official reports' narrative style construct a sense of historical accountability? In what sense is this historical justice? Though transitional truth reports generally disclaim a role in judgment,[73] such disclaimers can only refer to a narrow view of judgment. For the form of the truth inquiries and reports, formal rituals with their detailed indictments, share certain affinities with criminal indictments. The reports might be said to offer a form of judgment in that their account of history uses the language of law in responding to past individual rights violations. The historical accounting is written in legal language, in terms of status, rights, wrongs, duties, claims, and entitlements. When perpetrators are not individuated, as is often the case in the truth reports, the subject of the reports' judgment is the society at large. This type of accounting is more comprehensive than that of the criminal justice system. At the very least, such truth accounts enable a broad sense of historical justice, if not in holding perpetrators accountable, in rehabilitating and vindicating victims. Within criminal justice, the accounting is, like adjudication itself, case by case, whereas the administrative inquiries have the advantage of focusing the historical lens more widely, better comprehending a state's historical legacy, social structures, and policies, all relating to the question of responsibility for wrongdoing. Within a broader historical inquiry, perpetrators and victims are linked up again in the inquiry into the state's persecutory policy.

Truth commission processes illuminate the historical response to a distinctive repressive rule and, more particularly, the relation of historical and political regimes. By offering critical responses to a predecessor regime's historical, legal, and political representations of past repression, official truth reports provide a form of accountability in the transition and respond to and delimit the claim that all was political. In the truth commission processes, political truth is constructed all at once, demonstrating how change in truth regimes corresponds to change in political regimes. The express nature of the transitional historical forms and processes reveals the often instrumental, and significantly politicized, nature of these measures, politicized in the sense that the relevant truth is that public knowledge needed to advance the particular society's transformation. In this perhaps most urgent of the transitional responses, a new story line is speedily produced; a "truth" is an overtly and explicitly political construction shaping the direction of the transition.

Let us return to the question with which the chapter begins: what is the nature and role of history in transitions? Transitions illuminate historical inquiry's social frameworks. Although it is generally understood that present social and political frameworks affect the construction of collective memory,[74] the ordinary relation does not pertain in transition. The construction of collective memory in times of radical transformation is distinguished by the sense in which the relevant framework is transitional. Official truth processes, such as the commissioned state histories, are expressly designed to advance a more democratic future. Here the histories' transformative purpose, their forward-looking political role in national reconciliation and liberalization, is evident. The truth produced is a "workable" past for a changed future. Transitional histories perform the twin functions of discounting and of reappropriating what was repressed, even to the point of disappearance under prior rule. What remains is a performative narrative of liberalization. It is a story that is liberalizing in the context of the states' political legacies.

## Historical Justice in the Legacy of Totalitarianism

> The fundamental pillar of the present totalitarian system is the existence of one central agent of all truth and all power, an institutionalized "rationale of history."
>
> . . .
>
> In the post-totalitarian system, truth in the widest sense of the word has a very special import, one unknown in other contexts. In this system, truth plays a far greater (and, above all, a far different) role as a factor of power, or as an outright political force. How does the power of truth operate? How does truth as a factor of power work? How can its power—as power—be realized?
>
> Václav Havel, *Open Letters: Selected Writings, 1965–1990*

> Hegel remarks somewhere that all great world-historical facts and personages occur, as it were, twice. He has forgotten to add: the first time as tragedy, the second as farce.
>
> Karl Marx, *The Eighteenth Brumaire of Louis Bonaparte*

> The struggle of man against power is the struggle of memory against forgetting.
>
> Milan Kundera, *The Book of Laughter and Forgetting*

"Living within the truth" was the slogan of much of the opposition in its challenge to the Communist regime.[75] Yet, after the political change, what exactly would it mean to "live within the truth"? How to move from "living in the lie" to an open society? Traditional dictatorships, such as the military in Latin America, tended to wield power through the forces of secrecy, disappearance, and impunity, to rule outside history. When this was the prior regime's relation of knowledge to power, the transitional response is to visibly construct a collective historical account of the period. By contrast, after communism, official truth-tellings have not been the common response. This response seems all wrong in the context of transition from totalitarian rule, in which official state histories played an integral role in the repression. Marxist ideology of progressive history rationalized the totalitarian state. Beyond the Berlin Wall, the greatest symbol of totalitarian repression was the state security apparatus and its methods of surveillance. What distinguished totalitarianism was the totality of state power, including the totalizing attempt to control culture and history. The totalitarian legacy involved the overtly political uses of state history.[76] An agonizing question, then, was what to do with the accumulated ancien régime state histories? The word *archive* itself hints at its significance: "arche" meaning "beginning," as well as "government." Nowhere is the archival link between government and its normative beginnings more evident than in transition.[77] While after dictatorship there appeared to be consensus about the value of exposure of the past history, in the post-Communist transitions, there was no such consensus. With the regime's collapse, the question arose of how to deal with the legacy of these official state histories. After Communism, the notion that official accountings were necessary to successful transition seemed flatly wrong. In the legacy of repressive totalitarian rule, what would an official transitional truth mean? Because of the legacy of totalitarianism's political uses of official history, the transitions out of Communism generally eschewed official history making about the past repression.

The movement away from totalitarian rule has not witnessed the massive historical investigations associated with the political shifts away from military dictatorship. The meaning of transitional historical justice appears to be contingent and peculiar to the regimes succeeding to Communist rule. While repression under dictatorship in Latin America and elsewhere denoted disappearances and uncertainty, under Communist rule, repression took another, more material form, in the totality of state control over the construction of historical events. This legacy affects the historical response in transition. In the brooding omnipresence of the totalitarian regime's documentation, in which history, like virtually every other realm, belonged to the state, what could freedom mean? In what sense was knowing history liberating? Whose history? What knowledge?

While there was little interest in reconstituting an official history of the protracted period under Communist rule, the transitional response is directed, instead, to exposing the truth about critical political moments in the prior repression and to gaining access to previously repressed history. The post-totalitarian historical inquiries focus on clarifying the imposition of repressive rule. Just this knowledge is anti-totalizing: As with postmilitary successor histories, the post-Communist inquiries were intended to counter predecessor representations of controversial historical moments. The meaning of transitional historical justice is defined in the context of prior state history. To the extent that they are responsive to prior state representations, such accountings provide a form of critical judgment.

Historical accountability devolved on the state's politically defining moments when the line between freedom and repression was drawn. In Russia, the opening of the KGB and party achives would remain highly politicized.

They played a role in the trial of the constitutionality of the Communist Party, where access to the files enabled establishing the party's unlawful action over the years.[78] The heady politicization of the archives in Russia is also seen in the absence of legislation; what guides access are presidential decrees transferring the materials from the archives of the party and the KGB to those of the state.[79] For the East European states making the transition out of totalitarian rule, the central question of historical justice was, Whose repression? The period could be fairly understood as external occupation or as internally imposed repression. The historical question has profound political and legal ramifications. Throughout the region, the effort is to reconstruct the period's critical historical gaps and the ensuing political turning points relating to the imposition of repressive Communist rule: for Hungary, the 1956 suppression of the uprising; for Czechoslovakia, 1968 and 1989; and for Poland, 1981. Historical inquiry was intended to shed light on the cold war's murky glitches.

In the former Czechoslavakia, there were at least two such defining moments: One was the crushing of the Prague spring. The full historical truth of the invasion became the subject matter of the Czechoslovak Government Commission for the Investigation of Events in 1967–70, made possible by the collapse of Soviet control in the region, which freed state files from the countries involved in the August 1968 invasion. Set up in 1989, the commission completed its work at the end of 1992, turning its documentation over to the Institute of Modern History. Another puzzle concerned the 1989 so-called Velvet Revolution. A related investigation concerned the events of November 17, 1989, and the government's attempted repression. A special government investigation by the parliamentary "November 17 Commission" was launched, which culminated in a report about the 1989 events, released at a special televised session of the Federal Assembly. The commission's report was read before the Federal Assembly on March 22, 1991. This highly public and politicized form of exposure led to "lustration"[80] and epitomized the uses of knowledge about the past as a purge, a policy discussed in chapter 5.

In Warsaw, the hope of political change was raised and extinguished on December 13, 1981. On that day, Poland's then-political leader, General Wojciech Jaruzelski imposed the martial law that crushed the opposition Solidarity movement. After 1989, the historical moment became the subject of a specially convened parliamentary (Sejm) Constitutional Accountability Commission.[81] While Poland had in large part eschewed a policy of retribution, the Parliament's investigation into the events of December 1981 was a rare look back. The burning question driving the historical investigation was, Who was responsible for the repressive period known as "the internal invasion" of Poland, "we" or "they"? To what extent was the country's repression attributable to internal or external responsibility? Whether external or not, to what extent was the nineteen-month crackdown on Solidarity justifiable to avoid a Soviet invasion? Was it justified by necessity? Even in the absence of further criminal inquiry, Jaruzelski's regime would at least be held historically accountable.

October 31, 1956, the date of the violent suppression of the popular uprising against dictatorship, was the turning point in Hungary. What drives transitional inquiry is the question of who was responsible for the suppression of 1956. The predecessor regime or the Soviets? We or they? The promise of an independent history of the uprising was fanned by newfound access to Soviet files. Nevertheless, ultimately, access to the archives did not much clarify and certainly did not settle the question of historical accountability, such as whether 1956 was an invitation to an occupation or a full-fledged invasion?[82] There was enough to suggest cooperation and collusion between the Soviets and the domestic Communist Party apparatus in the 1956 suppression. The reports revealed that leaders of the Communist Hungarian Socialist Worker's Party and military commanders were responsible for the deaths of thousands in the 1956 uprising.[83] Though the investigation into the invasion began with an inquiry into the foreign occupier ("they"), pursuant to an externalized concept of responsibility, it ultimately led to a more internalized concept—and the question, Who are "we?" This historical inquiry would lead to the pursuit of criminal accountability discussed in chapter two of this book.

In unified Germany, as elsewhere in the region, historical inquiry began with the question of national collective responsibility. Here, a more sweeping historical inquiry was undertaken than anywhere else in the region. The Eppelman Parliamentary Commission, named after its chairman, a leading former East German dissident, had a much broader mandate than other East European commissions to explore not merely responsibility for the occupation but also the broader reasons for the repression.[84] The commission was charged with exploring popular support for the Socialist Unity Party (SED) regime, even going as far as to review the role of *Ostpolitik*—West Germany's accommodationist policies in supporting the East German dictatorship.[85] The focus of the investigation was the attribution of broad historical accountability, and then, as the investigations unfolded, they gave way to more individualized investigations of collaboration and resistance. Both the Czech November 17 Commission and Hungary's 1956 inquiry sparked criminal investigations,[86] and ended in widespread administrative purging from political office.[87] The truth of what had happened in the country ultimately came down to tests (or trials) of political loyalty—what one might regard as the truth of its subjects. These continuities in the historical and administrative responses in the transition throughout the region suggest that the critical law acts or promulgations are reconstructions of truth and displays of collective knowledge that are inextricably connected with political power and reconstruction of the political.

## Historical Justice in Communism's Shadow

> Who controls the past controls the future; who controls the present controls the past.
>
> George Orwell, *Nineteen Eighty-Four*

To what extent should archives created under repressive rule be relied on in transition as if they were in ordinary administration shifts in working democracies? Archives refers both to government records and to the place where they are housed—the seat of government. So it is that in the transitions out of totalitarian rule, the control of state history became utterly conflated with the control of political power. Truth inheres in the context of coerced ideological control. In this context, what is the meaning of normative transformation? This is the central question concerning the past state archives in the region. The question of how to treat archival historical knowledge has become deeply enmeshed in the politics of transition: The secrets of the political past are inextricably linked to control of the political future; historical inquiry quickly gives way to the politics of exposure.

How to resolve the dilemma of the legacy of totalitarian state histories? The most radical measure would be to destroy the files, as an auto-da-fé.[88] Burning the files would mean drawing a bright line between regimes. History could begin again. Burning the files seemed justified by the sense that they were at least in part unreliable and at worst ridden with lies. Protecting the old state files gave the succeeding regimes enormous power to destroy individual reputations thus perversely continuing the totalitarian legacy, while burning the files seemed to forever ensure against history's repeating itself.

Still, burning the files also seemed too radical. What if destroying the files did not necessarily quell suspicions about past collaboration? Suspicions could well persist, fueled by other sources. A more troubling consequence of burning the state archives was that the record of a long period of national history would be destroyed. Ordinarily, administration shifts in democracies presume succession in the archives,[89] precisely because state archives—like other state property—are elements of national identity. The analogy to working democracies militated for continuity of the files and the opening of the old archives. Indeed, such continuity seemed to be the hallmark of a rule-of-law system. But was the analogy appropriate? Competing rule-of-law considerations, instead, pointed toward discontinuity and breaking away from the old archives. Consider the ethics of a successor regime's relying on information previously gathered coercively and surreptitiously by invasion of privacy or, even worse, grave rights abuses. In established democracies, there are constraints in place on governmental information gathering, in part, relating to the protection of individual reputation and dignity rights. In a liberal state, there would be no space for archives such as those created in the post-totalitarian countries. Should the violations by its predecessor regime matter to the successor? Arguably these concerns are less vital for a successor regime; however, when fact-finding was conducted under a prior repressive regime, by its reliance on the prior regime's records, the successor regime operates as if it is an ordinary administration shift under continuous rule of law. Ongoing reliance on the ancien régime files complicates the consolidation of liberal rule.

At the same time, however, as the succession of the files poses a lingering threat to the legitimacy of the regime, opening the ancien régime's files offers an appealing symbol of the open society. Close to a half century of repressive state security militated for entirely open access. The alternative was a Latin American–style "truth commission," which would take control of the files. Yet, after Communist rule, the truth commissions that captured the public imagination in transitions from military dictatorship had little or no currency.

The varying transitional responses are not well explained in terms of the prevailing realist perspective, for diverse state responses do not appear to turn on a simple calculus of the balance of power. The question of whether there are public inquiries is hardly explicable in terms of ordinary understandings of political power. In the transition, knowledge and power are inextricably connected, mutually constituted and constituting. The post-Communist bloc's pursuit of measures varying from those of other transitions is thus better explained by the social meaning of party, of ideology, and of the locus of control of history and truth in that community. The construction of transitional histories is shaped by historical and political legacies in the region. The converse is also true; the present political context and culture affects the selective nature of historical retrieval, as well as the form of the truth production processes.

The former Communist bloc has struggled desperately to find its own way to deal with the old archives' terrible legacy. The question of what to do with the state files sparked the greatest public debate in countries with the most repressive security apparatus. This again reveals the ongoing force of legacies in shaping the direction of the transitional response. Unified Germany and the former Czechoslovakia in particular struggled with varying approaches to their repressive security states' legacies. Each country experimented with varying levels of freedom and access to the ancien régime archives. Ultimately, the resolutions in both countries were compromises, involving neither destruction of the archives nor full access.

Behind the Berlin Wall, there was no greater symbol of Communist repression than the miles of East German state police ("Stasi") files. For forty years, the state, through its security ministry and under the aegis of the Communist Party, had amassed documentation on its own citizens. The numbers alone were staggering; out of a country of eighteen million, more than a third were subjected to state surveillance.[90] There were said to be "six million" files, the same figure cited for victims in the Holocaust, fueling the historical analogy to World War II repression and supporting the argument that this time around, Germany would "deal" with its past.[91]

With the political change, the question arose of what to do with the state files. If repression depended on secrecy, justice depended on exposure. So it was that from the beginning of German reunification, there appeared to be strong societal support in favor of opening the files. Thus, the Act Regarding the Records of the State Security Service of the Former German Democratic Republic (Stasi Records Act) was adopted "to give the individual citizen the possibility of access to the personal data stored concerning him, so that he can clarify what influence the state security service has had on his personal destiny."[92] Yet, what became clear was that even for the victims of prior state persecution, freedom of information was not necessarily desirable. Opening one's file could mean finding that one had been spied on by family or friends, to the ruin of careers, friendships, even marriages.[93] Moreover, from the start, the opening of the Stasi files defied easy expectations, revealing their strange two-sidedness. Though in name a victims' rights measure, the Stasi files legislation never transferred the state's custody over the state files, allowing even victims only limited access. Moreover, though the files documented victims of state surveillance, they also implicated many in the security apparatus. Given their ambiguous Janus-like aspect, the opening of the files could hardly be said simply to vindicate victims. Other purposes were to "ensure and promote the historical, political and judicial reappraisal of the state security service."[94] Accordingly, files were deployed in the purging of the public administration.[95] The work of the independent commission created to regulate access to the Stasi files soon became the conduit to the purging of collaborators. Once the policy was put into motion, the Stasi files law seemed inadequate to its subject. The question of what was the societal interest in the files could hardly be answered in the abstract; and it was disingenuous to pretend that there existed a societal consensus on opening the files. Even victims had conflicting interests in the files, but the law regulating the files offered no guidance for reconciling these interests. When, in the transition, the state files were used once more to exclude persons from public life, the legacy of the repressive past cast its long shadow.

Whose archives and whose truth? Who had a legitimate stake in the old state histories? To what extent did the old regime's files "belong" to the individuals whose names they bore?[96] Or should access be granted perhaps as well to third parties, such as journalists, historians, and others? The old state files triggered all sorts of questions that transcended the perpetrators and victims. Resolving these dilemmas necessitated somehow accommodating the societal and individual interests in clarifying the past, while also protecting other privacy rights, as well as other societal interests in controlling access. The question was whether the policy regulating victims' access ought to regulate access to the files for less-benign purposes. Privatizing the old state histories, as exemplified in unified Germany, constituted a critical response to the prior regime. If, before, information was entirely in the state's hands, the successor policy was to let it go instead to the private domain.

The Czech approach appeared the opposite, as even the successor regime continued to perpetuate state control over the files. In the Czech Republic as in Germany, the principle guiding the old state files was nominally disclosure: evident in the Czech policy known as "lustrace" or "lustration," from the Latin *lustrare*, "to shed light" on the past.[97] Yet, from the very beginning of the transition, lustration's purposes and its risks were clear, as opening the state security files could well mean clarifying the past but also its attendant purging, excluding Communists and collaborators from participating in political life. Thus, perhaps paradoxically, greater access would still mean political exclusion. In the first free elections, conducted in the shadow of the files, the files themselves became the democracy's predominant political test. When the files were used as a form of blackmail to induce political candidates to self-purge or engage in "voluntary" self-disqualification, the attendant enormous political controversy culminated in the enactment of a law to regulate the files. Under the lustration law, access to the files remained squarely under governmental control. Even more troubling, the very same commission that controlled the files for the purpose of lustration also had the power to decide whether "lustrated" persons would be purged from their employ.[98] The powers to establish the truth about the past, as well as to shape the present political domain, were concentrated in the same institution—hauntingly, just as under Communism, in the Ministry of the Interior. This persistence of past legacies appeared also to be true elsewhere in the region. Lustration evinced the thin line between the politics of memory and the politics of disclosure. In the very institution which state documentation had been wielded as a weapon under Communism, it continued to be so used during the transition. While in the past the files had documented charges of subversion of the Communist state, in mirror fashion they now documented charges of collaboration. So it is that the old state archives were still being used to control politics in East Europe. The past state histories were still being used to punish, to exclude, and to disqualify. The specter of new purges grounded in old state histories and past purges evoked the Marxist vision of a recurring history.

What is evident in wrenching struggles throughout the region is that the question of what rule ought to govern the old state histories could not be separated from the question of their prospective transitional uses. In radical political flux, the pursuit of historical justice underscored the contingency of what is considered salient knowledge. While especially apparent in transitional periods, the contingency in how we know what we know is also present in established democracies and in legal systems in ordinary times. Thus, what rule governs knowledge in the law always depends on its purposes and uses; the rule is a function of knowledge's relation to prospective uses under the law. Thus, the relevant question in the law becomes, knowledge as a predicate for the definition and exercise of what legal claims, rights, or duties? Legal rules structure the relation that knowledge bears to power. Thus, for example, when historical knowledge serves as a basis for criminal justice, American law demands the highest standard of proof, "beyond the shadow of a doubt." For other public purposes, such as conditions for participation in the public sphere, the determination must be supported by "clear and convincing evidence." Finally, the historical knowledge that is a basis of civil rights or duties must amount to a "preponderance of the evidence," the standard of truth adhered to more broadly by journalists and historians. In its constitutional review of lustration, the Czechoslovak Constitutional Court held that the question of what evidentiary rule applied to the files depended on their reliability and their prospective uses. Though it upheld the lustration law's constitutionality, some parts of the files were considered unreliable and, therefore, constitutionally impermissible bases for the imposition of political disabilities.[99] The standard of historical knowledge as a constitutional matter was said to be related to the files' purposes. In its ruling, the court drew a thin line of discontinuity between the past totalitarian system and the rule of law. The principle of historical justice was not a question to be decided in the abstract but guided by varying evidentiary standards that related to particular political problems. The question of what rule governed access to the ancien régime archives depended on their prospective political uses. The approach taken ultimately follows an American case-by-case approach toward governmental information largely eschewing a general rule.[100]

The long shadow of the totalitarian state histories can be seen in the region's ongoing struggle with its legacy of inherited state archives. Whereas, after decades of repression, political change meant opening the ancien régime's archives, opening the old state files would not automatically bring about the open society. Propounding a new rule of law regarding the old archives was inherently paradoxical, for it meant maintaining the fiction of full legal continuity with the prior regime, even as the change in the rule regulating the archives through new, more permissive rules of access constituted a form of liberalizing discontinuity. The ancien régime's archives have a profound symbolic force, recalling again the paradoxical ongoing legacy of totalitarianism: at the same time evoking that repressive rule and holding out the promise of a knowledge that is potentially transformative of the public sphere.

## Freedom of Information: Entrenching Future Access

The truth regime associated with the totalitarian security state has ongoing implications for the approach to governmental information in the transition, as is seen in the responsive measures taken in liberalization that are peculiar to the legacies in the region. The change in rules regarding citizens' access to information responds critically to the repressive past. Under totalitarian rule, the state controlled its archives, and access to the archives was on a largely arbitrary basis.[101] In the transition, as the move to democracy is seen to depend on civic participation predicated on freedom of information held by the state, there is political impetus toward greater access to the state archives.

Even in working democracies, weighing interests in access to information against those of privacy is a delicate balance. Freedom of information is regulated by a rule of law. It comprises a balance of rights to freedom of information and expression and other individual rights, as well as state interests.[102] Thus, in the United States, for example, governmental documentation is controlled by law protecting an open government's information policy, while also protecting individual privacy interests. Under American law, for example, agency records not exempted from disclosure for reasons of privacy or national security are, in principle, open to citizens. Whatever conflicts may exist are reconciled by a balancing test: The balance struck weighs individual privacy rights against the public's interest in disclosure.[103] In the United States, "informer's" privilege may well be analogous to the problem of secret police collaborators in East Europe. Even when formerly confidential police records are revealed in the United States, the government has a privilege to maintain the confidentiality of its informers by blacking out their names.[104]

The sense in which the response to the predecessor Socialist legacy is "critical" is seen in the successor regimes' attempts to shore up what had been eviscerated, to reconstruct the public and private spheres. This reconstructive work occurs largely through the recognition of constitutional rights to privacy and freedom of information. Many of the new constitutional protections expressly respond to the problem of the absence of privacy under the predecessor regime by controlling the extent to which the post-Communist states can collect information on their citizens. Thus, for example, the Czech and Slovak Constitutions provide: "Everybody is entitled to protection against unauthorized gathering, publication or other misuse of personal data."[105] The Slovenian Constitution prohibits the "use of personal data in conflict with the purpose of their collection."[106] The Hungarian Constitution provides that everyone "shall have the right to good reputation, the inviolability of the privacy of his home and correspondence, and the protection of his personal data."[107] The Croatian Constitution declares, "Without the consent from the person concerned, personal data may be collected, processed and used only under conditions specified by law."[108] Nevertheless, despite these provisions, without more, these efforts at constitutionalizing constraints on governmental control over documentation appear to be unenforceable, for they neither prohibit the state from collecting data nor set a standard regulating archives. These constitutional constraints appear to require only the minimal rule-of-law standard—that any state collection of information be according to law. Other types of constitutional constraints on governmental data would limit its collection based on a voluntariness standard. Thus, the new Russian Constitution states that "[i]t shall be forbidden to gather, store, use and disseminate information on the private life of any person without his/her consent."[109] The Estonian Constitution similarly prohibits "state or local governmental authority or their officials from collecting or storing information on the beliefs of any Estonian citizens against his or her free will."[110] Controlling the creation of state data is one way the constitutions in the region attempt to transform the prior legacy of state histories. The idea is to limit the state's unfettered access to the individual, thereby drawing a new line to delineate a fledgling private sphere.

At the same time as they seek to redefine the terms of the control over individuals and their privacy, transitional constitutions enact critical transformation of the terms of the citizen's access to the state and expand this freedom. Thus, for example, Russia's constitution requires state and local government to "provide each citizen access to any documents and materials directly affecting his/her rights and liberties."[111] Slovenia's constitution provides that "all persons have the right to acquaint him/herself with personal data."[112] Estonia's constitution gives a citizen the right to obtain information about himself or herself "held by state and local government authorities."[113] According to the Bulgarian Constitution, "Citizens have the right to obtain information from a state authority or establishment on matters of legitimate interest to them, provided that such information is not a state secret and does not violate the rights of others."[114]

Constitutional changes elaborated after Communism point to simultane-

ous attempts to forge new boundaries limiting state access to citizens and
expanding citizens' access to the state. In the post-totalitarian transitions, the
critical transformative response to prior abuses is to deprive the state of power
previously abused and to limit the potential for abuses through constitutional-
ization of individual rights to privacy and access to information. The critical response by constructing freedom-of-information standards is a step toward a
more open society.

The struggle over the ancien régime's files after Communism reveals the
extent to which the meaning of historical accountability in transition manifestly depends on the nature of prior legacies of injustice. Historical justice
after Communist rule, as after other sorts of repressive regimes, seeks greater
disclosure of documentation of state wrongdoing suppressed under prior rule.
Beyond that, there are differences. In the postmilitary transitions, when the
predecessor dictatorship acted with utter impunity, failing even to concede the
fact of the wrongs committed, historical justice signified a *construction* of
state history, a *building up* of documentation, largely through testimony
witness by witness, fact by fact. In the former Communist bloc, such official
narratives have largely been eschewed, for documentation abounds; historical
justice implies a *tearing open* of amassed state history, file by file. In the postmilitary transitions, successor institutional changes respond chiefly to the uncertainty created by the absence of state documentation, concentrating new
power in institutions charged with the investigation and documentation of
rights abuses. Other changes of a legislative and regulatory nature, particularly regarding the law of defamation, seek to protect nonstate actors in their
investigation and publication of information, in particular, political speech,
though this may well be at the price of other rights and interests in transition.
In the post-Communist transitions, by contrast, institutional change has been
directed to controlling public investigations, protecting individual privacy, and
constitutionalizing citizens' right of access. These disparate responses reveal
that the content of historical justice is forged in the context of transition and
in the legacy of repressive rule. The meaning of historical justice is itself
highly contingent on past persecution and, in particular, on the predecessor
regime's uses of history and knowledge.

Experiences in periods of political transformation suggest that, despite
varying legal cultures, states frequently turn to some form of historical accountability. The question arises: What is the relation between historical justice in transition and accountability in established democracies? It is this:
Legal responses to tyranny forged in the crucible of transition illuminate background values underlying established democracies' governance of official
documentation and information. The transitional dilemmas and related legal
responses discussed above reveal issues and resolutions that often transcend
these extraordinary periods. Thus, for example, in contemporary times, the
boundary between the "public" and the "private" spheres is often in flux, and,
therefore, the questions are in public debate. The historical response has long-
range implications that transcend the individuals involved, and reach the collective and the nation. Indeed, the historical response helps construct the col-

lective's political identity. The above responses to the transitional dilemma may help inform the way societies think about the significance of these boundaries in nontransitional times.


## History's Law

"History will be the judge"—the truth will withstand the passage of time. Common sayings reflect popular intuitions regarding the relation of historical interpretation to time, suggesting that somehow historical judgment evolves with its passage. Certainly at the descriptive level, this appears true. Often many generations pass, whether after war or repressive rule, before societies are able to confront their history. Though the struggle for historical justice rages in transitional periods, its meaning is often revisited and subject to change. With the passage of time, interceding political events and historiographical developments all bear on historical interpretation, which means that such interpretations undergo change. Thus, the passage of time presents a dilemma for the possibility of attaining historical justice. To what extent do transitional understandings of historical justice, whether produced through individual trials, commissions, or other processes, endure over time? Do changed readings over time challenge the possibility of establishing any single, fixed understanding of past state repressive legacies? Does this mean transitional historical justice is merely transient and political?


## The "Historians' Debate": Drawing a Line on the Past

The transitional productions of history discussed so far illustrate the significance of both political legacies and contemporary political frameworks in shaping collective history and memory. Nevertheless, these constructions, too, have their limits. The debate over revisionism in World War II–related history illustrates the limiting of permissible historical accounts.

The paradigm of the problem of historical justice after the passage of time is contemporary Germany's attempt to integrate its World War II past into national history. At the heart of the German debate, more than a half century after the war, was the question of whether there is a historical understanding that can withstand the test of time. The *historikerstreit*, "historians' debate," began in 1985 with the publication of Joachim Fest's *The Guilt-Laden Memory*, challenging the prevailing understanding of the war and contending that the real enemy was the Soviets, not Germany. Other historians joined in the debate with similar challenges to the prevailing postwar account of Nazi wartime responsibility. In *The Past Which Will Not Pass On*, Ernst Nolte compares Nazi crimes with Soviet action in the Gulag, intimating by the comparison that there was nothing special about the Nazi persecution. If Fest and Nolte attempt to normalize the prevailing historical understanding of Germany's wartime responsibility, Andreas Hillgruber's *Two Kinds of Ruin: The Shattering of the German Reich and the End of European Jewry* is an even more forceful challenge to the established understanding, for Hillgruber's account transforms Germany from perpetrator of genocide to its victim.[115] The challenge from within academia coincided with political efforts of the Helmut Kohl administration that also seemed intended to transform the prevailing understanding of the German past. From the apposition within the same diplomatic trip of two highly publicized visits—a concentration camp together with the Bitburg military cemetery—the highest echelons of the German government sent the message of the equivalence of Germany's military casualties with its persecution of civilians.

Another example following the Soviet collapse are accounts of the horror of the Gulag drawing from newly opened Communist archives juxtaposing the evils of fascism and communism as "two kinds of totalitarianism."[116]

What is at stake in these challenges? The historians' debate has been characterized by philosopher Jürgen Habermas as a "campaign for the revision of the Nazi past."[117] The question was whether, after the passage of time, the historical account of the World War II genocide of the Jews would be preserved as the official account or whether, over time, the account could legitimately change, perhaps in the light of contemporary human rights abuses.[118] New versions of wartime persecution challenged the established account in a number of respects: as to the nature of the wrong, the status and responsibility of perpetrators, and the rights of victims. The significance of the hermeneutical debate over the Nazi past lies in its implications for the state's self-understanding. Some historians, like Charles Maier, suggest that the significance of this historical development lay in the beginnings of "comparative genocide." The challenge was to the prevailing understanding of Germany's calculated, systematic extermination of its wartime enemies as sui generis. Comparisons to Soviet persecution undermined the established view of the singularity of German criminal responsibility. Other historians and philosophers, like Habermas and Martin Broszat,[119] suggest that what is at stake instead is a different perspective on historical justice, not as it relates to interpretation of perpetrators' responsibility, but with profound implications for victims' historical due. Even historical justice is potentially restorative, with the liberal potential of affording victims' dignity and even ultimate corrective justice.

Are changed readings of the Holocaust and other persecution inevitable with the passage of time? Can historical justice really be fixed for all time? The problem of changed readings of the war arose in the context of a much broader scholarly debate over historical interpretation and representation. Contemporary historical theorizing presumes the inevitability of changes in interpretation, particularly over time; indeed, the historians' debate poses the challenge in terms of changes in interpretation. In this line of theorizing, historical interpretation can never be considered neutral or objective but is always situated in a particular political context.[120] Yet, the question of the permissible parameters of characterization of World War II persecution, after the passage of time, framed this interpretive debate in its most extreme form.

When the question of whether there were principles defining the permissible bounds of historicization was leveled at Nazi atrocities, the theoretical debate was brought into grim focus: Were there no principles to guide historical truth, even of a history whose truth seemed so self-evident? Were there to be no limits to the parameters of historical interpretation, relativization, revisionism, and ultimately, "denial?" If not in the case of genocide, then when? Even for arch relativists, Auschwitz posed the limiting case. Despite the apparent inevitability of change in historical interpretation after time, the question posed is whether there were any limits on the sort of narrative that could be told.

The danger of the reinterpretation of critical political events—the crux of the historicans' debate—underscores what is at stake in the successful transition from an oppressive unjust system to a liberal democracy: For political and social change is predicated on change in interpretation. What changes is how persons interpret events around them. Yet, what the historians' debate pointedly raises is that the line, as it were, between interpretations is not always clear. The attempts to control historical interpretation speak to the significance—in the face of new challenges of racism and xenophobia—of preserving a liberal state narrative.

## Preserving Historical Justice through the Law

Though there are occasional challenges to revisionist interpretations of historical accounts, ultimately, the limiting principles that cabin permissible historical interpretations have not come from within the academe; to the extent limits have been leveled in the affected societies, it has been through and by law. Even when the historical production is unofficial, legal processes are often resorted to so as to preserve an established historical account. A look at these legal responses illuminates how historical narratives become entrenched.

How to fix an enduring historical account of an evil past? Transitional societies commonly attempt to entrench historical accounts of past persecution, and, as the experiences discussed above reflect, the very production and preservation of historical accountings are regulated through law. Most explicit are the trials and truth commissions used to create official records, which in and of themselves limit possible counteraccounts. Yet, amnesty laws too, in and by their silencing effect, can be used to protect a single historical account. Preserving a particular national narrative depends on ongoing control of the official history, as well as of the alternative historical accounts. Maintaining such control becomes increasingly difficult after the passage of time. An illustration is the revival of the issue of the disappearances in Argentina, more than a decade after the transition, with a former navy captain's confession of participation in disappearances.[121] So, despite a consensus struck at the time of transition to limit the confrontation with past wrongdoing, one person's struggle with his conscience reopened the question. Challenges after time reflect the dissatisfaction with transitional compromises—and a willingness to entertain other accounts.

The adjudication process with its evidentiary standards also enables the creation and protection of an established account. Principles of legal adjudication, case by case, delimit the parameters of historical debate. One such strategy is the principle of "judicial notice," whereby courts accept, without formal proof, the truth of particular facts. "Judicially noticeable" facts are those generally known in the community or capable of determination through ordinary sources. Instances of application of this principle concerning World War II persecution lead all the way back to the Nuremberg trials, where the tribunal was under obligation to take "judicial notice" of "facts of common knowledge."[122] United States cases concerning war-related offenses have taken judicial notice of persecution. When they take judicial notice, courts are saying that such facts are so notorious as not to be disputable.[123] Through the adjudicative principle of judicial notice, the judge recognizes those historical events known and incontrovertible in the community and assumes the power to decide what historical controversy belongs outside the parameters of legitimate legal challenge and outside reasonable historical debate. Through this mechanism, individual victims' memories can be formally recognized, appropriated, and incorporated into a greater, formally acknowledged, collective history.

The entrenching of a particular historical account can also be effected through legislation regulating and controlling counteraccounts. One way this process has been accomplished in transition, previously discussed, are amnesty laws that quite literally enable the official repression of past mistreatment. For this reason, amnesty legislation often sparks conflict, with some objecting that such legislation censors the voices of victims who seek fuller accountings, dissident perpetrators, and others in the society who might seek an independent account of the past. Countries directly affected by Nazism have also turned to regulation to preserve a particular account. Since the war, many countries in Europe have civil laws providing causes of action for defamation relating to wartime genocide. For example, propagation of the so-called Auschwitz lie, the attempt to deny the historical truth of the Holocaust, has for some time been treated as a form of group defamation giving rise to civil liability. These censorship laws have generally been justified in terms of the historical justice owed persecution's victims and of the potential harmful impact of a counteraccount. Since the advent of the historians' debate, there has been a flurry of criminal lawmaking designed to preserve the prevailing account of wartime persecution. Race-hatred writings were previously against the law.[124] Holocaust denial now creates a basis for criminal prosecution. According to the new laws, if a person "approved, denied or made light of acts of genocide perpetrated under the Nazis" and the insulted party is a member of a group persecuted "under the National Socialist or another violent and arbitrary dominance," this act gives rise to criminal liability. These censorship laws, like the civil laws, are justified in terms of the duties owed victims and the harmful impact of such counteraccounts.[125] Thus, in recent years, Germany's Federal Constitutional Court held that the denial of the Holocaust is not protected under the Basic Law's guarantee of "freedom of opinion." The use of the expression "Auschwitz lie" (Auschwitz *Lüge*) constitutes a punishable violation of the rights of Germany's Jewish citizens.[126] In Germany, the courts have treated the facts of the Holocaust as established, requiring no formal proof.[127] Similarly, a French law first enacted in 1990 criminalizes "revisionism," or the denial of the Nazi genocide.[128] In Canada, similar criminal sanctions barring "knowing falsehoods" have been deployed to censor revisionist World War II–related writings.[129] By shifting from civil to criminal sanctions, contemporary legislation moves beyond concern with the harm of such speech for victims of World War II to its effect upon the society. Criminalizing revisionist history expresses a conviction that the competing accounts are not merely insults to individual victims but also wrongs done to the community. The harshest form of law is being used to ensure a distinct conceptualization of historical justice: one affording victims of grave state persecution the right to an enduring historical account, with its protection ensured and enforced under the criminal law. For example, in a prosecution brought under French law, the court held that "the necessary limits to freedom of expression include respect for the memory of victims."[130] And a German case holds that "anyone who denies the murder of Jews in the 'Third Reich' insults every one of them."[131] Yet, it is unclear how this justification will weather the passage of time. Contemporary European legislation expands upon the Holocaust-denial legislation to regulate denial of all persecution, such as crimes against humanity or genocide, whether perpetrated under Nazis or subsequent repressive regimes.[132] Other contemporary criminal legislation is primarily aimed at protecting persecution's victims. The laws are also premised on a broader view of the harm, namely, that there is a larger societal interest in protecting a historical account.

The law is used to protect an entrenched account of state persecution by circumscribing other accounts. Thus, for example, in Europe after World War II, a broad array of speech legislation was enacted, linking past and present, criminalizing "hate speech" against protected victims of wartime persecution. Hate-speech laws link prior persecution with contemporary events that, in some way, revive contested histories or the operative political abuses. Hate-speech norms criminalize propaganda reviving the country's past persecution. These forms of legal responses appear prominently in existing international law. Thus, the Universal Declaration of Human Rights, Article 20, provides that "any advocacy of national, racial or religious hatred that constitutes incitement to discrimination, hostility or violence" shall be prohibited by law.[133] Article 4 of the International Convention on the Elimination of All Forms of Racial Discrimination provides that states should prohibit the "dissemination of ideas based on racial superiority or hatred, incitement to racial discrimination."[134] The International Covenant on Civil and Political Rights at Article 20 similarly provides that "any advocacy of national, racial or religious hatred that constitutes incitement to discrimination, hostility or violence shall be prohibited by law."[135] Many European countries have similar laws. Germany's Criminal Code prohibits "attacking the dignity of others by inciting hatred against parts of the population, calling for violent measures against them, or insulting them, maliciously exposing them to contempt or slandering them."[136] In Denmark, making racial or ethnic slurs is a criminal offense.[137] Publicly threatening or expressing "contempt for a group of a certain race, skin color, [or] national creed" may result in a prison sentence of up to two years in Sweden.[138] Britain's Race Relations Act made criminal any "stirring up hatred, publishing, distributing, or using in public any threatening, abusive or insulting material against others on the basis of color, race or ethnic origin."[139] In the United States, a history of slavery, segregation, and enduring racism has spurred a spate of "hate-crime" legislation. Though the legal tradition is heavily speech-protective, hate-crime laws increase the penalty of crimes when they are committed because of racial bias or similar persecutory motive.[140] In a constitutional challenge, a law censoring hate speech was upheld because "this conduct is thought to inflict greater individual and societal harm."[141] Though the circumscribed conduct may be private action animated by racial animus, against a prior history of state action, it is a revival of prior persecution, hence the heightened condemnation. Responding to such wrongdoing revives and reentrenches the transitional moment.

The turn to the law to protect a particular historical account can occasion profound dilemmas, because such regulation often competes with other societal interests associated with the liberal state, such as unbounded freedom of expression.[142] How these dilemmas are resolved varies in transitional societies depending on the political context, as well as on the particular legacies of injustice. Thus, for example, in Germany's constitutional scheme, the dilemma is resolved by a normative principle providing for the overriding of speech interests deriving from the wartime abuse of racist propaganda.[143] "Whoever abuses freedom of expression . . . in order to combat the free democratic basic order, shall forfeit the basic rights." By contrast, in Anglo-American history, in which tyranny took the form of curtailment of expression,[144] the balance in the jurisprudence tends to come out the other way. Absolutism and censorship are the primary evil. What constitutes the primary value of historical justice, as the above practices suggest, is not universal but contingent, relating instead to distinctive legacies of injustice. Transitional responses to repressive rule helped to forge contemporary norms structuring the diverse conditions of liberal political discourse.

The attempt to entrench any one historical account itself raises questions for liberalism. This question arose in the wave of transition following the Communist collapse, when there were those advocating with the conceded fall of Communism that this was at long last the time to entrench the identity of Western capitalism, supposedly bringing to an end a central historical dialectic.[145] Nevertheless, these claims did not fully capture the extent to which even "post-Communist" history was not posthistory but was itself situated as part of a transitional dynamic and a historical identity and within a particular context deemed progress by virtue of the immediate repressive past and the transitional circumstances of justice. Might it not be a normative imperative of the liberal state that it allow for ongoing historical change?

Poetic Justice: The Narratives of Transition

Let us again return to the question posed at the beginning of this chapter: What is the relation of historical processes to liberalizing political transformation? The chapter began with discussion of what role historical inquiry plays in responding to a state's evil legacies and whether there is any correspondence between a state's historical inquiry into its illiberal past and its prospects for democracy. In this analysis, the normative question of whether historical inquiry constitutes the ideal transitional response seems beside the point; for even without self-conscious historical productions, such as trials, investigatory commissions, and reports, there is always a historical narrative. Transitional narratives follow their own rhetorical structures, which are in and of themselves constitutive of identity change. Transitional histories—the accounts of past tyranny in liberalizing periods—constitute a distinctive narrative.

It is the narratives constructed at the time of transition that most clearly bear out the normative claim about history's relation to democracy. The very narrative line propounds the notion of historical knowledge's relevance to the possibility of personal and social change. The historical accountings of transition in and of themselves constitute an account of the relation of knowledge to the move from dictatorship and the prospects for a more liberal future. These accountings propound a sense of justice that is "poetic."

Transitional narratives are of a distinct form or genre, what might be regarded a mixed tragic-comedy, or tragic-romance.[146] While the narratives of transitions commence in tragedy, they end in a comic and romantic mode. In the classical understanding, tragedy comprises the elements of catastrophic suffering involving the fate of entire groups, cities, and countries, followed by some discovery or change from ignorance to knowledge, a moment of clarification.[147] Just as ancient tragedy focused on the plight of individuals, whose fate, due to their status, implicated entire collectives, contemporary stories of suffering similarly concern affliction on a grand scale.

Whereas transitional narratives begin in a tragic mode, at a certain point, they switch over to a nontragic resolution; in classical literary categories, they are characterized by a turn to a comic phase. The country's past suffering is somehow reversed, culminating in a happy ending of peace and reconciliation. In tragedy, the role of knowledge seems only to confirm a fate foretold; however, transitional accounts begin with terrible suffering, injustice, slavery, murders, and so on, and something happens in these accounts, causing the persons enmeshed in the story to ultimately avert tragic fates and somehow adjust and even thrive in a new reality. In the convention of romance associated with transitional accounts, the change involves a critical juncture of self-knowledge, where—unlike tragedy—the revelation of knowledge makes a difference. Transitional narratives in the context of changing politics take on a distinctive form and fulfill a distinct role in the political change. Through commission processes, in legal action, the polis as a whole is caught up in a plot of transition.

As discussed below, the structure of transition is evident in both fictional and nonfictional accounts of transformation. Reports of these periods, as well as fictionalized accounts, commonly adhere to a distinct narrative that runs along the following lines: Though the prior regime saw massive state suffering, that suffering is somehow transformed into something good for the country, into greater national self-knowledge and enhanced prospects for an enduring democracy. The national narratives read as tragic accounts that end on a redemptive note. Consider the stories told in the reports following repressive rule. Begin with the reports' names: Entitled *Never Again*, the Latin reports promise that truth accountings can deter future suffering. For example, in the first report of the Argentine National Commission on the Disappeared, the account of the country's repression begins with a prologue declaring that the military dictatorship "brought about the greatest and most savage tragedy" in the country's history. Nevertheless, the preface asserts that "[g]reat catastrophes are always instructive." Catastrophic history is said to provide lessons. "The tragedy which began with the military dictatorship in March 1976, the most terrible our nation has ever suffered, will undoubtedly serve to help us understand that it is only democracy which can save a people from horror on this scale."[148] According to the account, knowledge of suffering plays a crucial role in the nation's ability to make the political transition to democracy.

The narratives in other transitional reports follow a similar story line. A society's confrontation with its past is deemed necessary to its transition to democracy. The report of the Chilean National Commission on Truth and Reconciliation asserts that historical accountability is necessary for the country's reconciliation. Disclosure and knowledge of suffering are said to have been instrumental in bringing the country together. The decree establishing Chile's National Commission declares that "the truth had to be brought to light, for only on such a foundation . . . would it be possible to . . . create the necessary conditions for achieving true national reconciliation."[149] According to Chile's report, the truth is the necessary precondition for democracy. This is also the organizing thesis of the report of the El Salvador Truth Commission. The story line is manifest even in the report's optimistic title: *From Madness to Hope* tells a story of violent civil war, followed by "truth and reconciliation." According to the report's introduction, it is the truth's "creative consequences" that "settle political and social differences by means of agreement instead of violent action." "Peace [is] to be built on transparency of . . . knowledge." The truth is characterized as a "bright light" that "search[es] for lessons that would contribute to reconciliation and to abolishing such patterns of behavior in the new society."[150] Even the unofficial reports similarly claim that the revelation of knowledge in itself constitutes a measure of justice. Thus, the preface to the unofficial Uruguayan *Never Again* report asserts that it is writing itself that constitutes a triumph against repression. This account could be understood to make a number of claims about the relation that historical knowledge bears to democratic prospects. The claim is that the transitional truth-tellings will deter the possibility of future repression. It is the lack of "critical understanding which created a risk of having the disaster repeated . . . to rescue that history is to learn a lesson. . . . We should have the courage not to hide that experience in our collective subconscious but to recollect it. So that we do not fall again into the trap."[151] In transitional history making toward liberalizing rule, the story has to come out right. Yet, the stories told imply a number of poetic leaps. Is it the truth that brings on liberalizing political change, or the political change that enables restoration of democratic government and the truth-telling? And how exactly is the truth to deter future catastrophe? The theoretical claim that it is the truth that is liberating—and that the "truth" enables the move to democracy—seemed wrong almost everywhere. For the move out of dictatorship did not await the truth; indeed, the movement to free elections and a more democratic political system generally precedes processes of truth production. Nevertheless, despite the ongoing processes of political change, the idea is that, until there is some form of clarification of the deception and ensuing self-understanding, the truth about the evil past is somehow hidden, unavailable, even external. So it is, for example, that in the post-Communist transitions, the national histories tell a story of evil as outsider. The accounts begin with the occupation and popular resistance but culminate in collaboration. Transitional narratives of dictatorship and repression begin with the representation of the foe as foreign, unknown, and proceed to the progressively ever more troubling discovery of collaboration closer to home and pervasive throughout the society. In narratives of transition, whether out of repressive totalitarian rule in the former Soviet bloc or out of authoritarian military rule, what is most pronounced is the tragic discovery.

Told this way, the profound implication of the revelation of knowledge is that it introduces the possibility of future change, through the potential of human action. Knowledge revealed somehow suggests that there is a logic to the madness, to the evil, and even intimates that there is something to be done. The notion is that had this knowledge been known, then matters would have been different and, conversely, that now that the "truth" is publicly known, the course of events will be different. This hope is the essence of liberalism. Accordingly, transitional accounts of a newly revealed knowledge regarding evil legacies are themselves glimmerings of a redemptive truth hitherto unknown in which lies the possibility of liberalization. Indeed, revealing the possibility of future choice is what distinguishes the liberal transition. In the transitional accounts lie the kernels of a liberal future foretold.

In the stories told in the reports, it is the revealed truth that helps bring on the switch from the tragic past to the promise of a hopeful future. How does this occur? The story told is of a catastrophe, which is somehow turned around. An awful fate is averted, as in dramatic narrative, by the introduction of a magical switch. Transitional justice operates as such a device through the introduction of persons with special access to privileged knowledge, such as judges in trials, commissioners, experts, and witnesses. Mechanisms of liberation and correction enable the shift in the societal story to move away from catastrophe to redemptive future. The move to a more liberal society is enabled by a reckoning with the past; transitional narratives are generally progressive and romantic. There is also often a competing undertone of irony, of defeatism, of conservatism. This is seen clearly in the narratives of East Europe, in which the subjects of transitional processes are seemingly beside the point: Those prosecuted (or purged) simply happen to have been in a given place and moment in time, so that they could serve a role in the legal processes; the apparent role is that of the sacrificed,[152] as, for example, in the border guards prosecutions at the lowest echelon of power in unified Germany. In these accounts, the transitional processes are laid bare, and the legal enterprise risks losing its presumptive legitimacy. Should the narrative be one of historical repetition, of cyclical state evil, these times will not be maximally transformative periods, but rather conservative transitions.

The literature of evil periods is comprised of literal accounts with a distinctive structure. Across political cultures, the representations in literature of state persecution take a highly literal form. This form is seen in writings about the Holocaust and World War II persecution and has tended to be largely testimonials, following a literal style. A prominent example is Elie Wiesel's *Night*.[153] The horror of the concentration camps is told in a dry literal account, adhering closely to the author's personal experiences. Another example in cinematic form is *Shoah*, which goes to extremes to present a realm of unrepresentability. This tension is captured by a hybrid form termed *novela-real*; an illustration concerning Argentina's dictatorship is Miguel Bonasso's *Recuerdo de la Muerte* in Spanish. A work of fiction that is most illustrative relating to the Stalin-era repression is Aleksandr Solzhenitsyn's *The Gulag Archipelago, 1918–1956: An Experiment in Literary Investigation*.[154] As its suggestive title, *Literary Investigation*, reveals, thousands of incidents of violence occur within one narrative; the structure reads like an official report. The pervasiveness of the chronicle as a style of accounting for atrocity is thrown into relief when it is deployed in the form of poetry. When poetry represents mass suffering, it does so in miniature by means of the "microreport."[155]

The literature of transition concerning evil legacies, like the official accounts discussed above, reveals a similar transitional structure. Beginning as tragedies of the country's history, the narratives commence with a sense of political or economic disorder that ostensibly explains or offers reasons for the military takeover. The narrative continues with a period of suffering shrouded in repression, culminating in discovery and self-knowledge, which is the turning point that enables future change. A haunting example is Jacobo Timerman's autobiographical *Prisoner without a Name, Cell without a Number* concerning the period of Argentina's military repression. In the book, Timerman recounts the sad story of how he, as part of the Argentine elite, supported the military takeover, expecting it would restore order. Instead, the military plunges the country into greater bloodshed and, ultimately, even goes after Timerman. It is only after experiencing personal betrayal and suffering that Timerman comes to understand the depths of the military savagery. A reversal of personal fortune enables deeper understanding of the country.

Narratives of transition suggest that minimally what is at stake in the transformation from an oppressive to a more liberal system is a change in interpretation. Societies begin to change politically when citizens' understanding of the ambient events change. It is the change, as Václav Havel has written, of "living within a lie to living within the truth." So it is that many of the fictional works coming out in this period are stories of precisely this change, of living within a lie, tales of deceit and betrayal, to the revelation that a newly gained knowledge and self-understanding affect and reconstitute identity and relationship. Often these are stories of affairs, such as Bernhard Schlink's *The Reader*, allegories of the citizen/state relation.[156] Transitional histories are not simply fact-seeking in a vacuum but accounts that build on prior national narratives. They are better understood, not as foundational, but as transitional, as the change in truth regimes constructed in the change in political regimes. When varying interpretations of governmental repression among those living under oppressive rule coexist under a political regime, the existence of "dissident" interpretations is itself a sign of the glimmerings of political change, helping to spur further transformation. Understanding the interpretive function in political change clarifies that the pursuit of historical accountability is not simply a response to political change but is itself part of the construction of the political change, constituting what we expect of a liberal politics.

The transitional accounts discussed above reveal continuities in historical and other forms of transitional justice. For the conceptions of justice explored here incorporate a similar story line regarding the role of knowledge revealed. The historical accounts construct a normative relation in connecting up the society's past and its future; narratives of transition begin with the backward-looking and the reflection on the meaning of the past, but it is always in light of the future. There is always something to be done. This is the quintessential liberalizing hope. Like other legal responses previously discussed, such as the punitive, the shared affinity is the corrective aim through legal processes; in creating a change in social knowledge, there is a pronounced shift from past evil and suffering to redemption.

## Of River Crossings and Sea Changes, of Exile and Return

The above accounts point to common structures and features of societal transition. These structures are also evident in classical literary forms associated with transitions; that is, they imply a move from tragic to comic-romantic convention. The expectations are those of ultimate possibility, of the pragmatic reconciliation of life's circumstances with desire.

The biblical account of the brothers Jacob and Esau is an ancient story of confrontation with an evil past, reconciliation, and political change.[157] In the biblical story of transition, a settling of accounts occurs between brothers after the return of Jacob, who has been living in exile and estranged from his brother, Esau. Their bad relations dating back to childhood relate to rivalry over their birthright and to Jacob's deception of Esau.

As Jacob plans his return home, he is concerned about meeting his brother and that Esau will avenge himself.[158] Upon being informed that Esau is coming toward him, armed with a large contingent of men, Jacob tries to appease his brother with gifts but then undergoes the personal transformation that ultimately leads to reconciliation with his brother and the building of a nation.

The story of the brothers' meeting and reconciliation begins with Jacob leaving his place of exile. After crossing the River Jabbok during the night, Jacob becomes locked in a wrestling bout with an unknown man of a supernatural quality. During the wrestling, his hip socket is wrenched, so that after it is over, he limps. And, once the wrestling match is over, he is blessed and given a new name; it changes from "Jacob" to "Israel," and the new identity symbolized by the new name he is given signifies his struggle with God. After the struggle, as he limps toward his brother, approaching him in a spirit of supplication, he is manifestly transformed in body, as well as in spirit. When his brother, Esau, sees him coming toward him, they tearfully embrace, and there is a reconciliation.

This ancient story of reconciliation begins with a river crossing, followed by a night of struggle, an encounter with a numinous force, and a change in identity. It is only after Jacob emerges from this struggle, symbolized by both a physical loss—the loss of use of his thigh muscle—and the symbolic gain of a new name, that reconciliation with his brother occurs. It is recounted that, though Esau came in anger with armed men, upon facing a transformed Jacob, a new man named Israel, Esau makes peace with his brother.

What are the predicates to transition? The ancient account evokes key symbols of passage: a water crossing of the River Jabbok in the night—spatial and temporal border crossings. Night is a quintessentially liminal time, a time of reconfiguration of one's circumstances, of confrontation and struggle, and water an ancient symbol of passage.[159] Beyond water and night, there is the physical loss and gain. In the biblical story of Jacob becoming Israel, the transformation in political identity is written on the body and reflected in the name change.

The distinctive structure of transitional narratives is well illustrated in romances, such as those of William Shakespeare's, for example, in his later work *The Tempest*. Like the biblical story of Jacob and Esau, *The Tempest*, too, is a narrative of transition through exile and return. Beginning with its characters in exile and ending with their return home, they find themselves estranged from their home, literally "at sea." *The Tempest*, like the biblical story, begins with the recounting of a story of political injustice. As with Jacob and Esau, there is the antagonism between Prospero, the "right" Duke of Milan, and Antonio, the usurping Duke of Milan. The story concerns their rivalry over the regime's leadership and a dissolving society. The transition to another political state, as in the biblical account, is a narrative of return, from exile to home. The change depends on the revelation of various truths so that the characters are ultimately able to return to their "true state." "And Ferdinand her brother found a wife where he himself was lost; Prospero his dukedom in a poor isle; and all of us ourselves when no man was his own."[160]

The play begins in Act I with its characters recounting stories of past political injustice: Prospero's loss of his dukedom, Ariel's capture and subsequent enslavement to Prospero. By Act II, alternatives are imagined to the existing regime. The shift occurs, in Act III, with the beginning of a reckoning with history. The confrontation occurs through a supernatural force (Ariel as a "harpy") with Ariel's recitation indicting "three men of sin" and sentencing them to "[l]ing'ring perdition."[161] With the revelation of truth, in Act IV, there is the contemplation of transition and revenge.[162] In Act V, there is a reckoning with history, forgiveness and grace. "The rarer action is in virtue than in vengeance."[163] Reconciliation means Prospero exercises forbearance in the further use of his powers. That the unfolding events involve a human choice to accommodate to circumstances, to reconcile love to reality, is symbolized by the play within the play: of Ferdinand and Miranda's game of chess—a symbol of the possibilities of deliberation and individual action.

At the play's end, almost all is restored, and injustice is seemingly rectified. In *The Tempest*, as elsewhere, transition to the new regime implies losses. While in *The Tempest*, the brothers, Prospero and Antonio, do not fully reconcile, there is reconciliation among the other characters. Indeed, through the play we come to understand that the very notion of a transition means that as a new interpretation is gained, the old one is cast off. The change epitomizing transition implies a visible loss as well as identity change.[164]

Transitional narratives take a familiar form. In both the biblical story and Shakespearean romance, the narrative line moves from exile to home, the true, natural state. Revelation of knowledge of truth often occurs through supernatural processes; there is a ritual disowning, a purging of the past, and, finally, a reappropriation of a newly revealed truth, enabling corrective return to the society's true course. Transitional truth has its valence. Previously secreted knowledge is confronted and, ultimately, worked through, charting a new course.[165] Societal self-knowledge is not an end in itself but, rather, the predicate for the potential of prospective change in human behavior and consequent liberalizing transformation.

## Transitional Historical Justice: Some Conclusions

The practices discussed here suggest that the role of historical inquiry is not foundational but transitional. History is ever present in the life of the state but, in political flux, it helps to construct transformation. For state histories that are ongoing, what is the distinctive part of the transitional historical narrative? What renders these accounts liberalizing?

One sense in which the histories discussed here are not foundational but transitional is that they are discrete histories, "mini" and not metanarratives, situated within the state's broader narrative. Transitional truth-tellings are not atomized narratives, not radical new beginnings, but, rather, always stand in contingent relation to the state's existing historical legacies. The transitional history necessitates negotiating between contested accounts and is deployed within a broader narrative and state history. Transitional accounts are produced within a context—the country's history—and are critical in response to prevailing historical conflict. Thus, transitional histories generally imply a displacement of one interpretive account or truth regime by another, even as the political regimes change, while preserving the narrative thread of the state.

Legal processes of truth-tellings construct collective memory in transition. The visible turn to the law, its processes, and framework occurs at a time when the social consensus is otherwise frayed. Law offers a canonical language and established symbols and rituals of passage. In contemporary times, legal rituals and processes through trials and public hearings enable transitionally produced histories that are social constructions of a democratic nature with a broad reach; the audience is potentially the entire country. These rituals of collective history-making are part of what constructs the transition and so divides political time, creating a "before" and an "after."[166] The turn to law means that historical claims are made in the language of justice, in shared terms relating to rights and responsibilities for past wrongs. The use of this language performs the critical undoing responsive to the prior repression, the letting go of discrete facts justificatory of the prior regime, which is critical to enabling political change. The practices of historical production associated with transition often publicly affirm only what is known implicitly in the society. Processes of historical inquiry bring forward and enable a public letting go of the evil history. The narratives of transitional history are discontinuous stories of corrective justice; transitional histories take a redemptive liberalizing turn.

Transitional historical narratives, whether through trials or other forms, highlight the role of knowledge, choice, and agency. Though the received wisdom on historical responses to past wrongs is that these are popular in liberalizing states emphasizing broad structural causes and solutions,[167] transitional histories are densely layered narratives weaving together complex accounts that mediate individual and collective responsibility. By introducing the potential of individual choice, the accounts perform transitional history's liberalizing function. In revealing a past truth, the account suggests things would have been different had it been previously known, adverting to the potential of individual action. This is the understanding represented in the contemporary political order of avoidable tragedy. Elucidation of the potential of individual choice and human action is itself liberalizing.

Historical accountings have become a feature of liberalizing transition, connected to change in the state's political identity. So it is that the transitional narratives advance construction of the contemporary political order. In the transitional narratives, the direction of the story is neither tragically preordained nor merely a question of brute power. It neither comports to preexisting world order nor merely to realist politics. Structured narratives emphasize the possibility of constrained choice, of individual agency in politics situated within parameters of broader political circumstances. The notion that there are redemptive possibilities of societal self-understanding, despite past legacies of wrongdoing, is profoundly definitional of the contemporary liberal state. Historical narratives emphasizing the possibility of societal self-understanding and averting tragic repetition are associated with the liberal political order. The structure of transitional histories follows a redemptive form, a tale of hope.

Liberalization through truth-tellings implies instability, which is closely associated with periods of transition. But the danger here is in telling the story too well, in rationalizing too far—in rendering past catastrophe somehow necessary as a consequential matter for its ultimately liberalizing effects for future prospects. How the history is told over time is a delicate matter. The historical narrative constructs the state's understanding of its political order. Transitional historical justice is linked up to the preservation of a state's political identity over time. So it is that, with the passage of time, a state's self-understanding itself becomes the controverted subject of political debate. The "historians' debate" reviving transitional deliberations suggests that when the state narrative is explicitly discontinuous from prior repressive legacy, it reaffirms the liberalizing transitional identity.

The historical practices discussed suggest that all the legal responses produce transitional narratives. Though it may not always be explicit, there is always a historical account. Transitional practices of history-making in periods of radical political change illuminate the more backgrounded role of historical narrative in established democracies, the historical accounts undergirding our political order.[168]

A defined historical genre is, by now, associated with a liberal political identity. As discussed here, there are common recurring features of these liberal historical narratives. Transitional histories are also inextricably connected with political context and circumstances. When history is marshaled in the service of political change, its aims are chiefly prospective, and modern historiography affirms the inescapably politicized nature of the act of writing history. Nevertheless, the parameters of historical discourse are set within preexisting societal contexts. Transitional historical productions are set in a context of preceding accounts, and when they displace these they become, in turn, the reigning accounts (only to be later subverted). So the transitional histories are mechanisms of continuities but also implied discontinuities. Cycles of displacement of truth regimes are evident in the contingency of historical responses to past evil. And, further, what will make for the subversion of, and discontinuity from, the reigning regime is nonessential and politically contingent.

To what extent is the cycle necessarily ongoing? What is the relation between transitional and nontransitional history making? The wish is often heard for a final accounting—for a fully entrenched historical consensus—to be "beyond history" as it were. This was nowhere more true than after the last wave of political change in the collapse of Communism. Yet, the impetus to fix the past, to be "posthistoire" is a futile attempt to stop the state's historical accounting, to exhaust its politics and its potential for progress. The attempt to entrench an identity based on a particular historical view for all time is itself an illiberal vision—no choice remains but plurality of narratives, instability, and political dialectic.

## CHAPTER FOUR

# Reparatory Justice

*I*n contemporary times, most transitional regimes—whether following war, military dictatorships, or communism—have undertaken some form of reparatory justice. The review of reparatory practices pursued here suggests this response is widely prevalent, despite divergent legal cultures. How do societies think about such efforts at reparation? What is their purpose and function? What is the meaning of transitional justice for victims of past regime wrongs and for the society?

The threshold dilemma confronted by successor regimes in transitional periods is whether new regimes are obligated to redress victims of state wrongs. Under international law, wherever states have violated duties, there is a clear legal obligation to repair.[1] Nevertheless, in national debates over what to do about past evil legacies, the question of reparatory justice is a more complicated problem generally inherited by the successor regime, raising conflicts between the backward-looking purposes of compensating victims of past state abuses and the state's forward-looking political interests. Reparatory practices raise the prospective/retrospective, individual/collective dilemmas characterizing transitional periods. Yet whether in ordinary or transitional periods, reparatory justice is always in some sense backward-looking, as it implies rectification of past wrong. Transitional reparatory justice, as is elaborated further on in this chapter, reconciles the apparent dilemma in the extraordinary context of balancing corrective aims with the forward-looking goals of the transformation. Similarly, transitional reparatory justice mediates individual and collective liability, shaping the political identity of the liberalizing state.

The vocabulary of "reparatory justice" illustrates its multiple dimensions, comprehending numerous diverse forms: reparations, damages, remedies, redress, restitution, compensation, rehabilitation, tribute. Precedents going back to ancient times illuminate transitional reparatory justice's complex role. Transitional reparatory measures mediate repair of victims and communities, past and present, laying a basis for redistributive policies associated with radical upheaval.

## Biblical Reparations: The Exodus from Egypt

> Know of a surety that thy seed shall be a stranger in a land that is not theirs, and shall serve them; and they shall afflict them four hundred years; and also that nation, whom they shall serve, will I judge; and afterward shall they come out with great substance.
> Genesis 15:13–14

The biblical account of the political shift—from oppression to freedom—of the Israelites in Egypt offers an ancient story of transition. According to that account, the ancient Israelites dwelled in Egypt for about four hundred years, suffering slavery and other persecution. Years of slavery were followed by freedom from the Egyptians, punishment meted out against the Egyptians, and ultimately establishment of nationhood. The story of the Exodus and the punishment of the Egyptians and the plagues is known, but less is known about the Exodus-related reparations. Its elusive meaning evokes the ongoing mystery and rich ambiguity of reparatory practices in times of political change.

In the biblical account of reparatory justice, on the fateful night of the Exodus, the Israelites "borrowed from the Egyptians objects of silver and gold, and clothing."[2] God told the Israelites to take valuables from the Egyptians: "The Israelites had done Moses' bidding and borrowed from the Egyptians objects of silver and gold, and clothing. And the Lord had disposed the Egyptians favorably toward the people, and they let them have their request, thus they stripped the Egyptians."[3] The text suggests the valuables were not taken by force but willingly given up by the Egyptians. However, the biblical story is open to divergent interpretations, for the same account that refers to "borrowing" and "request" also says the Israelites "stripped the Egyptians."

Another aspect of the night's events is reiterated in a biblical section that elaborates on the "stripping" of the Egyptians: "Each woman shall borrow from her neighbor and the lodger in her house objects of silver and gold, and clothing, and you shall put these on your sons and daughters, thus stripping the Egyptians."[4] This account suggests there was an exchange of dress between the Egyptians and the Israelites. Stripping the Egyptians implies that the freed slaves had assumed the dress of their slave owners, in turn, leaving the owners virtually naked—as slaves. The sequence harks back to the very origins of the term *redress.* "Redress," according to the word's origins, relates to the attire worn in public ceremonies, signifying distinct status. In its earliest usage, in the Middle Ages, "redress" links attire, status, and the restoration of dignity. The stripping of the Egyptians and the "re-dressing" of the Israelites signifies more than a material settlement, it is a setting straight, a ceremonial redressing, a rehabilitation in the public eye. This ancient symbolic aspect of reparatory measures is manifest in subsequent precedents throughout history.

What is the meaning of the Exodus epoch's reparations? The biblical account supports alternative understandings. The taking of the valuables could be understood as a gift; a loan; an inducement to leave, for example, a bribe; a mutual property exchange, for example, Egyptian movables traded for the Israelites' real property left behind; compensation for back wages and other abuses relating to years of slavery in Egypt; or, as symbolic redress, a rehabilitation of political status. In one interpretation, the story is about the ancient Hebrews' taking advantage of the chaos of the transitional moment and pillaging stolen goods. In another interpretation, this is not the action of runaway slaves but the implementation of a divine plan. The Egyptians gave the valuables as reparations, as part of a divinely ordained justice.[5] This interpretation builds on earlier biblical allusions to the fleeing nation's becoming one of "great substance," foreshadowing the claim to the Egyptian treasure.

How to make sense of the account? Was the stripping of the Egyptians backward-looking, the valuables taken to settle for past enslavement and persecution? Or was the "re-dressing" of the Israelites forward-looking, the valuables taken to amass capital necessary to nation-building? The language of the biblical text and subsequent commentary support both views. If the biblical account of the night of the Exodus is interpreted in its historical and political context, that interpretative context is the particular hermeneutics of transition, including the years of enslavement before the eventful night and also the subsequent history in the biblical account of the transition out of slavery to nationhood. The transitional context has both backward-looking and forward-looking aspects that color interpretation of the reparatory practices. As we shall see, the biblical story has enduring resonance, for it illustrates the paradigmatically multiple quality of reparatory justice.

## Postwar Reparations and Total War Guilt

At the end of World War I, the reparations exacted of Germany squarely raised the question of the meaning of reparatory justice. At Versailles, responsibility for the war was conceived in totalizing terms: The peace settlement made Germany responsible for "total war guilt" and concluded with Germany's agreement to pay huge reparations.[6] In the peace settlement, the reparations levied on Germany were punitive but justified on the basis of deterrence—that is, to cripple Germany so that it could never again wage war. The Treaty of Versailles attributed the crime of "aggressive war " to the state of Germany. Its understanding of responsibility was in collective terms, and the sanctions' impact, too, would fall on the state. After four years of war, the Allies might have demanded the entire cost of the war as a matter of right, but, ultimately, the claim to reparations was framed, not in terms of the Allies' "right," but, rather, in terms of Germany's "duty." The so-called war-guilt clause of the Versailles treaty emphasized Germany's total liability, forcing Germany to accept responsibility for "causing all the loss and damage to the Allies . . . as consequence of a war imposed on them by . . . aggression." The Versailles treaty at Article 231 provides: "The Allied and Associated Governments affirm, and Germany accepts, the responsibility of Germany and her Allies for causing all the loss and damage to which the Allied and Associated Governments and their nationals have been subjected as a consequence of a war imposed upon them by the aggression of Germany and her Allies."[7] According to the treaty's war-guilt clause, all responsibility for the war—its total costs—was to be shouldered by Germany.

Versailles' heavy reparatory burden raised a number of questions. There was the practical problem raised by onerous sanctions so heavy that, as recognized at the time, there was little likelihood that Germany could make its payments.[8] There was also the crudeness of economic sanctions. Their undifferentiated nature meant their impact fell on the state as a whole. The reparations' magnitude raised a host of questions about their nature and function: To what extent were such remedies intended to fulfill a compensatory function, for war-related offenses? To what extent punitive? The formulation of the reparations provisions in the Versailles treaty was ambiguous, reflecting multiple purposes. The postwar treaty intriguingly separated the question of responsibility from that of ultimate liability. Total war guilt pressed at the interstices of criminal and civil liability; while the reparations at stake appeared to be civil in nature, the Versailles treaty's "total war-guilt" clause explicitly distinguished responsibility from its enforcement, from execution of judgment. Despite the treaty's statement of total liability at Article 231, Article 232 conceded the problem of the scarcity of resources. Though there was substantial Allied debate over the question of the extent of liability and at what level to set the reparations, the language of the treaty suggested there was an understanding that—beyond payment for material losses—Germany would be held morally, politically, and legally responsible for the war. Nevertheless, the same treaty recognized that Germany would not pay. The treaty's peculiarly phrased two clauses signaled the profound ambiguity raised by reparatory practices in periods of transition.

Postwar reparations, like those in ancient times, reflect a hybrid, complex view of the nature and role of these practices, which simultaneously advances the repair of present damage and the sanctioning of past wrongs, assertedly intended as corrective of the past, while advancing the broader future-related political goals of the transition.

## Wiedergutmachung and Shilumim

Out of World War II's unconditional surrender and the ashes of the camps arose a reparatory project that still remains the most sweeping in history, totaling in the tens of billions of dollars in the last half century. After this war, two sets of widely disparate reparatory claims were made of Germany—one from its triumphant enemies, the other from its most pathetic victims. Early on in the peace process, even before World War II ended, the Allies demanded Germany pay for waging unjust war. As discussed above, in the aftermath of World War I, the norm was for defeated nations to pay reparations to the other parties; the origins of the German reparation scheme derive from these postwar restitutions. In the transition from occupied territory to sovereign state, a major provision of the 1952 Transitional Treaty with the occupying powers was the obligation to make restitution for war-related property confiscations as well as for other losses.[9]

The other impetus for reparations came from the victims and survivors of the millions who had died in the death camps. The accounts of the negotiations leading up to the reparations agreement among Germany, Israel, and survivor groups tell a tale of two peoples in transition, one, a defeated nation with a profound sense of moral bankruptcy, and the other, a newly created nation of survivors in fiscal bankruptcy. After extensive negotiations led by Chancellor Konrad Adenauer yielded the 1952 Luxembourg agreements, Germany agreed to pay a sum to an organization representing victims of Nazi persecution,[10] as well as reparations to the new state of Israel. The Federal Compensation Law was sweeping in the scope of its redress to victims of the Nazi oppression, compensating for physical injury and loss of freedom, property, income, professional, or financial advancement if the loss resulted from persecution for political, social, religious, or ideological reasons.[11]

Payments to victims, their representatives and the state of Israel were not contemplated by the international law of the time, nor were there precedents for such payments. Perhaps, the closest analogy was the traditional postwar reparations, in which the laws of war ever since the 1907 Hague Convention required the belligerent state violating the norms of war to pay compensation. However, this view implied adopting the fiction that Germany and Israel were "belligerent" states. Yet, not only had Israel not participated in the war, but the state did not even exist at the time of the war. Payments promised in the 1952 agreements by the Federal Republic of Germany, as in contemporary agreements after Unification,[12] diverged from the traditional understanding of war-related reparations as national in nature. The designated beneficiaries of the reparations were not a triumphant nation but, instead, the citizens of the very nation doing the compensating. They were also potential citizens of Israel, represented by the beneficiary nation. These were no ordinary postwar reparations.

The post–World War II payments changed forever the concept of reparations. After Nuremberg, dramatic developments in international law extended the norms relating to the law of war beyond the international sphere to apply to states' internal conflicts. At the war's end, the 1949 Geneva Conventions spurred the development of international humanitarian law, contemplating reparations for violations of civilians' rights in all sorts of armed conflicts.[13] The newly developing obligations under the law of war regarding reparations to abused victims of other states led to the national obligations to compensate citizens for violations. A contrary result would have meant greater remedies afforded for aliens under international law than afforded for citizens under their own national legal systems. The emergence of these obligations under international humanitarian law, in turn, led to the transitional reparatory obligations for past state wrongs assumed by successor regimes. Reparatory standards associated with the law of war have evolved and extended beyond the circumstances of international conflict to purely internal conflict.

How to understand the German reparations scheme? *Wiedergutmachung* was Germany's term for the reparations, literally meaning "to make good again," that is, to return to former conditions.[14] With the failure of denazification, reparations drew political support in Germany as a way to regain credibility in the eyes of the international community. By contrast, rejecting the notion that reparations could ever make anything "good" again, victims' groups called reparations by a Hebrew term *shilumim*,[15] meaning "to make amends, to bring about peace." For the victims, reparations were a matter of economic necessity, and so, for them, the point of departure in the negotiations was the refugees' cost of resettlement. For perpetrators and victims alike, reparations were about settling accounts, but for each in a different way. Nevertheless, despite completely different understandings of the nature and purposes of the reparations scheme, negotiations over the varying concepts culminated in a political agreement.

Germany's reparation scheme is paradigmatic of the complex conception of transitional reparations. Transitional reparatory practices are infused by mixed, backward and forward-looking, moral, economic, and political justifications. Perhaps not altogether surprisingly, reparations originating in postwar and other transitional agreements, products of political negotiations and compromise, advance divergent, and even apparently conflicting purposes. The postwar reparatory project illuminates that transitional reparatory schemes have multiple purposes, advancing the interests of individuals and collectives, victims and societies. As we shall see in exploring other similar practices in periods of political transformation, this hybrid multiple function distinguishes transitional reparatory schemes.

## Dirty Wars, Disappearances, and Reconciliation: The Role of Reparations

The disappearance and presumed murder of a young man, Velásquez-Rodríguez, in Honduras in the 1980s set off a chain reaction throughout Latin America, stimulating a continent-wide reparatory policy. When Honduras failed even to investigate the disappearance, it appeared to be clearly state-sponsored, and the country was taken before the Inter-American Court of Human Rights. In a series of landmark decisions, the Inter-American Court held that Honduras had violated the American Convention on Human Rights and that states had a "duty to prevent, investigate and punish" violations of rights guaranteed by the convention.[16] The court held, moreover, that whenever such rights had been violated, states were obligated to ensure victims' compensation. *Velásquez-Rodríguez* held that the failure to pursue criminal justice was not simply a matter within the state's discretion. Rather, failure to enforce norms was understood to imply the loss of important victims' (citizens) protection rights, triggering international law duties to reparations.

The duties that *Velásquez-Rodríquez* recognized are manifestly transitional—that is, they both transcend and bridge regimes. Though the original right relates to the duty to equal protection under the law, once the prospective duty to protect is abrogated, subsequent "curative" duties fall on the successor regime, such as duties of investigation and of compensation. *Velásquez-Rodríquez* suggests that when the obligations of investigation and compensation are not fulfilled, the violations are potentially ongoing and successor regimes are responsible. While the first duty, to protect, is prospective and forward-looking, the other duties, of investigation and compensation, are retrospective and backward-looking; they are therefore potentially ongoing, open-ended, and the responsibility of subsequent regimes until satisfied.[17] The very duties recognized in the case law mediate the predecessor and successor regimes, expanding the meaning of human rights protection in the transition.

*Velásquez-Rodríguez* set a high standard of reparatory obligation. Characterizing the disappearance as a "wrongful death resulting from serious acts imputable to Honduras," the Inter-American Court said that the state had a duty to make both "moral" and "material" compensation to the survivors for damages suffered relating to the disappearance.[18] Moreover, the expansive reparatory scheme elaborated in *Velásquez-Rodríguez* was a departure from Latin American legal culture, which lacks a tradition of payment for damages for official wrongdoing.[19]

*Velásquez-Rodríguez* shed a new perspective on the nature of transitional justice, reparations illuminating affinities in the criminal and civil remedies. The uses of the reparatory measures in the wake of criminal justice are evinced when, in principle, the failure to prosecute grave state wrongs is seen to implicate victims' rights and related states' duties, reaffirmed in subsequent decisions holding that amnesty laws violated victims' rights under regional human rights law.[20] Throughout Latin America, the meaning of *Velásquez-Rodríguez* was that when criminal justice was unavailing, other reponses could be brought into play; that is, other legal responsibilities were owed to victims, chiefly, some form of reparations.

The norm adumbrated in *Velásquez-Rodríguez* raises many questions. What sort of duty is implied here, that is, what is the relation between a state's duty to protect citizens equally and its duty to "restore" such rights? Even more threshold questions are raised: In what sense were the human rights recognized in *Velásquez-Rodríguez* traditional "rights"? To whom did they belong? On this view, who is harmed when equal protection rights are violated, the victims alone? Their survivors? And to what extent are there ramifications for the society? These questions arose as a part of the broader consequences of impunity policy, when many countries in the region amnestied past regime wrongdoing.

Given that amnesty policies were adopted throughout Latin America, the message of *Velásquez-Rodríguez* sounded insistently. After the horrors of repressive military rule, torture, executions, and disappearances, the ultimate question was whether successor regimes could "disappear" even their own pasts to oblivion? Given the region's political past, this type of policy would be particularly perverse. When Chile returned to democratic rule, the fragility of its balance of power challenged the possibility of punishing its military, and the successor Aylwin regime turned to an alternative form of justice. As in *Velásquez-Rodríguez*, the state promised an official investigation into military repression, and reparatory remedies.[21] Chile's remedial scheme helps to further explicate the relation between transitional understandings of criminal and reparatory justice. When the governmental Truth and Reconciliation Commission reported that, during military rule, there had been thousands of forced disappearances and extrajudicial executions, Chile's president, in presenting the Truth Commission's report to the country, ascribed these crimes to official wrongdoing and went on to characterize reparations as "acts expressing the state's admission of, and responsibility for, the events and circumstances discussed in the report."[22] In assuming the obligation to pay reparations, the successor regime took responsibility for the past regime's wrongdoing. Despite the initial opposition to redress and the absence of a legal culture with a tradition of punitive damages for official wrongdoing, such remedial schemes became more common throughout the continent. After Chile, Argentina assumed an even broader reparatory policy, undertaking to compensate not only for disappearances but also for wrongful internment under prior junta rule.[23] In related precedents in the Inter-American Commission of Human Rights, Uruguay was also ordered to pay reparations.[24]

Transitional precedents redefine the nature of the state's obligation to its citizens. Much as transitional constitutions and criminal sanctions delimit changes in state sovereignty, these changes can also be defined through reparatory measures. Transitional reparations were intended to restore victims, but they also hold additional significance in the public sphere. When reparations are part of a formal public successor policy, they can critically respond to predecessor policy by correcting the derogation from equal protection under the law. Victims of military repression have been accused of subversion and annihilated as enemies of the state. They were abducted, tortured, and executed and disappeared; their children were ransomed, their property confiscated. Thus, Chile's Truth and Reconciliation Commission recommended "moral" reparations "to publicly restore the good name of those who perished from the stigma of having been falsely accused as enemies of the state."[25] In keeping with this mandate, just days after taking office, President Patricio Aylwin addressed the Chilean people in a public commemoration event held in the very stadium where, under the military junta, political prisoners had been detained. As the president recited the names of the disappeared in a national public address, their names simultaneously flashed on the stadium's electronic scoreboard in a publication of retraction and apology to the victims of governmental wrongdoing.

As with ancient redress, Latin America's "moral reparations" are intended to set things straight in the community and to restore dignity. The moral reparations, are intended as compensatory, not punitive.[26] Moral reparations are intended to repair the shame and humiliation previously inflicted on victims and to restore their reputation and equal status in the public eye. In the ordinary, common-law understanding of defamation, liability does not survive the victim, but it does in the case of the disappeared. Moral reparations transcend redress to the affected individuals and their survivors for injury, reaching the public eye. This restoration of reputation suggests that reputation serves a broader function than in ordinary times; it serves the societal interest in the political transition. When political defamation and persecution are at stake, more than the victim's personal reputation is on the line. While rehabilitating the disappeared, the state is also publicly acknowledging its responsibility for wrongdoing. Further, in taking responsibility, the successor regime recharacterizes the nature of the wrong; indeed, state assumption of responsibility even has the effect of reducing the amount of moral damages.[27] These remedies are explicitly intended to enable societal reconciliation, to bring peace to the politically riven societies of Latin America. Transitional reparatory practices display multiple purposes: backward-looking, in repairing victims of past state wrongdoing, but also forward-looking, in advancing the purposes of peace and reconciliation in the transition.

The Latin American reparations illustrate the complex roles for reparatory policies in transition. Transitional reparations serve multiple purposes. When reparations emerge as explicit alternatives to punishment, they reveal alternative ways to advance the vindication and rehabilitation accomplished through the criminal sanction. Transitional reparatory measures assume the burden of responsibility for past wrongdoing in public fashion. Indeed, the shift in emphasis from victims' harm to state's wrongdoing is particularly clear in moral reparations. As with criminal justice, in the state's assumption of responsibility expressed through its public redress, wrongdoing is identified and, relatedly, blame is assumed for past wrongs. In addition to sanctioning wrongdoers, reparations vindicate victims.[28] Through formal legal responses recognizing the juridical status of the disappeared, reparatory justice reconstructs the borders of political community.

Because of their versatility, reparatory practices have become the leading response in the contemporary wave of political transformation. "Truth and reparations," a response combining reparations with the historical inquiry discussed more fully in the previous chapter, has become the dominant way to resolve agonizing conflicts throughout Latin America and elsewhere. Protracted civil war was settled in El Salvador on the promise of an investigative commission and reparatory remedies.[29] A similar formula brokered the peace in Guatemala.[30] In South Africa, an amnesty became part of the transition agreement in exchange for "truth and reconciliation." The country's 1993 Constitution, entitled "National Unity and Reconciliation," provides: "In order to advance such reconciliation and reconstruction, amnesty shall be granted in respect of acts, omissions and offenses associated with political objectives and committed in the course of the conflicts of the past."[31] As interpreted by the country's Constitutional Court, amnesty's core minima include the clarification of past political crimes and their reparation;[32] thus, in South Africa, the two are concededly connected. Despite the legislative rule, the amnesties are conditional in South Africa and, therefore, imply case-by-case determinations predicated on some investigation into the past wrongdoing. The promise of reparations served as incentives for victims to testify in the country's public proceedings; and, as the South African Truth Commission's report nears finality, reparatory measures are known to be part of its proposed recommendations. In all the transitions above discussed, the criminal sanction was eschewed for a hybrid form of reparatory justice.

The uses of transitional reparatory measures, as discussed above, by successor regimes as alternatives to punishment challenge our intuitions about what distinguishes civil and criminal sanctions. Supposed criminal/civil antinomies do not well account for transitional practices. For transitional reparatory practices redress individual rights violations, even as they express responsibility for past criminal wrongdoing, these combined aims defy conventional categorization as either criminal or corrective justice. The transitional reparatory practices discussed above enable the public recognition and condemnation of wrongdoing in a way that is generally considered the criminal sanction's distinguishing feature. At common law, the nature of the wrong was considered to be bound up with the nature of the harm, hence, public and private to correspond to criminal and civil. As William Blackstone wrote, "[P]rivate wrongs, or civil injuries, are an infringement or privation of the civil rights which belong to individuals, considered merely as individual, public wrongs, or crimes and misdemeanors, are a breach and violation of the public rights and duties, due to the whole community."[33] Though this distinction is the point of departure at common law; nevertheless, in the modern state, the way we think about these ostensible differences in criminal and corrective justice has undergone change. This is dramatically vivified in transition.

Transitional reparatory practices challenge the understanding that the distinguishing feature of criminal justice (as opposed to civil justice) is the dominant role of the state, as these reparatory schemes imply substantial state involvement.[34] This understanding is also challenged by the many private initiatives in transitional criminal justice. In periods of political transition, private parties, such as victims or their representatives, have often taken the prosecutorial lead. This private initiative is true historically; virtually all efforts after the immediate postwar period to bring to trial World War II criminals resulted from private initiatives.[35] France is a leading example. In continental criminal law, the initiative in criminal justice is often left to private parties, usually the victim, as in a civil proceeding.[36] Victims' private involvement in criminal actions is also contemplated in the jurisprudence of the Inter-American system, in which the Inter-American Commission has recognized that when amnesty legislation is enacted, victims' judicial process rights are affected, potentially shutting off their investigatory and retributive avenues. "The petitioners, relatives or those injured by the human rights violations have their right to a recourse, to a thorough and impartial judicial investigation to ascertain the facts."[37] The guarantee of equal protection runs through the society and is vindicable by victims as a basic guarantee of the rule of law owed them.

Out of the dilemmas of the liberalizing regime's response to grave past state wrongs. Hybrid forms of justice emerge that assimilate the state's role in sanctioning public wrongs, together with individual redress; for the past wrongdoing is not merely a matter between victim and perpetrator but involves state policy in a community. Transitional reparatory practices enable recognition of individual rights violations and ensuing harm, as well as of public, governmental wrongdoing. The affinities between criminal and corrective justice are appreciable in both forms of legal responses in the paradigm of transitional jurisprudence. As previously discussed in chapter 2, even the limited form of criminal sanction advances the purposes of denunciation of crime, vindication of victims, and the legal system. There are affinities in the punitive and reparatory ideas of justice in periods of radical change. Law's overriding function is to advance the transition in such times. Law does so when it recognizes the state's own past wrongdoing, restores victims, and vindicates the legal system.[38]

## Reparations and Privatization after Communism

What distinguishes the transitions out of communism are the multiple, simultaneous radical transformations: constitutional, political, civil, and economic. It is in the midst of these multiple transitions, and as an integral part of the attempt to construct a free market, that the reparatory schemes in Eastern and Central Europe were adopted.[39]

Whether through restitution of confiscated property or compensation, the linkage to privatization manifests a complex role for transitional reparations after communism: to repair past state wrongs, mostly Stalin-era takings, and also to advance contemporary state privatization interests related to the economic transformation. These two purposes are often said to be in conflict, occasioning a dilemma peculiar to the former Soviet bloc and to states undergoing similar market transformations. The distinct question posed in these societies is, What redress is compatible with the interest in economic change, namely, the transition to freer markets? Ultimately, the reparatory measures adopted attempt to reconcile these purposes. In pragmatic resolution of political purposes in the transition postcommunist reparations challenge traditional understandings of corrective and distributive justice.

In early 1991, less than two years after its 1989 revolution, the debate in the Czech Republic over what to do about the former Communists' political crimes culminated in the Law on Extrajudicial Rehabilitation.[40] Intended to redress Communist-era victims of political persecution, the law required that wherever property had been obtained in a coercive fashion, it should be returned. In the parliamentary debate over the law, what became clear were restitution's dual purposes; many of the law's advocates argued for the legislation on economic grounds. Since in the former Czechoslovakia the state had had a virtual monopoly on the means of production, the return of confiscated property was justified as "natural restitution," as an efficient way to privatize, because it appeared to facilitate the transfer of state property to private owners. By contrast, the restitution law's opponents argued that it was a fundamentally backward-looking enterprise that detracted from the possibility of freer property relations. There was truth on both sides: Constructions of first property rights advanced the apparent expedient goal of the present need to create a private market, and the law constructed an understanding of private property rights. After the first steps in political transition, the country would wrestle with its vast restitution project.

That reparations in postcommunism served political purposes was made explicit in Hungary's Compensation Law. The law's preamble asserts that its "double purpose" is "to establish entrepreneurial security under conditions of a market economy, and to mitigate unjust damages caused by the state." Justification of the "new property" is made in terms of the protection of past property claims:

> [I]t is a moral duty of a state which recognizes and protects private property to take action and provide financial indemnification to those who suffered injuries in their property. In the interest of developing appropriately settled ownership relations in a modern market economy the state intends to remedy the earlier private property injuries suffered . . . by providing partial property indemnification to former owners."[41]

As the preamble of the Hungarian law makes clear, the very notion that there were "past" property rights is a judicial fiction being deployed in the region to justify and to advance the construction of instant property rights. And, while the recognition of such property rights may well be ex post, this construction serves a forward-looking economic interest. When the country's Constitutional Court upheld the constitutionality of the compensation scheme, it was characterized as a "novation," capturing the sense in which the notion of "rights" (and past violations thereof) is being used to justify present entitlements. Whatever conflict there is between the interests in restitution and privatization is reconciled in eschewal of the absolutes of all or none, that is, the dilemmas of whether there appears to be full restitution of confiscated property. Instead, the resolution is to opt for the compromise of so-called partial indemnification.

Squaring reparatory goals with economic concerns is a balancing act that is being worked out on a country-by-country basis in the region. Indeed, the balance of interests is ever-changing in the transition. Thus, in the Unification Treaty, the two Germanys agreed to broad restitution: According to the treaty's "principle of restitution before compensation," whenever property was confiscated, other than during the Soviet occupation, it would be restored to its former owners or their heirs.[42] The project commenced, and its broad restitution principle was challenged for holding up privatization, thus spurring conversion of restitution to compensation claims. When the compensatory scheme was challenged under Germany's Basic Law's protection against property takings, its constitutionality was upheld. According to the court, the constitutional ban on takings, vindicated against past Communist confiscations, required neither the return of the original property nor any particular measure of compensation.[43] Similarly, when the so-called partial compensation law was challenged in Hungary, its Constitutional Court upheld the scheme, declaring that there were no "rights" to restitution and, therefore, the legislature had to show that special entitlements to benefits were in the public interest.[44]

In this way, regimes' successors to one-party communist rule reconcile the mixed purposes of their restitution programs. The guiding principle is harmony, so that reparations for past wrongs are justified in juridical terms, as legal entitlements and "rights" to the extent and insofar as they are compatible with the goals of the economic transition.[45]

The problems of privatization through reprivatization that surfaced in Germany and the Czech Republic may well have been dissuasive of similar attempts at large-scale restitution.[46] Thus, though Poland debated the restitution of the property claims of those dispossessed by the Communists ever since the political change, it failed to garner a consensus on restitution policy. Its Draft Reprivatization Law would have reconciled any conflict between reparatory justice and privatization policy by making the measure of compensation for wrongful taking the income obtained from privatizing state enterprises.[47] Once again, the measure of damages strikes an accommodation between reparatory and distributive purposes.

Postcommunist reparations illustrate the paradigmatic transitional conception of reparatory justice. Rather than an ideal foundational basis, the measures reflect the multiple purposes animating extraordinary times of political flux. Transitional practices effect a transfer of payments that is justified on the bases of both righting past wrongs and simultaneously advancing the state's transitional economic goals. As the state repairs the ancien régime's takings, past entitlements are used to justify contemporary property distributions. In this way, reparatory principles do the work of transition to a market economy. Reparatory obligations are assumed and rights claims vindicated when they are compatible with the other political purposes of the transition. Ex post facto property "rights" are constructed and justified to the extent that they are otherwise compatible with the economic transformation. In this complex conception, transitional reparatory schemes advance simultaneously multiple and diverse forms of change.

Insofar as transitional reparatory measures are intended to advance economic reconstitution, the schemes create a new class of property holders with corresponding consequences for the political transformation. Obviously, amassed capital offers an important and renewed stake in the political community. Moreover, whenever reparatory schemes condition governmental benefits on a political basis, they can effect reconstruction of political and economic membership. So it is that restitution interest groups have shaped the development of the fledgling political party system in the Czech Republic, Hungary, and Bulgaria.[48] Whenever restitution policies are conditioned on past political persecution, the policies display affinities with other transitional responses, such as administrative measures that overtly reconstruct the boundaries of the political community.

## The Dilemma of Transitional Reparatory Justice and the Rule of Law

What rule-of-law principle guides reparatory justice in transition? The reparatory projects of societies in the extraordinary context of political flux advance purposes related to radical political change other than those conventionally considered remedial, such as societal reconciliation and economic transformation. Transitional reparatory justice advances political aims concededly external to conventional corrective justice principles. In these complex reparatory schemes, what guiding principle does the work of justifying transitional reparatory justice?

The question of what should be the guiding principle surfaced in debates concerning restitution after communism. The recurring challenge to reparations in the region, in the words of Czech Republic President and former dissident Václav Havel was, "If everyone suffered, why should only some be redressed?"[49] Generally, the guiding normative value was past harm. Harm under prior rule is understood (as one might expect given the legacy in the region) in universalist and egalitarian terms. These premises derive from the central value of rule of law under communism. Thus, Jon Elster, observes that "the main issue . . . is . . . equal treatment. . . . [I]t is important to keep in mind that essentially *everybody* suffered under communism. . . . Full compensation to some of the victims cannot be defended as a second-best approximation to *the ideal of universal* compensation."[50]

Beginning with the claim that under prior totalitarian rule *everyone* suffered, those opposing postcommunist reparatory measures reason that the only fair reparatory scheme is a universal one. Since such a scheme is frankly unrealizable because of the scarcity of resources, the universality argument ultimately appears, perhaps paradoxically, as a not so thinly veiled basis for the denial of all redress. Whatever the case for reparatory justice in the former communist bloc, the project is said to be fatally undermined by the lack of full compensation. The central egalitarian assumption that "everybody suffered" under the prior regime implies at least two claims regarding reparations based on harm, a claim of universality and a claim of equivalence. When universal reparations are posited as the ideal, transitional reparatory schemes are relatedly all or none. In the aftermath of the failed socialist experiment, the egalitarian arguments marshaled against transitional reparation have a painful and almost perverse resonance.

Yet, in working democracies, doing something ameliorative, even if it is partial, is an accepted feature of corrective projects.[51] The rule of law generally applicable to governmentally administered policies is that they fairly proceed one step at a time.[52] Equal protection values suggest that like cases should be treated similarly; a just corrective policy would need to account for the fairness of individual claims and for equivalent treatment of similar claims.

The challenge to postcommunist reparatory schemes also sounds in distributive concerns. From this perspective, a just distributive policy ought take account of other claims within the community. Though universality is not conventionally the criterion guiding corrective justice, it has a certain resonance after communism.

To the extent that harm is often the basis for reparatory justice in transitional periods, the schemes seem vulnerable for their open-endedness, potentially sweeping in all sorts of past injuries. In the face of the potentially limitless claims given the nature of prior rule, the apparent constraints appear to be those imposed by the scarcity of resources. However, this concern may be somewhat mitigated by the political legacies of the controlled economy in the region, as the property in question is largely in the hands of the state: the state is implicated either as the property owner or as the enforcer of restitution schemes that depend on the cooperation of third parties. This affinity between corrective and distributive schemes in transitional circumstances goes some way toward explaining the urge toward universality as the guiding rule of law.

The critique of transitional reparation from ideal theory challenges the schemes for their lack of universal reach, given harm as the basis for reparations, yet, while harm may well be justificatory of transitional reparations, other restrictive principles come into play, principles that shift the focus from harm to rights. With the injection of new liberal principles constructive of rights, reparatory claims are said to derive not merely from past injury but also from the present recognition and legitimation of individual property and bodily security rights. The liberal case for reparations is justified in the recognition and protection of individual rights. In the liberal state, these are the bases for corrective justice.[53] Indeed, the centrality of individual rights as a predicate of liberal legal systems is evinced by the dominance of corrective justice in working democracies. Thus, transitional schemes, particularly after communism, when they occur during simultaneous political and economic transformations, transcend conventional understandings of corrective and distributive justice. Property rights entitlements arising out of past wrongs are constructed ex post and are simultaneously self-referential and justificatory of present property distributions. Indeed, recognition of past violations lays the basis for contemporary constructions of new property rights. So it is that reparatory schemes mediate both backward- and forward-looking purposes of the transition.

### The Case for Political Reparations: The Transitional Priority of Political Equality

Across legal cultures, reparatory practices are common in periods of political flux. There is a remarkable convergence on reparations as the most popular legal response in transition, even in societies that are generally inhospitable to such remedies. Compensation is somewhat controversial in countries outside the common-law tradition; in continental legal culture, grave rights abuses are not generally considered assuagable through monetary damages.[54] Similarly, for reasons related to policies associated with the command economy, discussed earlier in this chapter, there has been some aversion to reparations after communism. Socialist legality placed little or no value on the vindication of individual property rights.[55] The project, therefore, of making up for past political treatment under the prior regime by compensating or restituting on a political basis constitutes a real break from the past.

The central question of justice is, Of all the wrongs committed under past repressive rule, which inequalities merit redress? What is a compensable difference in prior state treatment justifying successor reparations? Harm alone, as above discussed, as a practical matter rarely serves as the exclusive basis for reparations in transition; for following systemically repressive rule, it seems potentially limitless and thus does not offer a restrictive principle. Reparatory precedents regarding divergent treatments under past repressive rule suggest that the relevant principle regarding compensable differences determining what harm is repaired is the principle of political persecution. Transitional practices discussed above suggest that past state treatment subject to compensation primarily relates to past discrimination on a political basis; the salient principle of compensable wrongs in the transition attempts to correct for past political persecution. Compensation is often justified on the basis of rights created under natural law or international law, as sources of continuous norms that take no notice of political change.[56] Under international law, the greatest support is for the most grave abuses, the "jus cogens" norms.[57]

Reparations justified on the basis of a political persecution principle mediate backward- and forward-looking purposes of the transition. Reparatory policies grounded in the principle of protection against political persecution are justified on the basis of the state's mandate to equal protection. All governments owe their citizens equal protection of the law; the duty's abrogation lays the very basis for revolution.[58] Thus, equality under the law is often the value animating revolution, but, in its aftermath, where do equal protection rights go? When redress is effected along the lines of past political persecution, it revives the basis for revolution and advances reconstruction of equal citizenship rights. Vindicating threshold political equality rights has significance that transcends the affected individuals and reaches the wider society. When the successor regime pays reparations for the predecessor's political persecution, the act affirms that citizens' rights will be protected on an equal basis. Vindication of individual rights delineates a newfound line of security between the individual and the state, itself a sign of liberalizing change. Transitional reparatory measures draw a line on past, political persecution and, in so doing, perform the acts and rituals associated with the legal system of the liberal state.

### The Dilemma of the Baseline

Successor reparatory undertakings are commonly adopted on the basis of a principle of political persecution, of rights recognized retroactively by transitional regimes. In this constructive process, accordingly, the key question of reparatory policy is where to draw the line.

How do transitional societies resolve this dilemma of the baseline? In established democracies, successor administrations ordinarily succeed to prior state obligations;[59] the assumption is state continuity and successor governments are deemed presumptively responsible for acts of their predecessors. But when a successor regime follows a series of repressive governments, what are the duties of the first successor rule-of-law administration? Do intuitions about legal continuity in governmental succession imply the assumption of all such obligations? To what extent does the successor regime inherit a legacy of obligations arising from the past regime's rights violations? Reparatory justice relates to past wrongs, but the recognition of rights by the successor regime raises the question, What guides these reparatory undertakings? Transitional precedents reveal selective succession to obligations generated by the unlawful acts implied by a prior regime's wrongdoings. States differ on the degree of commitment to liabilities arising from past wrongs.

What is the right baseline in the redress calculus? The problem is illustrated in contemporary transitions that followed successive occupations and waves of political persecution. In the postcommunist bloc, the question of the baseline sparked heated debate. A history of repeated invasions, of World War II Nazi occupation immediately followed by Soviet occupation, meant that after the collapse of the Soviet empire the debate over baselines for political persecution and which victims would be compensated moved to the fore of public debate all over the region. Though the region's past is often portrayed as a seamless period of sustained persecution, the deliberations on reparatory measures forced the first public debate on the consequences of a legacy of successive occupations for the baseline of liberalizing transition. The question and choices are politically freighted, as they relate to the Nazi and Soviet occupations and to the drawing of the line of return to domestic control. The baseline debates implied a political struggle over the social significance of recognizing transitional reparatory rights. When the line of successor responsibility was drawn as that coincident with the return to internal control, this baseline might have been justifiable from a legal perspective, that is, the return to rule of law; nevertheless, the choice remained politically controversial. For the choice of restitution baselines implies choosing among victims of varying persecutions and their political interest groups. The dilemma proved so divisive that in some countries, like Poland, it became an obstacle to the adoption of any restitution policy. Prolonged and heated debates over the baselines in Eastern Europe suggest that reparatory policies in such periods could hardly resist politicization, particularly when compensatory schemes are used to do other work, such as economic reform and privatization.

In much of the region, 1948 was settled on as the cutoff date, justified as the date foreign occupation ended and domestic rule was restored. In Germany, for example, pre-1949 confiscations were not originally part of the country's restitution program;[60] only in response to outside (American) pressure was the restitution program broadened to include Nazi-era takings. While takings going back to the date the German Democratic Republic (GDR) came into existence were to be restituted to former owners, property taken during the Soviet occupation of eastern Germany between 1945 and 1949 was only partially compensated. The Czech Law on Extrajudicial Rehabilitation similarly drew the line at 1948, justified as the date of the Communist seizure of power and the beginning of one-party rule.[61] Though the Czech restitution law would recognize the "various injustices from previous periods," such as World War II-related takings, it did not allow for return of Jewish property expropriated by the Nazis or for return of the property of two million Sudeten Germans confiscated upon their expulsion after the war.

The discriminatory potential of the drawing of the baseline rose to constitutional dimensions in the region. The issue brought the political branches into conflict with the courts. In Hungary, the question of the baseline became the focal point of protracted, contentious struggle between the Parliament and the Constitutional Court. Hungary's Compensation Law would have restituted only those whose property was forcibly nationalized after 1949. In a series of controversial decisions, Hungary's Constitutional Court held that the law lacked a "constitutional reason" for its 1949 baseline, excluding anyone whose property was taken in pre-1949 confiscations, such as the Jews during the war or the Germans right after the war. Equality principles, the Constitutional Court held, necessitated extending the 1949 baseline back to 1939 and treating the victims of Nazi-era takings in the same way as victims of Stalin-era takings.[62] In a similar ruling, the Czech Constitutional Court, reviewing the Law on Extrajudicial Rehabilitation, held that the baseline should be rolled back to allow restitution to victims of Nazi-era takings.[63]

After forty years of Communist rule and its pronounced ideological opposition to property rights, the question of how to recognize property rights in the law is politically freighted. Accordingly, the constitutional jurisprudence concerning the baseline controversies attempts to depoliticize the issue and to move it off the table of political deliberations in the transition. In the constitutional courts, the baseline controversies underlying postcommunist restitution were treated as a problem of constitutional dimensions, with the salient issues being adherence to principles of equal protection and the rule of law. Yet in the absence of clear preexisting property rights protection under the law, successor parliaments and courts in the region have turned to notions of higher law, for example, in international law, to construct rights. Thus, for example, in the judicial review of the Hungarian compensation scheme, the constitutional justification given is grounded in the language of "rights"; compensation claims are said to derive from the "novation of old promises."[64] Similarly, the Czech Law on Extrajudicial Rehabilitation roots the law's protection of property rights in international law protecting against takings without compensation.[65]

In the context of political transition, the baseline dilemma poses a profound puzzle. Drawing the line on state liability for past wrongdoing constructs a social understanding of legal continuity and adherence to the rule of law. Conversely, however, drawing a baseline also constructs legal discontinuity from evil regimes and a form of "undoing" of past wrongs. Examples are the

Hungarian and Czech cutoffs, where the relevant baselines are drawn and justified on the basis of the purported commencement of the "unlawful" regimes.
On this view, the baseline implies some degree of juridical discontinuity regarding the Communist regime while otherwise reaffirming continuity.

The reparation baseline controversies raise the ultimate issue intrinsic to
the transition of the vivid construction of state continuity relating reparatory
liability to political identity. For example, in Germany's Unification Treaty, the
line drawn at 1949 was justified by the end of Soviet occupation. Nevertheless,
this line-drawing could not be rationalized on the basis of the lawfulness of
the prior regime, for the period under Soviet control was at least as repressive
as that under domestic one-party rule. Instead, the principle guiding the baseline is justified by introducing the notion of the dichotomy of internal versus
external control and the guiding principle of the extent to which there is continuity of control, that is, legal continuity and the premises for regime succession. A state's willingness to assume the debts of predecessor regimes is a symbol of continuity in state identity. The converse is also true, underscoring the
relation of reparations to state identity as exemplified in post–Civil War
America's posture toward the Confederacy's Civil War debts, an act of discontinuity from this regime.[66] Transitional reparatory remedies are operative acts
that demarcate continuity of obligation and, as such, are constructive of political identity.

Across political transformations, as the postmilitary and postcommunist
cases illustrate, reparations comprise a plausible social response to persecution as well as a means to prospective political and economic transformation.
They afford a way to draw a line on the past. This is the role of transitional
reparations at their most symbolic, advancing the purpose of political transformation. Reparatory efforts are linked with the reconstruction of political identity. Reparatory schemes lend victims a restored juridical and political standing. Thus, for example, in the Latin American reparations, where the prior loss
of political and juridical status occurred through means outside the law, the
form that political rehabilitation assumes is the public apology, that is, the
public, formal repeal of the stigma of political defamation,[67] for example,
President Aylwin's address to the Chilean people, apologizing on behalf of the
nation in the public arena. By rehabilitating the disappeared, reparations draw
a line on past wrongdoing, forging a new political identity. Reparatory justice
in the form of political rehabilitation is also prevalent in the postcommunist
schemes. After the political changes in the region, many laws were passed rehabilitating the victims of Stalin-era persecution.[68] Beyond legislative rehabilitation, there have been case-by-case reviews of close to a million criminal
cases of persons previously deprived of citizenship and forcibly expelled from
the country.[69] Rehabilitation of victims of political reprisals has meant payment of compensation, as well as, where relevant, the restoration of citzen-
ship. Restoration of political status is effected by the redress of symbolic trap-
pings, such as titles and medals—even property is used this way—as public
constructions of political status, identity, and membership in the commu-

nity.[70] Entire collectives that had been previously persecuted have been rehabilitated by presidential decree.[71] Most broadly, countries' histories are being
rehabilitated in the renaming of its streets and monuments. Political rehabilitation laws explicitly recognize and endeavor to undo political persecution by
means ranging from conventional reparations to collective memorials.[72] Here
is evident the constructive role of redress in defining the state's history salient
to its political identity.

## Reparatory Justice Deferred: The Dilemma of the Passage of Time

This final part explores reparatory justice over time: What happens to transitional reparatory entitlements and obligations over time? What are the consequences of the passage of time for transitional justice? Our intuitions are that
such claims generally weaken over time.[73] Jeremy Waldron, in theorizing
about our intuitions about injustice over time, argues for the "supersession" of
injustice, for the fading of entitlements over time, as new circumstances over-
take past injustice.[74] Yet these intuitions do not appear to pertain to the transitional case; for many of the reparatory projects discussed in this chapter were
undertaken long after the relevant state persecution and often after the passage of much time. The consequences of time here seem to go against our intuitions. Indeed, as some of the practices discussed here suggest, transitional
dilemmas, in some instances, have been averted through temporizing. Thus,
for example, more than a half century after World War II atrocities, survivors
continue to receive redress. Reparatory efforts in the former Soviet bloc also
occurred after the passage of extended periods of time. Occurring after wars
and occupations, transitional redress is often long deferred; yet these reparatory practices do not appear to be diminished by time.

The experiences discussed in this chapter (and throughout the book) suggest that time operates paradoxically regarding transitional redress, and, moreover, that the primary reason is the hitherto largely unanalyzed role of the oppression of the state. Where the wrongdoing is that of the state, the passage of
time has unexpected consequences for the possibilities of transitional justice.
Time affects political change with ramifications for the conditions of justice,
but our intuitions do not well account for its effect upon victims' reparatory
rights, as well as for the state's obligation to pay compensation—consequences
that once again underscore core features that distinguish corrective justice in
the abstract from reparatory justice in transitional circumstances. The salient
feature is the role of the state in past evil and this legacy's ongoing consequences for the possibility of repair. In these circumstances, time's role is
paradoxical. The passage of time can facilitate the establishing of the fact of
past wrongs, as there is a greater political distance from the predecessor
regime and broader access to the archives of the state. Moreover, the greater
the documentation, the greater the likelihood of compensation, though the

passage of time also augments the likelihood of death. However, in these instances, redress is often made to survivors, descendants, and even victims' representatives.

After time, the dilemma of transitional reparatory projects that are temporized or postponed raises profound problems of intergenerational justice. Whereas, in conventional corrective justice, victims are repaired by their wrongdoers, and, even when not from identified wrongdoers, by the wrongdoer's political generation, in transitional reparatory projects, victims' payments ordinarily come from general government funds. The passage of time implies change regarding the identities of not only the beneficiaries but also those doing the paying. Yet, with the passage of time, what is troubling is that those paying for past wrongs are successor generations that are supposedly personally unimplicated in the prior wrongdoing. Is it just that the present generation should pay for the wrongs perpetrated by regimes long gone?

The question raises a serious problem of intergenerational justice. In general, the central problem of intergenerational justice concerns the fairness of the present generation's making sacrifices for future generations. A quarter of a century ago, John Rawls characterized the problem thus: "How much better off are we to make our successors?"[75] Nevertheless, of late, the question of justice between generations is reconfigured, and a less-rosy picture of the future takes shape. The direction of future societal resources concerns less the question of accumulation than of degradation. The question of justice between the generations is formulated anew.[76] The transitional problematic introduced here illuminates yet another dimension to the question of intergenerational justice. Reparatory justice after time raises the peculiar intergenerational questions of what obligation the successor regimes owe victims of earlier generations and whether it is fair to lay this burden on the present or later generations.

The fairness of reparations after time is a profound question for transitional societies struggling with these obligations. The precedents examined here shed light on what justifies a successor regime's assumption of responsibility after the passage of time, clarifying what are salient considerations to a state's inherited legacy of wrongdoing. For example, contemporary reparatory schemes intended to redress Stalin-era injustices illustrated the dilemma of the passage of time, as these have been challenged as a case of one generation's paying for the losses of another and generally justified in moral terms.[77] In another example, more than a half century after the war, in Germany, the legacy of state wrongdoing is characterized as the country's "moral deficit."[78] The question is interpreted as involving the inheritance of a moral legacy. This intuition has several implications. For example, despite the apparent absence of personal wrongdoing, in the successor generation, there is, nevertheless, the sense that successor generations succeed to bad predecessor policies by which they have unjustly benefited. Another way to think about this is as the prior generation's having squandered precious national moral resources, a deficit passed on to subsequent generations, which, ultimately, must assume the debt. Societies in transition deliberating over reparatory schemes after time reflect just this understanding of moral deficit. Debates over whether reparatory measures are justified treat the problem of transitional reparatory justice between generations as involving the inheritance of a "deficit" in the country's moral resources. It is just this sort of moral language that justified reparations in the deliberations concerning Germany's war-related payments to victims of Nazi persecution.[79] Reparation payments appear to serve as cancellations, or exchange, for the buildup of moral capital. Similarly, in the postmilitary Latin American redress schemes, reparations' stated purposes include restoration of the state's moral credibility.[80] Similar language resounding with moral considerations appears in other reparatory policies, such as in the American compensation scheme for citizens of Japanese-American descent interned during World War II. Almost a half century after massive governmental violations of the civil rights and liberties in the wartime detention and internment of American citizens of Japanese ancestry, an investigative commission established that racial prejudice, not military security, was the basis for the internment and recommended an apology and governmental reparations.[81] The Japanese Civil Liberties Act of 1988 formally acknowledged the injustice to Japanese-Americans during World War II and provided for compensation to individuals of Japanese ancestry who were interned.[82] In 1990, a full forty-eight years after President Franklin Roosevelt's original discriminatory executive order, President George Bush formally apologized for the country.[83] Restoration of the country's moral standing was given as the reason for the congressional reparation.

After the passage of time, reparatory acts become increasingly symbolic, often taking on the form of an apology, which is illustrated in the responses to wartime inhumanity half a century later in the form of the congressional apology. Apologies are also seen in responses to other historic struggles, such as slavery and segregation. As time passes, the harm inflicted is largely a reputational one in the public eye and, therefore, redressable by political apology. After the passage of time, transitional justice is more likely to take this form. Despite prevailing theorizing that views the emergence of the apology response as a function of culture,[84] the experiences reviewed here introduce another, perhaps more salient, factor, namely the association of transitional justice with the passage of time.

The ongoing concern with moral standing underscores the profound force of evil legacies as challenges to the legitimacy of liberalizing states. This concern goes some way towards explaining why successor generations assume heavy obligations for the past. Though the initial wrongdoing and liability originate in predecessor generations, such evil legacies imply long-standing societal concerns, often with grave implications for contemporary and future successor generations. In considerations of criminal justice, similar conceptions of collective responsibility emerge in transition. When unaddressed after time, the sense of injustice is only heightened. Moreover, after time the reparatory measures serve as symbols of transition and can be used to consolidate the liberalizing gains of the transition. Indeed, a contemporary regime's succession to old obligations demonstrates how the assumption of collective responsibility constitutes a state's political identity over time.

## The Persistence of Unresolved Reparatory Justice and Contemporary Politics: The Dilemma of "Affirmative Action"

With the passage of time, reparatory projects move farther from the traditional model of corrective justice. After time, wrongdoers don't pay; innocents do. And, after time, redress goes not to original victims but to their descendants. With the passage of time, therefore, reparatory schemes look less like conventional corrective justice and more like a social distribution and political question. Policies for reparations that are not directed at identifiable victims but to victims' representative groups identified along the lines of past persecution look more like distributive schemes. Such distributive schemes are controversial, because the allocations seemingly collide with principles of liberal democracy and rule-of-law systems. At issue, for example, is the fairness of allocating public and private benefits along racial lines in the United States—the issue of "affirmative action."

Consider the contemporary controversies over race-based affirmative action as an as yet unresolved problem of transitional reparatory justice. Grave official persecution of African Americans was perpetrated in the United States over different centuries, first, through government-tolerated slavery and, then, through official segregation. After the country's Civil War, there were reparatory proposals, the most well known being "forty acres and a mule."[85] Nevertheless, as of yet, there has not even been any formal acknowledgment of state wrongdoing or reparations for past rights violations, though the question remains a matter of contemporary controversy and debate.[86] There has been a call for governmental apologies, as previously discussed, that could serve as a symbolic reparation. There is also ongoing debate over affirmative action remedies, for example, whether some form of governmental benefits allocated along a racial basis is justified to remedy prior official discrimination.[87]

In the prevailing approach, the issue of affirmative action is generally framed doctrinally as a problem of conventional corrective justice. Race-conscious remedies are justified only insofar as those who have suffered wrongful race-based harm have a right to recover from those who have wronged them. The current constitutional approach conceives of the rights as harm-based; that is, there must be ongoing effects of prior official discrimination and, as in traditional corrective justice, some connection to the entity doing the remedying.[88] In the prevailing approach, there must be a specific finding connecting the governmental entity administering the remedial scheme to the prior discrimination; the actual wrongdoer must pay.[89] But after the passage of time, analogizing the affirmative action problem to conventional corrective justice seems inapposite. The "original" wrongdoers are gone; the "original" victims, too, have dropped out of the question. How, then, to account for what remains? It is the legacy of unrepaired political persecution, an instance of unresolved transitional reparatory justice after time.

Let us rethink the problem posed by affirmative action, guided by the transitional precedents and principles. The experiences reviewed in this chapter suggest that successor governments frequently undertake obligations to redress victims of the predecessor regime's persecution and that such obligations are often assumed after the passage of time. In the former Soviet bloc, it is close to a half century since some of the relevant (Stalin-era) state wrongs. While the prevailing approach to affirmative action is frequently justified on the basis of ongoing harm or persistent effects of persecution, transitional justice is not dependent on such a showing. After the passage of time, while there often remains only an attenuated link to the originally aggrieved parties, what nevertheless persists in the society is the sense of an unrepaired state wrong. The persistence of the political issue and the incidence of reparatory measures over time attest to the state's recognition and assumption of obligations to repair the political wrongs inflicted by prior regimes. Out of the precedents emerges a conception of transitional reparatory justice characterized by a distinct historical legacy. When the state has turned on its own citizens along racial, ethnic, religious, and political lines, the need for the vindication of the rule of law and the attendant political transformation is not extinguished by the mere passage of time.

While in most of the instances discussed, the reparatory issue is generally dealt with by the first successor regime, in the United States, the question has by now become the legacy of repeated successor governments. An example relates to American treatment of Native Americans after World War II.[90] Reparatory schemes have been haphazard, athough, at the very least, there has been some official recognition of past wrongs. Reparations for the wartime internment of Japanese-Americans have been more comprehensive. In the case of the Japanese-American internees, reparations were assumed as a national obligation, despite the passage of time. What triggered the right to redress was the governmental acknowledgment of a hitherto unacknowledged and unrepaired state wrong. The conventional affirmative action question, whether there are "ongoing effects" of past persecution, was not even raised. Instead, psychologically stigmatizing effects were simply assumed to result from state-sponsored discrimination and from repeated successor governments' ongoing failure to remedy. As in other transitional precedents discussed in this chapter (regarding disappearances), the successor governments' continued failures to respond in and of themselves are deemed part of the ongoing wrong. If enduring wrongs have been taken notice of in the Japanese-American internment involving ethnic persecution over a relatively short period, so much more so does this militate for addressing the far more sustained African-American experience of slavery, segregation, and discrimination.

Transitional practices, principles, and values discussed in this chapter could illuminate and help guide contemporary affirmative action schemes.[91] Perhaps the most controversial feature of reparatory practices after time is the awarding of benefits, not to original victims, but to their descendants and representatives. Here, transitional practices offer useful comparative experience.

Thus, for example, many of the post-Soviet schemes adopted more than forty years after the beginning of the political persecution contemplate entitlements to the original victim's heirs. Czech law expressly recognizes claims belonging to the original victims' children's children—fully two generations removed from the original persecution.[92] Perhaps the best example remains the post–World War II German reparatory scheme, under which reparations have been issued redressing past persecution despite the fact that, in many instances, entire families and villages were exterminated and that, therefore, the survivors or heirs could not inherit. The German reparations precedent exemplifies the successorship to victims' rights of special representative bodies created for this purpose.[93]

The historical precedents reflect practices that this book terms "representative reparations," awarded by successor governments to successor classes of victims to vindicate past state wrongs. Recognizing the significance of representative reparations helps to explain the persistence of affirmative action and similar controversies, despite the passage of time. Representative reparations signal that what justifies a successor government's assumption of reparatory policy after time beyond the original wrongdoing is the distinctive violation of unrecognized and unrepaired state persecution, an ongoing threat to the rule of law. Transitional reparatory precedents across legal cultures reveal a core reality: Legacies of state oppression do not simply go away of their own accord, though they are often temporized over a nation's lifetime.

## The Dilemma of the Transitory Tort

What of reparatory justice when the state fails to recognize such rights? Where do the rights go? Is their vindication tied to the successor regime, or are they vindicable elsewhere? A series of cases in the United States concerning the most serious wrongs, "gross abuses" of human rights, suggest that in the worst cases of persecution, the vindication of victims' rights is not confined to the borders of the implicated state. This is often seen in the beginning, at transition's incipience, since during this time those implicated in prior wrongdoing commonly flee their countries seeking safe haven.

When Joel Filartiga's death by torture in Paraguay was denied by the regime in power, his family's relentless search for justice led them to the United States, where the perpetrator, Paraguay's former police chief, had fled. In a case that would become a landmark precedent for victims of state abuses to vindicate their reparatory rights in American courts, the family relied on a two-hundred-year-old law, the Alien Tort Act, dating back to the country's founding, which created jurisdiction in the United States courts for suits against foreigners for violations of the "law of nations."[94] Guided by the analogy to piracy, the appellate court held that "official torture" was a violation of the "law of nations" and, therefore, that suit could be brought anywhere.[95] "For the purposes of civil liability, the torturer has become—like the pirate and slave trader before him—*hostis humani generis*, an enemy of all mankind."[96]

Compensatory claims deriving from rights protected under the "law of nations" traditionally were considered transitory causes of action and, as such, could be brought in jurisdictions other than where the claim arose. Deliberate torture, like piracy, violated the law of nations; accordingly, reparatory rights arising out of official torture were to be treated as transitory claims.

The case of Joel Filartiga spawned a long line of so-called alien tort cases, generally involving either official torture or unlawful executions. In *Forti* and *Siderman*, suits were brought against Argentine torturers found in the United States. Acts of torture attributed to Argentina were held to constitute violations of "jus cogens" norms; peremptory norms of international law are those from which no derogation is permissible and that have universal applicability and protection.[97] *In re Estate of Marcos* concerned a suit regarding torture in the Philippines brought against Ferdinand Marcos, its former president.[98] In all these cases, victims or their families initiated suits against their perpetrators in the United States. The jurisdictional principle followed is that in cases of political persecution, civil liability is transitory and follows the perpetrator.

The Alien Tort Act precedents, guided by the piracy analogy, relied on the fiction of an individual outlaw and a seemingly traditional idea of corrective justice whereby civil liability follows the lone wrongdoer. Perhaps the extreme case is epitomized by a recent alien tort suit, in which Radovan Karadžić, the Bosnian Serbs' top political leader, is being held civilly accountable for thousands of atrocities committed under the policy of ethnic persecution he advanced in the Balkans.[99]

The central conception of the transitory tort, that liability follows the tortfeasor, is paradoxical. Where does wrongdoing fairly lie? Regarding torture generally committed under color of state law—encouraged or condoned by the state—who should be held responsible? To what extent are transition-related reparatory claims arising out of modern state persecution fairly attributable to an individual wrongdoer?[100]

To some extent, the alien tortfeasor is a juridical construct best understood as a sort of pragmatic resolution characteristic of justice in nonideal circumstances. When a regime is responsible, it cannot be so held in the implicated country's domestic courts.[101] Furthermore, foreign governments are largely immune from suit in American courts for reasons of sovereign immunity. The practical resolution is to resort to concepts of traditional private civil liability. Yet the paradox of the resort to the "alien tort" for redress of human rights–related wrongs is that, while the cause of action allows for individual liability, it also recognizes that the wrongs at stake are committed against a background of state policy. Though the Alien Tort Act creates a cause of action against individual wrongdoers, jurisdiction is largely based on "official" wrongs perpetrated under color of state law. Only a small class of perpetrators fits this bill, as they have to have acted in their official capacity, under color of state law, and their actions must have clearly violated the law of nations. At the same time, the claims must have somehow circumvented the defense of sovereign immunity, that is, the immunization of foreign states from jurisdiction, subject to exceptions. Violations on which there is the greatest consensus are torture, summary executions, and genocide,[102] characterized as "jus cogens" norms with the highest status within international law, assuming a backdrop of state, or statelike, policy.[103]

It is almost two decades since *Filartiga's* landmark holding, and during that time there have been many declaratory judgments holding liable human rights violators. Indeed, the remedy has been ratified into federal law: The Torture Victim Protection Act authorizes civil actions for monetary damages for abuses such as official torture and summary executions if the perpetrator is within the jurisdiction.[104]

Over the years, declaratory judgments have been much more frequent than payments.[105] Recognition of civil liability has an impact beyond monetary judgment. In these cases, civil liability has implied public sanction because of the media attention that attends civil actions involving high-level foreign public officials. Publicity's impact is such that, during the pendency of litigation, defendants generally flee the country. The attribution of individual liability, notwithstanding its civil nature, results in something of the stigma and social censure associated with the criminal sanction. The incidence of reparatory justice-seeking measures across state borders, like its incidence after the passage of time, exemplifies these remedies' complex and dynamic role. Though civil remedies are ordinarily intended to vindicate victims' rights, to make them whole, like other transitional measures previously discussed, the alien tort suit serves purposes ordinarily associated with the criminal sanction, such as the recognition of governmental wrongdoing and the exclusion of perpetrators from the community. Indeed, the transitory tort elucidates the linkage between vindication of victims' rights, recognition of individual wrongdoing, and state persecution. The emergence of the transitory tort in cases of persecution points to a conception of reparatory justice with affinities to other transitional legal responses.

In mediating the public and the private, the individual and the collective, the national and international, the alien tort effectively responds to the offense of persecution characterizing modern repression. Like the "crime against humanity," the transitory tort for human rights abuses illuminates a similar conception: a cause of action that somehow transcends the jurisdictions of time and space, conceived here as the "tort against humanity." This tort emerges as a response to a distinctive form of contemporary governmental persecution, in a cause of action that brings together the individual implicated in a broader persecutory policy. Furthermore, the tort against humanity challenges ordinary intuitions whereby civil causes of action are related to particular jurisdictions, which only inaptly captures instances of grave wrongdoing that implicate the state itself in persecution. With the breakdown of ordinary jurisdictional parameters, the "foreign" is rendered "domestic," and the international offense is redefined. And though they may well be vindicated outside the national legal system, by recognizing victims' rights, these actions nevertheless commence a process of transition. Even where there is not yet regime change and the circumstances associated with political change are largely absent, the affirming of core human rights norms can nevertheless play a constructive role. These transitional legal responses evince the emergence of fluid, nuanced approaches to sovereignty and jurisdiction. These departures from conventional principles are rationalized in terms of the nature of the state behavior and the extent to which it adheres to the international community's rule of law.

## Transitional Reparatory Justice

The practices discussed point to a paradigm of reparatory justice associated with transitional times. The paradigm of transitional reparatory justice is a complex conception, as it does work advancing multiple purposes mediating and constructing the transition. Transitional reparations publicly recognize and instantiate individual rights that are, in a sense, predominantly symbolic. Often they are not truly compensatory, bearing little or no relation to the material loss, exemplified in the Latin American "moral reparations" or postcommunist rehabilitations. Transitional reparations take many forms: They can be in kind, as in property restitutions, monetary payments, or nonconventional redress, such as education vouchers or other collective public benefits, such as memorials, legislative rehabilitations, and apologies.

The transitional reparatory paradigm differs from our prevailing intuitions about corrective justice in a number of respects.[106] The transitional conception lacks the symmetry of the private tort system, as it reconceives the relation of victim to wrongdoer, of individual to collective.[107] Whereas in the prevailing understanding, the repair of victims falls to the offenders, transitional reparatory measures provide official recognition of victims' rights and yet without necessarily individuating wrongdoing. Rather than the individual wrongdoer or even the culpable regime, it is successor regimes that assume liability for prior wrongful acts.[108] Transitional reparations transform the conventional civil action in differentiating and separating the attribution of responsibility for the individual rights violation from the assumption of redress. In traditional compensatory principles, harmful behavior and related liability are attributed to identified persons, but transitional reparations are generally obligations undertaken by the state. The shift in reparatory principle affirms the transcendence of the conventional principle of individual responsibility, replaced by collective responsibility in the transition. Notions of joint individual/collective responsibility emerge in many of the transitional legal responses discussed throughout this book, complicating understandings of state wrongdoing and shedding light on the problematized circumstances of justice in such times.

Further, reparatory understandings implying state assumptions of responsibility are ways to construct continued political identity. Transitions, unlike ordinary administration shifts, are not instances of simply succeeding to prior state obligations, for the prior regime failed to assume such obligations. This is the paradox of reparatory transitions. Whereas between ordinary shifts in administration, the assumption of debts simply expresses continuity in state identity and in the rule of law, when there are transitions between political systems, the determination of whether to assume responsibility allows for the construction of political continuity, or discontinuity and normative change.

Transitional reparatory justice is not justified primarily by conventional corrective concerns, but, rather, by external political values related to the political exigencies of the time. A related normative principle emerges concerning what is a compensable difference regarding prior state treatment. In transitional practices, however, the law in its reparatory function advances purposes that are explicitly political. The state's justifications for reparations are multiple and complex, based on traditional corrective aims, as well as on transformative redistributive purposes. The "political persecution" principle guides transitional reparatory justice, serving as a restrictive principle, cabining potentially limitless reparatory projects, as well as mediating individual and collective responsibility. Reparations are even used to justify the transition, for such claims are said to derive from past derogations from equality justifying the break with the prior regime. Redress constitutes a primary symbol of discontinuity with the past, exercising the new regime's critical transformative potential. The significance of redress goes beyond vindicating individual claims, constructing the transitional society's move to the liberal state. As signs and practices of liberal rule of law, remedial measures enable a renewed commitment to political equality and against repression. Even after the passage of time, these practices persist in highly symbolic forms, capable of reviving liberalizing individual rights norms. Even where there is not yet political transition, reparations comprise modern symbols of liberalization, illustrating a dynamic approach toward rights instantiation in a global age.

## CHAPTER FIVE

# Administrative Justice

*T*his chapter turns to where the law itself is the engine of revolutionary change. In negotiated political transitions, the transformation often depends on the force of law. Politicized public law can effect radical change when it distributes power explicitly on the basis of the new ideology. Sweeping politicized administrative measures have been pervasive in periods of political change worldwide: after the American Civil War, in the shift from slave to free state; in postwar Europe, in the shift from fascism to democracy; in postcommunist Europe, in the shift from totalitarian to freer market economies; in postmilitary Latin America, in the shift to civilian rule. The asserted purpose of the politicized exercise of administrative law is always the noble one of guarding the transition; nevertheless, this use of the law, grounded as it is in categorical judgment, resembles the political justice of totalitarian regimes. Such measures raise the question, What is the relation of illiberal means to liberal ends? Where an illiberal ideology has permeated society, what is the hope for moving that society toward a more liberal political system? What is the potential for revolution by law? To what extent do transitional societies rely on past political behavior as the basis for transformation? What if any are the normative parameters? What justifies the overtly political measures? How can the successor regime's interest be reconciled with concerns for individual rights? The inevitable dilemma is one of means and ends. Is transitional administrative justice a necessary evil on the road to societal transformation?

The core dilemma is eloquently captured in an exchange between Arthur Koestler and Maurice Merleau-Ponty about the Stalinist purges. In their argument, Koestler and Merleau-Ponty invoke the figures of the "commissar" and the "yogi" to represent opposing sides: The commissar defends political purges because he believes in revolution and that "the end justifies the use of all means;" the yogi opposes the purges because he believes in the impossibility of revolutionary change, which leads him to conclude that since "the end is unpredictable, . . . the means alone count."[1] It is this question, What are the uses and justifications for explicitly political measures adopted in periods of radical political change? This is the subject of this chapter.

After repressive rule, a central question is, What is the relation of an evil regime to its subjects? Revolution implies change at the top; nevertheless, to effect substantial political change, mere personnel change at the highest echelon is often not enough, and transitional societies rely on administrative measures broadly to redistribute power among classes of citizens. How do societies undergoing massive transformation reason about the uses of political class-based measures? Our intuitions are to conceptualize such measures in sharply antinomic fashion: as retrospective punishment versus prospective conditions on the political order. These transitional administrative measures appear paradoxical, defying intuitions premised on law in ordinary times. In some sense, the measures seem forward-looking, intended to effect political transformation. In another sense, however, transitional administrative measures appear backward-looking, like punitive sanctions. In their backward-looking features, these responses resemble criminal justice; whereas in their forward-looking features, the measures are sweeping attempts to shape the political community, institutions, and processes, and in this way administrative justice resembles constitutional measures.

Related to the tension of their simultaneous backward- and forward-looking nature is the way the subjects of regulation are both the individual and the collective. Criminal justice primarily seeks to establish individual responsibility for wrongdoing, but the tyranny of the modern bureaucratic state diffuses responsibility throughout the polity; thus the ordinary workings of criminal justice are inapposite, particularly when those implicated in prior repression go not only unpunished but also on to positions of power under the new regime. Whereas criminal sanctions are generally predicated on individual wrongdoing, civil sanctions of an administrative nature are based on exclusionary conditions, chiefly of political loyalty, systematically disqualifying entire classes from participation in the new government.

The categorical judgments that recur over and over in these transitional measures assume a harsh form: a negative politics of exclusion, evocative of the political theory of Thomas Hobbes, later more pronounced in the writing of Carl Schmitt, where "political actions and motives can be reduced [to] that between friend and enemy."[2] A politicized public law easily instantiates a new political regime, as it demonstrably shifts the site of the sovereign constitutive power.

Collective responses of an ideological nature are inextricably bound up in the politics of transformation. The dilemmas of administrative justice are illustrated in experiences spanning ancient times, post–Civil War United States, postwar Europe, postmilitary Americas, and contemporary decommunization in the former Soviet bloc. The measures illustrate that practical resolutions at the juncture of law and politics are elaborated in periods of upheaval. Considered together, common processes and justifications reveal how the forms of these measures are not dichotomous, at war with their purposes but intimately bound up in their transformative purposes. Exploration of these historical instances below illustrate these practices' role in the radical work of transformation.

## Sodom and Gomorrah: The Purges of the Evil Cities

The central question pursued in this chapter concerns the relation of the individual to the political collective and how the relation is normatively reconceived and restructured in times of radical political transformation. Going back to ancient times, this question is understood to be central to the possibility for political change. It appears in the biblical account of the famous dialogue over the proposed destruction of Sodom and Gomorrah, two ancient cities said to be corrupt.[3] The cities mistreated alien visitors by a range of offenses—from the absence of hospitality owed visitors to the far more heinous offense of rape. After these atrocities were committed, the questions were, What response is appropriate? and, Should the cities be destroyed for their sins? The dilemma was whether to destroy the cities, if it would mean destroying righteous persons along with the wicked. The central questions were, What is the relation that the citizens bear to the political identity of the city? and, At what point does the existence of virtuous citizens affect the identity of the city?

The biblical story suggests nuanced, textured relations between the political identities of the cities and that of its citizens, between the individual and the collective. The city cannot be saved by the existence of merely one virtuous person. In the ensuing negotiations, the number of righteous necessary to save the city beginning with fifty, "If I find in Sodom fifty righteous within the city, then I will spare all the place for their sakes," is argued down to ten, "I will not destroy, for the sake of the ten."[4] There is a turning point in the relation between the identity of the individual and that of the city that stakes out a threshold for the identity of the political collective.

Moreover, is the mere existence of some good persons enough? Saving the city raises a question not just about sufficient numbers of good men but about what it takes to constitute a political community. The account says that virtuous persons need be found "within the city," understood to mean that they must participate in the public sphere.[5] In the city worth saving, there are at least ten citizens making up a politically participatory community. Indeed, this understanding of political virtue as implying a predicate of participation in public life is borne out in later political (Aristotelian) theory. The message of what constitutes community as a normative matter is reinforced elsewhere in the biblical story. Beyond this question is that of the appropriate relation of the individual to the collective, established in the redefinition of political affiliation in terms of threshold membership and participation. The sins committed by the corrupt cities are in and of themselves relevant to a perversion of community, for they have violated basic principles of social justice involving the mistreatment of aliens. Going back to ancient times, foreign civilians falling outside the political community are nevertheless owed, as a normative matter, a threshold level of protective treatment across national lines. The question of what response is owed—to the persecution of outsiders, outside the community's protection of the law—becomes a trope that resonates from ancient times up to the modern period.

In the biblical account, the cities' legitimacy is a matter to be established. The cities are ultimately destroyed but not sight unseen. "The outrage of Sodom and Gomorrah is so great, and their sin so grave! I will go down to *see*."[6] Even when one might have assumed omniscience, there is investigation. Political truth, that is, loyalty, is a matter that is established in public processes, in its circumstances and over time. As in this ancient illustration, it is these processes of "evaluation" that comprise administrative justice, epitomized in more contemporary political rituals of lustration, discussed later in this chapter.

Though liberal intuitions emphasize the significance of individual action, the predicate for change to a civil society as suggested in the ancient account is not simply an individual matter but involves a relation between individual and collective. The biblical purges of the evil cities suggest that the polity's identity is predicated on the notion of a threshold political collective. There is also the relation of the cities' past to their future: The cities' past evil legacies have profound implications as their legacy is fateful for their political future. The verdict is radical and absolute. Because of their evil past, the cities have no future. Political transformation is necessary to political survival, and, despite liberal intuitions that are often construed to privilege the role of the individual, the project of political transformation is predicated on the existence of a participatory body. The ancient biblical purges of the corrupt cities is an early instance of the role of collective sanctions in political transition. Ultimately the biblical purges illustrate the boundedness of and limits on the possibility of change.

## Reconstructing America

Perhaps the greatest experiment in the reconstruction of political identity through the public law occurs in the nineteenth century. It is of particular relevance because it illuminates both the role of ongoing political conflict over the scope of political change and the sort of constraints placed on overtly political measures applied in a constitutional democracy.

After the American Civil War, the period known as Reconstruction was a time of national struggle over the transformation of the Union. The period presented the dilemma of how to respond to an agonizing, bloody conflict and a bitter time in the country's history, when political differences were resolved outside the Constitution. It is this illegality—the extraconstitutional nature of the Civil War—that was the Reconstruction's point of departure. If the Civil War and the Confederate secession were conceptualized to have occurred outside the law, the question became how to characterize the South's broken allegiance. How was the Union wronged? By the "rebel" states, as states, or by their constituent members, as "rebel" citizens? And, whether by individuals or states, what did Reconstruction imply? It implied more than restoration—to "reconstruct" meant greater political change. It raised the question of what ought to be the new relation between the Union's past and its future, rebel states and citizens. Reconstruction illuminates the possible restructurings of individual, citizen, and state, in radical political upheaval.

To what extent could rebel states become full and equal participants in the new Union? Should past political loyalty be relevant to future political representation in the Union? Should the rebel states, and their citizens, be considered treasonous and criminal? And, despite their wartime criminal status, would Confederates and sympathizers be restored? Criminal measures were largely eschewed, other than the prosecutions of Confederate leader Jefferson Davis and Captain Henry Wirz, chief of Andersonville prison camp. Could a democratic Union, nevertheless, be forged by unreconstructed Confederates? Even if one might imagine reconstitution with Confederate supporters, at the very least, a line would be drawn at the top echelon predicated on change in southern leadership and representation. Post–Civil War America reveals the profound struggle over how to respond to disloyalty and how to secure fidelity to a newly unified national government.

The foundation of Reconstruction policy was the secession and its illegality. As a threshold political and juridical parameter, new constitutional amendments were passed declaring the illegality of the secession. The secession's illegality implied legal discontinuity between regimes, the Confederacy and the Union. This illegality was made explicit in a constitutional provision repudiating responsibility for the debts incurred by the rebel states during the war.[7] Even if it was beyond debate that the Confederacy had been destroyed as a legal entity, the seceding states persisted as political and juridical entities, raising the questions of how their rights would be restored and how they would be reincorporated into the Union. In the reconstituted Union, sweeping public measures placed political disabilities on the Confederate states and their citizens, redefining the political parameters of the Union largely through constitutional law.[8]

Throughout Reconstruction, ever present were the seemingly paralleling questions about how to treat the rebel states and their citizens and what transitional policy guided this relation. American Reconstruction implied a change in the relations of the individual and the collective, the citizen and the state. Indeed, the displacement of the slave regime and the consolidation of the republic depended on a restructuring of the relation. Throughout history, test oaths have been used to help consolidate a fragile and divided political community. The more fractured the polity, the greater the pressure to unify. In the lenient form of Reconstruction policy advocated by then-President Abraham Lincoln, prospective oaths were imposed on prior Confederate supporters only to secure their future allegiance to the Union. Moreover, Lincoln's proposed loyalty oaths, would have been universally applicable, intended as public acts of consent to the new government, as constitutive oaths of allegiance.[9] Such oaths harked back to the earlier transition from England, whereby the American Constitution provides for oaths to the Constitution by individuals as predicates to their holding public office, representing the reconstruction of allegiance from a faraway king to a constitution. Whenever 10 percent of a Confederate state agreed to take an oath of allegiance to the United States, the new state government would be recognized, and pardons and property restitution would follow. Lincoln's loyalty oaths were intended to enable transformation from rebel states to the legally restored southern states, but the plan was short-lived, and another more punitive policy followed.

Reconstruction policy predicated on constitutional conditions in the Fourteenth Amendment was largely prospective in nature; the conditions placed on the southern states and their citizens for reentry to the Union implied a broad commitment to a core principle of equality under law. Rehabilitation of states was conditioned on compliance with the Fourteenth and Fifteenth Amendments, and terms ratified by state legislatures before eligibility for congressional representation in the Union.[10] Similarly, constitutional conditions disqualified from public office anyone who had previously broken his oath to support the Constitution, by engaging in rebellion. The legislative history makes clear that the constitutional disabilities were intended to exclude former Confederate leadership and others from public office.

> No person shall be a Senator or Representative in Congress, or Elector of President and Vice-President, or hold any office, civil or military, under the United States, or under any state, who having previously taken an oath, as a member of Congress, or as an officer of the United States, or as a member of any State legislature, or as an executive or judicial officer of any State, to support the Constitution of the United States, shall have engaged in insurrection or rebellion against the same, or given aid or comfort to the enemies thereof.[11]

These constitutional disabilities were given force by the enactment of "ironclad" oaths, whereby deponents would attest to past allegiance to the Union as a condition for future public service. With rehabilitation predicated on these ironclad oaths, the country's political identity was defined chiefly in response to the former regime. While Lincoln's loyalty oaths were affirmative expressions of forward-looking future allegiance, the so-called ironclad oaths were just the reverse, backward-looking expressions of renunciation. Like ancient canonical oaths,[12] the ironclad oaths served as tests of political truth, employed to clear persons of a charge or suspicion of guilt by assertion on oath. Despite the ironclad oaths' harshness, the Reconstruction amendments' constitutional language reflects deep ambivalence about their imposition. Unlike other constitutional provisions that are apparently self-enforcing, operation of the political disabilities is predicated on the existence of an ongoing political consensus. Even more telling, in the constitutional amendments, Congress is explicitly given power to remove the constitutional disabilities,[13] suggesting the Reconstruction amendments lacked the usual constitutional status and, instead, always were considered provisional measures—to last only as long as deemed politically necessary.

Reconstruction's political disabilities were ultimately short-lived. Over a period of years, Congress regularly exercised its removal powers, enacting amnesty legislation, steadily lifting disabilities.[14] In the Forty-second Congress, the disabilities were refined to exclude only a higher political echelon. In 1872, at the urging of then—President Ulysses Grant, Congress exempted everyone from the constitutional disabilities except top political officers, such as congressional representatives and federal judges. Finally, in 1878, six years after their enactment, even these limited disabilities were removed, leaving only the constitutional disenfranchisement provisions. Nevertheless, the constitutional disabilities continued to operate as warnings, as de facto disqualifications from public employ on a political basis. Reconstruction-era political disabilities remained forever in the text of the American Constitution, where they stand as an enduring expression of the historical politics that shaped the identity of the American Union.

Reconstruction policy was controversial for its basic realigning of federal-state relations, which accordingly would be challenged in the courts. The constitutional question at issue concerned what principles governed relations between the federal and state governments, governments and citizens. In a federal system, what government has the authority to determine the status and rights of citizens, and to whom do citizens owe their allegiance? Moreover, what bearing did these questions have for the reconstitution of the states' political identity?

In its review, the United States Supreme Court generally deferred to the political branches and their Reconstruction agenda. In *Mississippi v. Johnson*, *Georgia v. Stanton*, and *Texas v. White*, cases involving challenges by secessionist states to new governmental limits, the Supreme Court affirmed Reconstruction policy.[15] The constitutional guarantee of a "republican" form of government was held a political obligation that formed the basis for Reconstruction legislation. Generally upholding policy transformative of the Union's federal-state balance of power, the Court also reaffirmed the role of the political branches by allowing Congress to control access to judicial review on Reconstruction issues through its constitutional removal powers.[16] While largely deferential to Congress, the Court nevertheless drew the line on Reconstruction policy in some instances. Despite congressional attempts to extend postwar military justice, the Supreme Court insisted on access to peacetime courts and due process.[17] In the so-called test oath cases, *Ex Parte Garland* and *Cummings v. Missouri*, decided in 1866, the Court considered and struck down the constitutionality of political disabilities on Confederate sympathizers. *Ex parte Garland* concerned the constitutionality of the congressional ironclad oaths, challenged by an attorney precluded from taking the oath because he was an officer of the court in Arkansas, a Confederate state. The oath's impact was to exclude him from the practice of law because of past status.[18] A companion case, *Cummings v. Missouri*, concerned a challenge to a similar oath imposed under a state constitution. As a condition of eligibility to vote in the state, as well as of holding public office, teaching, and engaging in other professions, including the priesthood, the Missouri State Constitution required affiants to attest to whether they had ever been "in armed hostility to the United States" or "had ever, by act or word manifested . . . adherence to the cause of [its] enemies."[19]

In *Garland* and *Cummings*, a divided Court struck down the Reconstruction-era oaths, holding that despite their superficial resemblance to civil sanctions, in effect, these constituted impermissible punishment. The relevant question of whether the test oaths could be considered valid qualifications to public employ, the Court said, depended on the nature of the connection between the relevant conduct and the affected employment, that is the strength of the relation between the legislative means and the asserted ends. Pursuing this inquiry, the oaths' sweeping breadth, the Court held, belied the asserted governmental purpose of assuring loyalty to the Union. The imposition of political conditionality was deemed, in effect, to be a punitive policy. Thus, despite the oaths' civil form, the deprivation of rights previously enjoyed constituted punishment. Blanket disabilities without a more specific connection to the organization's unlawful purposes posed an unconstitutional burden on freedom of association. Freedoms of speech and rights were at issue as well as whether there was a sufficiently direct nexus between the political disqualification and the conditioned employment. Rejecting the government's asserted Reconstruction-related purposes, the Court said that, as a constitutional matter, such measures could not simply be rationalized in terms of the transformation.

The post–Civil War disabilities hardly comport with our intuitions about punishment in ordinary times: Indeed, constitutional interpretation of the Reconstruction-era measures was guided by other transitional precedents deriving from other periods of radical political change in Anglo-American history. Reconstruction-era laws were analogous to those forbidden by the Constitution's "bill of attainder" clause. Like bills of attainder, Reconstruction-era oaths were considered to constitute punishment inflicted without the usual judicial process. The absence of judicial processes ordinarily associated with punishment, such as protection against retroactivity, rendered the oaths unconstitutional. Throughout Anglo-American history, similar measures had been imposed, first, by the English Parliament in periods of monarchical excess and, again, by the states after the Revolution. What characterized the measures was that they were legislatively imposed, politically based deprivations. Throughout history, such legislative sanctions were traditionally used to repress the political opposition. As the Court observed, these were "[m]ost usually passed in England in times of rebellion, or gross subserviency to the crown, or of violent political excitements; periods, in which all nations are most liable . . . to forget their duties, and to trample upon the rights and liberties of others."[20] Whereas English bills of attainder lacked transformative justification, Reconstruction's political disabilities might have been so justified and yet, nevertheless, were held impermissible legislative punishment, despite the existence of transformative rationale.[21]

Today, the conventional understanding of Reconstruction-era jurisprudence is to consider it as obstructionist to the project of transformation of the time.[22] The period is generally considered a low point in the Court's jurisprudence and frequently omitted from constitutional law surveys. Yet, the above analysis invites rethinking the doctrine of this period. Considered in the light of similar transitional phenomena in other societies, the Reconstruction-era exemplifies a politicized jurisprudence characteristic of periods of political upheaval. This jurisprudence exposes the tensions and incoherence of the supposedly autonomous categories of criminal and civil law, of punishment and administrative law. It also tests the limits of constitutional law, in particular, the extent of the politicization. Reconsideration of Reconstruction case law from a transitional perspective challenges the accepted scholarly understanding of the nature and role of this politicized public law. For the Reconstruction Court, the points of reference doctrinally are the past periods of political transformation in the country's history. These historical precedents suggest that, even at the time, the measures were treated as extraordinary and peculiar to transitions, as the Court balanced these exigencies with adherence to conventional rule of law.

The Reconstruction-era jurisprudence is guided by compromise; American Reconstruction jurisprudence, like that of other countries in periods of substantial political flux, reflects a limited, partial constitutional justice. In such periods, constitutional adjudication reflects a pragmatic balance of the values of continuity and discontinuity and of the potentially competing rule-of-law values of security and equality. Reconceptualizing the constitutional politics of the period has implications for contemporary debates about the relevant principles guiding constitutional interpretation of the Reconstruction amendments.[23] Recognition of the Reconstruction amendments' relation to the broader political agenda of the time has implications for the question of how these should be interpreted in light of the Reconstruction legislative program, as well as what relation the historical understandings of Reconstruction-era civil rights standards bear for present-day rights controversies. The Reconstruction-era jurisprudence is best understood from a transitional perspective; the period's transformative purposes clarify the salient decision-making jurisprudence and shed light on its relevance to constitutional jurisprudence.

## Law's Liberation

> I do not know a method of drawing up an indictment against a whole people.
>
> Edmund Burke, Speech on Conciliation with America,
> March 22, 1775

Historically, the next such massive project of political transformation was denazification, attempted at World War II's end, when the Allies insisted that supporters of National Socialism be removed from positions of influence in Germany. Whereas postwar trials policy was rationalized as retributive measures designed to avenge Nazi wrongs, at Potsdam, the proposed denazification was justified instead, by the forward-looking purpose of democratization. Denazification was deemed necessary in these terms, to ensure those with fascist leanings were not handed the reins of power. But how to reach all those with undemocratic leanings? Though postwar denazification began with the idea of barring high-ranking Nazi Party officials, SS, Gestapo, and SD from the top power echelons of the new regime, with time, the policy appeared to expand to near universal proportions.

Despite denazification's asserted democracy purpose, which was forward-looking, the scheme also seemed inherently backward-looking. Advancing the conception of pervasive evil under the Reich, the Nuremberg trials appeared to offer a novel approach to the question of what was the relation of individual to collective responsibility for wartime persecution. The innovation known as "Bernays' brain child" used individual trials to criminalize Nazi organizations, and organizational convictions to reach individual members to resolve the practical problem of reaching all those responsible. After certain organizations were found "criminal" by the International Military Tribunal, in follow-up Allied trials, organizational convictions became the basis for individual convictions.[24] Individual trials would not be necessary; proving membership in criminal organizations would be enough. The idea was controversial for its fluid approach to individual responsibility, challenging intuitions of the rule of law, whereby principles guided designations of status, of rights, and of responsibilities in terms of the individual. After Nuremberg, the idea that Nazism was "criminal" would become true as a matter of law. The punishment policy of the Tribunal helped shape Allied denazification: What characterized the law's uses in this period were Nuremberg's fluid continuities in the attribution of individual and corporate responsibility, as well as its mediating of the boundaries of criminal and civil sanctions.

At its inception just after the war, denazification policy under the aegis of the Allied military government in Germany was explicitly linked to the policies of postwar criminal justice developed at Nuremberg, grounded in corporate notions of responsibility. In its first phase, denazification was limited to the disqualification of those in the higher ranks of the Nazi Party and the other organizations found "criminal" at Nuremberg. But when power was transferred back to Germany, a more ambitious stage of denazification began. True to its name, the Act for Liberation from National Socialism and Militarism of March 5, 1946 was intended to free Germany from Nazi ideology. National Socialist tyranny was to be excluded from "influence in public, economic and cultural life." To that end, through the so-called *fragebogen,* "questionnaire," the entire adult population was vetted about its wartime service. The Liberation Act's broad scope ranged from excluding "major offenders," those actually implicated in war crimes and crimes against humanity, down to "followers," nominal supporters of National Socialism.[25] The gravamen for sanctions under the law was entirely class-based; knowing membership was enough. With its elaborate framework of sanctions ranging according to varying levels of responsibility, the Liberation Act took the form of a sentencing scheme, evincing denazification's punitive side. Sanctions that caused deprivations of civil rights—from imprisonment to the deprivation of employment in public and other sectors—appeared to constitute punishment. Nevertheless, despite denazification's punitive impact, the civil sanctions lacked individual focus; the procedures were noncriminal and predicated only on an administrative process. While, as discussed in chapter 2, criminal justice in transition often implies judicial processes that do not culminate in full punishment, transitional administrative measures seemingly present the obverse picture: the imposition of punitive sanctions without full judicial process.

By all standard accounts, denazification policy failed. Most persons vetted under the scheme were dubbed "followers"—the lowest level of political responsibility. Those sanctioned were subjected to fines only; few were excluded from public office and then only for short periods. Long after denazification, many of the collaborationist elite still held on to jobs they had had under the Nazi regime; even institutions like the judiciary remained dominated by former Nazis.[26] Years later, the question of how to treat the prior Nazi civil service was so controversial, it continued to elude consensus; in the country's new Basic Law, the question was left for the political branches and for another day. Paradoxically, the very same justifications that animated denazification easily rationalized the reinstatement policy. Nazi Party membership was so pervasive that continuing denazification policy would have meant eliminating many of the sitting judges. Prior experience in government, albeit under the Nazi regime, became the basis for integration into public service. Indeed, shortly after the initiation of denazification policy, the Reinstatement Act was passed, reintegrating Nazi officials and, as such, putting the lid on denazification.

In the standard critique of denazification policy, its flaws lay in the failure of implementation because of the political context: the sheer numbers placing unworkable demands on the screening tribunals, the absence of political will, in particular, in light of the cold war, and the difficulty of self-vetting, of the "autopurge." There was also the implied relation of Allied denazification to punishment policy, so that after the prosecutions gave way to clemency policy, denazification became difficult to pursue.[27] The sweeping breadth of denazification policy over the entire public service seemed to elude enforcement. Thus, denazification's standard critique derives from a realist perspective; denazification policy's aborted cause is explained in terms of its political circumstances.

However, the standard critique of denazification begs the question of whether there may have been something wrong with the policy, as it raised the relevance of Germany's political past to the new regime's construction of public service and democratic transformation. With this question in mind, one might further ask about the breadth of denazification policy's scope. In this regard, one might distinguish degrees of past complicity as well as differentiate among the affected governmental positions, thus, for example, distinguishing broad-scale purging of the entire public service from the screening of the top political echelon and discrete sectors like the security apparatus. Posing the normative question necessitates justifying transitional administrative justice policy. Postwar denazification's asserted justification is that of "democracy building." Excluding Nazis from public service was said to be necessary to reconstruct German democracy. Maintaining the existing administrative apparatus was thought to subvert the possibility of making the transition to a more liberal system. Yet, what exactly is the relation between past political conduct under a prior repressive regime and the ability to participate in a successor liberalizing regime? Our intuitions are that establishing a liberal democracy would not be possible under the Nazi Party's top brass. In working democracies, political change at the higher governmental echelons occurs through regular elections. However, in societies in between political systems, regular methods of political representation are frequently not yet in place. Moreover, elections do not reach all the public service. Thus, a regime's change following peaceful negotiations relies heavily on the law to redefine the new political boundaries of the public domain. In these political circumstances, the change of regime through the removal of those entrenched in positions of power is largely advanced by the law. Common justifications for the political purges are exclusion of the prior regime and its supporters from political participation in democracy.

What is the role of political conditionality in the liberalizing regime? The central claim in the democracy argument prevalent in transitions is the forecast that those who acted to further the past repression would be likely to do so again, in this way subverting democracy's consolidation. The democracy justification is at its most compelling when the affected positions are most similar to those held under the previous regime and when there is a likelihood of repression rearing its head. Accordingly, though mere party membership may not justify exclusion from low-level civil service positions, that would not be true of higher policy-making positions in the successor regime or positions in the state security apparatus enabling the perpetration of rights abuses. The closer the connection between the political disabilities and the affected positions, the more relevant the democracy justification. Yet, on this account, denazification lacked closely justified transitional policy, as there did not appear to be much relation between sweeping political disabilities and democracy. On the contrary, moral considerations aside, competence for prospective employment in the successor democratizing regime was in some sense arguably greater among those with prior political, administrative, and managerial experience. Ultimately, the democracy argument seemed misguided and internally incoherent: For the force of the democratic justification for political disabilities was seemingly premised on the assumption that democracies were shaped more by their personnel than by their structures, institutions, and procedures. Yet this reasoning appears to run counter to liberal political theory.

Postwar denazification, like the Reconstruction-era political disabilities, is best understood from a transitional context. Considering the course of the policy over time underscores its transitoriness and ever-shifting balance over the course of the transition. Denazification policy begins at war's end, lasting for a circumscribed period of time. The policy tapers off after about five years, in 1950; and by 1951, the transitional phase ends. That sequence tells us something about the processes by which the administrative state reconstitutes itself. Though the frequent critique of denazification policy focuses on the failure to effect permanent exclusions, nevertheless, the policy suggests that the law's role here was to advance transformation and, as such, its partial and provisional nature is a recurring feature of these politically dynamic periods.[28] Though right after the war, the association with the Fascist regime was fatal to political participation; after the passage of time, such past political service became acceptable, and even desirable, in subsequent successor regimes. Governmental experience, albeit under the Nazis, became the basis for integration in public service.[29] Participation in the prior regime became normalized after an ordinary administration shift. Treatment of the predecessor regime shifted from discontinuity to continuity. In the beginning, denazification legislation was animated by the dominant purpose of restoring legitimacy; as the successor regime consolidates, public policy gives way to other purposes.

Considered as an isolated instance, denazification has generally been viewed as a failed attempt at transformation. Yet, when considered in a comparative/historical perspective, together with other measures applied during periods of radical political upheaval, the postwar experience turns out to be closer to the transitional norm. Administrative purges occur in periods of fragile and unstable political order; these measures are provisional and often temporized over the period of political transformation. From the start, these measures are pragmatic resolutions intended as transitory for a particular political period of reconstruction. They are always understood as transitional justice.

## *Epuracion* and *Zuivering:* The Politics of Exclusion

Whereas in Allied-occupied Germany, there reigned a sense of pervasive collective responsibility, by contrast, elsewhere in postwar Europe, there was an enemy to purge. Liberation from Nazism went hand in hand with wholesale purges of supporters of the prior regime. And the basis of these purges is explicitly ideological: Postoccupation justice is forged in terms of we/they, friend/foe, collaborator/resistance; it is reconstitution by deconstitution.

After the collapse of the occupying regimes in postwar Europe, societies responded to a public sphere utterly compromised by its support of fascist power. In the transitions out of fascism, newly reconstructed friend/foe lines went beyond the reconstruction of the administration to a broader public sphere comprising all civil society. Postwar Europe's purge practices reveal how administrative justice involves a turning away from regular criminal processes to those more sweeping and informal, moving away from the judiciary to other tribunals or bodies, often isolated within vast governmental entities. The departure from established criminal law and regular judicial processes highlights the purges' politicization. Throughout the region there is the attempt to impose measures of political conditionality and judgment, a move toward informal processes and vague political offenses, such as "national degradation" and "national indignity."[30] Although, ordinarily, penal judgment is based on past unlawful behavior, the new offenses were predicated simply on the finding of a political condition declared by a body given this authority during the transition. Establishing collaboration and other political crimes entailed only proving the political status of supporting totalitarian doctrine. The gravamen of the investigations was not past criminal conduct as in a trial but, rather, membership or support of past so-called subversive political associations. Along with the reconceptualization of offenses came special procedures, laws, courts, and forms of action.[31] The purging tribunals were not the ordinary courts of law but military courts and administrative bodies composed of judges, nonjurists, and lay persons. Though the penalties sometimes appeared to be traditional criminal sanctions, others affected civil status, such as the loss of the franchise, rights to political participation, and even citizenship. Both in its processes and effect, this was extraordinary justice.

As a historical matter, purges are visited on the ancien régime leadership, yet the postwar purges went further, reflecting a broad understanding of the scope of responsibility and transformation. Postwar measures expelled individuals from a broader segment of society, including sectors not previously considered part of the administration, such as education and the media. As such, the purges reconstitute the domain of the public sphere, as they attempted to restructure the various corporate sectors: business, the media, and those intellectual elites, which, in one fashion or another, had supported the Nazi regime. The purges, therefore, were radical restructurings of the professions with special purging committees for educators, writers, and musicians. Though purges regulated the private sector, they did so pursuant to governmental decree. Offenses were vaguely stated, and failure to have "the proper attitude" during the occupation made for newfound liability.[32]

Nowhere were the purges more radical and sweeping than in the media.[33] In the case of the press, the offense of collaboration was easy to prove— with proof texts—and publication kept the issue of collaboration in the public eye. In a series of purgings and reenactments, the media was rededicated to the new political regime in the public eye. When collaboration papers became the object of purge orders, the parameters of free expression were reconstructed in response to the past. Even newspapers' names were subject to critical changes, like that of the French newspaper *Libération*, symbols of changed identity.

The postoccupation purges of the public sphere go far beyond the civil service; the attempt is nothing less than to "purify" society. These political purges in the public sphere critically respond to the distinct nature of fascist repression that is achieved by the hegemonic control of the sectors of ideological production, such as education and the media.[34] Accountability for the intellectual elite recognized its role in hastening the fascist takeover and attempted to reorient this sector to the liberal ideology of the successor regime.

Postwar purges reconstruct the relation between the individual, mediating associations, and the state. Defined in terms of the collective, political disabilities are, nevertheless, brought to bear against the individual. These processes' informal approach to the identification of past fascist affiliation suggests that group-based exclusions are not primarily aimed at individual wrongdoing. They are not justified in these terms but, instead, as defining cognizable institutional change for the transformation of the public domain. Individuals are a means to expurgate publicly the ideology of the ancien régime from the future public sphere. The postwar purges challenge our intuitions about the rule of law, as the administration of justice is not applied in known regular procedures but through highly informal, irregular procedures. The measures' diminished due process, along with their nontransparent and politicized nature, reflect a compromised understanding of the rule of law. And, though the purposes are forward-looking, sounding in democracy, the means are in some sense just the old ones associated with repressive regimes: of categorical judgments made on an ideological basis, at odds with liberal thought. Though paradoxical, it is the critical response—the explicit undoing through the old forms that best signals the ideological switch. Moreover, the tension of illiberal means directed to liberal, forward-looking ends is reconciled by these measures' limited impact on the legal system. Postwar purges lasted only a short while, from as little as a year to five years.[35] These radically politicized measures were bounded *ex ante*, as from the start they were intended to be provisional transformative mechanisms. The temporizing seen here, as in earlier instances, for example, American Reconstruction, is also manifest in contemporary political transformation discussed in this chapter. What emerges is that even the most radical politicized responses to repressive rule are intended as provisional from the start and constitutive of transition.

## *Lustrace* and *Bereinigung:* Political Purges in East and Central Europe

> Everyone, however, is in fact involved and enslaved, not only the greengrocers but also the prime ministers. Differing positions in the hierarchy merely establish differing degrees of involvement: the greengrocer is involved to a minor extent, but he also has very little power. The prime minister, naturally, has greater power, but in return he is far more deeply involved. Both, however, are unfree, each merely in a somewhat different way. The real accomplice in this involvement, therefore, is not another person, but the system itself. Position in the power hierarchy determines the degree of responsibility and guilt, but it gives no one unlimited responsibility and guilt, nor does it completely absolve anyone.
>
> Václav Havel, *Open Letters: Selected Writings: 1965–1990*

Contemporary transitions throughout East and Central Europe were largely negotiated and, therefore, relied on radical public law measures to decommunize; as such, they test law's role in the transformation of party politics. Totalitarianism is characterized by repressive control pervading society. Whereas rule by dictatorship is characterized by drawing a line between ruler and ruled, under totalitarian rule, there is no such clear line, with repression diffused throughout the society. In totalitarianism's wake, accordingly, the question becomes who is responsible for past wrongs? The legal responses to communism's collapse tell us about the contemporary understanding of individual responsibility for repression, of the relation of citizen to party, and of party to state. The evil of totalitarian rule is seen as pervasive, perpetrated by an occupation force and by widespread collaboration.

Throughout the region in the wake of political change, the response focuses on the prior security apparatus and its secret collaborators. The purges' object goes beyond official power; for totalitarian rule was characterized by an exercise of power that was not transparent, and a repression that was ambiguous as to whether private or public. Throughout East and Central Europe, those implicated in the prior system were subjected to political disabilities, although decommunization measures varied in their harshness and sweep. Unified Germany, the former Czechoslovakia, Bulgaria, and Albania all enacted bans against former Communist Party hierarchy and state security apparatus in the public domain.[36] Hungary adopted milder measures, such as the publication of lists of those implicated in Communist rule. In the new republics, forward-looking measures were adopted, such as oaths of allegiance.

The idea of being tested by one's political past began informally. In the summer of 1990, in the first free elections in the former Czechoslovakia, political parties screened their candidates for evidence of ties with the former state security. When a parliamentary commission formed to screen Parliament for collaborators with ties to state security, the inquiry became entirely politicized. A year later, the attempt to systematize the screening culminated in legislation, in Czech, known as "lustrace" or, "lustration." "Lustration," deriving from the Latin *lustrare* for "purification," refers to the processes of investigation and screening intended to "shed light" on the past. Historically, these investigatory processes were associated with taking a count, or census, of the population.[37] Czech lustration law would purge anyone with prior ties to the state security apparatus from a wide range of appointive positions in government, army, Parliament, courts, state-owned businesses, academia, and media. Under the law, mere membership in the state security apparatus sufficed to imply involvement in the organization's repressive goals.[38] As such, the law codified the presumption that supporters of the past Communist regime endangered democracy. The lustration law was challenged by ninety-nine parliamentary deputies who had previously opposed the law in the Parliament. Other opposition included outside human rights organizations, the International Labor Committee, and Czech President Václav Havel, who proposed amending the proposal to allow for individualized review.[39] In its most notorious decision, the country's short-lived unified Constitutional Court would uphold lustration's policy, though circumscribing its scope.[40]

Decommunization also began informally in unified Germany with the German Democratic Republic's (GDR's) first free elections. While in the other negotiated transitions in the region, the purges of Communists appeared to be supported by some level of social consensus in the political branches; in unified Germany, the purges began as a form of "victor's justice." For the East, there would be little choice in the matter. As with the Confederate South's reentry in the Union, when East Germany was subsumed into unified Germany, its return was conditioned on renunciation of its ideological past. The country was "divided by unification,"[41] as the Unification Treaty set out the terms for reunification unified the German civil service, creating a system of review for those employed in the former GDR administration, and disqualifying from civil service those in the Communist Party hierarchy, as well as the

Stasi, the dreaded secret police.[42] The Unification Treaty authorizes disqualification on two bases: "unacceptability because of past political acts" and "technical incompetence." As in postwar denazification, once again questionnaires were used to vet individuals for membership in the secret police, and local commissions were empowered with exclusion. The 1991 passage of the Stasi Files Act provided for access to the files of the former secret police and background checks of the prior regime, leading to massive purges of former East German civil service at all levels. Exclusion from public office, state security, and education meant sweeping discharges of thousands of public officials, judges, schoolteachers, and former university professors.

Of the two schemes, Czech decommunization on its face appeared to cast a wider net, for the law penetrated all the way down to the lowest echelon of past regime supporters, even those attending security school or "candidates" for collaboration, thus potentially affecting tens of thousands. Moreover, Czech lustration's enforcement was centralized in the historically dreaded Ministry of the Interior, while Germany's purges operated on a more local level. Nevertheless, ultimately, Germany's purges had the greater impact, since they were systematically enforced by a preexisting fully functioning administrative apparatus, and a substitute labor pool was readily available.

The uses of political disabilities were sweeping and apparently justified only by the presumptive (and inverse) relation between past political affiliation and competence to participate in the democratic regime. Nevertheless, the normative question the schemes raised was, Just what was the relevance of past political conduct to the shaping of the new public order? In both the former Czechoslovakia and Germany, this question was controversial and culminated in constitutional review. Constitutional review necessitated ongoing public justification of decommunization policy. In unified Germany, political disqualifications were justified by the presumption that former Communists could not serve in a democratic political system. In other countries, like Hungary, political disqualifications along similar lines were justified by its judiciary on democracy grounds.[43]

In upholding lustration's constitutionality, the Constitutional Court of the Czech and Slovak Federal Republic analogized it to security clearances in working democracies. Like security clearances, lustration conditioned employment on past conduct; the law "merely specifie[d] some further prerequisites for the discharge of certain sensitive functions in the State administration and economic apparatus." To allow "persons who participated in the violation or suppression of human rights and freedoms the . . . means which could serve serious destabilization of democratic development and the threat of the security of citizens would be an irresponsible risk."[44] Consider the analogy of lustration policy in transformative periods to the role of security in established democracies. In working democracies, trustworthiness as condition of employment is generally limited to security-related or other similarly sensitive positions involving access to classified information. Ordinarily, few public positions necessitate greater security; such disqualifications are generally considered unjustifiable and punitive. Moreover, ordinarily the government bears the burden of showing the relevance of the screening process to the affected position. The analogy to security clearances might well justify screening for select governmental positions in the region, such as those involving human rights, and human rights concerns might have justified an earlier, milder precursor to the lustration law, which would have screened out those personally responsible for human rights violations. But security concerns hardly supported the sweeping scope of lustration.

Historically, the state had plenary power to condition public employment on a political basis. In American constitutional law, for example, this discretion is captured in a landmark judicial opinion that "[a person] may have a constitutional right to talk politics, but he has no constitutional right to be a policeman."[45] Nevertheless, the modern position has moved away from the historical view. Though political conditions on the practice of law relating to Communist Party membership were once upheld, this was during the cold war, and U.S. law has changed since then.[46] Modern liberal democracies are generally constrained from decision making in the public domain on purely political grounds. In working democracies, only top governmental positions are thought justifiably chosen on a primarily political basis and, therefore, by electoral processes. Though public employment or benefits may be denied altogether, the state generally lacks discretion to condition such benefits on a political basis. In the liberal state, political conditions must be justified by weighty interests and closely drawn to advance those interests. Governmental efficiency concerns are ordinarily considered inadequate to justify politically based appointments.[47] Political loyalty, in and of itself, is also rarely adequate to justify patronage politics. The relevance of political affiliation depends on the nature of the affiliation that is the basis for the disqualification, and it is predicated on a governmental showing of a close relation between the affected position and political basis, with political affiliation considered in employment-related decisions only when relevant to effective performance.[48] The general principle against politically driven decision making in the public sphere protects political association and speech rights important to working democracies.[49] Moreover, in the European social welfare democracies characterized by greater regulation of employment, political conditionality implicates other rights such as labor-related entitlements and freedoms in the public domain.[50]

Though ordinarily our intuitions about the rule of law would militate against the adoption of such political measures, special transitional concerns may well support such measures in limited periods. Thus, in upholding the country's screening policies, the Constitutional Court of the former Czechoslovakia rationalized lustration policy on the basis of the extraordinary needs of the period. Warning of the "possible relapse of the totalitarian regime" and the need to prevent "destabilization of the democratic development of the state," the court's justification for the purges was explicitly transitional. The measures were justified by the necessities of constructing a more democratic regime:

Every State, especially one which had been obliged to suffer the violation of basic rights and freedoms by the totalitarian power for more than forty years has the right to apply such legislative measures which aim to foil the risk of subversion on the return of, or possible relapse into the totalitarian regime in order to establish a democratic system.

Other transitional precedents from prior postwar periods were invoked: "Measures of this type . . . taken also by other European states after the collapse of the totalitarian regime . . . are a legitimate means . . . not to threaten the democratic character of the constitutional system . . . or the . . . rights and freedoms of the citizens . . . but for their protection and consolidation."[51] That the extraordinary justifications for political disabilities are confined to limited periods of political shifts is conceded in the law, in which the measures are expressly circumscribed in time. Thus, in the former Czechoslovakia, though lustration was at the start intended to last five years, in the Czech Republic it would be extended for another five. Unified Germany's disabilities were also explicitly provisional from the start.[52]

Complicity in the past political regime is often considered relevant to the holding of public office in transitional societies during fragile periods of political transformation from repressive to liberal rule. But what are the parameters of the relevance of past political allegiance? Historically, after dictatorship, purges were leveled against the top political rung. Yet, the purges after the Communist collapse responded to a different kind of repression, to a totalitarian rule that penetrated all sectors of society, seemingly implicating everyone. The character of totalitarian repression might have justified the purge of an entire political generation, and the question thus became where to draw the line.

For some, nothing less than past dissident status would be a sufficient sign of the moral integrity necessary to high-ranking public service under the new regime. In the contemporary wave of political change, dissident status would become the unspoken de facto condition of high political office. In many of the transitional administrations of East Europe and Latin America, presidents have been former dissidents. Thus, Václav Havel campaigned for human rights in the former Czechoslovakia; so did Arpad Göncz in Hungary; in Poland, Lech Walesa led the opposition. In Latin America, Argentina's Carlos Menem was imprisoned under the former military regime. Brazilian President Fernando Cardoso was a political exile during the country's period of military rule. Bolivia's former President Gonzalo Sánchez de Lozada, too, came from a family in exile. But how far to go with this line of reasoning? Beyond a new regime's leadership, to what extent is complicity in a past regime's wrongdoing material to public service under a liberalizing regime? Might there be a principle of rule of law guiding the transitional purges and justifying limited politicized decision making? This question was considered by the former Czechoslovakia's Constitutional Court, when it reviewed the lustration law's reach to the many who appeared in the secret police files as potential candidates for collaboration. Tens of thousands fell in this group, of which only a tiny number knowingly volunteered to collaborate with the previous regime. Such "unknowing" membership, the court held, was insufficient to disqualify them from the prospective political order.[53] At the very least, the line was drawn at "knowing membership."

The next question confronted by decommunization policy was whether "knowing" participation could serve as a basis for dismissal. This question arose in a case arising under unified Germany's disqualification law.[54] To justify political exclusions, such involvement had to be more than the degree of knowing membership general to East Germany's citizenry. As a constitutional matter, the court held, suitability for public service could not be determined solely on the basis of position in the GDR hierarchy or identification with the German Socialist Union Party (SED) regime. Since "loyalty to the socialist order . . . [was a] prerequisite for public service employment in the GDR, . . . the loyalty and cooperation that were necessary and normal for remaining and rising in the public (civil) service . . . cannot be the sole justification for lack of suitability."[55] Suitability for the newly unified public service ought to be justified by special circumstances, on a case-by-case basis. In similar cases, the rule of law drawn by the courts supports the liberal principle that public law should be constructed in terms that transcend mere adherence to political ideology; there has to be something more.

Where a law structuring a successor judicial system would have disqualified the judiciary on the basis of "political decisionmaking under the prior regime," these political conditions, the court held, were too vague to apply.[56] Poland's Constitutional Court put a rule-of-law limit on what could have been a highly politicized lustration of the country's judiciary.

In reviewing a case concerning a former police chief, Germany's Constitutional Court overturned his dismissal as unconstitutional, challenging the breadth of decommunization policy. Vindicating the principle of judicial review, anticommunist disabilities were treated as legislative presumptions of incompetence but not as presumptively irrebuttable . The court required an inquiry that looked beyond mere past conduct, to make an individual determination about the public officials' prospects for service in a democratic regime. In the case of the police officer, there was evidence of his prospects for reform so that he could serve in a democratic regime. The potential for reform seemed particularly pertinent in the German context in which, given the GDR's incorporation into preexisting democratic structures, there were diminished justifications for sweeping exclusion. In recognizing a baseline of political affiliation with the prior totalitarian regime, judicial notice was taken of an acceptable baseline level of past regime support. When there was mass societal support for a regime, without more, such support in and of itself was not enough to disqualify an entire political generation. This normative principle would guide a bounded relation to the past in the transitions after communism. The case of the reformed police officer exemplifies the potential of constitutional courts in periods of political flux. When it rejected the irrefutability of the legislative presumption, Germany's high court affirmed a principle central to liberal democracy, of individual rights protected within a system of judicial review. If totalitarian rule was marked by the total penetration of the private sphere, an independent judiciary epitomized the liberal hope of limiting state power.

The reasoning in these cases illuminates the contingency in transitional justice and its relation to past legacies. After repressive rule, restructuring the public service means reconstructing the normative relation of the individual to the political order. But of what relevance is past political behavior to public decision making in transitional regimes, when other things are changing too? Change at the individual level ought to be considered in light of broader structural change. With changes in political context and a shift in political system, past individual conduct may well be largely irrelevant to a society's democratic prospects. Yet, insofar as the logic of political conditionality is largely justified in forward-looking terms, the democracy justification seems internally incoherent: For leveling political conditions on individuals based on past behavior largely elides the potential of newly created political institutions. So, it is that transitional justice defies reductive categorization, as it responds to political exigencies as well as to particular legacies of repressive rule.

### Administrative and Distributive Justice

Generally, the political schemes here discussed are justified on democracy grounds for the purpose of construction of a new political order. Yet, there are other purposes invoked by transitional societies in redirecting public goods on a political basis, which are, at least in part, redistributive. The group-based political disabilities discussed above make operational a distributive principle for political participation on the basis of political system preference. Thus, for example, decommunization, or other such similar political disqualifications, could be reconceptualized as a massive preference scheme based on political affiliation. Such an argument is being made in the ongoing transition in postapartheid South Africa.[57] Political conditions could be reconsidered as preferences, an automatic thumb on the scales. What are the justifications for some form of collective judgment on a political basis, for example, for "affirmative action"? When political systems undergo liberalization, what state interest justifies remedial preferences on the basis of political adherence?

Transitional preferences can be analogized to patronage systems in older democracies. While there is now a presumptive antidiscrimination principle, historically, patronage was used to organize public administrations. After World War II, governmental discrimination on a political basis raised the specter of past persecution, and, as such, was proscribed in most domestic and international law. Most postwar international human rights legislation ensures equal protection on the basis of political opinion. Antidiscrimination principles provide that wherever legislation discriminates on the basis of political opinion, there ought to be a weighty governmental interest. Ordinarily, the constitutional legitimacy of such political disabilities would depend on the nature of the state's justifications, on whether there is a state interest justifying departure from principles of equality of opportunity. From this perspective, anticommunist political disabilities in East Europe are often rationalized as a form of affirmative action.[58] The argument goes something like this: In postcommunist Europe, to make political system adherence relevant to prospective participation in state administration does not merely imply burdening present freedom of expression of political opinion, but it is also historically freighted. So it is that in contemporary transitions, political preferences are justified, because like the question of racial preferences in the United States, the legacy of political system adherence in East Europe has played a distinctively divisive and repressive role throughout the region's history. Whatever the commitment to political equality in the successor regime, the historical context for the political purges in the region is one of long periods of sustained political discrimination. Indeed, the significance of historical political discrimination is recognized by the region's constitutional courts in their review of the transitional screening measures. In upholding lustration policy, the Constitutional Court of the Czech Republic reasoned:

> A democratic state . . . cannot be inactive in the situation in which the leading posts on all levels were staffed on the basis of political criteria. A democratic state has the duty to endeavor to eliminate unjustified preference of a group of citizens, based on the principle of their membership in a certain political party as well as to eliminate the discrimination of their citizens.[59]

Past political discrimination has a certain justificatory appeal but, in and of itself, is generally not sufficiently weighty to justify political discrimination. While decommunization schemes imply transfers from communists to noncommunists, such schemes are not closely drawn to advance the goal of political diversity in the fledgling democracies. To what extent was the affirmative action analogy appropriate? Could one say that there had been "rightful" owners that were unjustly treated? Not all public employment was wrongfully expropriated from noncommunists; for example, not all present jobholders wrongfully hold their jobs. Decommunization measures barring employment from the public sector were challenged for violating individual rights, such as rights relating to work.[60] Yet, these challenges were themselves controversial, since political changes went hand in hand with economic change and radical cuts in the civil service. Whether, and in what way, political disabilities threaten employment entitlements raises controversial questions about the social understanding that the market transitions have brought into contention. Forward-looking redistributive interests have been used to justify sweeping disqualification legislation that penalizes communists to the benefit of anticommunists in the region. When political categories are redrawn to undo past preferences, all to the benefit of the prior political opposition, the asserted state interest in redistribution in the public sector appears to be not only politically discriminatory but also pretextual.

Decommunization legislation is simultaneously backward- and forward-looking as it mediates the transition. So-called past entitlements are deployed to justify the present allocation of employment in the successor regime. These transitional redistributions themselves reconstruct the distinctions upon which past entitlements were putatively based, redefining social relations in the past system, a system with few established understandings of private property entitlements. The interaction of transitional and distributive justice criteria in the restoration of those whose opportunities were previously wrongfully taken is more fully discussed in the next chapter.

### Redrawing the Party Line: The Social Meaning of Purgings in the Public Sphere

The public purges construct the political transformation by redefining the boundaries of the political landscape as the effect of political disabilities plays out in the public sphere. Their effect is a function of transitional legacies. So it is that, for the most part, decommunization's bite came down primarily to exposure of past collaboration through publication and the attendant political accountability and social censure.[61] Though employment bans might be lifted after a time, this was often not true of the often lingering stigma of being named an "enemy of democracy" during the transition. In the former Czechoslovakia, the lists of so-called excludables read over television caused a profound societal stir; in Poland, the leaks prompted a political crisis that almost brought down the government. Thus, lustration began as de facto disclosures in the public sphere; and even when regulated by law, ultimately its implementing legislation eschewed the traditional sanctions associated with lawmaking and instead largely depended on exposure in the public sphere. For example, in Hungary, the lists of those said to be implicated in past repression were published in the daily civil service paper.

Czech lustration was similarly concededly largely declaratory. In its review of the Law on the Illegality of the Communist Regime, the country's Constitutional Court expressly recognized and affirmed decommunization legislation's hortatory nature:

> The so-called lustration law, for example, does not impose sanctions, rather it merely sets the conditions for certain offices. . . . The constitutional foundation of a democratic State does not deny the Parliament the right to express . . . its moral and political viewpoint by means which it considers suitable and reasonable within the confines of general legal principles and passably in the form of a statute.[62]

Referring to law's "crediting" and "blaming" functions, the legislation was understood to operate as a normative declaratory measure, though not formally ascriptive of criminal responsibility, nevertheless, effecting the social condemnation associated with criminal judgment. In its expressive stigmatizing aspects, lustration's potential effect is similar to that of criminal legislation.[63] Ordinarily, such stigma would be supported by the ascription of individual responsibility characteristic of the criminal process. The political exclusions draw attention to the significance of publication: The purge begins with the list. When the list of those to be disabled is published, the list itself constitutes a stigmatizing political judgment. Perhaps the least formal approach to lustration is Poland's, where prospective candidates for top positions in the public service are expected to self-purge via declarations about their relation to the secret service in the years between 1944 and 1990.[64] Decommunization legislation lays bare the social meaning of regulatory measures lacking in the formal sanctions, changes in rights or duties ordinarily associated with law. Against the context of the region's legacies, political purges in the public sphere have force.

How exactly do political conditions and disabilities enable transformation? Successor purges are deployed to undo a past regime's repression, law is used to reconstruct the political parties relevant to participation in the public sphere. In the transition, successor regimes deploy as categorical disqualifications the very same political categories that previously served as definitional qualifications under the predecessor regime. The force of the political reconstruction is clarified against this background; the postcommunist purges are performative as they explicitly invert the bases of the processes supporting the past regime. Nevertheless, the reliance on predecessor regimes' documentation comes at a cost. Screening a person's past is done against the old regime's state security files; with the files of the ancien régime constituting the successor regime's political test. "Lustration" or verification is effected through the old regime's files; the "truth" is thought to emerge from the old regime's records. In ordinary administration shifts in working democracies, reliance on predecessor regimes' archives would not be exceptional; however, in shifts between political systems, particularly in the move from dictatorships to more liberal regimes, reliance on ancien régime archives implies maintaining continuity in the material foundations of the prior regime and, therefore, appears utterly paradoxical. For even as they intend to purge the past, the processes are firmly steeped in that past. Even the jargon deployed harks back to the predecessor regime's procedures. "Lustration" is the very term that was used by the Czech secret police for their background checks on citizens' loyalty to the Communist Party during its forty-year rule. Seen this way, the post-1989 purges are just the most recent in a line of purges: 1970; the purges of the 1968 reformers, where a half million communists were thrown out of the party; and, before that, 1948 and the Stalinist purges.[65] Even in its mild form, lustration evokes the dreaded lists of the totalitarian regimes; as such, it seems to reconstruct society just as in the old way, by redefining political parties along the very same lines. Lustration appears profoundly enmeshed in the ways of the old regime even as it pursues its transformative purposes.

If the chapter begins by questioning the relation of illiberal means to liberal ends, the political purges of East and Central Europe illuminate the problem. Here is the paradox of the social construction of decommunization in transition, of the political purgings that condemn past evil, even as they reenact past purgings. In the new democracies, decommunization laws eerily evoke their totalitarian past. To some degree, resorting to these forms cannot help but recall the prior repression, in which revolutionary change occurred through the purge. Predecessor means and successor responses look all too similar, so highlighting the rationale for these processes. For these purges show that, though paradoxical, it is often through a society's traditional ritualized processes that political change is most clearly expressed. Transitional practices bear out a well-known sociological observation relating to the social rituals of preservation and reform: It is through the old forms that the change in political message is made manifest,[66] though these may be distinguished by the minimal procedural guarantees and liberal justifications. Analysis of these controlled forms of change clarifies how it is that in the transition performing established political rituals can nonetheless advance the purposes of transformation.

## Demilitarizing in the National Security State

Given persistent authoritarian rule, how is the move from militarized regimes to more liberal systems achieved? Perhaps the greatest challenge is the use of administrative measures to change the national security state. The end of World War II ushered in an invigorated urgency to preserve the peace and a democratic impetus. The peace purpose animated a range of initiatives, from the founding of the United Nations and its peacekeeping commitment, to demilitarization among the losing powers. Unconditional surrenders in Germany and Japan were translated into the yielding up of all prospective war-making power in their postwar constitutions.[67] In countries perceived to be warmongering, new postwar limits chiseled away at established military power.

Despite the heightened postwar impetus for demilitarization, with the advent of the cold war, it would be short-lived. This was particularly so in Latin America, where growing global polarization affected the continent, as the attempt to adhere to a Western-style economy went hand in hand with oppression, as the capitalist powers supported dictators insofar as they resisted communism. Well into the 1950s, about half the Latin American republics were subject to military rule. The 1960s and 1970s ushered in a new increase in military power, when even long-standing democracies, like Chile, fell to military rule. By the early 1980s, virtually the entire continent was plunged under repressive military rule.[68] This was the heyday of the national security state. With the military seemingly entrenched in power, mere party politics as usual was not a plausible solution; elections, not a full answer. Even when the military officially handed over the reins of power, a growing culture accepting military rule allowed a de facto retaining of the balance of power, which was often achieved under the guise of maintaining civilian rule.

In the Americas, transition from authoritarianism meant a struggle over subjecting the military to civilian rule. The failure of simple party politics spurred other structural responses in the transitions. Despite political liberalization, few attempts were made to hold the military accountable as a body.[69] Though one country, Costa Rica, eliminated its entire military power.[70]

Post–civil war El Salvador offered a more circumscribed form of demilitarization on the continent. When United Nations–brokered peace accords brought to an end the country's bloody, protracted civil war, there was a call for an overhaul of the country's security apparatus. The very possibility of peace between the government of El Salvador and the Frente Farabundo Martí para la Liberatión Nacional (FMLN) hinged on purges of the military and the police. The FMLN agreed to give up its arms only on condition of the "purification" of the military, and so demobilization of the opposition was exchanged for the purging of the national security apparatus. Demilitarized, purged of its weapons, the opposition was allowed entry to the political sphere and freedom to form a political party as a trade-off for the exclusion of the national security apparatus from the legitimate political domain.

The question remained, How to transform the military? What was the appropriate relation of individuals to the military, particularly, as concerns past wrongdoing and the military's potential role in the democratic transformation? Transformation of the army in El Salvador was effectuated by a combination of systemic change and individual purgings. Institutional transformation of the security apparatus occurred through two kinds of purges: individual expurgations and corporate restructurings of the military body. Purging individual transgressors was one path to expurgating the military, to ridding the body of its nondemocratic elements.[71] In Spanish, *purificación*, "purification," involved screening the military for past participation in human rights abuses in an inquiry to ascertain the likelihood of prospective democratic behavior.[72]

Though the stated intention was speedy change of the security apparatus, getting the military to yield to civilian rule would become a protracted struggle. When the so-called ad hoc commission identified individual wrongdoers, the lengthy list included numerous top-level officers, even the country's defense minister, implicated in the well-known Jesuits' murder. Even more ominous, among those identified for dismissal were the officers who had led the peace negotiations. Military resistance to the proposed purges, and a threat of a coup d'état, slowed down the purging. A half year after the schedule agreed to in the peace accords, the top echelon of the armed forces was finally removed from duty. Salvador's military purges had weighty justifications generally sounding in deterrence. Perpetrators of past human rights abuses were considered likely to repeat their behavior and, for this reason, excluded from their positions of power. Though such individualized exclusions rested on strong justifications, in ordinary times, these exclusions would have obtained only after due process. Ultimately, the conflict between weighty interests and the rights to individual due process was reconciled in a compromise, a partial purge that excluded individuals but lacked the stigma associated with criminal justice.

Transformation of the military is predicated on a distinct, close relation between the individual and the body that is inextricably bounded up to societal understandings of the military as an institution. Indeed, the very turn to collective transitional measures assumes a close nexus between the implicated individuals and the collective. Within the military, there is a particularly close relation, as evident in the understanding of criminal responsibility, discussed in the prior chapter on criminal justice. Within the military structure, understandings of the construct of "chain of command" implied command responsibility, assumptions of responsibility that transcended merely those of individuals, to the actions of others in the body.

The struggle over Salvador's military purges illuminates how purges, though often punitive in their consequences, lacked the processes that usually go hand in hand with punishment. This is evident even in what constitutes the first purge. Publication of the list in the public domain is, like lustration after communism, the first public condemnation of the prior wrongdoing. The list of those to be purged is itself artifactual of the subsequent purge; accordingly, graduating the dismissals so that the exclusions were dissociated from the wrongdoer's identification softened the censure of being on the "ad hoc" list. Once the purges were dissociated from the list and the removals subsumed to routine transfers and retirements, the stigma of judgment was dissipated. Lacking judgment, the sanctions lost their harsh punitive aspect, leaving only the change in civil status. This accommodation mitigated the tension in the exclusions—and kept the peace.

Transformation of the national security state would also imply change in the police, as not only the military but also the security police had been implicated in the past wrongs. The old police would be purged, demobilized, and replaced by a new civilian-controlled police force and reconstitution, not through exclusions, but by forced inclusion. "Purge" in this context takes on its historic meaning, signifying ridding one fluid by infusion or flushing with another.[73] Transformation of the police was premised on an influx of "clean" civilian recruits. Transformation of the body meant more than a majority of the force had to not have been implicated in the prior civil war. A supermajoritarian sixty/forty formula for proportional personnel change was considered necessary, with political quotas, of former rebel combatants, and military to ensure this political transformation. More than half of the institution had to be free of taint with the past, so that roughly equal parts remained: screened veterans of the former police and a demobilized rebel army.[74]

What constitutes political transformation after military rule is, in part, structured by the regime it displaces. Thus meaningful change is, in part, "critical" or discontinuous with past practices. Otherwise it is residual or continuous with the predecessor regime. There is a transitional fluid conception in the relation of structural to individual change. Institutional transformations occur in these instances through a hybrid of structural and individual change, with the aim of creating checks and balances of political factions. Restructuring the security apparatus by opposing political factions of roughly equal representation of governmental supporters and former rebel combatants is a way to control an endless cycle of repoliticization, by checks to avert partisan domination of the institution. The fear of factional political domination, is quintessentially American, and its control through a form of checks and balances (through diverse political representation) is long-standing in the region.[75] The path to institutional transformation ran a spectrum from the individual to the collective, by way of the individual purgings of "evil soldiers" and the influx of "good soldiers." In the military, the relation between individual constituents and the military body is especially close, as is evident in its command structure. It follows that demilitarization in the Americas involving a blend of the individual and the structural, reflected the especially close connection between the individual and the collective, epitomized by the corporate understandings of responsibility that distinguish the military. Therefore, transitions out of military rule tolerate lesser adherence to individual due process than contemplated in our intuitions about the rule of law in established democratic systems.

### Of War and Peace

Attempts to reform the national security apparatus are commonly rationalized by the peace. Purges easily become the gravamen of peace agreements, wherever the predicate for initial political change is justified in the purposes of peace and reconciliation. Indeed, the peace justification is bound up in the means deployed in the Salvador purges. According to the peace accords, military demobilization would move the country to the next stage. Purges of the security apparatus went hand in hand with a new security doctrine, whereby the military was made subject to the constitution.[76] The Salvador purges advance weighty interests in the peace, as their provenance lay in the peace agreements. Moreover, the attempt to ascribe individual responsibility lifts guilt from the collective to relegitimate the military.

Other military reconstitution in the region has been similarly rationalized in the name of the peace. The relation among transformation, security, and peace is manifest, for example, in nearby Haiti. After years of military rule and the withdrawal of multinational forces, the question arose of what to do with Haiti's security apparatus. Its interim police force, still composed of former members of the repressive military, had not been subjected to even the screening mechanisms that might have excluded human rights violators.[77] Failure to vet rights abusers and the simple transfer of personnel from one part of the security apparatus to another fostered the perception of an utter lack of authority and legitimacy in the force.[78] The perceived absence of a legitimate law enforcement body signified an attendant absence of security and peace. A similar agreement was made regarding Cambodia, which authorized United Nations Transitional Authority In Cambodia (UNTAC) to make personnel decisions.

Though transitional purges are generally controversial, those involving the security apparatus have been widely supported.[79] Transformation of the security sector justifies the most radical measures, for here the nexus between the purge response as means and the purpose of prospective rule of law seems to be its tightest. Where the threat to security lies in a discrete sector, the security apparatus, political transformation depends on its restructuring and legitimation. Conversely, when such changes are not carried out, security forces are apparently rendered unable to guarantee security. Transitional practices concerning the security sector point to an especially close relation between structural change and the transformation to a rule-of-law system under civilian rule. The security apparatus purges highlight the specially close relation of the individual to the collective in particular spheres of affiliation, suggesting heightened justifications for such measures in the attempt to structure political transformation from the national security state. Indeed, grounded as they are in security, postmilitary purges are ultimately the means that come closest to the ends of political transformation. Even in established democracies, political purges are often rationalized as expedients to national security and peace, particularly true of wartime. For example, during World War II, mass internment of citizens of the United States based on ethnic origin was said to be justified on the grounds of "national security."[80] The basis for the ethnical internment measures was later found to be a pretext for the political exclusions. Politicized exclusions were similarly justified during the cold war. While ordinarily security justifications ring hollow, they take on greater force in wartime, as well as in transitional periods of radical change.

Postmilitary purges remain extraordinary transitional measures, presenting responses to a distinct perception of the sources of institutional weakness, that is of a "critical" nature, for demilitarization necessitates clarifying the particular relation security bears to legitimacy and authority. When the security apparatus fails to subject itself to civil law, the singular threat posed is that the very institutions intended to provide security, instead, perpetrate repression and insecurity. Indeed, the struggle over the military purges in the transition itself reveals the region's pervasive rule-of-law problem. Military purges reveal the difficulty of reforming deeply politicized law enforcement institutions, offering a cautionary tale about the limits of administrative justice. Nevertheless, for regimes moving out of national security rule, demilitarization instantiates threshold newfound constraints on military power and the triumph of civilian rule and, therefore, offers a facet of the reinstatement of the rule of law.

## Militating Democracy

In contemporary transitions since the postwar period, public law has been the site of somewhat anomalous protection against past evil that takes the form of what is sometimes known as "militant democracy."[81] Militant democracy is a transitional response peculiar to the paradox of modern repression, whose origins are often democratic in that they are preceded by free elections. When repressive rule emerges out of the simple workings of democracy, how to understand the evil: To what extent is it in the people, the party, the state? And what bearing for the direction of the transformation? After the horrors of fascism, this was a central question of transitional justice. For Nazism had apparently taken hold in Germany through simple parliamentary politics, with a political majority vigorously opposed to the prevailing political order.[82] Fascism and its horrors were attributed to the weakness of the prior Weimar Republic and to extremist political parties that became populist movements subverting democracy. With this perverse legacy of democratic politics gone awry, after the Nazi collapse, the question became how to guard democracy for the future. There, the greatest threat to the possibility of liberal order was perceived to be the party that operated from within the democratic political system, only to subvert it. It is this peculiar historical legacy of political repression that animates the response known as "militant democracy"—the attempt to guard from within against the subversion of the democratic system.

"Militant democracy" responds to a distinctive prior tyranny but, in so doing, redefines democracy. For militant democracy justifies the constitutional suppression of political parties that, if left unchecked, would jeopardize the democratic order; within the scheme of militant democracy, the "unconstitutional" party lies outside permissible politics.[83] Putting certain political associations outside the bounds reconstitutes the parameters of the political system.

The dilemma raised by militant democracy is the restriction on democracy in the name of democracy. This is but a more extreme form of the political conditions and disabilities already discussed. To some extent the scheme is mitigated by its processes: Though party banning may be initiated by the political branches, it is ultimately predicated on action by the Constitutional Court. Accordingly, what is "antidemocratic," and outside the constitutional scheme, will be a matter for constitutional interpretation. Thus, in its interpretation of militant democracy, the Constitutional Court operates as the guardian of the new democratic order. Just after the war, in the Socialist Party case, there is only one issue: the extent to which there is continuity of identity with the Nazi Party, requiring party exclusion. The neo–Nazi Party is the paradigm of the anti-democratic party, which in its membership, structure, and ideology, is nothing other than the revival of the old Nazi Party.[84] Yet with the advent of the cold war throughout Europe, the potential threat to democracy went beyond neo-Nazism. When Konrad Adenauer's government initiated Article 21, the constitutional action to ban Germany's Communist Party, the relevant question, the court said, was whether the party's purpose was to combat the "democratic" order. There had to be a showing of "actual danger" to the democratic system; "antidemocratic" purposes had to be made manifest "in political action." This was similar to the "clear and present danger" standard applied by the United States Supreme Court in reviewing similar legislation enacted to ban the Communist Party in the United States during the cold war period. Militating against democratic party politics might seem perverse, but Germany's Constitutional Court reasoned, it was justified by the country's historical experience and repressive legacy. Constitutional suppression of a party occurred only twice in the seven-year period since the country's establishment in 1949, with the banning of the neo–Nazi Party in 1952 and the German Communist Party in 1956.[85] With the passage of time, the need for hypervigilance appeared to pass. Thus, by 1968, when the Communist Party of Germany gave way to its successor, such political representation no longer appeared controversial. In both Germany and the United States, repression of the Communist Party occurred for a limited time after the war; when the principle of militant democracy appeared to hold sway.

Constitutional suppression of a party would rarely be exercised in Germany; and, as a practical matter, it was largely limited to the transitional period. Nevertheless, all over the region, throughout postwar Europe's changing constitutional systems, the response to totalitarianism frequently took the form of militant democracy. Constitutional limits were placed on political associations on the basis of democracy. Thus, for example, Turkey's constitution provides that "political parties must accord with the principles of democracy." While Portugal's constitution limits freedom of association specifically in postwar terms, as it proscribes "organizations which adopt fascist ideology."[86] Throughout the region, the response to the historic fear of democratic politics gone awry is constitutional repression. Through this structural response, dangerous forms of political expression are put outside the established political order. Limiting permissible politics becomes the rule of law of the transition, though its exercise by this transitional constitutional standard makes a more lasting contribution as it informs the country's identity.

The postwar response to fascism is to take the opposition to democracy outside permissible politics. Militant democracy raises the dilemma of what to do with political parties that endanger the very democracy that spawned them. The transitional case illuminates a broader pathology of democratic politics: of illiberal rule resulting from democratic means. Indeed, the case illuminates the sense in which democracies raise a quintessential form of the dilemma of means/ends discussed in this chapter. The militant democracy case exposes the tension and suggests that at least in transitional times, illiberal processes are tolerated, when there are extraordinarily weighty democracy-building purposes.

## The Party and the People

Perhaps the most radical party-driven attempt at political transformation is evidenced in the contemporary postcommunist transitions. During the fall of the Soviet Union, auto-purges of the Communist Party were the leading sign of political change. Indeed, the collapse began in 1991 when then-President Mikhail Gorbachev called on the Communist Party of the Soviet Union (CPSU) Central Committee to dissolve itself. Throughout the various republics, Communist Parties ceased to exist, either by outright banning, presidential decrees, or constitutional reform. The end of one-party rule, as well as the circumscribing of its other privileges, signaled the beginnings of the opening of the political order. Since the party's status had been previously entrenched in the region's legal scheme, its collapse, too, was formalized through the law. Political transformation could occur only by breaking the linkage between the party and state power, so that sovereignty could visibly shift from the party to the people.[87] Through constitutional change, the Communist Party was stripped of its assets and barred from exercising privileged public power.[88] Even the term Marxism-Leninism was purged from the constitution. Delegitimated and corrupt, the regime seemed virtually to collapse of its own accord.

After the critical political changes, the question became what to do with the Communist Party? Could a party accustomed to one-party rule adapt to democratic party politics? Might this weakened entity somehow undermine the attempt to consolidate a liberal democratic order? To what extent should the Communist Party be treated like other political parties and allowed to vie for state power? After repressive one-party rule, did the Communist Party have any legitimacy? Or, was the party's identity essentially synonymous with the totalitarian state? On the latter view, meaningful change meant that the party ought to be dissolved. While if the party's identity was not conflated with the state, it could continue to play some part in the transition to more democratic politics. The question was pivotal, with potential repercussions all over the region.

The issue came to a head in 1991, when Russia's newly formed Constitutional Court ruled on the constitutionality of its Communist Party. In August 1991, soon after an attempted coup, then President Boris Yeltsin challenged Russia's Communist Party on grounds of unconstitutionality, through presidential decrees that shut down the leadership apparatus of the party, the Politburo and policy-making Central Committee, as well as local party structures.[89] Yet Russia, unlike Germany, had no preexisting constitutional scheme allowing the suppression of extremist parties. Accordingly, there were several issues before the court: the constitutionality of the Communist Party of the Soviet Union, as well as the constitutionality of the executive exercise of authority outlawing the party on constitutional grounds.[90] It had been only after political actors turned to the Constitutional Court to quash Yeltsin's ban that an obviously self-interested Parliament hastily amended the country's constitution to allow high-court review of the constitutionality of political parties.[91] Under the German model of constitutional suppression of a party, the Constitutional Court was the ultimate arbiter of what behavior was deemed "undemocratic." But in post–Soviet Russia, whatever would constitutional review of the parties mean?

The question was whether Yeltsin's attempted party ban was based on the abstract likelihood of subversion, whether "the actions of the President were dictated by the objective need to prevent a return to the earlier situation."[92] Coming so soon after an attempted coup, Yeltsin's decree raised a question about party wrongdoing. Alleging party leadership responsibility in the attempted putsch, his decree alleged, "It has become clear that while the CPSU structures exist there can be no guarantees against another putsch or coup taking place."[93] In the party ban proceedings, witnesses testified in daily hearings to about a half century of party corruption and power abuses, revelations of criminal wrongdoing in Katyn and Afghanistan, establishing responsibility at the top party structure level. After decades of repression, the party's threatening nature was made real.

Coming out of a repressive totalitarian system in which the party was not subject to the rule of law, the question was how to transform party power and create a stable multiparty system. Constitutional suppression of the party put some of the responsibility in an independent court. In considering Russia's party ban, the Constitutional Court would ultimately strike a Solomonic compromise, holding that democracy justifications supported the party ban for its higher echelons, the ruling Politburo and policy-making Central Committee, but that a similar ban would not abide at the local level. Through a judicial process adverting to the bases that constituted party wrongdoing, the justifications for the state action were made public. The Constitutional Court played a significant part in the minimal rule-of-law processes rationalizing what otherwise appeared to be a political purge.

## Militant Democracy and the Liberal State

Consider constitutional suppression of a party and its underlying principle of militant democracy. In the above examples, certain political parties were censored as threats to the liberalizing state. The threats are collective in nature, as are the sanctions—dissolution of the party and confiscation of its property. Sanctioning political parties expresses political judgment on a collective basis and, as such, is seemingly incompatible with our intuitions about the workings of the liberal state. Accordingly, the question raised is, Are these justified protections against genuine threats to the constitutional order or simply politicized constraints on unpopular political minorities? To begin, when a political majority limits a political minority from participating in the public sphere, this policy will always appear suspect.

However, whether the converse may be a scenario within the realm of possibility, will depend upon the role of the courts. Militant democracy is a transitional response premised on a particular view of the pathology of democratic politics: of the paradox of democratic and, yet, nonetheless illiberal rule. Militant democracy ultimately exposes a tension present in democracy and liberalism, indeed, one that is recurring in constitutional democracies. Just how generalizable is this dilemma of democracy? In the contemporary wave of transition and constitutionalism, the questions arose of how to respond to illiberal rule and whether to follow Germany's constitutional example. To what extent should the militant democracy response be emulated and guide transformative party politics elsewhere? This question arose in the postcommunist transitions. Militant democracy is a response to tyranny bound up with a distinctive European history. In East Europe and Russia, repressive rule originated not in Weimar-like politics, but in totalitarianism. In the region, the particular historical political pathology has not been the problem of too much democracy, for example, the control exerted by fringe parties, but its converse—one-party rule. Nevertheless, the argument for extension of the militant democratic view is that when repressive rule inheres in patently undemocratic processes, such one-party rule regime often perpetrates its hold over a protracted period only by virtue of societal acquiescence. Yet, militant democratic schemes in the absence of a strong democratic tradition may well threaten incipient democracies. When such constitutional suppression power of a party is not cabined, other than through judicial interpretation, the power is a transient phenomenon.

The transitional phenomenon of vigilance raises a broader question, of whether and to what extent democratic conditionality ought posit a normative guide of such political systems on a more permanent basis. The postwar model implemented in Germany depends on the judiciary for its operation. Judicial interpretation reflects the attempt to move away from vague notions of political extremism to more objective bases, such as political violence. Modern constitutional jurisprudence reflects this interpretation. Though constitutional standards regarding party banning have tended to move in a liberalizing direction, protective of freedoms of association and expression, there is always the danger of the courts' politicization. Even in established democracies, there are periods when the countries' high courts have been more vulnerable to politicization, such as the United States Supreme Court during its cold war period.

The transitional questions raised by conditional democracy frameworks also arises in similar questions regarding more enduring arrangements in the liberal state. Thus, for example, the contemporary examples of party banning in Europe and the Middle East, such as in Algeria and Turkey, involved extremism and religious factionalization.[94] Throughout Europe, there have long been political parties that are nominally religious; yet, the question is where to draw the line. How should these parties be treated in the liberal state? In the contemporary wave of postcommunist transition, the question takes on a new urgency. Identity politics poses a profound challenge to the transitioning state, with the conflicts in the former Yugoslavia grim illustrations. However, transitional justice offers a way to reconstruct the state, rather than along an identity politics, instead along an assertedly political and juridical rights-based identity.

The transitional dilemmas, though they pertain to extraordinary times, expose the tension latent in democratic theory, of the potential for head-on conflict between democratic processes and democratic purposes. This potential conflict often comes up in questions concerning the limits of tolerance in the liberal state.[95] For example, in *"The Law of Peoples,"* John Rawls contends for a "tolerance" approach to political threats to democracy.[96] Yet, recall the dilemma that frames this chapter, of the tension that is exacerbated in transitional times, where in periods of shift from past repression, the very construction of democracy constitutes a justification for limiting majoritarian processes and compromising on ideal rule of law. This tension is rationalized in the constitutional schemes defined by militant democracy, because the extremist party must be suppressed or it threatens the political order. On this view, only constitutional suppression allows transitional regimes to reconstruct their political identities. The explicitly political aspect of these measures is mitigated somewhat by the availability of judicial review. The line that is reconstructed here is of a "critical" transformative nature, as it concerns the role of the political and its redefinition in relation to the state's constitution. When transitional administrative measures go beyond political to constitutional processes, these measures are explicitly rationalized by the normative justifications of democracy. Although in ordinary times, the question and role of such measures is often somewhat backgrounded, defining the state's constitutionally entrenched political parameters of membership, of participation, of exit; in transitional times, these processes of state building are exposed and come to the fore.

## Justice between the Generations

The practices here discussed, associated with periods of radical political change, shape the very societal understanding of political transformation. These practices advance the sense of social constitution of delimited times as periods of political change. These are the rituals that define political time, of political periodization that construct a "before" and "after." Such periods are generally understood in temporal terms, What is the role of time in political transformation?

An ancient story recounted in the Bible illuminates the role of time in political transformation. In Exodus, there is the account of the movement of a people—to freedom. In the biblical account, the ancient Israelites spend forty years in the wilderness, before they can move from slavery in Egypt to their new life as a free people. This transformation is said to take forty years.

> 22] none of the men who have seen My Presence and the signs that I have performed in Egypt and in the wilderness, and who have tried Me these many times and have disobeyed Me, 23] shall see the land that I promised on oath to their fathers none of those who spurn Me shall see it, . . . 29] Of all of you who were recorded in your various lists from the age of twenty years up, you who mutter against Me, 30] not one shall enter the land in which I swore to settle you . . . 31] Your children who, you said, would be carried off— these will I allow to enter; they shall know the land that you have rejected. 33] while your children roam the wilderness for forty years, suffering for your faithlessness.[97]

Of what significance is the forty years in the wilderness? In the biblical paradigm, the transformation from an enslaved to a free people takes time—apparently two generations. And the transformation appears to imply an interim, transitional stage characterized by the time in the "wilderness." "For a sudden transformation from one opposite to another is impossible."[98] The impact of the generational, time-based purge is universal and absolute. Not one person who knew slavery in Egypt would reach the Promised Land. Even Moses, the liberation's leader would die before the polity's entry to the new land and, therefore, is excluded from participation in the new political freedom. The passage of time defines the political generation forming the new nation.[99]

Another illustration of time's operative role in defining the phases and generations of political transformation is seen in the shift from monarchy to republicanism. Time-based conditions of a generational nature are the predicates for meaningful change. Thus, in the 1787 American Constitution, are embedded qualifications for political leadership in defining the participating generation of the nation. The U.S. Constitution, at Article II, defines the qualifications for candidates to the presidency, "natural" citizenship and a minimum age of thirty-five.[100] These two constitutional qualifications, of age and natural citizenship, combine to exclude likely Royalist sympathizers or their children. Together, these qualifications serve to construct an eligible political generation. This constitutional rule, conditional on political generation, precludes from eligibility for the highest political office those presumed likely to be lacking in a firm commitment to the country's independence and to its transition to republican rule. Although these qualifications were adopted at a time of substantial political change, they remain constitutional parameters for the highest political office today.

Another instance emerges in the contemporary transitions out of Communist rule in East Europe, where time before and after is punctuated by the proxy for political trust. Age-based disabilities were deployed in the attempt to transform the emerging political parties in the move to the multiparty system. In Hungary, the political party "Fidesz," is founded after the revolution, translated literally as "young democratic union," it also signified "trust." Claiming to stand for political trust in the transition, Fidesz adopted a party disqualification rule excluding from its ranks anyone over thirty-five. The party's age condition was a symbol of clean, noncollaborationist party membership and considered to ensure trust. The limit was dropped about five years after the political change. There are also the time-based conditions seen in the revanchism in which former Communists have regained power in the region. Thus, for example, in Bulgaria, when the socialists regained political power, legislation was enacted requiring five years' experience for public employment.[101] Time-based conditions were an easy proxy for ideology based on adherence to Communism, as those meeting the necessary qualifications could only be those supportive of the prior regime. Thus, qualifications drawn on the basis of time can operate as proxies for overt political disabilities.

Conditions for political participation and representation are often pervasively time-based even in ordinary times. Indeed, one need only think of the requirements for political franchise, often predicated on citizenship based on a five-year naturalization period. Such a period is commonly considered the predicate necessary showing of loyalty and political affiliation associated with political membership, and participation. Beyond citizenship, implying conditions for mere membership, are other sorts of age and time requirements for other positions of political representation. The transitional rituals of political purification are more exaggerated forms of those regularly associated with taking stock or the census that defines the political community. Historically (in Roman times), as well as up to the present, in ordinary times, these measures of counting the population are commonly deployed at five year intervals.[102] Indeed, the census constitutes the embedded form of political lustration that is ordinarily used to evaluate and define the parameters of the political community.

Time-based disabilities can be sweeping, and the impact of such exclusions radical, enabling exclusion of entire political generations. Nevertheless, since these exclusions are not explicitly drawn on the basis of ideology, time-related disqualifications appear politically neutral and not expressly normative. Time-based conditions are hidden and yet pervasive. They can be sweeping, often excluding entire political generations. Such conditions can operate to prevent all members of a political generation, whether or not compromised by the prior regime, from participating in the new political order. In this way, time-based qualifications operate as proxies for disqualifications that discriminate explicitly on a political basis. Though outwardly politically neutral, time-based disabilities can effect tremendous political change. Through time-based conditions, societal transformation occurs over time. States' political identities are constituted in time.

When age- or time-based conditions are placed on political participation, an entire generation bears the burden of political transformation. The transitional generation is asked to sacrifice itself for the sake of the future. Thus, problems of intergenerational justice are not solely the purview of periods of transition; yet, insofar as these arise they do so in the context of issues of distributive justice. Paradoxically, the ordinary inquiry is framed in terms of whether the present older generation is benefiting itself at the expense of future generations.[103] The issue that arises most frequently relates to the environment or other resources. But in the case of transitional justice, in periods of shifts from repressive to more liberal regimes, the usual intergenerational justice problem and its directionality are inapposite; it is the present generation whose sacrifice favors future generations. Considered within an intergenerational context, sanctions or property confiscations emerge as sacrificial, even redemptive. In transitional times, as previously discussed, political purges and similar measures are often justified for the sake of the political future.

It is often said that for true and lasting political change, time must pass. At the intuitive level, no doubt, the passage of time has cognizable political consequences. The practices discussed above illuminate the affirmative use of time as a basis for political change. Whether or not other conditions are placed on the political order, when time passes, it has consequences for societal and political change. The mere passage of time may effect political transformation.

## Transitional Administrative Justice

"Lustration," "lustrace" "epuracion," "purification," "zwiering," "reconstruction," "demilitarization," "depuración"—the recurring transitional purge practices discussed in this chapter suggest that political conditionality through the law is endemic to periods of political transformation. Transitional practices reveal the pervasive uses of the public law to define a new polity. For a time, a provisional public law redefines status by reconstructing core understandings of supporter and opposition, of friend and foe. Despite diverse societies and legal cultures, legal purges are persistently used to effectuate political change. Radical public measures critically reconstruct the parameters of the political community, as well as the terms of participation in a changing political order, for these political purges and other political conditions bear the law's imprimatur, albeit provisional in nature.

The measures discussed in this chapter challenge our intuitions about what it means to move to a liberalizing rule-of-law state: for their procedural irregularity, for their lack of prospectivity, for their fluid approach to individual and collective responsibility, and last, for their explicit politicization. For all these reasons, the practices discussed in this chapter challenge our bedrock intuitions about liberalization. Recognizing the role of these practices in transition sheds light on the absence of a fixed core value in the liberalizing state, as well as drawing attention to the political realities surrounding the building of the liberal state coming out of dictatorship. The practices raise questions about the extent of successor regimes' discretion to shape the new administration on an ideological basis and to temporize on political liberties for a time until a more liberal regime consolidates.

To begin, consider what the chapter teaches about how these informal politicized measures emerge; in transitions, de facto purges outside the law commonly precede their regulation. These measures are irregular, in part informal, in part formal law. As such, transitional measures illuminate that, in shifts between regimes, there is often no one norm to apply. This is the central political fact with which this book begins, the shift in regimes. The change in political regimes and its attendant normative shift imply a number of ensuing dilemmas for adherence to the rule of law. The transitional administrative measures here discussed mediate periods of radical political upheaval in their critical reconstruction of status, rights, and responsibilities in the society working for political transformation.

Though states often enjoy substantial latitude in the shaping of the public administration; nevertheless, in ordinary times, such decision making is not usually openly partisan. Politicized measures enable radical political change by instantiating it, effecting political reconstitution through the speedy redistribution of rights to political membership, representation, and participation. These measures are truly the machinery of the revolution in their capacity to dislodge existing power structures, as they consolidate the prevailing regime in its progress toward liberalization.

Despite their strong connection to the political circumstances of the transition, the measures here discussed also challenge standard accounts of law's relation to political and social change. To begin, the turn to law, rather than to frontier justice, is a response to past wrongs that is measured and controlled and that follows formal processes. For the course of the law proceeds not merely as a function of political circumstances but, rather, is from the start intended as part of the transitional design. Here, law is not merely responsive but instrumental to political change producing shifts in the balance of the power. Though liberal regimes strive for a law that is independent from politics and agnostic on matters of political opinion, in transitional times, law is invariably politicized. For a set period, circumscribed public measures reconstruct the very contours of the nation. Transitional measures are bounded; their finite nature cabins and delimits an extraordinary period in the life of the state, itself constructive of transition.

This most radical use of the law can effect speedy and far-reaching political change. In their most deliberately politicized transformative functions, administrative measures are "critical" in their modality. When they effect deliberate repoliticization of the public sphere, these practices posit a critical response to prior evil rule. Responses to prior political discrimination and persecution shape the liberalizing states' enduring normative commitments by undoing the predecessor regimes' political structures, by inverting the prevailing power relations. How does return to transitional practices effect transformation? The practices reviewed here suggest that this transformation occurs by inversion, by a recombination of the traditional forms, through measures structured along collective categorical criteria, the very fault lines of political dissensus enabling the constitution of consensus. These most transformative functions of the law, in practice, are delegated, informal, discretionary, political. If public law is the way the expanded modern state ordinarily achieves its regulatory goals, its potential is even more pronounced in periods of radical change. Transitional periods reveal a sharply politicized public law, whereby the law's regulatory uses are thin, often apparently symbolic, relying largely on law's rhetorical force. Transitional administrative measures are at the same time justificatory and performative of political transformation, with wide force as they penetrate public bureaucracy. At a time of political flux, the regulatory regime enables public reconstruction of the new political ideology. Through these measures, political judgment is passed upon the predecessor regime; establishing new standards for public justification and rationalizing the normative transition, the old regime is delegitimated, the old ideology disowned, and the new legitimated. Delegitimation of the old regime is effected by the categorical reconstruction of who is a political insider and who is a political outsider through the public law. Through these measures, a past political order is purged, and a new political order is injected with new reasons and bases given for political loyalty and affiliation. "Bans," "purges," "oaths," "purification," "lustration," "trials," and "publications" all constitute a form of public proclamation that lays the basis and is itself performative of a normative shift.[104] These ritualized forms are the ways in which law effects change in power relations to reconstruct the political community and individuals are tested and purged to express the new political truth. These public measures compose a new regime, both constituting and legitimating of the successor regime.

The political justifications (i.e., the law's "purposes") for transitional regulatory measures are an express part of the regulation's political conditionality. By explicitly conditioning on a political basis, these measures transform state identity. Reconstruction of the public law in categories that explicitly respond to the predecessor political regime constitutes critical transitional transformation. The undoing of persecutory collective measures—perpetrated on a racial, ethnic, or religious basis—is performed by measures propounded along political criteria. Predecessor regulatory regimes serve as an important background, throwing into relief the meaning and normative force of the transitional measures. What constitutes liberalizing political transformation in the successor regime comes into focus only in the light of predecessor political identity. While constructing national identity, along ethnic, national, or religious lines may well be in tension with core liberal precepts, liberal states do permissibly discriminate on a political basis; there is some latitude to legislate on the basis of political opinion. Indeed, decision making on a political basis in the public domain is often permissibly related to legitimate state interests; a fortiori, this would be even more true of transformative periods of heightened change.

Transitional administrative measures challenge our intuitions about the liberal state, but the uses of these measures in societies are not without justification. For the paradox here, as is plainly seen in the transitional judicial review, is that the very justification for these seemingly illiberal measures is liberalism. The measures are justified by the very values that underlie the threatened rule-of-law principles: political freedom and equality. Though such measures threaten the conventional rule of law, what supports their use, at least as a temporary matter, is that they are justified in the successor regulatory regime by the future aim of constructing a more liberal state.

Short-acting administrative measures by their very radical form—highly politicized, sweeping, collective—present profound challenges to the rule of law associated with the liberal state, in a number of ways. To begin, it is an axiom of the liberal state that its citizens are treated as individuals, rather than as members of groups and on an ascriptive basis; further, notions of guilt by association are antagonistic to liberalism. These liberal intuitions are often thought to apply in the transition, whereby new freedom from communally based oppression creates expectations of eliminating the group-based difference. Nonetheless, these expectations notwithstanding, the measures discussed in this chapter depart from these ideal liberal intuitions by perpetuating collective judgment, lacking individualized due process, in what amounts to a collapse of lawmaking and judgment procedures challenging to ideal rule-of-law and liberal values. When transitional administrative measures sanction a political class, they pass political judgment. Our intuitions about such judgment generally are that conduct that rises to the level of individualized criminal wrongdoing is permissibly relevant to prospective participation in the liberal state; nevertheless, judgments on a collective basis ordinarily challenge fundamental liberal tenets regarding individual accountability. Yet, transitional administrative measures bridge the individual and the collective, effecting change at a broader structural level of a changing political system. These measures elide conventional categories of the law. Transitional administrative measures raise a confluence of entitlements, of property, reputation, and political rights; yet, it is precisely in periods of political and economic change that little societal consensus exists on the status of these entitlements and, relatedly, on what process is due.[105] Though administrative sanctions are often considered to constitute "punishment," yet, unlike traditional punishment, these procedures generally do not ascribe individual responsibility but, instead, define a responsible class along political lines. Whatever the ideal expectations about the role that individual responsibility plays in the liberal state, these are inapposite to transitional times, where there emerges a more fluid transitional understanding of the relation of individual to polity. In so doing, these measures bridge a central transitional debate regarding whether responses to past evil rule ought to be individual or structural.[106] By sweeping uses of the public law, transitional jurisprudence effects both individual and structural change.

These measures shed light on our intuitions about the perceived significance of core rule-of-law tenets: of law's prospectivity, of the circumscribed relation of the individual to the collective, and, more broadly, upon the role of the political in the liberal state. The study of transitional law undertaken here exposes the tension in the often conflicting rule-of-law values and in opposing individual and structural approaches in the law. The tensions revealed give rise to new mediating forms. These measures are transitional, defining a bounded space for law that is partial, failing to comport with the full rule of law. Here is the most pervasive form of resolving the transitional dilemma, temporizing:

transitional measures are frequently short-lived and distinguishable by their simultaneous lack of retrospectivity and prospectivity, that is, circumscribing the parameters of an extraordinary boundedness. Postwar denazification and purification, post–Civil War Reconstruction, and Eastern and Central Europe's post-Communist lustration, postmilitary measures, all legislated for a limited time period, correspond to periods of the greatest political transformation lasting about five years after the regime's changeover. As such, these purge measures are definitional of the political transition. This legislation of heightened transitionality is designed to apply only to a circumscribed period of political change; in their simultaneous retrospectivity and nonprospectivity, these measures delimit and structure the period's transition.

The energetic uses of the public law discussed here suggest a way to think about administrative law over time. From a comparative and historical perspective, across legal cultures, the most energetic uses of the public law correspond to periods of greater reform. An empirical approach from a historical and comparative perspective goes beyond prevailing theory to account for these uses of the law. Transformative uses of the law in these periods go beyond bare political realities but also depart significantly from ideal theorizing that abstracts from established rule-of-law systems.

Transitional constitutional measures such as those adopted after the Civil War in Reconstruction and in postcommunist unified Germany illuminate affinities between administrative and constitutional measures, discussed in the next chapter. The practices here discussed relate to a short period associated with the greatest political transformation, but the transitory measures often have a more long-lasting legacy. Through these measures, the state's reconstruction of political membership, participation, and leadership visibly turns on renewed political commitments. It seems right that public officials uphold core constitutional norms as a condition of public office, and these values are generally backgrounded in constitutional law. Beyond periods of upheaval, these core structural political parameters are simply taken for granted, while they become more manifest in transition. By the last half of the twentieth century, the normative conditions of political status, membership, and participation have almost universally become constitutionalized the core agreements guiding the nation's political life constitutionally entrenched. In periods of political upheaval, public regulatory law serves, like constitutional law, to redefine the normative parameters of the political community in flux, conditions of political membership and participation in the public domain. These transitional measures suggest that periods of political change imply a somewhat backgrounded deconstitutionalization. Even in the general absence of constitutional consensus, these administrative measures critically redefine the political order.

## CHAPTER SIX

# Constitutional Justice

*T*his chapter turns to the nature and role of constitutionalism in periods of political change. The central dilemma is how to reconcile the concept of constitutionalism with revolution: Revolutionary periods and their aftermath are times of political flux and, as such, present tensions with constitutionalism, which is ordinarily considered to bind an enduring political order. Consider the prevailing conception of the relation of constitutional to political change and, in particular, the modern claim for constitutionalism as foundational to democracy. This model, it is argued here, best describes an eighteenth-century view of the relation of the constitutional to the political; hence it cannot capture the constitutional developments associated with political change during the last half century and, as such, needs to be supplemented.[1] This chapter explores contemporary manifestations of constitutionalism, particularly of the last wave of substantial political change, and contends that these give rise to another paradigm of transitional constitutionalism, providing an alternative account of constitutionalism in its third century. The alternative paradigm proposed here should have ramifications beyond the transition for prevailing understandings of constitutionalism, judicial review, and relevant interpretive principles.

Constitutionalism in periods of political change it is contended stands in "constructivist" relation to the prevailing political order. Transitional constitutionalism not only is constituted by the prevailing political order but also is constitutive of political change. This is the constitutional document's constructivist role. Transitional constitutions arise in a variety of processes, often playing multiple roles: serving conventional constitutions' purposes, as well as having other more radical purposes in transformative politics. Transitional constitution making is also responsive to prior rule, through principles that critically refine the prevailing political system, effecting further political change in the system. Transitional constitutions are simultaneously backward- and forward-looking, informed by a conception of constitutional justice that is distinctively transitional.

## The Prevailing Models

Theorizing about the nature and role of constitutionalism in periods of political change is commonly guided by competing realist or idealist perspectives. In the realist view, constitutions in periods of political change are thought simply to reflect the prevailing balance of political power and, therefore, are epiphenomenal with, and arise by virtue of, the provenance of the political change.[2] Under this view, it is not at all clear what distinguishes the making of a constitution from other lawmaking; what, if any, is the distinctive value of constitutions in the transition? As such, this approach offers little to the project of discerning the significance of the nature and role of constitutionalism in such periods.

It follows that the dominant approach to the study of constitutionalism in periods of political change derives from idealist constitutional theorizing, where there is a normative claim for a strong connection between revolution and constitution making. This strong connection first appears in the classical constitutional model in Aristotle's writings. Although the classical understanding of constitutionalism generally is not considered to follow an idealist model, in its view of the relation of constitutions to political change, it shares affinities with the model discussed herein. Its modern expression appears in Hannah Arendt's work, and a contemporary articulation can be found in the work of Bruce Ackerman, discussed in this chapter. Although these are different in important aspects, there are affinities among these claims for the potential of constitution making in effecting political change. Below, these views are explored and discussed as a triad in the intellectual history of constitutional politics.

Constitutionalism in periods of political transformation raises a basic tension between radical political change and the constraints on such change that would appear to be the predicate of constitutional order. In the idealist model discussed more fully below, the dilemma is reconciled by positing that constitutionalism functions as the very basis of the new political order: a claim for constitutional foundationalism.

### The Classical View

In the classical view, the constitution is understood as the state's fundamental political arrangements, the distinctive form or organization determining its structure and function. In the Aristotelian view, constitutions are organic entities: "The 'constitution' of a state is the organization of the offices . . ."[3] On this understanding, the constitution is at once normative and descriptive. "[T]he association which is a state exists not for the purpose of living together but for the sake of noble actions."[4] Accordingly, in the classical view, revolutionary political change means constitutional change. Radical political transformation does not necessarily require a change in political leadership, representation, or membership, for it is the constitution that determines the identity of the polis. When the constitution changes, so does the polis: "For the state is a kind of association—an association of citizens in a constitution;

so when the constitution changes and becomes different in kind, the state also would seem necessarily not to be the same."[5]

The classical account of constitutional politics is organic constitutionalism. In the classical view, the unity of the acts of revolution and constitution mediates the dilemma posed by the relation of constitutionalism to political change. Issues of justice remain, despite the move to a more democratic order. Yet this account leads to the following questions: What is the relationship between reconstitution and political change? How does the new constitutional consciousness that defines the transition occur? The classical paradigm invites, but does not elaborate, a theory of the role of constitutionalism in the process of political change.

### The Modern Claim

As distinguished from the classical view, modern constitutional theory emphasizes normative limits on state power of a structural and individual rights nature. Nevertheless, as we shall see, aspects of the classical conceptualization remain pertinent to the modern model, at least with regard to the reigning vision of the nature and role of constitutions in periods of political change. The classical view equates constitutions with political arrangements, with implications for the preeminent nature and role of constitutionalism in periods of political change. The paradoxical role of modern constitutions is that they are considered to provide such limits on government despite periods of political change. How is one to reconcile the modern view of constitutionalism with constitutional change?

This is the dilemma of constitutionalism in the context of massive political change. For Hannah Arendt, the dilemma is resolved through a rethinking of the theory of constitutionalism. Rather than conceptualizing constitution making as counterrevolutionary and the opposite of political change, the "truly revolutionary element in constitution-making" is "the act of foundation."[6] The Arendtian vision of revolutionary constitution making draws heavily from American constitution making. In this version, the apparent dilemma of the incompatibility of revolution and constitution disappears; the two political acts merge. The constitution is deemed the culmination of revolution; it is the "deliberate attempt by a whole people at founding a new body politic."[7]

The Arendtian vision resolves the tension between revolution and constitutionalism through the mediating idea of foundation. America's revolutionaries are described as "Founding Fathers" preoccupied with "permanence." In constitution making, their purpose is "the deeply felt desire for an Eternal City on earth," and the wish to create a government that "would be capable of arresting the cycle of sempiternal change, the rise and fall of empires, and establish[ing] an immortal city."[8] The notion of a founding elegantly reconciles the dilemma of political change with constitutional permanence. Though paradoxical, the very nature of the revolutionary change sought is the constitutive act of founding. American constitutionalism is distinguished by the paradox of constitutional change: It is revolutionary but lasting. The American posture toward its revolution ushered in a new paradigm of constitutionalism as foundational to its democratic order. In this paradigm, constitutionalism was something other than its classical sense, identified with the political order. It was also more than constitutionalism in the Magna Carta sense, as protective of negative liberties. The idea of constitutional democracy transcended the protection of individual rights. "Constitution-making" is considered by the framers as "the foremost and the noblest of all revolutionary deeds."[9] An idealized foundational constitutionalism had the potential to embody the full normative sweep of the revolution.

Building on the Arendtian account, American constitutionalist Bruce Ackerman also makes a strong normative claim for constitution making as foundational to democratic revolution. On this view, constitution making is the necessary and final stage of liberal revolutions, a revolutionary "constitutional moment" of rupture from the ancien régime and the founding of a new political order.[10] "If the aim is to transform the very character of constitutional norms, a clean break seems desirable. . . ." For Ackerman, a "legitimate order" depends on "a systematic effort to state the principles of a new regime." In the more contemporary constitutional theorizing, transformative constitution making is not limited to the revolution; instead, there are potentially many more such constitutive moments. By extending the possibility of transformative constitution making beyond the revolution, Ackerman contributes to the modern model a helpful categorical distinction between ordinary and constitutional politics. Within the "dualist democracy" framework, ordinary political change and constitutional change proceed on separate tracks, offering a neat resolution of the dilemma posed by constitutionalism in revolutionary periods. By a move defining "dual" categories of "ordinary" decision making by government as opposed to "higher" lawmaking by "the People," the dilemma with which this chapter begins, of constitutionalism and radical political change, seemingly falls away.[11] In a dualist democracy, the dilemmas of constitutional beginnings, constitutional change, and constitutional review are made to disappear.

In the contemporary model, constitution making relates to revolution through higher lawmaking, yet the distinction between higher and lower lawmaking remains ambiguous. What distinguishes higher lawmaking is a distinctive process, a particular timing. There is considered to be a constitutional onset period, a window of time for constitution making or "constitutional moments." Constitution making occurs before the establishment of other laws and institutions.[12] Higher lawmaking also implies heightened, deliberative decision making. "The higher lawmaking track . . . employs special procedures for determining whether a mobilized majority of the citizenry give their considered support to the principles that one or another revolutionary movement would pronounce in the people's name."[13] Foundationalists embrace the view that the special status of constitutional politics derives from its popular sovereignty, expressed through special constitutional convention processes. Constitutional politics is considered to correspond to a higher level of popular deliberation and consensus and, as such, is distinguishable from ordinary politics. This conception relies heavily on the circumstances of the American founding.

This conception of constitutional politics depends on the view that the American constitutional conventions implied broad popular consensus. Yet this claim is somewhat controversial. Perhaps the processes considered to be predicates of constitutional foundationalism ought to be interpreted at a higher level of generality. Understood this way, low participation in constitutional ratification processes would not be fatal, as long as participation is better than the ordinary political participation of the time. A transitional perspective helps to explain why in periods of political upheaval, even limited popular participation may well suffice to legitimate constitutional transformation.[14] In the prevailing contemporary paradigm, there is a strong claim for linkage between meaningful political change and constitutional change. The constitutional ideal is forward-looking; the purpose is to put the past behind and to move to a brighter future. Constitution making is conceived as the foundation of the new democratic order.

Although its claims have been universalized, contemporary constitutional theory itself derives from a distinctive political context, specifically the eighteenth-century revolutions. Whereas the modern understanding does not define constitutionalism as a state's political arrangements, as in the classical understanding, the modern vision of constitutional politics is inextricably connected to particular revolutions and past political orders. Although the American experience is thought to exemplify foundational constitution making, in recent years a broader prescriptive claim has been leveled at other states in the process of transition. Thus, in *The Future of Liberal Revolution*, the foundationalist vision is extended to the contemporary post-Communist transitions. Invoking the United States's constitution making, Ackerman exhorts fledgling East European democracies to put aside ordinary politics and to cap their revolutions with a constitution.[15] Yet the view of constitutions as foundational to liberalizing political change offers only a theoretical resolution to the dilemma posed by postrevolutionary constitution making. Further, despite the contribution of contemporary constitutional theory to the political science debate over the criteria for liberalizing change, this book contends that liberalizing political change is associated with varieties of legal responses, beyond the constitutional response. The dominant model is highly idealized and, as such, cannot account for many constitutional phenomena associated with periods of political transformation. Instead, contemporary constitutionalism necessitates rethinking the prevailing theorizing about the relation of political to constitutional change. With constitutions in their third generation, constitutional precedents of the late twentieth century suggest that the model overstates the differences between ordinary and constitutional politics. As suggested below, instances of constitutionalism in periods of substantial political change reveal diverse manifestations of constitutional politics.

### A Transitional Counteraccount

This part proposes another account of transitional constitutionalism that better captures the constitutional politics associated with transformative periods.

Constitutionalism in periods of radical political change reflects transitionality in its processes, as developments in periods of political upheaval suggest. Constitutions are not created all at once but in fits and starts. Constitution making (as discussed below) often begins with a provisional constitution, predicated on the understanding of subsequent, more permanent constitutions. Despite prevailing notions of constitutional law as the most forward-looking and enduring of legal forms, transitional constitution making is frequently impermanent and involves gradual change. Many of the constitutions that emerge in periods of radical political change are explicitly intended as interim measures. Whereas prevailing theorizing conceives of constitutions as monolithic and enduring, some features of transitional constitutions are provisional, and others become more entrenched over time.

The "constructivist" account proposed here bears a certain similarity to the processes characterized in more idealized form in Rawlsian theory elaborating gradual construction of political consensus. John Rawls uses the term *political constructivism* to describe the gradual emergence of constitutional consensus as a result of a step-by-step decision making process that narrows the area of parties' political differences. The analysis here is constructivist in a somewhat different sense. While (with Rawls) the view proposed here posits that new constitutional elements gradually emerge over time through the political process, here each change in the constitutional order itself produces change in the participants' perspectives, in turn changing their sense of what is politically possible with consequences for the potential for constitutional consensus.[16]

The notion of transitionality has a number of normative implications. Within prevailing theory, constitutionalism is commonly understood as unidirectional, forward-looking, and fully prospective. Once retrospective political understandings are included, the prevailing ideal becomes a poor model for transitional constitutional phenomena. While the picture of a polis at constitutional point zero might have been appropriate for describing constitutionalism in the eighteenth century, in the late twentieth century, constitutions associated with political change generally succeed preexisting constitutional regimes and are thus not simply created anew.

The construction of new constitutional arrangements in periods of radical political change is informed by a transitional conception of constitutional justice. Constitutional law is commonly conceptualized as the most forward-looking form of law. Yet transitional constitutionalism is ambivalent in its directionality; for the revolutionary generation, the content of principles of constitutional justice relates back to past injustice. From a transitional perspective, what is considered constitutionally just is contextual and contingent, relating to the attempt to transform legacies of past injustice.

The study of constitutionalism in periods of political change suggests that transitional modalities vary in constitutional continuity. The constitutional types proposed here, like Weberian ideal types, do not lay claim to comprehending all constitutional phenomena but, rather, are offered for their help in understanding diverse constitutional phenomena. These also resonate with other transitional legal responses that evince similarly varying modalities. Thus, other chapters in this book have previously discussed transformative legal responses in adjudicative and punitive forms. Whereas in its "codifying" modality, constitutionalism expresses existing consensus, rather than transformative purpose. In its transformative modality, by contrast, in what is here termed "critical" constitutionalism, the successor constitution explicitly reconstructs the political order associated with injustice. In yet another transformative form, in which successor constitutions are used to return to the pre-predecessor constitutional order, such constitutionalism might be considered as "restorative." When the successor constitution is a holdover from prior rule, one might consider these manifestations of constitutional continuity to be "residual." As a review of illustrative constitutional developments in periods of political flux will show, many transitional constitutions incorporate aspects of more than one of the proposed types. These constitutional constructions mediate periods of political change.

My aim here is to interpret how states move from illiberal regimes to those that are more liberal and to explore the role constitutions play in constructing these political changes. Below, a number of cases are explored that illuminate the nature and role of constitutionalism in periods of political transformation. The phenomenon of transitional constitutionalism goes back to ancient times, to the account of the constitution written after the Athenian revolution. With the revolution, there was much debate about the nature of the desired political system, a debate that culminated in two draft constitutions, one for the "immediate" crisis and another "for the future."[17] With such historical transitions came the dilemma of squaring revolutionary political change with constitution making. As we shall see, similar gradual constitutional processes take place in contemporary transitions.

## Brokering Out of Authoritarian Rule

In contemporary theorizing, the constitutional ideal is the culmination of the revolution and the foundation of the new democratic order. The constitution somehow transcends its politicized origins, as constitutional politics transcends ordinary politics. By contrast, in the realist model, the nature and role of constitutions in negotiated transitions is largely conceived in political terms, and constitutions are conceived as extensions of ordinary politics.[18] The two prevailing views take opposing positions on the place of constitutionalism in transformative politics. Neither model, however, adequately explains the nature of constitutional politics in contemporary political change. Examining the roles of constitutions in periods of postauthoritarian rule illuminates the constructivist constitutional paradigm. While constitution making is shaped by periods of radical political change, it also helps construct the political opening that allows transition.

Transitional constitutions broker the political shifts from authoritarian rule. They construct interim periods of substantial liberalizing political change, albeit not equivalent to a fully democratic order. Such constitutions are transitional in a number of senses: Their processes are plainly transient; their instruments are at least in part provisional. Such constitutions frequently suffer from features held over from the predecessor constitutional regime, features one might consider residual. Examples of such constitutions arise in Europe's historical negotiated transitions, as well as in the more recent wave of political change.

Although war provides the distinct break frequently considered a threshold to constitutional foundation, political shifts often occur without such ruptures, following prolonged and tortuous political negotiations. Transitional constitutions may emerge in the negotiated shifts out of authoritarian rule. When the prior regime has not collapsed and the political shift occurs only as a result of negotiations, constitutions play a role not well accounted for within prevailing constitutional theory. Transitional constitutions are not simply revolution-stoppers, but they also play a role in constructing the transition. Early in the process, constitutions can jump-start and instigate political change. Insofar as such constitutions destabilize rather than stabilize a political order, the transitional constitution's "disentrenching" role is analogous to the ordinary codifying constitution's "entrenching" role in this respect.

A contemporary illustration of the "disentrenching" constitution is postapartheid South Africa. Likened to a "historic bridge between the past of a deeply divided society characterized by strife, conflict, untold suffering and injustice, and a future founded on the recognition of human rights, democracy and peaceful co-existence . . . for all South Africans,"[19] South Africa's postapartheid constitution exemplifies the uses of transitional constitutions following authoritarian rule. Its constitution embodies the political agreement and shift from minority rule over a disenfranchised population to a representative democracy. This constitutional pact enabled the political transformation to occur. To what extent can new constitutional legitimacy derive from an agreement ratified by the old apartheid-era Parliament? To what extent would the procedural linkage to the past regime compromise constitutional processes? The transitional constitution's origins in the apartheid regime are mitigated by its express provisionality. Constitutional change began with the old Parliament's enactment of an interim constitution, itself predicated on the making of another, prospective constitution. The 1993 Constitution's preamble contemplated that it will be in force pending a final constitution.[20]

South Africa's 1993 transitional Constitution reflected complex modalities. While generally provisional, it also included binding constitutional principles. In its structure, South Africa's first postapartheid constitution shares affinities with Germany's postwar constitution.[21] Despite its transitional nature, Germany's Basic Law also entrenched core provisions guiding the state's liberal political identity. These binding principles related in large part to equality and representation rights. By reaffirming the protection of racial and ethnic groups, the South African constitution transformed the legacy of racial prejudice in the move out of repressive apartheid, setting forth enduring liberal constitutional values.[22]

Transitional constitutions have been particularly useful in political movements from military rule. In the southern European transitions, for example, the post-Franco Constitution of 1978 helped to steer Spain out of military rule.[23] The successor constitution's transitionality is reflected in the absence of a complete withdrawal of military power; while the military is made subject to constitutional rule, much about the new power sharing is left undefined. Though the threshold question in Portugal's 1974 transition was the military's place in the successor regime, there the army had been a force against the dictatorship for liberalization. By creating a constitutional structure that made room for the armed forces, the first postrevolutionary constitution enabled the transition to democracy by restructuring the allocation of military and civilian power.[24] Throughout Latin America, transitional constitutions have served to broker the way between military and civilian regimes. An example is Brazil after military rule.[25] Through the constitution's limits on state power that previously led to abuses, the authoritarian structure was reconstructed to effect political transformation.[26] The 1988 Brazilian Constitution was concededly provisional: After five years, there was to be constitutional review with an eye to amendment. According to reigning constitutional theory, the provisional nature of the 1988 Brazilian Constitution appeared to defeat a written constitution's basic purpose, of preserving a distinct vision of state power over time.[27] Yet, from a transitional perspective, the critique is inapposite. If a political regime is not yet consolidated, it makes little sense to insist on constitutional permanence. To the contrary, the constitutional opening may well be contingent on its transience. The possibility of reform associated with the first interim constitution is often predicated on and bounded by the assumption of a deferred, more plenary constitutional process. Chile's contemporary constitution dramatically illustrates this possibility. Its 1991 Constitution helped to extricate the country from rule by military dictatorship but only at a constitutional cost. The first transitional constitution maintained some residual continuity with past rule by accommodating military dictatorship within its constitutional structure. In a delicate series of constitutional amendments negotiated between the ruling military junta and the opposition groups lay the glimmerings of the return to democracy in Chile. The constitutional amendments limited the power of the military, as well as other institutions supporting military rule, and lifted the ban on opposition parties in the Senate. This transitional change enabled civilian/military power sharing and the move to a more liberal democratic regime.[28] Similar gradual constitutional reform occurred in Argentina, where it would not be until the second successor regime after military rule that a new constitution was adopted. Even when it was, the new 1994 Constitution continued to hold over many articles from the prior 1853 Constitution, whereas other sections explicitly sought to amend prior areas in need of reform, such as concerning new limits on executive power. As such, the new constitution illustrates a mix of "residual" and "critical" features.

Colombia provides a good historical illustration of disentrenching constitutional change. Analogized to a treaty, the recent Constitution of Colombia truly enabled the peace. A long-standing political crisis between the government and the guerrillas exploded in the 1980s with the partial collapse of the state.[29] The political crisis signaled the need for overhaul of the constitution, but the problem was how to enact constitutional reforms without the support of the Congress and in contravention of existing constitutional law. As is characteristic of transitional constitution making, Colombia departed from its pre-existing constitutional procedures to allow interim constitutional change, pending greater constitutional reforms. By a referendum on constitutional change, a popular decision was made to elect a constituent assembly to redraft the constitution. The referendum was followed by elections to the constituent assembly. By then, the former guerrilla movement had demobilized, had made a strong showing as an independent force in electoral politics, and ultimately would play an active role in the constitution making.[30] These ingenious measures structured the transition; they opened a political space and provisionally constrained the political process in a way that permitted the shift to freer democratic rule. The Colombian Constitution embodied a boldly constructive mechanism for political transformation. Self-consciously provisional, it was intended to restructure an unstable political order. Because the central abuses lay in the allocation of executive/legislative power, the new constitution gave the president extraordinary legislative powers, as well as created a new "mini-congress" to take effect until the installation of a new Congress. Transitory provisions laid down rules for the first free elections, reconstituted the political order, granted amnesty for past political crimes,[31] and reintegrated demobilized guerrillas. Constitutionalism first implied disentrenchment, followed by reconstitutionalism.

Transitional constitutions discussed above are explicitly political, in that they all ratify features of political agreements often contemporaneous with transitional constitutions and themselves directives of constitutional change. The fact that these agreements are frequently not subject to broad political participation challenges the sense in which such constitution making is fully democratic. Indeed, the politicized nature of such constitutions is also evident in their affinities with transitional criminal measures. In shifts out of harsh rule, transitional constitutions often ratify amnesties of past political offenses. The role of transitional amnesty agreements in brokering the transitions was previously discussed in chapter 2 on criminal justice. Thus, in transitional times, constitutions delineate the parameters of what is permissibly political as well as what is outside the bounds of the political community. In the context of these political changes, constitutions serve not as the culmination or end stage of revolution but, rather, as agents in the construction of the transformation. As such, these constitutions are frequently explicitly provisional measures that facilitate political transformation. Successor constitutions delimit provisional political agreements and structures, creating a new political space constructive of the political transition. Further, with the superentrenching of certain critical constitutional norms, successor constitutions can also comprise boldly constructive responses to past repressive rule. While the concededly transitional nature of the balance of these constitutions chiefly relates to the structures of state power, normative principles relating to individual rights norms are intended to be transformative and enduring, guiding the state's liberal democratic identity. There is a higher law, higher even than the constitution, that could be understood as the "constitution's constitution."

Transitional constitution making, to some extent, provides a reflection of prevailing ideas about the state and political change. Unlike the dominant constitutional model, the transitional constitution is flexible in the entrenchment of norms, as seen in the emergence of interim or provisional constitutional phases regarding controversial questions of a constitutional nature. Over time, a first round of constitutional changes further transforms the political scene, leading to more constitutional change. The constructivist constitutional paradigm discussed here draws from comparative analysis of political practices in transitional periods and inductive reasoning and bears similarities to some theoretical models of gradual constitutional consensus-building processes.[32] Finally, rather than expressing existing popular consensus, these constitutions' normative principles are best accounted for within a transitional account, their very purposes reflecting constitutionalism's transformative possibilities.

## Victor's Constitutional Justice

The course of constitution making after war appears to follow the idealized sequence of rupture and new beginnings. Although postwar constitutionalism implies a "clean break," it hardly implies the superdemocratic processes and popular sovereignty predicates of the contemporary constitutional model. Two illustrations discussed here are postwar West Germany and Japan, which adopted constitutional schemes following Allied victory and unconditional surrender. Both the West German and the Japanese Constitutions illustrate a distinctive transitional constitutionalism, namely the "victor's" constitution. To varying degrees, these are imposed constitutions. These postwar constitutions' transitional purposes are seen in their heightened critical function: As is reflected in their substantive mandates, both West Germany's Basic Law and Japan's 1946 Constitution were expressly designed to transform past repressive legacies.

Perhaps the extreme case of victor's constitutional justice is the postwar Japanese Constitution. Adopted under almost absolute American domination, drafted by a small group under General Douglas MacArthur's direction and forced on the Japanese Parliament for ratification,[33] the 1946 Japan Constitution cannot be understood as an expression of popular sovereignty in this occupation context. The significance of popular participation in constitution making may well be less in states with a tradition of authoritarian rule. Like MacArthur's constitution, Japan's previous Meiji Constitution had also been drafted in private by a handful of elites. Despite undemocratic constitutional beginnings, the postwar constitution's continuing authority suggests that other mechanisms operate to legitimate victors' constitutions over time. To some extent, the victor's constitution exemplified by postwar Japan is simply a more extreme version of a constitutional process that, in this century, is common to transitions. In periods of political transition, after war or repressive rule, constitutional processes are often mediated by occupying powers or other influential countries. Perhaps the mildest form of such mediation is the contemporary constitutional advisory role played by international, national, and nongovernmental actors.[34] The leverage of the mediating actor affects the sense in which such constitution making processes represent popular sovereignty. Perhaps the legitimacy of postwar constitutions devolves on their mandates and the degree to which these constitutional processes can nurture democratic norms to shape the transition's political structure. In this respect, much of the postwar Japanese Constitution reflects a transitional modality best understood as transformative and critical. The constitution's explicit purposes were to transform the political tendency toward militarism and imperial nationalism. Thus, Japan's warmaking power is renounced completely, and its emperor reduced from a near deity to a figurehead.[35] There is a broad attempt to displace the prior legal regime and to move Japan to a formally more egalitarian democracy.[36]

The 1946 Japanese Constitution evinces several critical aspects in presenting a retributive response to the prior regime. The constitution's delimiting of the emperor's powers appears as an express alternative to criminal justice. This response evokes the affinities between criminal justice and constitutional lawmaking in periods of political upheaval. As discussed earlier, constitutions have been used to recognize past criminal wrongdoing, while also pardoning such offenses. In such instances, the constitution circumscribes the parameters of permissible democratic politics. In limiting the emperor's powers, the new constitution provided a compromise for the threat of punishment that had destabilized the imperial role.[37] Like the eighteenth-century trials of kings, constitutional limits on imperial sovereignty drew a normative line between prior rule and the new regime. Successor constitution making, like trials, offered formal, public legitimation of the transformation from the implicated political systems.[38]

Victor's justice would not be as complete in Germany. Although Germany surrendered unconditionally, subsequent cold war political change gave it leverage over its constitutional reconstruction. The occupying powers instigated but did not control constitutional reconstruction. Thus, despite Allied calls for the convening of a constituent assembly to draft a constitution to be adopted by popular plebiscite, Germany resisted the demand for a permanent constitution, adopting instead the so-called Basic Law, which was avowedly enacted as a transitory document, "to give a new order to political life for a transitional period." The Basic Law was intended to be ratified by state legislatures, with plenary constitution making processes postponed until after the country's prospective reunification, but the constitutional moment of ratification never arrived.[39] Within the prevailing constitutional model, the Basic Law's provisionality is not well accounted for. The proposed paradigm of transitional constitutionalism, however, illuminates the Basic Law's provisionality and its normative commitments. Its dominant purpose was transformative: to counter the abuses of power that enabled the past regime's evil.[40] As such, the Basic Law follows the critical constitutional type introduced above. Further, unlike the eighteenth-century constitutions, in the Basic Law the normative constitutional concern regarding the potential threat to democracy transcends the abuses of state power to the policy itself. The sense in which this concern responds to the prior repression is best explained from a transitional perspective.

The meaning of constitutional justice from a transitional perspective is conceptualized and constructed in terms of prior constitutional and political regimes. In Germany, the lessons of the Weimar Republic steered the postwar constitutional course. Fascism's success is commonly attributed to the Weimar constitutional scheme, which combined a strong executive with a weak legislative branch, enabling the rise of subversive movements. Responding to this legacy, the Basic Law aggressively countered the fascist tendencies in the political order that culminated in Nazi dictatorship. In the Basic Law, presidential powers are rendered largely symbolic. Similar to the postwar Japanese Constitution's treatment of its wartime emperor, the federal president is bereft of power, the wartime institution deposed, and power diffused more broadly to the Parliament.[41] As with Japan's postwar constitution, Germany's Basic Law also reflects the sense in which criminal and constitutional mechanisms posit fully alternative responses to prior evil rule. Both punishment and constitution making construct normative limits on past abuses of state power. Postwar sovereignty would be restored when the Allies ended occupied trials and Germany committed to constitution making.[42] Thus, the Basic Law's rights provisions prohibit the racial and religious persecution rampant under the Nazi regime. For example, Article 3(3) provides that "no one may be prejudiced or privileged because of his sex, his descent, his race, his language, his homeland and origin, his faith or his religious and political opinions."[43] While such equality rights are common to modern constitutions, the Basic Law goes beyond the conventional protections. The normative structure created by the Basic Law has been characterized as a "militant" democracy.[44] "Militant democracy" may appear to be a paradoxical construct, but it captures the sense of the instrument's primary transformative purposes. Through the Basic Law's placing of democratic conditions on both individuals and political parties, illiberal elements were to be excluded from political life. A militant constitutional order is vigilant not only to the excesses of state power but also to those of popular sovereignty.[45] Transitional constitutionalism operates differently from our prevailing intuitions about the role of constitutionalism. Protection against similar future persecution is not limited to the enumeration of individual rights; transitional constitutions set limits not only on the political majority but also on an illiberal polity. The view that fascism was a political expression of a populist nature leads to the attempt to constrain such expression, even when it is that of a supermajority, a seemingly paradoxical endeavor in the service of constitutional democracy. Adopted as a provisional constitutional instrument, the Basic Law nonetheless reflects varying degrees of transitionality and constitutional entrenchment. Some constitutional norms are provisional, whereas others relating to the instrument's animating normative liberal values, such as protection of individual rights of dignity and equality, are utterly unamendable and superentrenched,[46] thereby defining the state's liberal political identity. Germany's Basic Law, as interpreted by the country's Constitutional Court, becomes the guardian of the liberal state. One might compare the role of South Africa's postapartheid 1993 Constitution.

These postwar constitutions illustrate constitutionalism in its third century. In the move from authoritarian rule, set against a backdrop of prior constitutional regimes, such constitutions plays a distinctive critical function: boldly reconstructive of past constitutional tendencies identified with illiberal politics. While postauthoritarian constitution making often lacks the legitimacy afforded by full constitutional processes predicated in the foundationalist model, delegitimation of the predecessor regime clears the path for constitutional reconstruction. The postwar constitutions pose a problem for the prevailing idealized constitutional model. These constitutions can hardly be understood as full-blown expressions of a heightened popular consensus and revolutionary agenda. Indeed, such constitutions would often seem to be just the reverse. The absence of popular consensus in constitution making processes and the failure of heightened democratic commitments implicit in the view of constitutions as political foundations are also borne out in such constitutions' normative principles. Modern constitutions are generally conceived and designed as structures to constrain state power, but transitional postauthoritarian constitutions counter illiberal tendencies more broadly. In realist theorizing, constitutions would be largely explained in terms of the balance of political power. Yet, the notion of constitutionalism as a product of the balance of political power does not well explain cases of total transition, such as those following war, unconditional surrender, and other regime collapse. Both the idealist and realist models assume that the triumph of the revolutionary regime over its predecessor implies fully forward-looking constitution making. However, as these constitutional normative structures are not well explained by idealized types or by explanations in terms of current political forces, they illuminate a distinctive transitional constitutionalism.

## Velvet Revolutions and Their Constitutions

What are the implications for constitutionalism of "velvet" revolutions? Like many of the postauthoritarian transitions, the fall of Communism occurred through the collapse of the prevailing Communist regime, or negotiated political change.[47] Political changes in the former Soviet bloc were largely peaceful and hence known as velvet revolutions. As such, constitutional change in the area did not follow the dominant constitutional model patterned on eighteenth-century-style revolution. The velvet revolutions generally lacked clean breaks and, as such, did not culminate in constitutional change of a foundational sort. Years after the political changes, and in much of the region, the story is of constitutional continuity. What emerges is an initial transitional constitutionalism displaying aspects largely of a residual type. Even states in the more advanced stages of economic reform still rely on amended Communist-era documents.[48]

What does smooth political change—or velvet revolution—imply about the attendant constitutional change? Whereas revolution by violent means implies rupture in the constitutional regime, velvet revolution implies forced continuity instead. The dilemma of the tension between constitutionalism and political change disappears, for there is no discontinuity, only constitutional continuity. As in other negotiated transitions, constitutions play a role in ratifying the agreements constructing the political shift,[49] as well as in restoring the prerevolutionary constitutional order.[50]

Post-Communist constitutionalism reveals several affinities between theories of political and constitutional change. Just as political change occurred in domino fashion after the Soviet collapse, so, too, there is a domino quality to the constitutionalism prevalent throughout the region. Constitutional change occurred through negotiation; as such, it did not rely on popular sovereignty. On the contrary, the first such constitutional change occurred through bargaining conducted by representatives of a political elite. In the velvet revolutions, the predecessor regime was dislodged rather than overthrown. Constitutional amendments ratified the move from one political regime to another. In the negotiated transitions, the first constitutional changes involved disentrenching the prior political order from power and constitutionalizing the move to power sharing. Throughout the region, constitutional amendments eliminated the constitutionally privileged role of the Communist Party. The amendment processes in Hungary and Poland, for example, first and foremost took power away from the dominant Communist Party and sought to protect those in the political minority. Thus, post-Communist constitutional change has less to do with delimiting state power than party power. Here there are affinities with Germany's postwar Basic Law and the constitutional responses to totalitarianism. This first round of constitutional change was provisional, reflecting affinities with other transitional legal responses. Constitutional processes in the region were not the culminating stage in revolutionary change but, instead, were inextricably linked to gradual political processes. Constitutional change was so closely associated with political change that it implies a constitutional politics not readily distinguishable from ordinary politics. Nevertheless, the legitimacy of constitutional changes did not appear to be affected by this similarity. Hungary's constitutional change is explicitly described as "transitional"; so, too, the amendments to Poland's 1949 Stalin-era Constitution were known as "the Little Constitution." Only five years after the revolution would Poland and Hungary begin to effect more comprehensive constitutional change, toward a bill of rights.[51] Rather than following the ideal of constitution making as a foundational expression of a preexisting political consensus, here constitutional amendment comes first, laying a foundation for further political change. Thus, the constitutionalism of the velvet revolutions challenges foundationalist understandings of the relation of constitution and revolution.

There is another face to post-Communist constitutionalism, that of "restoration" constitutionalism. In the former Czechoslovakia, the revolution began in November 1989 with a demonstration commemorating the fiftieth anniversary of the closing of the Czech universities by occupying German forces. These auspicious beginnings underscored the historical sense of political occupation pervading the region. At the end of political occupation, there was a virtually automatic revival of the constitutional order that preceded the occupation. I call this dimension of transitional constitutionalism "restoration constitutionalism."[52] In the post-Communist bloc, restoration constitutionalism is rampant, implying a partial return to the pre-Bolshevik constitutional regime. In the former Czechoslovakia, the Constitution of 1920 became the basis of drafts for the "new" constitution after the revolution. In Latvia, a constitutional hybrid of the 1922 Constitution, together with laws passed by the current parliament, has been in force since May 1990. The 1938 Constitution was the basis for Estonia's constitutional draft. The basis for constitutional drafts in Georgia was the Constitution of 1921.[53] Turning to restoration constitutions enabled countries to eliminate the constitutional regime associated with Communism. However, some countries returned to these old constitutional structures out of nostalgia and the desire for stability. Indeed, the very term *restoration* suggests the normative pull of the old order. Yet the post-Communist restorations offer dubious stability. Although these regimes may be expressions of traditional and national identity, they can hardly be regarded as an expression of true existing social consensus. Nevertheless, restoration constitutions have a normative pull that manages to evade the dilemma of constitutional beginnings. To the extent that such transitional constitutions are restorative, there are seemingly no constitutional beginnings, only returns. Such constitutionalism eliminates the tensions inherent in constitutionalism in periods of political change.

These cases illustrate varying modalities of transitional constitutionalism. When there is constitutional change, it has tended to occur not through special bodies or procedures but in piecemeal fashion, through negotiations and ordinary political processes. Such constitutional change has been inextricably bound up with the processes of political change. Much of the remaining constitutional order is residual, reflecting constitutional continuity. To the extent that there has been transformative constitutional change away from the prevailing political order, often it has been to revert to the constitutional and political order that prevailed before totalitarianism, a form of restoration constitutionalism.

## The American Constitution: A Transitional Account

Finally, I turn to the American Constitution, the paradigmatic case of foundational constitution making. Despite this status, the American case does not completely fit the dominant theoretical model, suggesting that the model is incomplete and must be supplemented.

Retelling the American constitution making from a transitional perspective adds a different narrative to the prevailing account. In its idealized version, the American Revolution culminates with constitution making. The Constitution embodies a putative immediacy bound up in the revolution, as well as a permanence.[54] Yet the relationship between the U.S. Constitution and the American Revolution reflects a transitional constitutionalism both in process and in its normative mandate. There was a stepwise progression from a backward-looking constitutionalism toward a more forward-oriented one. The Revolution did not immediately culminate with a foundational constitution but, rather, produced a number of constitutive documents. A sequence of constitutional changes put in motion by the Revolution led to the adoption of the Constitution of 1787. The chain of constitutive documents begins with the Declaration of Independence's statement of justification to break with the prior regime. Even when the framers convened in 1787, it was with the purpose to amend the previous constitutive charter.[55] In the first postrevolutionary five-year period, the Articles of Confederation constituted a transformative, critical response to a regime distinguished by minimal state power. Though some scholars suggest the 1787 Constitution incorporates the Declaration, comparable claims have not been made about the Articles of Confederation. Nevertheless, the Constitution implicitly assumes some continuity with the Articles of Confederation.[56] A more expansive scheme of state power was created only upon the adoption of the Constitution of 1787. The addition of the Bill of Rights and the post–Civil War amendments to the American Constitution represented yet additional constitutive stages.[57]

Told this way, the story of the U.S. constitution making shares some affinities with transitional constitutionalism. This transition was not as dramatic, however, given the passage of time between the American Revolution and the enactment of the Constitution and given the nature of the American transition from limited monarchy rather than from the worst of dictatorships. Such a transition seems markedly conservative compared to others discussed here; the American constitutional instrument itself reflects this. Indeed, one might consider there to be a continuum in transitions in regard to the variance and extent of liberalizing change. From a transitional perspective, the American Constitution is not a monolithic founding instrument but a nuanced document. The depiction of American constitution making as a self-conscious founding glosses over the pronounced conflict among the framers as to their purposes.[58] Transitional analysis exposes the unseen Constitution, those parts steeped in the historical and political contingencies of the day. That these provisions have been generally overlooked by contemporary scholars may well attest to their transient nature. A leading feature of the American Constitution's transitionality is its provision for amendment.[59] Because the amendment process is difficult to incorporate within the dominant account, it has occasioned lively scholarly debate. Much contemporary constitutional theory has focused on the question of how to reconcile the contemporary idealized foundationalist view of the enduring Constitution with constitutional change, whether predicated on the Article V amendment process, through principles of constitutional interpretation departing from the original understanding, or by other means.[60] The paradigm this chapter proposes suggests that the amendment process should not be considered in isolation but in light of other aspects of constitutional change. In the American constitution making sequence, the antecedent structural Constitution is the predicate to the ultimate recognition of individual rights.

Transitionality also marks the constitutional provisions regarding rights, the leading transitional feature of which was the controversial issue of slavery. The 1787 Constitution postponed any change regarding federal legislative regulation of the slave trade until 1808.[61] Thus, the Constitution's resolution is twofold. There is one Constitution for the moment, when political debate is constrained and a federal solution imposed. The provisional language of the document, however, leaves open the possibility of another prospective resolution. This reading seems to be supported by the express limitation in Article V on such amendments until 1808.[62] When it came to perhaps the country's most politically contentious issue, the Constitution offered only an interim guiding principle. A transitional perspective also illuminates the distinctive understanding of constitutional justice. The Constitution's protections of freedom and its related conception of tyranny are better understood in the context of colonial rule.[63] The primary such constitutional response, often considered the Constitution's crowning achievement, is the reconstruction of state power. Indeed, the Federalist defense of the new scheme of state power is made largely in terms of an argument from history, based on the experience of tyranny characterized by British parliamentary sovereignty.[64] The Constitution's critical response to monarchic rule is its definition of executive power; an even more pronounced response to strong executive power is evident in the interim constitutional measures adopted after the Revolution.[65] The same was largely true of the state constitutions, in which the governors' terms were limited and their powers few.[66] Most former monarchies move from strong executive systems to parliamentary systems, the United States is virtually unique in turning to a presidential system. The American anomaly is best explained within a transitional analysis.[67] Justifications for the structure of executive power relied on the historical experience of prior monarchic rule. The reasoning in the Federalist arguments for the proposed executive power works backward from the institution of the king. Whereas the king's rule was unbounded, the four-year limited presidential term prevents abuse of power. Other features of the proposed presidential powers have analogous justifications: Because the king's veto power was plenary, it followed that the qualified presidential veto is limited and appropriate. The extent of historical monarchic powers is used to justify the proposed qualified presidential treaty power, as well as the president's constrained war power.[68]

The Constitution's provisions concerning republican rule also suggest a transformative function. First, reconstitution of political order occurs through redefinition of political participation, membership, and leadership. Antiaristocratic features appear in a number of constitutional provisions, most prominently in the express prohibition of nobility. Qualifications and terms for political participation and representation indicate a critical response to the prior order.[69] The allocation of military and civilian power responds to abuses of military rule.[70] A transitional perspective illuminates the contemporary understanding of rights provisions, such as the Second Amendment.[71]

A vivid illustration of transitional constitutionalism is Reconstruction, a time of profound struggle over how to transform the Union. The Reconstruction Amendments appear highly backward-looking, as they normatively structure the constitutional status of the Confederate secession.[72] The amendments respond to the evil of slavery by imposing new obligations on the southern states; only by affirming the principle of equality under law could states reenter the Union and be equally represented in Congress.[73] Conditions for public office in the Fourteenth Amendment disqualified Confederate supporters.[74] Reconstruction's political disabilities would ultimately be short-lived. As provided for in the amendment itself, most of the disqualifications were removed by Congress by 1872.[75] Nevertheless, they remain forever in the text of the American Constitution as an enduring expression of extraconstitutional politics. Understanding the transitional relationship between post–Civil War constitutional law and politics has profound implications for contemporary debates concerning the interpretation of the Reconstruction amendments.[76] A transitional perspective evaluates the Reconstruction jurisprudence within its context of political transformation, with implications for contemporary controversies.

This chapter has suggested ways in which the American Constitution can be better understood from a transitional perspective. By offering a more nuanced view of the nature and role of constitutionalism, the above discussion complements the prevailing model. Transitional constitutionalism also has implications for constitutional interpretation. A transitional perspective contributes a unique view to debates over the ongoing relevance of "original intent" to the contemporary significance of relevant constitutional provisions.[77] The transitional perspective shares with the "fidelity" school of interpretation the understanding that constitutions are best examined in light of historical and political contexts. From a transitional perspective, however, the problem with originalist interpretative theories is that they generally assume a unitary, constitutional purpose over time and the preservation of meaning across time and context, missing other more transformative purposes of a dynamic nature. The transitional perspective adds to the understanding of constitutions as codifying, purposes that are transformative and dynamic. The relevant interpretative inquiry might be to what extent the relevant constitutional provision is considered transitional and whether it is transformative in purpose. With the passage of time, transitional constitutional features will operate in a dynamic fashion, either withering away or expanding in their transformative purposes. This mix of possible original purposes advises a more nuanced approach to the relevance of original intent. Thus the transitional perspective offers a distinctive principle of constitutional interpretation with consequences for prevailing approaches.

## Transitional Constitutionalism: Some Conclusions

Prevailing constitutional theorizing does not fully account for the constitutional phenomena associated with substantial political change, particularly true of the late twentieth century. The central ideas of modern constitutionalism are its eighteenth-century response to premodern rule and its restraint on political arrangements. Constitutionalism in its third century, however, is both normative and transformative in its response to the preexisting political order. Such constitutionalism displays a dialectical quality of varying modalities: critical, residual, and restorative. As such, this paradigm helps account for the threshold dilemma created by constitution making in revolutionary times. Transitional constitutionalism bridges radical political change by reconciling dichotomous understandings of the relation of law and politics. Moreover, transitions demonstrate how constitutionalism reinforces democracy. In ordinary times, constitutionalism often appears in conflict with simple democracy, but during times of transition, constitutionalism plays a unique role in facilitating the move to a more liberal regime.

Transitional constitutionalism provides an alternative paradigm. The paradigm's distinctive paradox is that, as in the premodern conception, constitutionalism does not stand independently from the political order but is inextricably enmeshed in transformative politics. Nevertheless, as in the modern conception, transitional constitutions also transcend political arrangements. The transitional paradigm elaborated a more nuanced relation between constitutional and ordinary politics: Transitional constitutions not only operate as codifications of prevailing consensus but also transform that consensus. Moreover, these two conceptions of constitutional purpose are not mutually exclusive; indeed, they may well coexist within a single instrument. They often do, as in the American Constitution. Thus the view proposed here complements prevailing constitutional theory. What distinguishes the transitional constitutional paradigm is its constructive relation to a political order in flux. Transitional constitutionalism comprehends different phases, ranging from provisional measures intended to shape the transient political order for a limited time to those entrenched and even superentrenched laws that guide a state's core political identity. In its disentrenching role, the transitional constitution ratifies new political arrangements to liberalize political space, enabling a more liberal order. Transitional constitutionalism varies from provisional to ultraentrenched, functioning as guardian of the future constitutional order.

The paradigm of transitional constitutionalism illuminates the special contribution of constitution making in periods of political change. In eschewing the prevailing tendency to collapse constitutionalism with revolutionary political change, the proposed paradigm has the virtue of creating a space and offering a vocabulary for the critique of the nature and role of constitutionalism in periods of transformation. The paradigm of transitional constitutionalism also has implications for our understanding of constitutionalism's normative force and its relation to other uses of the law. Critical constitutionalism implies an explicitly transformative response to prior repressive rule. To the extent that the constitutions discussed above reflect a critical response to the legacy of the ancien régime, transitional constitutionalism enables a sense of justice. Critical constitutional responses to the predecessor political regime also play a justificatory role for the transition by delegitimating aspects of the ancien régime and legitimating its successor. To the extent that these structural principles enable normative expressions of accountability, they overlap with other normative uses of the law, such as criminal law, in these extraordinary periods. Contemporary postmodern constitutional norms delimit and transcend the structuring of state power to guide broader normative understandings of the social order. Finally, a transitional constitutional perspective offers a glimpse of constitutional progress. This vision of progress is not essential or universal but limited and contingent. Understandings of distinct national legacies of injustice enable construction of constitutional constraints truly responsive to a state's political, historical, and constitutional legacies.

## CHAPTER SEVEN

# Toward a Theory
# of Transitional Justice

$\mathcal{T}$his book has explored two questions: What legal approaches do societies in transition adopt in responding to their legacies of repression? and What is the significance of these legal responses for these societies' liberalizing prospects? We are now in a position to examine what light *Transitional Justice* sheds on these questions and, more generally, on law's role in periods of far-reaching political change. In exploring states' legal responses to their illiberal legacies, *Transitional Justice* pursues an interpretative, historical, and comparative method in order to draw synthetic conclusions concerning what these practices convey about the conception of justice at such times. What emerges is a pragmatic balancing of ideal justice with political realism that instantiates a symbolic rule of law capable of constructing liberalizing change. This concluding chapter thus analyzes the legal phenomena discussed throughout this book in terms of a theory of transitional justice that bridges ideal conceptions of the rule of law and the contingent political exigencies of particular cases.

Legal measures during such periods follow a distinctive paradigm, guided by rule-of-law principles tailored to the goal of political transformation. The analysis undertaken in this book demonstrates the conceptual and practical channels through which an extraordinary paradigm of transformative law helps to construct liberalizing change. But it also goes further, arguing that law maintains an *independent* potential for effecting transformative politics. The various legal responses explored in the preceding chapters reveal common features in their nature and functions—and thus ramifications for an analytically coherent conception of transitional justice that transcends particular cases. Transitional justice's paradigmatic rule-of-law principles are intimately related to these periods' quintessential and defining feature, namely the grounding within society of a normative shift in the principles underlying and legitimating the exercise of state power. Accordingly, the understanding of transitional justice advanced here should have import beyond periods of political flux, shedding new light on contemporary questions concerning human rights law's potential for responding to international conflict, and core understandings of the relation politics bears to justice.

This book's exploration of the nature and function of law in transformative periods began by shifting the terms of debate and the relevant frame of reference, for transitional justice is not adequately captured within prevailing analytical frameworks used to examine law's role in periods of liberalizing political change. These accounts tend to be highly antinomic. They are either radically realist, with the course of developments in the transition simply following the balance of power (and thus denying law any independent significance in political transformation), or they offer idealized narratives in which law operates as an entirely self-enclosed inaugural and foundational force, implying a potentially universal sequence of legal and political development during transformative periods.[1] Neither of these profoundly dichotomized understandings provides a persuasive positive or normative account of law's role in periods of substantial political change. Drawing on a historical and comparative perspective across societies, the analysis pursued here argues for an alternative way of conceptualizing law's role at such times.

Consider, for a start, the prevailing scholarship's implicit conceptualization of the relevant subject matter: Law's role is either simply reduced to the balance of political forces that shape the onset of regime change or extrapolated from the end point at which "liberal revolution" putatively aims.[2] As a result, law's role in the salient period—understood in political terms to correspond to an interregnum, that is, to a period between regimes[3]—has eluded understanding, for each of these approaches *by definition* excludes the phenomenology of law in liberalization as a discrete subject of analysis.

This analysis is by no means to deny or minimize the importance of structural constraints and normative goals in shaping legal processes and political outcomes. On the contrary, legal phenomena are obviously never either autonomous of their context or purely responsive to it. Why, then, is there any reason to assume, as each of the prevailing approaches does, that law's operation is any less interactive and dialectical during periods of far-reaching political change? Indeed, a systematic analysis of the legal processes occurring during the passage from one political regime to another is *precisely* what is required in order to clarify the nature and extent of their role in the transitional period. Rather than our simply describing outcomes as a mere residuum of the balance of political forces or deducing ideal legal responses from a revolutionary end point that presupposes democracy and the rule of law, it is necessary for us to examine transitional legal responses' relation to societies' historical legacies of injustice and the extent to which this relation shapes their paths to liberalization. The usefulness of this approach will become more apparent as we turn to a discussion of the legal phenomenology and applicable rule-of-law principles that are characteristic of contemporary instances of radical political transformation.

## Transitional Justice and Transitional Jurisprudence: A Paradigm

Law in periods of radical upheaval is commonly conceived as antistructural, as eluding principle and defying paradigm.[4] The period of normative shift is commonly thought to be antiparadigmatic. Yet, the legal phenomenology that characterizes periods of political flux reveal patterns pointing to a paradigm. As we have seen, the manifestations of justice seeking during transformative periods are diverse: retributive, reparatory, bureaucratic, constitutional, and historical. Nevertheless, across diverse legal responses, regularities become evident, revealing the distinctive processes associated with political change. Across legal categories, a paradigm of law emerges—a transitional jurisprudence.

Because transitions' defining feature is their normative shift, legal practices bridge a persistent struggle between two points: adherence to established convention and radical transformation. Ultimately, a dialectically induced position emerges. In contexts of political upheaval, transitional jurisprudence comprises a partial and nonideal conception of justice: provisional and limited forms of constitutions, sanctions, reparations, purges, and histories. Across categories of law, a distinctive legal form mediates the move between regimes. Law's role here is transitional, and not foundational, constructive of critical changes in individual status, rights, and responsibilities—and, more broadly, of shifts in power relations. As law's function is to advance the construction of political change, transitional legal manifestations are more vividly affected by political values in regimes in transition than they are in states where the rule of law is firmly established. Thus, the jurisprudence of these periods does not follow such core principles of legality as regularity, generality, and prospectivity—the very essence of the rule of law in ordinary times.[5] While the rule of law in established democracies is forward-looking and continuous in its directionality, law in transitional periods is both backward-looking and forward-looking, retrospective and prospective, continuous and discontinuous.

Ordinarily, the values of prospectivity and continuity, as well as general applicability and equal protection, are thought to be fully compatible in established legal systems. However, in periods of substantial political flux, these values are vividly seen to be in conflict. This was manifestly apparent in both the immediate postwar period and following the Communist collapse in jurisprudential debates over the relation of law and morals and over the meaning of the restoration of the rule of law. The struggle is over the extent to which pre-existing procedures are adhered to or new regime values are advanced. Which rule-of-law values ultimately take precedence in transition is a function of the particular historical and political legacies—that is, of the primary understanding of the sources of fear, insecurity, and injustice that gains authoritative normative force in the society. While the balance of power between key political actors may be viewed as constraining the range of possibilities, the profound challenge and distinctive role of transitional jurisprudence remains to somehow bridge conventional legality and the normative shift entailed by liberalizing transformation.

In periods of political change, there is no singular site of operative legal action, and there are no seamless foundational ideals. Nevertheless, transitional experiences do not necessarily follow the course postulated by political realists on the basis of balance-of-power considerations. Instead, the salient question is, What institution has the legitimacy to carry out substantial normative transformation? As is discussed in preceding chapters, the role of reinterpreting the meaning of the rule of law in periods of substantial transformation is frequently assumed by constitutional courts, particularly when they are *entirely new* institutions brought into existence by the transition itself. The transitional judiciary exercises considerable interpretive freedom, crafting a nuanced rule of law that simultaneously adheres to aspects of conventional legality while doing the work of normative change. Thus, adjudication in these periods typically reveals a dynamic combination of conventional and transformative imperatives. Though not acts of political decision-making bodies, these adjudicatory responses, nevertheless, constitute significant symbols of the liberalizing rule of law. When the constitutional courts predate the transition, other institutions imbued with newfound legitimacy and authority, such as public commissions, become the sites of transformative practice.

At the same time, transitions vary in their extent of normative transformation and in their adherence to conventional legality. A theory of transitional justice must, therefore, develop a vocabulary with which to comprehend the transformative continuum along which transitions are arrayed. The possible modalities range from "critical," denoting a maximally transformative legal repertoire aimed at repudiating prior regime policy, to a "residual" modality, which aims at preserving the preexisting legal order. In contrast, a "restorative" modality draws normative force from a return to the state's prior legacies. As this typology suggests, the varying modalities relate to differences in the extent of *novel* political transformation, although not necessarily in the extent of liberalization, particularly when a "restorative" repertoire can credibly draw on an appropriate preexisting tradition.

As the discussion in preceding chapters sought to demonstrate, the rule-of-law principles associated with transformational modalities are evident across legal categories. Indeed, we may take this point still further. Whereas rule of law principles associated with ordinary times include clear distinctions in categories of the law regarding procedural and evidentiary rules, as well as the determination of individual status, rights, and duties, the extraordinary nature and workings of transitional law frequently blur the boundaries separating criminal, civil, administrative, and constitutional law. In operating across legal categories, paradigmatic transitional rule of law principles may also tend to dissolve these conventional boundaries in the law.

For example, establishment of the rule of law within a liberalizing state is often considered to depend on exercises of individual accountability. Thus, punishment most clearly instantiates the concern with individual responsibility central to law within the liberal state. Yet, as chapter 2 demonstrates, this perspective on the nature of punishment does not accord with its role in times of radical political flux. The transitional criminal form is instead informed by values related to the distinctive circumstances and project of political passage. Criminal justice is ordinarily theorized in starkly dichotomous terms as animated by either a backward-looking concern with retribution or a forward-looking, utilitarian concern with deterrence, considered internal to the justice system.[6] In its transitional variant, however, not only is punishment informed by a mix of retrospective and prospective purposes, but also the question of whether to punish or to amnesty, to exercise or restrain criminal justice is rationalized in overtly political terms. Values of mercy and reconciliation commonly considered to be external to criminal justice are an explicit part of the transitional deliberation. The explicit politicization of criminal law in these periods challenges ideal understandings of justice and turns out to be a persistent feature of jurisprudence in the transitional context.

The extraordinary transitional form of punishment characterized in chapter 2 as the "limited" criminal sanction is directed less at penalizing perpetrators than at advancing the political transformation's normative shift. The transitional limited sanction is exemplified wherever criminal processes are partial and truncated and ultimately culminate in little or no penalty. The limited sanction is well illustrated historically, not only in postwar policy, but also in the course of punishment following more recent cases of regime change, during which the limited sanction performs important operative acts—formal public inquiry into and clarification of the past, the indictment of past wrongdoing, and so forth—advancing the normative shift central to liberalizing transition. Even its arch limited form is a symbol of rule of law that enables expression of a critical normative message.

In terms of the argument advanced here, it is especially important to note the affinities that the operative effects advanced by the limited criminal sanction, such as establishing, recording, and condemning past wrongdoing, display with other legal acts and processes constructive of transition. The massive and *systemic* wrongdoing that is particularly characteristic of modern repression implies a recognition of the mix of individual and collective responsibility. Hence, there is a pronounced overlap of punitive and administrative institutions and processes. Individualized processes of accountability give way to administrative investigations and commissions of inquiry, the compilation of public records, and official pronouncements about past wrongs. Frequently, these are themselves subsumed in state histories commissioned pursuant to a political mandate for reconciliation, as in South Africa and in much of postauthoritarian Latin America.[7] Whether bureaucratic forms of public inquiry and official truth-tellings are desirable and signify liberalization is contingent on state legacies of repressive rule. The role of the production of social knowledge regarding a state's past is no original or foundational matter, for successor truth regimes' critical function is to respond to the repressive practices of the prior regime. Thus, for example, in transitions after military rule, when the truth was a casualty of disappearance policies,[8] the critical response is the concerted pursuit of an official story, whereas state histories have been largely eschewed in the postcommunist transitions, as their production was itself an instrument of repressive control. Transitional historical inquiries reveal that the relevant truths are those that are implicated in a particular state's legacies of injustice. These are not universal, essential, or metatruths. As is demonstrated by the generalized transitional use of independent accounts in contemporary human rights law to dislodge the predecessor truth regime and establish a primary form of accountability, a marginal truth may be all that is needed to draw a line on the prior regime.[9]

New historical accounts about past legacies rehabilitate, as well as condemn, particular individuals. In its transitional form, the reparatory remedy does important work of the normative shift by instantiating changes regarding political status, for example, the rehabilitation and restoration of individual dignity associated with liberalism, which may accompany other legal remedies of a distributive nature. Across cultures, the call for reparatory measures as a display of equal protection under the law is pervasive, spurring changes in rules relating to individual status and rights. In ideal theory, principles of corrective justice are largely backward-looking, relating chiefly to individual victims' due. In their transitional form, however, reparatory measures have a "hybrid" nature, with corrective goals linked to broader societal concerns related to the normative entrenchment of liberalizing political change. The transitional reparatory project's hybrid combination of backward- and forward-looking purposes is most evident in countries undergoing simultaneous political and economic transitions, departing radically from ideal theorizing about principles of distributive and corrective justice.[10] The transitional compromise is thus most vivid in the postcommunist transitions, when even so-called first property rights were not structured on an ideal basis.[11] Transitional reparatory remedies advance "entitlements" that seek to correct violations of rights in the past precisely in order to embed them simultaneously in the future. Once again, through broad legislative projects, often broadened or amended by the judiciary, the liberalizing state adopts a form of *systemic* repair for past *systemic* derogations from equal protection of the law.

In their bureaucratic form, transitional measures' political and collective basis is most overt, law is at its most radically transformative, and the boundaries separating legal categories are most blurred. Public regulatory measures that condition association, membership, and participation effect real change in the status, rights, and duties of citizens in the new regime and, accordingly, can have radical and wide-sweeping impact on a state's political order.[12] To be sure, transitional administrative justice comprises conventional legal forms, once again demonstrating the transitional compromise. Yet, by relying on past behavior as a basis for prospective treatment in the public sphere, these measures display the punitive aspects of criminal law. When public law is deployed on express bases of political conditionality, it critically responds to legacies of persecution perpetrated on ideological grounds, radically reshaping the boundaries of political legitimacy and thus redefining the contours of the successor society's changing political identity. Indeed, in their structuring of future behavior on a political basis, these measures also appear to be largely constitutional in nature.

Transitional constitutionalism also does not follow an ideal conception[13] but is hyperpoliticized, displaying affinities with other transitional reponses. Our intuitions are to envision constitution making as a thoroughly forward-looking project designed to structure future government. But transitional constitutionalism performs additional functions entwined with the normative shift, as it is, at the same time, backward- and forward-looking, retrospective and prospective, and continuous and discontinuous with the prior political order. It is also in this area of the law that the transformative continuum, ranging from "critical" to "residual" in terms of adherence to the status quo, is most evident. Transitional constitution making comprehends the codifying, entrenching purposes associated with constitutionalism and also the transformative, disentrenching purposes peculiar to transitions. In pursuing these purposes, transitional constitutions may be entirely provisional, intended to operate for only a finite period of heightened change, as is exemplified in South Africa's interim 1993 Constitution, or aim immediately for superentrenched, unamendable constructions of lasting political identity, as in the case of postwar Germany's *Grundgesetz*.[14]

The paradigmatic affinities discussed here bear on the recurrent question in debates surrounding transitional justice concerning what response to repressive rule is most appropriate to ushering in a lasting democratic system. The subtext of this question assumes a transitional ideal and that normative concerns somehow militate for a particular categorical response. However, this is simply the wrong question: There is no single correct response to a state's repressive past. Which response is appropriate in any given regime's transition is contingent on a number of factors—the affected society's legacies of injustice, its legal culture, and political traditions—as well as on the exigencies of its transitional political circumstances. Indeed, beyond the contingency of responses appears the general irrelevance of which particular ones are adopted. The paradigmatic fluidity of transitional legal responses highlights this jurisprudence's heightened political character.[15] For law's function in these periods is largely symbolic, so that multiple and diverse responses can and do mediate the normative shift. Let us now consider in greater detail how the paradigm of justice discussed here is constructive of this shift.

## Transitional Constructivism

How is transition constructed? What is law's role in political passage? The question of law's constructive role generally arises in the context of the more conventional problem of social reproduction and transmission of authoritative norms across time. Indeed, the problem of institutional reproduction and related questions of legitimation have been well studied.[16] Fundamental political and social change, however, involve shifts in normative orders that render such theorizing inapposite, for generalizing from established systems of law and politics misses what is particular to law's role in such periods.[17] Rather than how law preserves a system capable of reproducing existing legitimizing norms, the problem is how these are radically transformed within and through the law.

The paradigmatic form of the law that emerges in these times operates in an extraordinary fashion and bears a constructive relation to the transition. It both stabilizes and destabilizes. In these circumstances, law's distinctive feature is its mediating function, as it preserves a threshold level of formal continuity while instantiating transformative discontinuity. The extent to which formal continuity will be maintained depends on the modality of transformation as set forth above, while the value content of the normative shift will be a function of history, culture, and political tradition, as well as the society's receptiveness to innovation.

Just what do transitional legal practices have in common? Law constructs through numerous diverse processes, including legislation, adjudication, and administrative measures. Transitional operative acts include pronouncements of indictments and verdicts; the issuing of amnesties, reparations, and apologies; and the promulgation of constitutions and reports, for transitional practices share features namely as ways to demonstrate publicly new collective understandings of truth. Historically, the transitional processes, whether of prosecuting, lustration, or inquiry, shared a similar sense. These were all transitional actions taken to share new public knowledge, to manifest change.[18] Law here appears to function at the margin, as it performs the work of separation from the prior regime and integration with its successor. Transitional law has a "liminal" quality, as it is law between regimes. Indeed, analysis of the salient legal practices suggests that their peculiar efficacy lies in the ability to effect separation and integration functions—all within continous processes.[19]

At the same time, transitional rule of law implies procedures that do not seem fair or compelling—trials lacking in regular punishment, reparations based on politically driven and legally arbitrary temporal (and often property) thresholds, and constitutions that do not necessarily last. What characterizes the transitional legal response is its limited, partial nature, embodied in the provisional constitution and purge, the limited sanction and reparation, and the discrete history and official narrative. Transitional law is above all symbolic—a secular sanctification of the rituals and symbols of political passage.[20] Although ritualized forms of operative action and communication are often thought to characterize primitive societies and to have waned in modern times,[21] the inquiry undertaken here suggests otherwise, offering a comprehensive understanding of the phenomenology of political passage and inviting comparison and evaluation of the nature and role of the rites and symbols it entails.[22] The evident legal patterns discerned in the preceding chapters evoke and frame political passage, notwithstanding the confluence of historical, legal, and political traditions on which they are contingent.[23] Yet, what sets these transitional practices apart from other rites and rituals? In what does their paradigmatic core consist?

Transitional legal processes are the leading such acts in transition for their ability to convey publicly and authoritatively the material differences that constitute the normative shift between regimes. The language of law imbues the new order with legitimacy and authority.[24] In its symbolic form, transitional jurisprudence reconstructs the relevant political differences through changes in status, membership, and community.[25] Through these processes, what is being constructed is the relevant political difference in the illiberal and liberal regimes. The relevant critical difference will be contingent, defined, and recognized as legitimate in light of a given successor society's past legacies.

In modern political transformation, it is through legal practices that successor societies make liberalizing political change, for, in mediating the normative hiatus and shift characterizing transition, the turn to law comprises important functional, conceptual, operative, and symbolic dimensions. As a threshold matter, law epitomizes the liberal rationalist response to suffering and catastrophe: that there is, after all, something to be done. In the liberal society, rather than resignation to historical repetition, the hope of change is put in the air. Even by their engagement in transitional justice debates, successor societies signal the rational imagining of the possibility of a more liberal political order.

Yet, the symbolizing legal practices examined here invoke as well as evoke the rationalism that lies at the core of the liberal rule of law.[26] In what has been characterized as these practices' paradigmatically limited form, the turn to legal symbolism thus offers the leading alternative to the violent responses of retribution and vengeance in periods of political upheaval. The transitional legal response is deliberate, measured, restrained, *and* restraining; in their transitional form, ritualized legal processes enable gradual, controlled change[27] The very turn to legal processes in order to redefine status, rights, and responsibilities and to delimit state power is, to some degree, an exercise of the rule of law associated with established democratic systems. It is performative of the acts of the liberal state. As the question of transitional justice is worked through, the society begins to perform the signs and rites of a functioning liberal order.

In this sense, transitional law transcends the "merely" symbolic to be the leading rite of modern political passage. Ritual acts enable the passage between two orders here, of the predecessor and successor regimes.[28] In contemporary transitions, characterized by their peaceful nature and occurence within the law, legal processes perform the critical "undoings," the inversions of the predicates justifying the prevailing regime, through public processes that produce the collective knowledge constitutive of the normative shift. Thus, legal processes simultaneously disavow aspects of the predecessor ideology and justify the ideological changes constituting liberalizing transformation. While in the prevailing understanding the relation between law and politics is viewed as consisting in adherence to conventional legality and stability, these cannot mediate normative shift. A one-sided emphasis on law's stabilizing function in periods of flux is, therefore, erroneous,[29] for transitions raise the problem of how the legal order—generally considered a closed and self-validating system[30]—nonetheless enables normative change to proceed. Prevailing theorizing often conceptualizes transition as being predicated on foundational change in the rules, hence, the theorizing regarding transitional constitutionalism discussed in chapter 6. Yet, transitions sometimes occur without such meta-level change. Indeed, the challenge is how law both maintains and, at the same time, transcends the conventional idea of law as stable, even obdurate, to construct normative change.

Change within and through the legal system depends on either a reinterpretation of the salient justifications underlying the prevailing normative order or a turn to an independent source of alternative legal norms. The first alternative corresponds to the lawyer's familiar choice of whether to rely on the facts or on the law, whereas the latter—introduction of an autonomous normative source—is effected through change in the recognition rule regarding the sources of valid law.[31] The question of which institution best lends itself to the advancement of legal normative change has been the subject of substantial debate in the literature of transition.[32] Yet, as the discussion throughout this book suggests, there is no one right answer, for the outcome of this choice is contingent on political circumstances of competence and legitimacy spanning both predecessor and successor regimes. Often, the legislatures previously under repressive rule are compromised, opening the way for newly created constitutional courts and activist judiciaries to incorporate international human rights norms.[33] The judicial turn to international human rights law enables preservation of a sense of continuity and even the forging of a constructive prospectivity, thereby reconciling the goals of transformation and normative change within an established legal system. Human rights law's significant normative force in periods of transition derives from its extraordinary potential to mediate the supposed theoretical divide of positivism and natural law, thus transcending law's conventional relation to politics.

More common, however, is normative change without alteration in the recognition rules, a strategy that depends on a reinterpretation of the normative bases rationalizing prevailing definitions of status, rights, and duties. These transformative processes are, to some extent, ordinarily backgrounded, playing an ongoing role in our legal systems. In established rule of law systems, the differentiation of legal categories and rules relates to varying standards of knowledge and reasoning that justify definition and change in status, duties, and rights under the law. Yet, as we have seen, the transitional paradigm departs from the epistemological principles associated with the conventional rule of law by leveling evidentiary standards and justificatory processes across legal categories—a de-differentiation in law.[34] The paradigmatic feature of transitional law is that it visibly advances the reconstruction of public knowledge, comprehending operative affinities and continuities that enable the separation from, and integration of, changing political identities.

Establishing a shared threshold knowledge regarding past legacies is something of a trope in the literature and discourse of transitions.[35] Nevertheless, the very meaning of "truth" and its relation to the transition, the analysis undertaken here suggests, is not universally shared but, rather, contingent and dynamic. The paradigmatic transitional legal processes rely on discrete changes in salient public knowledge for their operative transformative action. Changes in shared public justifications underlying political decision making and behavior reveal the centrality of interpretative innovation in the construction of transition.[36] What is politically relevant to transformation is plainly constituted by the transitional context and, in particular, by legacies of displacement and succession of predecessor truth regimes.

Legal processes offer established means of changing public reasoning in the political order, for they are themselves predicated on authoritative representations of public knowledge. Transitional legal processes thus contribute to the public epistemological and interpretative changes contributing to the perception of transformation. At the same time, transitional legal processes vividly demonstrate the contingency concerning what knowledge will advance the construction of the normative shift underpinning regime change. Yet, in the cases examined here, the potential normative force of changes in public knowledge depends on critical challenges to the policy predicates and rationalizations of predecessor rule. Accordingly, what "truths" there are in transition are often discrete and yet of disproportionate significance. For example, the mere identification of a victim's status as a civilian rather than as a combatant can topple a regime (at least on the normative level) by undermining a key ideological predicate of the national security state responsible for past repression.[37] Indeed, the reinterpretations themselves displace predicates to prior rule and offer a newfound basis for the reinstatement of the rule of law.

## A Theory of Transitional Justice

A paradigm of transitional jurisprudence defines periods of political passage. The transitional paradigm proposed here seeks to clarify law's relation to political development in periods of radical flux, as it demonstrates processes that reconstitute societies on a basis of political liberalization. Whether trials, constitutions, reparations, administrative tests, bans, or historical inquiries, the legal measures pursued in periods of political transition are emblematic of normative change, for all are operative acts that aim at proclaiming the establishment of a new political order.

The comparative and historical perspective adopted here suggests that what is deemed true and just in transitional periods is politically contingent but not in an arbitrary sense. Despite realist claims, transitional phenomenology is not *simply* the product of its abiding political circumstances but is, instead, a function of contemporary political circumstances *and* historical legacies of injustice. Thus, the conception of transitional justice advanced here implies a reconceptualization of the prevailing theorizing about law and politics and, also, of critical legal theory's emphasis on a progressive role for a rule of law fully enmeshed in politics.[38] For transitional law's distinctive contribution to the construction of political passage is that it is both constrained by and transcendent of politics. As critical theory would predict, law plays an explicitly constructive, ritualized role by structuring the interpretative changes that are perceived as political transition. Nevertheless, political appropriation of the language and processes of justice signifies the symbols and rituals of legitimate and measured change. Transitional law's distinctive contribution is its ensemble of established, measured processes of legitimation and gradual political change.

The paradigm of a provisional, hyperpoliticized transitional jurisprudence is linked to a conception of nonideal justice that is imperfect and partial. What is fair and just in extraordinary political circumstances is determined not from an idealized archimedean point but from the transitional position itself. This vantage point has certain ramifications for which principles of justice guide periods of political change. What is deemed fair and just during periods of radical political innovation is not necessarily arrived at in deliberations under idealized conditions and regular procedures.[39] Even in liberalizing periods, deliberative processes are often truncated, and the electoral or constitutional consensus structuring political decision making weak and short-lived. When lacking in fully representative processes, democratic legitimation of transitional decision making depends on subsequent ratificatory processes. Accordingly, the account of transitional justice put forward here has implications for reconceptualizing theories of democratic development, as legal constructions that characterize these periods gradually alter the political landscape and the agreements struck affect the subsequent course of politics. Indeed, by modifying the conditions of decision making and consensus, transitional legal constructions bear little resemblance to idealized democratic theory.[40] The imperative of normative discontinuity often trumps the protection of other values in the hope that whatever departures from conventional legality this entails will pay off in democratic consolidation. The enterprise is risky, as arguments for limiting conventional legality are often pretextual. Only the crucible of time will reveal whether, and to what extent, the transitional compromises this book discusses are justified in the consolidation of liberal democracy.

Authoritative determinations of what is fair and just in moments of transition do not occur in a vacuum but, rather, are forged against the backdrop of historical legacies of injustice. Justice seeking is situated in the political conditions of transition. In this context, the very meaning of the rule of law is historically and politically contingent, and its content is informed by a society's self-understanding of the nature and sources of coercion and repression in its past. These legacies are the springboard for the society's imagination of transitional justice. Across cultures, the meaning of transitional justice is infused with restorative and transformative dimensions.

From this perspective, even procedural departures from values internal to conventional legality and theories of justice can be clarified. Thus, for example, transitional criminal justice is not justified in the language of individual accountability and retribution but, rather, contains an explicitly political rationalization. Similarly, transitional reparations reconcile ideal corrective aims with distributive or other goals related to the political exigencies of the moment. Transitional phenomena reflect a balancing and accommodation of ideal theories of law and the political circumstances of the transition. Recognizing this has significant definitional consequences that allow a more comprehensive positive account of these periods, as well as a more compelling normative evaluation and critique of transitional legal phenomenology. The reconception proposed here characterizes transitional law in terms of imperfect and partial justice but one that for precisely this reason preserves a critical space relating to the extraordinary political circumstances that define the context of justice in these times. The availability of a vocabulary of transitional jurisprudence and a conception of transitional justice may also illuminate conceptions of justice associated with nontransitional circumstances.

## Transitional Justice and Liberal Identity

The justice-seeking phenomena discussed here are intimately tied to the fashioning of a liberal political identity. As our earlier discussion suggests, the turn to legalism, however contingent, is emblematic of the liberal state, with transitional justice reconstructing political identity on a juridical basis by deploying the discourse of rights and responsibilities. Moreover, while there appears to be diminished adherence to an ideal rule of law in transition, there is, nonetheless, a palpably heightened sense of the public interest, evident across a spectrum of paradigmatic transitional responses, including constitution making, amnesties, reconciliations, and apologies.[41]

These responses point to a fragmentary but shared vision of justice that is, above all, corrective. What is paramount is the visible pursuit of remedy, of return, of wholeness, of political unity—an impetus incorporating values external to those of ideal theories of justice. For example, transitional constitutionalism comprehends not just forward-looking but also backward-looking remedial dimensions; it operates in corrective fashion, constructing a normative (if not historical) "return" to a state's liberal political identity. Similarly, transitional criminal justice goes beyond punishing individual perpetrators to serve the society's prospective corrective purposes. To the extent that transitional justice implies a turn to the corrective, it offers an alternative successor identity that centers on political unity. Transitional justice offers a way to reconstitute the collective—across potentially divisive racial, ethnic, and religious lines—that is grounded in a political identity that arises from the society's particular legacies of fear and injustice. While this is necessarily based on an evolving critical self-understanding, it nonetheless draws on a juridical discourse of rights and responsibilities that offers both a transcendent normative vision and a pragmatic course of action.

The transitional legal phenomena discussed throughout this book suggest that meanings of freedom, security, and the rule of law vary across states and cultures, for, in reflecting responses to particular manifestations of repressive rule, they also indicate that the rule of law means something more than nonarbitrary rule and adherence to regular, generally applicable procedures. What is distinctive about contemporary transitional jurisprudence is that its constructions of the rule of law respond to systematic persecution under legal imprimatur. Underlying contemporary transitional legal phenomena is a conception of state injustice as a *systematic* persecutory policy. When the state systematically persecutes its citizens on a racial, ethnic, religious, or political basis, this persecution is not simply an arbitrary derogation from the rule of law. Accordingly, contemporary transitional law responds to this particular sort of repressive rule. Transitional responses to systemic persecution under the law costitute a performative undoing of the prior wrongdoing perpetrated within the legal system. Transitional responses, such as the new constitutional courts,[42] constitutions, and other measures, declaim the political persecution emblematic of the latter half of the twentieth century.[43] Transitional legal processes of inquiry are well suited to establish the patterns and systematicity in state persecution policy; indeed, the full scope of persecutory policy is only made manifest in the legal response. Whether such persecution is perpetrated on the basis of race, ethnicity, nationality, religion, or ideology, transitional law derives from and responds to the political implications of repression as state policy.[44] The recurring transitional responses addressing systemic persecution seek to disavow the ascriptive hierarchies associated with the old regime. The "friend/enemy" distinctions ratified by legal regimes, as discussions throughout this book suggest, are endemic to authoritarian regimes. These responses constitute undoings of the persecutory logic of the ancien régime and, hence, repudiations of that authority.[45]

Transitional jurisprudence reveals the basis for democratic values operative in societies at the time of the political change.[46] Cycles of transitional justice illustrate the nexus between these legal phenomena and the construction of liberalization. Historically, in transitions from monarchical to republican regimes, the salient rituals of political passage were the trials of kings—a ritual that symbolized the subjection of the king to the will of the people and the triumph of popular sovereignty.[47] Twentieth-century successor justice further reconstructed the individual's relation to the state: thus, the postwar Nuremberg trials' generative principle of individual responsibility emphasized the role of the individual as subject of a sovereign international law. The same is true of the related constitutional changes of the time that protected individual rights.[48]

In contemporary transitional phenomena, the postwar democratic vision is now in the process of being superseded by more complex and fluid understandings of sovereignty and responsibility that mediate the individual and the collective, national and international orders. The increasingly dynamic relation of the individual and state in a fast changing global public sphere affects understandings of personal and collective responsibility, thus bringing about related changes in the conception of democracy. There entails an expansion of individual and state responsibility as a theoretical matter and, thus, shifts in sites of authority and agency, with transitional law mediating the individual/collective divide to reach nominally private action against a background of state policy.[49]

Expanded legal jurisdiction and changes in sovereignty help construct the shifts in authority that constitute political transition. But such changes often also put sovereignty, jurisdiction, and responsibility themselves in flux, depending on the character of state behavior, for example, its adherence to or derogation from duties under international law. Despite expanded liability as a theoretical matter, application of these principles is occasional and generally restricted to cases involving an additional limiting principle, such as a demonstrable pattern of persecution.[50] Nevertheless, by reinterpreting states' obligations toward their citizens through critical displacements of sovereignty and jurisdiction, contemporary transitional practices potentially invigorate human rights guarantees first adumbrated in the immediate postwar era.[51]

The reconceptualization of core ideas concerning the relation between the individual and the state holds important ramifications for understandings of the self as well. In transitional jurisprudence's advancement of normative shift, law's role is often largely symbolic. Yet, at the operative level, transitional justice affects the individual: Whether through trials, reparations, constitutions, administrative processes, or other measures, transitional legality reconstructs the rules and conditions of political membership, representation, and participation that are basic to the individual's place in the community. Liberalizing normative change depends on a redefinition of understandings of individual status, rights, and duties, as well as a circumscribing of the parameters of state power. The threshold effect of the successor regime's justice-seeking acts operates at the level of individual action, in turn altering the state's political identity and at least potentially charting a new liberal course.

The influence of transitional justice's phenomena on the development of states' political identities in periods of upheaval raises a related question concerning transitional versus nontransitional times. In fact, the question of transitional justice's relation to ordinary times has two dimensions. One is the question with which this book began: To what extent are ideal theories of justice pertinent to transitional times? This book replies that ideal theory is simply not the relevant yardstick by which we can judge legal action in these periods. The comparative and historical perspective pursued here compels an understanding of a nonideal, "compromised" justice that at once is informed by and constitutive of the conditions under which it is chosen.

Recognizing this conception of justice has ramifications for the second dimension of the question: To what extent ought transitional justice be generalized to ordinary times? The phenomena examined here occur largely under the first postrepression successor regime, whose responses are defined temporally as well as by the modalities of transformative change discussed above. It has thus been necessary to delimit a period of transition constructed by paradigmatic acts of jurisprudence that serve as rituals of political passage. Yet, despite the passage of time, intervening events, and political change, the problems of transitional justice, when they are left unresolved, do not simply disappear.[52] Transitional justice-seeking persists, failing to follow conventional understandings regarding the responses to wrongdoing, generally thought to diminish with time. Enduring rights problems and successor assumptions of obligations for past derogations from the rule of law often—notwithstanding time lag—obscure the sense in which these actions are appreciably the subject of transitional justice. Yet, the persistence over time of claims for past wrongs once again reveals the independence of these questions from the simple advent of changes in political power. It suggests that the assumption of ongoing state responsibility for past related claims goes hand in hand with stable political identity, indeed, realizing more than partial justice often awaits the passage of time.[53] Though the persistence of past-related claims also raises potential conflict, possibly pitting traditionalist claims against other more forward-looking liberal values.

Entrenching the transitional identity, however, holds a compelling normative as well as functional appeal; after all, it is a political identity that emphasizes the possibility of unity and corrective justice—a redemptive vision. Similarly, transitional justice offers a controlled means of reform, more measured than changes guided solely on the basis of other normative sources, such as morals.[54] Indeed, transitional resolutions appear to converge, at least provisionally, on transcendent values informed by human rights norms capable of mediating the transitional political divide.[55]

Though transitional jurisprudence posits a cognizable paradigm, it is one with affinities to law in nontransitional circumstances. Indeed, one might think of transitional jurisprudence as exaggerated instantiations that vivify conflicts and compromises otherwise latent in the law and, in particular, illuminate law's relation to politics. One place this is seen is in the connection between transitional jurisprudence and human rights law, because it is evident that the most vigorous enforcement of human rights law occurs in transitional periods. Although human rights norms are largely codified, their application commonly occurs in transitional times, when there is a greater readiness to experiment with alternative normative schemes. An example is the ad hoc war crimes tribunals established to prosecute human rights abuses during the Bosnian and Rwandan conflicts. While the full administration of justice is not possible, this paradigmatic symbolic form, nonetheless, performs the usual function of expressing the shift in the site of authority in the transition. Moreover, at a minimum, the responses in these periods emphasizing record keeping preserve the possibility of future more plenary justice. Nevertheless, these accommodations and temporizing should not be confused with ideal justice. The transitional response ought not to be generalized as the human rights standard of how to respond to violations, whether ongoing or in the past. Normalization of the transitional response would miss what is, after all, the core transformative message: the belief in the human possibility of averting the tragic repetition of the past in the liberalizing state. Indeed, human rights law's normative force is such that it enables transformation even in nontransitional circumstances.

The pursuit of an entrenched transitional identity poses two further risks. The first concerns the extent to which it appears to rationalize the past too much and too far. The quintessential transitional hermeneutics is a historicist self-knowledge available only ex post, and the danger is that this hermeneutics could be undermined if past wrongs are somehow justified by the ensuing progress toward liberalization. Second, the transitional state's search for unity can all too easily come to be premised on an inherently unstable formula rendered either as myth or as an unreachable normative vision. In both cases, the risk is that the state's assumption of a political identity based on unity may attenuate the possibility of political change. Such static entrenchments of identity are ultimately illiberal. A liberal posture, by contrast, necessitates nurturing—and thus sustaining—the transitional modality as a critical space between the practicable and the redemptive in the political imagination.

# Epilogue

## Transitional Justice and Its Normalization—Fin de Siècle

Consider to what extent the recurring discourse of the last years of the twentieth century is one of transitional justice. There is a persistent call for apologies, reparations, memoirs, (individual and collective), and all manner of account settling relating to past suffering and wrongdoing. Instances abound regarding settlements for World War II–related controversies, lost bank accounts, property restitution, reparations for slave labor, return of confiscated objects. Perhaps the most obvious instance of normalization of transitional jurisprudence is the entrenching of the postwar international military tribunal in the proposed international criminal court, the new international institution at century's end. There is apparently an ever-expanding discourse of rights claiming and accountability.

This turn to the rituals associated with political flux discussed in this book occurs at a time of periodization of centennial and millennial dimensions. The turn to these rituals in the context of meta-transition appears a pervasive attempt to construct collective passage. In the contemporary moment, the social rituals of passage appear not to derive from religion but from the law. These are the secular rites and symbols of passage, harbingers neither of apocalypse, nor of messianism, but of what appears to be the paradigmatic transitional conception: of *bounded change*. Transitional jurisprudence's appeal is that it offers the closure that passage brings. But it does so at a cost. Every act of transition implies an ambivalent resolution. These liberal rites perform political passage by constructing discontinuities and continuity, destruction and reproduction, disappropriation and reappropriation, disavowal and avowal. These rituals attempt to relegate to the past the worst of this century, while also propounding a workable shared narrative for the future. By these practices, a line is drawn delineating the parameters of that collective memory to be preserved: what is to be remembered and what repressed; what is to be abandoned and what validated; what is to be rendered incontestable and what will remain controverted. Renewal is forged by letting go of the century's historical injustices and moving from a plurality of controverted political identities to a narrative in common. As such, transitional practices have an ambivalent character, the resort to these practices in political flux is in the service of unity; yet, there is also a loss.

Transitional justice is partial and limited. The resort to such settlements implies compromise; their potential lies in their ability to reconstitute the community. The resort to transitional justice has its distinct politics—of forced consensus and an eschewing of a measure of the individualism characterizing modern constitutionalism—while the transitional forms comprise the tiny symbols of the habits of a rule of law state.

These practices reveal a mind-set peculiar to the contemporary moment. This is the turn to the transitional jurisprudence not of grand foundational projects of reform but of sober stocktaking, not of the modernizing belief in moral progress of the early twentieth century but also not a hopeless conservatism or fin de siècle decadence. Political compromise to be sure is a perennial sign of working democracies; yet, consider the significance of the normalization of this paradigm in and through the law. This quintessential form of bounded change is utterly self-conscious about law's constructive force and about its constraints. At the end of this bloody century, what is paradigmatic is the response to political catastrophe: justice as political, law without illusion, yet nurturing some small hope of amelioration.

# Notes

## Preface

1. See Ruti Teitel, "How Are the New Democracies of the Southern Cone Dealing with the Legacy of Past Human Rights Abuses? (paper prepared for Council on Foreign Relations New York, N.Y., May 17, 1990).

## Introduction

1. Works that move beyond the case study or regional approach often confine themselves to a particular historical moment. See, e.g., John Herz, ed., *From Dictatorship to Democracy: Coping with the Legacies of Authoritarianism and Totalitarianism* (Westport, Conn.: Greenwood Press, 1982) (focusing on postwar period). For the classic inquiry into the question of political justice, see Otto Kirchheimer, *Political Justice: The Use of Legal Procedure for Political Ends* (Westport, Conn.: Greenwood Press, 1980).

2. See Bruce A. Ackerman, *The Future of Liberal Revolution* (New Haven: Yale University Press, 1992); Carlos Santiago Nino, *Radical Evil on Trial* (New Haven: Yale University Press, 1996); John Herz, "An Historical Perspective," in *State Crimes: Punishment or Pardon*, ed. Alice H. Henkin (Queenstown, Md.: Aspen Institute, 1989). For comparative approaches, see the essays collected in Guillermo O'Donnell et al., eds. *Transitions from Authoritarian Rule: Comparative Perspectives*, (Baltimore: Johns Hopkins University Press, 1986). See also Juan J. Linz and Alfred Stepan, *Problems of Democratic Transition and Consolidation: Southern Europe, South America, and Post-Communist Europe* (Baltimore: Johns Hopkins University Press, 1996) (exploring processes of transition and consolidation from comparative perspective). See, e.g., Jaime Malamud-Goti, "Transitional Governments in the Breach: Why Punish State Criminals?" *Human Rights Quarterly* 12, NO. 1 (1990): 1–16.

3. Charles R. Beitz, *Political Theory and International Relations* (Princeton: Princeton University Press, 1979), 15–66; R.B.J. Walker, *Inside/Outside: International Relations as Political Theory* (Cambridge: Cambridge University Press, 1993), 123–24. For sound summaries of the realist school in international theory, see John H. Herz, *Political Realism and Political Idealism* (Chicago: Chicago University Press, 1951);

Martin Wight, *International Theory: The Three Traditions* (London: Leicester University Press for the Royal Institute of International Affairs, 1990); J. Ann Tickner, "Hans Morgenthau's Principles: A Feminist Reformulation," *in International Theory; Critical Investigations,* ed. James Der Derian (New York: New York University Press, 1995), 53, 55–57.

4. See generally Linz and Stepan, *Problems of Democratic Transition and Consolidation;* O'Donnell et al., eds., *Transitions from Authoritarian Rule* (collecting essays that adopt primarily regional approach). See also Samuel P. Huntington, *The Third Wave: Democratization in the Late Twentieth Century* (Norman: University of Oklahoma Press, 1991), 215; Stephen Holmes, "The End of Decommunization," *East European Constitutional Review* 3 (Fall 1994): 33.

5. For such an argument, see Huntington, *Third Wave,* 231.

6. See Ackerman, *Future of Liberal Revolution,* 69–73; E.B.F. Midgley, *The Natural Law Tradition and the Theory of International Relations* (New York: Barnes & Noble Books,1975), 219–31, 350–51.

7. Anne-Marie Slaughter, "International Law and International Relations Theory: A Dual Agenda," *American Journal of International Law* 87 (1993): 205. The liberal tradition in jurisprudence informs these approaches.

8. The paradigmatic expression of liberal theory's views on law and politics can be found in John Rawls, *Political Liberalism* (New York: Columbia University Press, 1993), and John Rawls, "The Domain of the Political and Overlapping Consensus," *New York University Law Review* 64 (1989): 233. On the relation of rights theory to democracy, see *Theories of Rights,* ed. Jeremy Waldron, (Oxford: Oxford University Press, 1984). See also Ronald Dworkin, *Law's Empire* (Cambridge: Harvard University Press, 1986); Ronald Dworkin, *Taking Rights Seriously* (Cambridge: Harvard University Press, 1977).

9. Prominent collections of critical legal studies (CLS) essays include James Boyle, *Critical Legal Studies* (New York: New York University Press, 1992), and David Kairys, *The Politics of Law: A Progressive Critique* (New York: Pantheon Books, 1990). See also Mark Kelman, *A Guide to Critical Legal Studies* (Cambridge: Harvard University Press, 1987); Roberto Mangabeira Unger, *The Critical Legal Studies Movement* (Cambridge: Harvard University Press, 1986); James Boyle, "The Politics of Reason: Critical Legal Theory and Local Social Thought," *University of Pennsylvania Law Review* 133 (1985): 685 (discussing legal realism, linguistic theory, and Marxist theory). For critical treatment of international legal issues, see Nigel Purvis, "Critical Legal Studies in Public International Law, World Order, and Critical Legal Studies," *Stanford Law Review* 42 (1990): 811. For critical analysis of American jurisprudence, see Mark Tushnet, *Red, White, and Blue* (Cambridge: Harvard University Press, 1988).

10. See Ackerman, *Future of Liberal Revolution,* 11–14; Hannah Arendt, *On Revolution* (New York: Viking Press, 1965), 139–78.

11. See Guillermo O'Donnell and Philippe C. Schmitter, *Transitions from Authoritarian Rule: Tentative Conclusions about Uncertain Democracies* (Baltimore: Johns Hopkins University Press, 1986), 6 (defining transition as "the interval between one political regime and another"); Juan J. Linz, "Totalitarian and Authoritarian Regimes," in *Handbook of Political Science: Macropolitical Theory,* ed. Fred I. Greenstein and Nelson W. Polsby (Reading, Mass.: Addison-Wesley, 1975), Vol. III 182–83. For the classical articulation, see Robert Dahl, *Polyarchy* (New Haven: Yale University Press, 1971), 20–32, 74–80. See also Huntington, *Third Wave,* 7–8, Richard Gunther et al., "O'Donnell's 'Illusions': A Rejoinder," *Journal of Democracy* 7, no. 4 (1996): 151–53.

12. See Huntington, *Third Wave,* 7.

13. For a critique of the teleological view, see Guillermo O'Donnell, "Illusions and Conceptual Flaws," *Journal of Democracy* 7, no. 4 (1996): 160, 163–64, and Guillermo O'Donnell, "Illusions about Consolidation," *Journal of Democracy* 7, no. 2 (1996): 34.

14. See generally Herz, *From Dictatorship to Democracy*.

15. This observation has implications for certain debates in political science and constitutionalism and may well share affinities with jurisprudential debates concerning what makes for the authority of law. See Joseph Raz, *The Authority of Law: Essays on Law and Morality* (New York: Oxford University Press, 1979), 214.

16. By "legal forms," I mean principles, norms, ideas, rules, practices, as well as the agencies of legislation, administration, adjudication, and enforcement. See Sally Falk Moore, *Law as Process: An Anthropological Approach* (Boston: Routledge, 1978), 54. On the significance of legal forms, *see* Isaac D. Balbus, "Commodity Form and Legal Form: An Essay on the 'Relative Autonomy' of the Law," *Law and Society Review* 11(1977): 571–72.

17. For a useful introduction to the constructivist approach, *see* Peter L. Berger and Thomas Luckmann, *The Social Construction of Reality: A Treatise in the Sociology of Knowledge* (New York: Anchor Books, Doubleday, 1966), 19 (describing approach from sociological perspective). On constructivism in the law, see Pierre Bourdieu, "The Force of Law: Toward a Sociology of the Juridical Field," *Hastings Law Journal* 38 (1987): 805, 814–40. See also Roberto Mangabeira Unger, *False Necessity–Anti-Necessitarian Social Theory in the Service of Radical Democracy* (New York: Cambridge University Press, 1987), 246–52 (analyzing legal and institutional responses to "context change"). For a subtle treatment of the role of law in constructing community, see Robert Gordon, "Critical Legal Histories," *Stanford Law Review* 36 (1984): 57. See generally John Brigham, *The Constitution of Interests: Beyond the Politics of Rights* (New York: New York University Press, 1996) (discussing law's role in constructing political movements).

18. See generally, Dahl, *Polyarchy*; David Held, *Models of Democracy* (Stanford: Stanford University Press, 1987).

## Chapter 1

1. Friedrich A. Hayek, *The Road to Serfdom* (Chicago: University of Chicago Press, 1944), 72 ("[G]overnment in all its actions is bound by rules fixed and announced beforehand-rules which make it possible to foresee with fair certainty how the authority will use its . . . powers in given circumstances and to plan one's individual affairs on the basis of this knowledge"). For a discussion of the general understanding of the role of rule of law in democracies as restraint on arbitrary power, see Roger Cotterrell, *The Politics of Jurisprudence: A Critical Introduction to Legal Philosophy* (Philadelphia: University of Pennsylvania Press, 1989), 113–14, which describes the danger of viewing the state as an entity above the law. For an exploration of the relation of the rule of law to democracy, see Jean Hampton, "Democracy and the Rule of Law," in *Nomos XXXVI: The Rule of Law*, ed. Ian Shapiro (New York: New York University Press, 1995), 13. The classic account of the minimum requirements of legality is found in Lon L. Fuller, *The Morality of Law* (New Haven: Yale University Press, 1964), 33–34. Ronald Dworkin offers the preeminent contemporary exposition of substantive rule-of-law theory. See Ronald Dworkin, *A Matter of Principle* (Cambridge: Harvard University Press, 1985), 11–12 (arguing that "rights conception" of rule of law "requires, as part of the ideal of law, that the rules in the rule book capture and enforce moral rights"). See also Frank Michelman, "Law's Republic," *Yale Law Journal* 97 (1988): 1493 (presenting

modern interpretation of government by law through reinterpretation of political theory of civic republicanism).

Margaret Jane Radin describes the philosophical underpinning of modern approaches to the rule of law as consisting of the following assumptions:

> (1) law consists of rules; (2) rules are prior to particular cases, more general than particular cases, and applied to particular cases; (3) law is instrumental (the rules are applied to achieve ends); (4) there is a radical separation between government and citizens (there are rule-givers and appliers, versus rule-takers and compliers); (5) the person is a rational chooser ordering her affairs instrumentally.

Margaret Jane Radin, "Reconsidering the Rule of Law," *Boston University Law Review* 69 (1989): 792. See generally Cotterrell, *Politics of Jurisprudence* (providing introduction to debate about nature of law); Allan C. Hutchinson and Patrick Monahan, eds., *The Rule of Law* (Toronto: Carswell, 1987) (collecting several essays discussing rule of law); Roger Cotterrell, "The Rule of Law in Corporate Society: Neumann, Kirchheimer, and the Lessons of Weimar," *Modern Law Review* 51 (1988): 126–32 (book review).

2. For an early discussion of the common themes in the concepts of the rule of law and of constitutionalism, see A. V. Dicey, *Introduction to the Study of the Laws of the Constitution* (Indianapolis: Liberty Fund, 1982), 107–22. See also E. P. Thompson, *Whigs and Hunters: The Origin of the Black Act* (New York: Pantheon Books, 1975).

3. *Planned Parenthood v Casey*, 505 US 833, 854 (1992); see Antonin Scalia, "The Rule of Law as a Law of Rules," *University of Chicago Law Review* 56 (1989): 1175 (advocating "general rule of law" over "personal discretion to do justice").

4. See H.L.A. Hart, "Positivism and the Separation of Law and Morals," *Harvard Law Review* 71 (1958): 593 (defending positivism); Lon L. Fuller, "Positivism and Fidelity to Law—A Reply to Professor Hart," *Harvard Law Review* 71 (1958): 630 (criticizing Hart for ignoring role of morality in creation of law).

5. Other theorizing about the nature of the rule of law in the works of Franz Neumann and Otto Kirchheimer also takes this period as its point of departure. See Franz Neumann, *Behemoth: The Structure and Practice of National Socialism* (Frankfurt am Main: Europäische Verlagsanshalt, 1977), 1933–44; Franz Neumann, *The Rule of Law: Political Theory and the Legal System in Modern Society* (Dover: Berg Publishers, 1986); William E. Scheuerman, ed., *The Rule of Law under Siege: Selected Essays of Franz L. Neumann and Otto Kirchheimer* (Berkeley: University of California Press, 1996). For an engaging exposition of the views of these scholars, see William E. Scheuerman, *Between the Norm and the Exception: The Frankfurt School and the Rule of Law* (Cambridge: MIT Press, 1994), which attempts to apply Neumann's and Kirchheimer's analyses to the twentieth-century capitalist welfare state.

6. See "Recent Cases," *Harvard Law Review* 64 (1951): 1005–06 (citing Germany, *Judgment of July 27, 1949*, 5 *Suddeutscher Juristen Zeitung* (1950): 207 (Oberlandesgericht [OLG] [Bamberg])).

7. See generally Fuller, *Morality of Law*, 245.

8. For a thoughtful exploration of the meaning of legal positivism, see Frederick Schauer, "Fuller's Internal Point of View," *Law and Philosophy* 13 (1994): 285.

9. See Fuller, "Positivism and Fidelity to Law," 642–43, 657.

10. See Fuller, *Morality of Law*, 96–97.

11. See Fuller, id. For discussion of the positivism/natural law debate, see Gustav Radbruch, *Rechtsphilosophie* (Stuttgart: Koehler, 1956); Gustav Radbruch, "Die Erneurung des Rechts," *Die Wandlung* 2 (1947): 8. See also Markus Dirk Dubber, "Judicial

Positivism and Hitler's Injustice," review of Ingo Müller, *Hitler's Justice, Columbia Law Review* 93 (1993):1807; Fuller, *Morality of Law*, 23.

12. For an excellent account of this historical debate, see Stanley L. Paulson, "Lon L. Fuller, Gustav Radbruch, and the `Positivist' Thesis," *Law and Philosophy* 13 (1994): 313.

13. See Hart, "Positivism and the Separation of Law and Morals," 617–18.

14. Fuller, *Morality of Law*, 245.

15. Ibid.

16. Ibid., 648.

17. See *Zentenyi-Takacs Law, Law Concerning the Prosecutability of Offenses between December 21, 1944 and May 2, 1990* (Hungary, 1991), translated in *Journal of Constitutional Law of East and Central Europe* 1 (1994): 131. See also Stephen Schulhofer et al., "Dilemmas of Justice," *East European Constitutional Law Review* 1, no. 2 (1992): 17.

18. See generally *Zentenyi-Takacs Law*.

19. See *Decision of Dec. 21, 1993* (Czech Republic, Constitutional Court, 1993) (on file with Center for the Study of Constitutionalism in Eastern Europe, University of Chicago) (upholding *Act on the Illegality of the Communist Regime and Resistance to It*, Act No. 198/1993 (1993)).

20. For discussion of Germany's statute-of-limitations debate, see Adalbert Rückerl, *The Investigation of Nazi Crimes, 1945–1978: A Documentation*, trans. Derek Rutter (Heidelberg, Karlsruhe: C. F. Müller, 1979), 53–55, 66–67.

21. *Judgment of March 5, 1992*, Magyar Kozlony No. 23/1992 (Hungary, Constitutional Court, 1992), translated in *Journal of Constitutional Law in Eastern and Central Europe* 1 (1994): 136.

22. Ibid., 141.

23. Ibid., 141–42.

24. Ibid., 142.

25. Compare Ingo Müller, *Hitler's Justice: The Courts of the Third Reich* (Cambridge: Harvard University Press, 1991) 68, 71–37, with Dubber, *Judicial Positivism and Hitler's Injustice*, 1819–20, 1825. See also Richard Weisberg, *Vichy Law and the Holocaust in France* (New York: New York University Press, 1996). For a thoughtful discussion, see Symposium, "Nazis in the Courtroom: Lessons from the Conduct of Lawyers and Judges under the Laws of the Third Reich and Vichy France," *Brooklyn Law Review* 61 (1995): 1142–45. For a discussion regarding South Africa, see David Dyzenhaus, *Hard Cases in Wicked Legal Systems: South African Law in the Perspective of Legal Philosophy* (New York: Oxford University Press, 1991), and Stephen Ellman, *In a Time of Trouble: Law and Liberty in South Africa's State of Emergency* (New York: Oxford University Press, 1992). For a discussion of the Latin American judiciary's interpretive strategies, see Mark J. Osiel, "Dialogue with Dictators: Judicial Resistance in Argentina and Brazil," *Law and Social Inquiry* 20 (1995): 481.

26. For a broader comparison of the American and English approaches, see Anthony J. Sebok, "Misunderstanding Positivism," *Michigan Law Review* 93 (1995): 2055. For analysis of jurisprudence under a slavery regime, see Robert M. Cover, *Justice Accused: Antislavery and the Judicial Process* (New Haven: Yale University Press, 1975), 26–29, 121–23. For a discussion regarding Nazi jurisprudence, see generally Müller, *Hitler's Justice*.

27. For an account of the history, see Friedrich A. Hayek, *The Constitution of Liberty* (Chicago: University of Chicago Press, 1960), 162–75. For an intellectual history of the German Rechtsstaat, see Steven B. Smith, *Hegel's Critique of Liberalism* (Chicago: University of Chicago Press, 1989), 145–48.

28. For a related discussion of tyranny and law, see Judith N. Shklar, *Legalism:*

*Law, Morals, and Political Trials* (Cambridge: Harvard University Press, 1964), 126–27.

29. See Henry W. Ehrmann, *Comparative Legal Cultures* (Englewood Cliffs: Prentice Hall, 1976), 48–50; James L. Gibson and Gregory A. Caldeira, "The Legal Cultures of Europe," *Law and Society Review* 30 (1996): 55–62.

30. On one such articulation of the conditions for law, see Fuller, "Positivism and Fidelity to Law," 638–43. See also Joseph Raz, *The Concept of a Legal System: An Introduction to the Theory of Legal System* (New York: Oxford University Press, 1970) (providing systematic effort to specify conditions for law).

31. *Judgment of Jan. 20, 1992*, Juristenzeitung 13 (1992): 691, 695 (F.R.G., Landgericht [LG] [Berlin]).

32. See Raz, *Concept of a Legal System*, 214.

33. See generally Boaventura De Soisa Santos, *Toward a New Common Sense: Law, Science, and Politics in the Paradigmatic Transition* (New York: Routledge, 1995) (articulating theory of law in light of dynamic law/society relation).

34. See Hans Kelsen, "The Rule against Ex Post Facto Laws and the Prosecution of the Axis War Criminals," *Judge Advocate Journal* (Fall-Winter 1945): 8–12, 46 (discussing nature of jurisdiction of Nuremberg Tribunal and other postwar trials); Bernard D. Meltzer, "A Note on Some Aspects of the Nuremberg Debate," *University of Chicago Law Review* 14 (1947): 455–57 ("The strict and automatic application of the rule against retroactivity to an underdeveloped legal system [such as international law] would, of course, have widened the gap between the developing moral sense of the community and its lagging legal institutions"). See generally Stanley L. Paulsen, "Classical Legal Positivism at Nuremberg," *Philosophy and Public Affairs* 4 (1975): 132 (arguing that Nuremberg Tribunal's rejection of Nazi defenses was justified by its rejection of classical legal positivism); Quincy Wright, "Legal Positivism and the Nuremberg Judgment," *American Journal of International Law* 42 (1948): 405 (arguing that criticism of Nuremberg trials as applying ex post facto law is rooted in critics' positivistic theory of international law).

35. *Judgment of March 5, 1992* (cited in note 21 above).

36. See *Act on Procedures concerning Certain Crimes Committed during the 1956 Revolution*, (Hungary, 1993) (on file with Center for the Study of Constitutionalism in Eastern Europe, University of Chicago).

37. See "Geneva Convention Relative to the Protection of Civilian Persons in Time of War," 12 August 1949, *Treaties and International Agreements Registered or Filed or Reported with the Secretariat of the United Nations* 75, no. 973 (1950): 287; "Convention on the Non-Applicability of Statutory Limitations to War Crimes and Crimes Against Humanity," 11 November 1970, *Treaties and International Agreements Registered or Filed or Reported with the Secretariat of the United Nations* 754, no. 10823 (1970): 73.

38. In Poland, the question of statutes of limitations was only settled when it became a matter of constitutional consensus. See Republic of Poland Const, Art. 43 (as adopted by the National Assembly, 2 April 1997), which provides that insofar as offenses constitute war crimes or crimes against humanity, they are not subject to limitations.

39. *Resolution of the Hungarian Constitutional Court of Oct. 12, 1993 on the Justice Law* (Case 53/1993) (on file with Center for the Study of Constitutionalism in Eastern Europe, formerly at University of Chicago). See Hungarian Const, Art 7, cl 1 ("The legal system of the Republic of Hungary . . . harmonizes the national law and statutes of the country with the obligations assumed under international law"). Compare Greek Const, Art 28, cl 1 (declaring that rules of international law shall prevail over contrary domestic law).

40. See *Border Guards Prosecutions Cases* (F.R.G., Bundesgerichtshof [BGH]), translated in *International Law Reports* 100 (1995): 380–82 (relying on *International Covenant on Civil and Political Rights*, 19 December 1966, *Treaties and International Agreements Registered or Filed or Reported with the Secretariat of the United Nations* 999, no. 14668 (1976): 171 (holding that domestic order infringed human rights protected by international treaty). See generally Stephan Hobe and Christian Tietje, "Government Criminality: The Judgment of the German Federal Constitutional Court of 24 October 1996," *German Yearbook of International Law* 39 (1996): 523. See also Krisztina Morvai, "Retroactive Justice Based on International Law: A Recent Decision by the Hungarian Constitutional Court," *East European Constitutional Review* (Fall 1993/Winter 1994): 33; "Law on Genocide and Crimes against Humanity Committed in Albania during Communist Rule for Political, Ideological, and Religious Motives," translated in Human Rights Watch, *Human Rights in Post-Communist Albania* (New York: Human Rights Watch, 1996), app. A (establishing basis for prosecuting former Communists).

41. See *Statute of the International Court of Justice, U.S. Statutes at Large* 59 (1945): 1031, Art 38(1). For an account of the positivist understanding, see Oscar Schachter, *International Law in Theory and Practice* (Dordrecht, The Netherlands, and Boston: M. Nijhoff, 1991; distributed in U.S. and Canada by Kluwer Academic Publishers), 35–36. The role of custom in the formation of international law is described in Michael Akehurst, "Custom as a Source of International Law," *British Yearbook International* 47 (1974–1975): 1. For a related discussion regarding elements of both natural and positive law in international law, see Shklar, *Legalism: Law, Morals, and Political Trials*, 126–28.

42. See J. M. Balkin, "Nested Oppositions," *Yale Law Journal* 99 (1990): 1669 (book review).

43. See *Judgment of Jan. 20, 1992* (cited in note 31 above), at 693.

44. See *Decision of Dec. 21, 1993* (cited in note 19 above).

45. For an account of the nature of such decision making in illiberal political systems, see the discussion of decisionism in Carl Schmitt, *Political Theology: Four Chapters on the Concept of Sovereignty*, trans. George Schwab (Chicago: University of Chicago Press, 1985), 53–66.

46. For description of the beginnings of this development, see Herman Schwartz, "The New East European Constitutional Courts," *Michigan Journal of International Law* 13 (1992): 741. See Ruti Teitel, "Post-Communist Constitutionalism: A Transitional Perspective," *Columbia Human Rights Law Review* 26 (1994): 167. For a wide-ranging collection of essays on East European constitutional courts, see Irena Grudzinska-Gross, ed., *Constitutionalism in East Central Europe* (Bratislava: Czecho-Slovak Committee of the European Cultural Foundation, 1994). See also South African Const, Ch VII (discussed in chapter on constitutional justice).

47. See *Judgment of Jan. 20, 1992* (cited note 31 above), at 694.

48. See *Judgment of March 5, 1992* (cited in note 21 above).

49. See Teitel, "Post-Communist Constitutionalism," 169–76.

50. See Ethan Klingsberg, "Judicial Review and Hungary's Transition from Communism to Democracy: The Constitutional Court, the Continuity of Law, and the Redefinition of Property Rights," *Brigham Young University Law Review* 1992 (1992): 62 (discussing remarkable access implied by Hungary's permissive standing rules). It is not alone in the region contemplating participation by political actors in constitutional litigation.

51. See Teitel, "Post-Communist Constitutionalism," 186–87.

52. See *Judgment of March 5, 1992* (cited in note 21 above).

53. See R. M. Dworkin, *Taking Rights Seriously* (Cambridge: Harvard University Press, 1977), 84.

54. Ibid., 84, 138.

55. On the traditional paradigm of the judiciary, see generally Martin Shapiro, *Courts: A Comparative and Political Analysis* (Chicago: University of Chicago Press, 1981). See also Mauro Cappelletti, *The Judicial Process in Comparative Perspective* (New York: Clarendon Press, 1989), 31–34 (observing that judges necessarily "make law" by interpreting it but distinguishing this function from that of legislators, who act in procedurally distinct manner). For the classic statements regarding the role of the judiciary in democracy, see generally Alexander M. Bickel, *The Least Dangerous Branch* (New Haven: Yale University Press, 1986); Jesse H. Choper, *Judicial Review and the National Political Process* (Chicago: University of Chicago Press, 1980); and John Hart Ely, *Democracy and Distrust: A Theory of Judicial Review* (Cambridge: Harvard University Press, 1980).

56. During the initial political shift, transitional parliaments are generally vestiges of the prior repressive period. *See* Andrew Arato, "Dilemmas Arising from the Power to Create Constitutions in Eastern Europe," *Cardozo Law Review* 14 (1993): 674–75.

57. For an illustrative discussion relating Russia's transitional plight to the absence of concentrated state power, see Stephen Holmes, "Can Weak-State Liberalism Survive?" (paper presented at Colloquium on Constitutional Theory at New York University School of Law, spring 1997, on file with author).

58. See Teitel, "Post-Communist Constitutionalism,"182–85.

59. See, e.g., Müller, *Hitler's Justice*, 201 (discussing compromised judiciary in postwar Germany).

60. See, e.g., Ronald M. Dworkin, *Law's Empire* (Cambridge: Harvard University Press, Belknap Press, 1986); Bruce R. Douglass, Gerald M. Mara, and Henry S. Richardson, eds., *Liberalism and the Good* (New York: Routledge, 1990).

61. See Philippe Nonet and Philip Selznick, *Law and Society in Transition* (New York: Harper and Row, 1978), 4–5; Richard L. Abel, ed., *The Politics of Informal Justice* (New York: Academic Press, 1982), 267; David M. Trubek, "Turning Away from Law?" *Michigan Law Review* 82 (1984): 825.

62. For exploration of the contrasting ideas of the rule of law from the perspectives of liberalism and critical legal theory, see generally Andrew Altman, *Critical Legal Studies: A Liberal Critique* (Princeton: Princeton University Press, 1990).

## Chapter 2

1. See Cesare Beccaria, *On Crimes and Punishments and Other Writings* (Cambridge: Cambridge University Press [1769], 1995); Jeremy Bentham, *An Introduction to the Principles of Morals and Legislation* vol. 2 (Darien, Conn.: Hafner Publishing [1823], 1970) (theorizing punishments in terms of the general good).

2. See Hyman Gross, *A Theory of Criminal Justice* (New York: Oxford University Press, 1979), 400–401.

3. See David Lagomarsino and Charles T. Wood, *The Trial of Charles I: A Documentary History* (Hanover, N.H.: University Press of New England, 1989), 25; Michael Walzer, ed., *Regicide and Revolution: Speeches at the Trial of Louis XVI*, trans. Marian Rothstein (New York: Cambridge University Press, 1974), 88.

4. For the contemporary argument, see Diane F. Orentlicher, "Settling Accounts:

The Duty to Prosecute Human Rights Violations of a Prior Regime," *Yale Law Journal* 100 (1991): 2537.

5. Walzer, ed., *Regicide and Revolution*, 88.

6. Ibid., 5.

7. Ibid., 78.

8. Judith N. Shklar, *Legalism: Law, Morals, and Political Trials* (Cambridge: Harvard University Press, 1964), 145.

9. Otto Kirchheimer, *Political Justice: The Use of Legal Procedure for Political Ends* (Westport, Conn.: Greenwood Press, 1961), 308.

10. See Ruti Teitel, "How Are the New Democracies of the Southern Cone Dealing with the Legacy of Past Human Rights Abuses?" (paper prepared as backgrounder for discussion at Council on Foreign Relations critiquing argument that democracy justifies an obligation to punish, New York, N.Y., May 17, 1990).

11. For an account of these failed national trials, see George Gordon Battle, "The Trials before the Leipsic Supreme Court of Germans Accused of War Crimes," *Virginia Law Review* 8 (1921): 1.

12. The Preparatory Committee on the Establishment of an International Criminal Court has concluded its work by adopting a framework for the establishment of an International Criminal Court. See U.N. doc. A/AC.249/1998/CRP.6–18; U.N. doc. A/AC.249/1998/CRP.21; U.N. doc. A/AC.249/1998/CRP.19; U.N. doc. A/AC.249/1998/ CRP.3/Rev.1. As of publication, the U.N. Diplomatic Conference of Plenipotentiaries on the Establishment of an International Criminal Court met in Rome from June 15 to July 17, 1998, to finalize and approve a convention to establish the court. See generally Christopher Keith Hall, "The First Two Sessions of the U.N. Preparatory Committee on the Establishment of an International Criminal Court," *American Journal of International Law* 91 (1997): 177; James Crawford, "The ILC Adopts a Statute for an International Criminal Court," *American Journal of International Law* 89 (1995): 404 (discussing International Law Commission's Draft Statute to create an international criminal court); Bernhard Graefrath, "Universal Criminal Jurisdiction and an International Criminal Court," *European Journal of International Law* 1 (1990): 67 (discussing United Nation's attempts to establish international criminal court).

13. See Norman E. Tutorow, ed., *War Crimes, War Criminals, and War Crimes Trials: An Annotated Bibliography and Source Book* (New York: Greenwood Press, 1986).

14. See note 12 above.

15. A notorious example was the United States's declining jurisdiction in the case brought against it by Nicaragua. See *Nicaragua v United States*, 1984 ICJ 392 (1984).

16. See Aryeh Neier, *War Crimes: Brutality, Genocide, Terror, and the Struggle for Justice* (New York: Times Books, 1998).

17. For a commentator taking this position, see, e.g., Hannah Arendt, *Eichmann in Jerusalem: A Report on the Banality of Evil* (New York: Penguin Books, 1964).

18. United Nations, General Assembly, *International Law Commission: Report on the Principles of the Nuremberg Tribunal*, Principle I , A/1316 (1950).

19. Ibid. Principle III of the Nuremberg Principles states: "The fact that a person who committed an act which constitutes a crime under international law acted as Head of State or responsible government official does not relieve him from responsibility under international law."

20. Both Nuremberg and a subsequent case, The *Einsatzgruppen* case, *Trials of War Criminals before the Nuremberg Military Tribunals under Control Council No. 10*, vols. 4–5 (Washington, D.C.: GPO, 1949–1953), rejected the due-obedience defense

and the doctrine of respondeat superior by which culpability is ascribed to the order giver. The opposite doctrine of "absolute liability" providing that superior orders never justifies an unlawful act was advanced in *Mitchell v. Harmony*, 13 How 115 (1851), and later incorporated into the Nuremberg Principles at Article 8. Under the manifest illegality standard, if a reasonable man would have understood the orders to be manifestly illegal, the due obedience defense is disallowed. Principle IV of the Nuremberg Principles states: "The fact that a person acted pursuant to order of his government or of a superior does not relieve him from responsibility under international law, provided a moral choice was in fact possible to him."

21. See *Judgment in the Tokyo War Crimes Trial, 1948*, reprinted in part in Richard Falk, Gabriel Kolko, and Robert Jay Lifton, eds., *Crimes of War: A Legal, Political-Documentary, and Psychological Inquiry into the Responsibility of Leaders, Citizens, and Soldiers for Criminal Acts in Wars* (New York: Random House, 1971), 113. General Yamashita's appeals were heard by the United States Supreme Court, which affirmed this principle. See *In re Yamashita*, 327 US 1, 13–18 (1945).

22. *United States v Wilhelm von Leeb*, reprinted in XI *Trials of War Criminals before the Nuremberg Military Tribunals under Control Council Law No. 10*, 462 (1950) (*High Command Case*); *United States v Wilhelm List*, reprinted in XI *Trials of War Criminals before the Nuremberg Military Tribunals under Control Council Law No. 10*, 1230 (1950) (*Hostage Case*).

23. See generally Telford Taylor, *Nuremberg and Vietnam: An American Tragedy* (Chicago: Quadrangle Books, 1970). See also Falk, Kolko, and Lifton, eds., *Crimes of War*, 177–415.

24. See *United States v Calley*, 46 CMR 1131 (1973). See also Gary Komarow, "Individual Responsibility under International Law: The Nuremberg Principles in Domestic Legal Systems," *International and Comparative Law Quarterly* 29 (1980): 26–27, for a brief discussion of the *Calley* case in this context.

25. Protocol I, "Protocol Additional to the Geneva Conventions of 12 August 1949 and Relating to the Protection of Victims of International Armed Conflicts," 8 June 1977, *Treaties and International Agreements Registered or Filed or Reported with the Secretariat of the United Nations* 1125, no. 17512 (1979): 609.

26. For a scholarly discussion see Theodor Meron, *War Crimes Law Comes of Age: Essays* (Oxford: Clarendon Press, 1998).

27. See Telford Taylor, *The Anatomy of the Nuremberg Trials: A Personal Memoir* (New York: Knopf, 1992).

28. Ibid.

29. E.g., Jaime Malamud-Goti, *Game without End: State Terror and the Politics of Justice* (Norman: University of Oklahoma Press, 1996).

30. Helsinki Watch, *War Crimes in Bosnia-Hercegovina*, vol. 1 (New York: Human Rights Watch, 1992), (Helsinki Rights Watch Report).

31. *Proceedings of Las Malvinas Trial* (on file with author).

32. See "Four Hardline Communists Investigated over 1968 Prague Invasion," *Reuters*, 17 April 1990, available in Lexis, News Library, Reuters File; "August 1968—Gateway to Power for Number of Politicians," *CTK National News Wire*, 18 August 1998, available in Lexis, News Library, CTK File.

33. *Act on the Illegality of the Communist Regime and Resistance to It*, Act No. 198/1993 (Czech Republic, 1993).

34. See "Velvet Justice for Traitors Who Crushed 1968 Prague Spring," *The Telegraph* (Prague 23 August 1998, (reporting no convictions despite eight-year investigations).

35. See "Polish Politicians Ask for Trial for Martial Law Instigators," *Reuters*, 9

December 1991, available in Lexis, News Library, Reuters File. See also Tadiusz Olsza-ski, "Communism's Last Rulers: Fury and Fate," *Warsaw Voice*, 18 November 1992, available in Lexis, News Library. For accounts of the testimony of Jaruzelski and others, see *RFE/RL Daily Report No. 49*, 12 March 1993, 4. See also "Walesa to Testify on Mar-tial Law," *Polish News Bulletin*, 25 May 1994, Politics section.

    36. As of the time of publication, Jaruzelski had been excused from trial for health reasons. See "Jaruzelski Will Not Be Tried," *Polish News Bulletin*, 9 July 1997, Politics section. The recent release of incriminating documents may, however, strengthen the position of the forces seeking a trial. See "Constitutional Accountability Commission Meets," *Polish News Bulletin*, 26 October 1994; "Russian Dissident Accuses Jaruzelski," *Polish News Bulletin*, 20 May 1998, Politics section. See also Tad Szulc, "Unpleasant Truths about Eastern Europe," *Carnegie Endowment for International Peace, Foreign Policy*, 22 March 1996, available in Lexis, News Library.

    37. See Michael Shields, "Hungary Gets Ready to Try the Communist Villains of 1956," *Reuters*, 5 November 1991, available in Lexis, News Library, Reuters File. See also Jane Perlez, "Hungarian Arrests Set off Debate: Should '56 Oppressors Be Pun-ished?" *New York Times*, 3 April 1994, available in Lexis, News Library.

    38. *Constitutional Court Decision on the Statute of Limitations*, No. 2086/A/1991/14 (Hungary, 1992).

    39. *Act on Procedures Concerning Certain Crimes Committed during the 1956 Rev-olution* (Hungary, 1993) (on file with Center for the Study of Constitutionalism in East-ern and Central Europe, University of Chicago). On November 3, 1993, investigations into the 1956 killings were ordered, "on suspicion of crimes against humanity." Since the passage of the law, arrests, trials, and convictions have been ongoing. See "Court Convicts Defendants for War Crimes in 1956 Uprising," *BBC Summary of World Broad-casts*, 18 January 1997, available in Lexis, News Library. See also "Hungary Arrests More in 1956 Shootings Probe," *Reuters*, 11 February 1994, available in Lexis, News Library, Reuters File.

    40. See, e.g., "United Nations Convention on Prohibitions or Restrictions on the Use of Certain Conventional Weapons Which May Be Deemed to Be Excessively Inju-rious or to Have Indiscriminate Effects," 10 October 1980, *Treaties and International Agreements Registered or Filed or Reported with the Secretariat of the United Nations* 1342, no. 22495 (1983): 137; Protocol I, "Protocols Additional to the Geneva Conven-tions of 12 August 1949 and Relating to the Protection of Victims of International Armed Conflicts"; "Geneva Convention Relative to the Protection of Civilian Persons in Time of War," 12 August 1949, *Treaties and International Agreements Registered or Filed or Reported with the Secretariat of the United Nations* 75, no. 973 (1950): 287. For a comprehensive analysis, see Theodor Meron, *Human Rights and Humanitarian Norms as Customary Law* (New York: Oxford University Press, 1989) (expanding on concept of crimes against humanity in international and internal conflict).

    41. See *Rome Statute of the International Criminal Court*, U.N. doc. A/Conf. 183/9,17 July 1998, Art 7 (defining "crimes against humanity" as part of a "widespread or systematic attack directed against any civilian population"). For an illustration, see gen-erally Helsinki Watch, *War Crimes in Bosnia-Hercegovina* (reporting on crimes against humanity committed in the Balkans). See *Statute of International Criminal Tribunal for the Former Yugoslavia*, Art 5, annexed to United Nations, General Assembly, *Report of the Secretary-General Pursuant to Paragraph 2 of the U.N. Security Council Resolution 808*, S/25704 (1993), reprinted in *International Legal Materials* 32 (1993): 1159, 1193–97. The various acts constituting crimes against humanity are "murder, extermination, en-slavement, deportation, imprisonment, torture, rape, persecutions on political, racial

and relegous grounds and other inhumane acts." The understanding of the Commission of Experts was that the International Tribunal had jurisdiction over crimes against humanity, whether the conflict was "international" or "internal." As a matter of international customary law, jurisdiction was considered to exist for crimes against humanity and genocide. See United Nations, Security Council, *Final Report of the Commission of Experts Established Pursuant to Security Council Resolution 780*, S/1994/674 (1992), at 13. See also *Prosecutor v Tadic*, Case No. IT-94-1-AR72, Decision on the Defense Motion for Interlocutory Appeal on Jurisdiction (Appeals Chamber, International Criminal Tribunal for the Former Yugoslavia, October 2, 1995), reprinted in *International Legal Materials* 35 (1996): 32. However, the appeals chamber drew a line as to its interpretation of "grave breaches," insisting on international armed conflict for purposes of this offense. The tribunal's jurisdiction extends to crimes not committed by agents of the state, as long as committed "under color" of the state. The statute of the tribunal is contained within United Nations, Security Council, *Report of the Secretary-General Pursuant to Paragraph 2 of U.N. Security Council Resolution 808*, (1993), reprinted in *International Legal Materials* 32 (1993): 1159. Article 2 on the competence of the International Tribunal provides: "The International Tribunal shall have the power to prosecute persons committing or ordering to be committed grave breaches of the Geneva Conventions of 12 August 1949." It goes on to list specific offenses. Article 7 defines "crimes against humanity" as part of a "widespread or systematic attack directed against any civilians."

42. For example, Human Rights Watch has been documenting abuses taking place in the former Yugoslavia nearly from the start of the conflict, publishing detailed accounts and calling for the prosecution of war crimes. See Helsinki Watch, *War Crimes in Bosnia-Hercegovina*, vols. 1, 2.

43. See generally Arnold J. Toynbee, *Armenian Atrocities: The Murder of a Nation* (New York: Tankian, 1975). See also Dickran Boyajian, *Armenia: The Case for a Forgotten Genocide* (Westwood, N.J.: Educational Book Crafters, 1972).

44. See Symposium, "1945–1995 Critical Perspectives on the Nuremberg Trials and State Accountability," *New York Law School Journal of Human Rights* 12 (1995): 453; Inge S. Neumann, *European War Crimes Trials*, ed. Robert A. Rosenbaum (New York: Carnegie Endowment for International Peace, 1951). See generally Randolph L. Braham, ed., *Genocide and Retribution* (Boston: Kluwer-Nijhoff, 1983). For a full bibliographic listing, see generally Tutorow, ed., *War Crimes, War Criminals, and War Crimes Trials*; Neumann, *European War Crimes Trials*. See also the Owen M. Kupferschmid Holocaust and Human Rights Project Seventh International Conference, "Judgments on Nuremberg: The Past Half Century and Beyond—A Panel Discussion of Nuremberg Prosecutors," *Boston College Third World Law Journal* 16 (1996): 193; Symposium, "Holocaust and Human Rights Law: The Fourth International Conference," *Boston College Third World Law Journal* 12 (1992): 1.

45. See Adalbert Rückerl, *The Investigation of Nazi Crimes: 1945–1978: A Documentation*, trans. Derek Rutter (Heidelberg, Karlsruhe: C. F. Müller, 1979). See "5,570 Cases of Suspected Nazi Crimes Remain Open," *This Week in Germany*, 3 May 1996 (reporting 106,178 persons have been prosecuted; 6,494 convicted).

46. Regarding the trial of Klaus Barbie, see, e.g., *Fédération Nationale des Déportés es Internés Résistants et Patriotes v Barbie*, 78 ILR 125 (Fr., Cass. Crim., 1985). The trial of Paul Touvier for crimes against humanity ended in conviction and life sentence. See Alan Riding, "Frenchman Convicted of Crimes against the Jews in '44," *New York Times*, 20 April 1994, sec. A3; *Judgment of Apr. 20, 1994, Cour d'assises des Yvelines*. Maurice Papon was, at eighty-seven, convicted to ten years in prison for his role in the deportation of Jews to concentration camps. Other indictments for crimes against humanity were

brought against Jean Leguay and Rene Bousquet, both of whom died during the proceedings. Judgment of Oct. 21, 1982, Cass. Crim. See Bernard Lambert, *Bousquet, Papon, Touvier, Inculpés de crimes contre l'humanité: Dossiers d'accusation* (Paris: Federation Nationale des Deportés et Internés Résistants et Patriotes).

47. See Timothy L. H. McCormack, and Jerry J. Simpson, "The International Law Commission's Draft Code of Crimes against the Peace and Security of Mankind: An Appraisal of the Substantive Provisions," *Criminal Law Forum* 4 (1994): 1; Ronnie Edelman et al., "Prosecuting World War II Persecutors: Efforts at an Era's End," *Boston College Third World Law Journal* 12 (1992): 199.

48. For a discussion of the Greek trials, see Nikiforos Diamandouros, "Regime Change and the Prospects for Democracy in Greece: 1974–1983, in *Transitions from Authoritarian Rule: Comparative Perspectives*, ed. Guillermo O'Donnell et al. (Baltimore: Johns Hopkins University Press, 1991), 138. For a discussion of the Portuguese transition, see Kenneth Maxwell, "Regime Overthrow and the Prospects for Democratic Transition in Portugal," in *Transitions from Authoritarian Rule: Southern Europe*, ed., Guillermo O'Donnell et al. (Baltimore: Johns Hopkins University Press, 1991), 109–37. See also John H. Herz, ed., *From Dictatorship to Democracy: Coping with the Legacies of Authoritarianism and Totalitarianism* (Westport, Conn.: Greenwood Press, 1982).

49. See, e.g., *Border Guards Prosecution Case*, *International Law Reports* 100 (1995): 366, 370. For discussion of some of the cases, see Stephan Hobe and Christian Tietje, "Government Criminality: The Judgment of the German Federal Constitutional Court of 24 October 1996," *German Yearbook of International Law* 39 (1996): 523. For a journalist's comparative account of the responses in the region, see Tina Rosenberg, *The Haunted Land* (New York: Random House, 1996).

50. See Symposium, "1945–1995 Critical Perspectives on the Nuremberg Trials and State Accountability," 453 (account of Ethiopia's trials).

51. See "Trial of 51 on Rwandan Genocide Charges Opens in Byumba," *Agence France-Presse* (Kigali), 18 March 1998. See also Payam Akhavan, "The International Criminal Court Tribunal for Rwanda: The Politics and Pragmatics of Punishment," *American Journal of International Law* 90 (1996): 501.

52. For the argument for selective prosecutions, see Diane F. Orentlicher, "Settling Accounts: The Duty to Prosecute Human Rights Violations of a Prior Regime," *Yale Law Journal* 100 (1991): 2537. See also Guillermo O'Donnell and Philippe C. Schmitter, *Transitions from Authoritarian Rule: Tentative Conclusions about Uncertain Democracies* (Baltimore: Johns Hopkins University Press, 1986), 29–30 (discussing Greece's selective prosecutions).

53. See H.L.A. Hart, *Punishment and Responsibility: Essays in the Philosophy of Law* (Oxford: Clarendon Press, 1968).

54. For exploration of some of these questions, see Sanford Levinson, "Responsibility for Crimes of War," in *War and Moral Responsibility*, ed. Marshall Cohen et al. (Princeton: Princeton University Press, 1974), 104; Richard Wasserstrom, "The Responsibility of the Individual for War Crimes," in *Philosophy, Morality, and International Affairs*, ed. Virginia Held et al. (New York: Oxford University Press, 1974), 47. See also Dennis F. Thompson, "Criminal Responsibility in Government," in *Criminal Justice: Nomos XXVII*, ed. J. Roland Pennock and John W. Chapman (New York: New York University Press, 1985), 201–40.

55. *Constitutional Court Decision on the Statute of Limitations*, No. 2086 /A/ 1991/14 (Hungary, 1992), translated in *Journal of Constitutional Law in Eastern and Central Europe* 1 (1994): 129, 136. See Republic of Poland, Const. Art. 43.

56. Before his trial for murder, Alexandru Draghici fled to Hungary, which refused to extradite him, citing the 30-year statute of limitations. See "Romanian Court Delays

Trial of Ex-Securitate Boss," *Reuters*, 28 June 1993, available in Lexis, News Library, Reuters File.

57. In November 1991, the Polish Parliament lifted the statute of limitations on crimes committed between 1946 and 1952 to enable the initiation of new criminal prosecutions. See "Former Security Officers Go to Trial for Torturing Prisoners," *UPI*, 13 October 1993, available in Lexis, News Library, UPI File.

58. *Law on the Illegality of the Communist Regime*, Act No. 198/1993 Sb (Czech and Slovak Federal Republic, 1993).

59. See "Erich Mielke Sentenced to Six Years for 1931 Murders; Faces Other Charges," *This Week in Germany*, 29 October 1993, p. 2.

60. See Adrian Dascalu, "Romania Jails Eight for 1989 Timisoara Uprising Massacre," *Reuters*, 9 December 1991, available in Lexis, News Library, Reuters File.

61. Miroslav Stepan, the former head of the Prague Communist Party, was tried first and convicted in 1990. See "Prague's Ex-Party Boss Guilty of Abuse of Power," *Chicago Tribune*, 10 July 1990, § 1, p. 4. Interior ministers—Frantisek Kincl, Alojz Lorenc, and Karel Vykypel—were convicted in October 1992. See "Czechs Allow Prosecution of Communist Crimes," *Reuters*, 10 July 1993, available in Lexis, News Library, Reuters File. See also "August 1998—Gateway to Power for Number of Politicians," *CTK National News Wire*, 18 August 1998, available in Lexis, News Library, CTK File.

62. See Howard Witt, "Russians Whitewash Blame for 1991 Coup," *Chicago Tribune*, 12 August 1994, § 1, p. 1. What had been termed the "Trial of the Century" when it began in April 1993 ended with the acquittal of the one defendant who refused to accept the February 1994 amnesty, insisting on having his name cleared.

63. See "Ousted Bulgarian Gets 7-Year Term for Embezzlement," *New York Times*, 5 September 1992, p. A2. See also "Bulgarian Former Prime Minister Sentenced to Ten Years," *Reuters*, 3 November 1992, available in Lexis, News Library, Reuters File. However, the country's Supreme Court overruled the seven-year sentence and acquitted Zhivkov in 1996. See U.S. Department of State, *Human Rights Country Reports* (1997).

64. See "Last Communist President Jailed for Five Years," *Agence France-Presse*, 2 July 1994, available on Lexis, News library, Curnws File.

65. See "Former German Labor Boss Convicted of Fraud, Released," *Washington Post*, 7 June 1991, p. A18.

66. See, e.g., "Czech Republic: Slovakia Asked about Communist's Tax Exemption," *Reuters*, 30 January 1995, available in Lexis, News Library, Reuters File.

67. Yuri Feofanov, "The Establishment of the Constitutional Court in Russia and the Communist Party Case," *Review of Central and East European Law* 19, no. 6 (1993): 623–637. For the English transcript of a press conference with prosecutors explaining the aims and legal strategy of the trial, see *Official Kremlin International News Broadcast*, 6 July 1992, available in Lexis, News Library. For a journalistic account, see David Remnick, "The Trial of the Old Regime," *New Yorker*, 30 November 1992, p. 104.

68. See Taylor, *Anatomy of the Nuremberg Trials*, 35–36. Though, ultimately, there was a turn to administrative proceedings. See chapter 5.

69. *Proclamation Establishing the Office of the Special Prosecutor*, Preamble, No. 22/1992 (Ethiopia, 1992).

70. Among human rights analysts, Greece's "torturers" trials have long been touted as a model of successor justice. See Orentlicher, "Settling Accounts," 2598. For a detailed account of the Greek military trials, see Amnesty International, *Torture in Greece: The First Torturer's Trial, 1975* (London: Amnesty International, 1977). For a discussion of Greece's selective prosecutions, see O'Donnell and Schmitter, *Transitions: Tentative Conclusions*, 29–30.

71. Rückerl, *Investigation of Nazi Crimes*, 48, 137.

72. See Judgment of Jan. 20, 1992, *Juristenzeitung* 13 (1992): 691, 692 (F.R.G. Landgericht [LG] [Berlin]), Stephen Kinzer, "2 East German Guards Convicted of Killing Man as He Fled to West," *New York Times*, 21 January 1992, International section.

73. Though former Communist boss Egon Krenz and party ideologist Kirt Hager were also indicted, it was difficult to marshal proof linking them to the shootings. Willi Stoph, a former prime minister, and Erich Mielke, a former chief of secret police, were severed from the trial for health reasons. See Steven Kinzer, "Honecker Release Is Now Expected," *New York Times*, 8 January 1993, International section. Charges against Honecker were dropped soon after. See Steven Kinzer, "Germany Frees Ailing Honecker, Who Flies to Chile," *New York Times*, 14 January 1993, International section. The three remaining defendants, Streletz, Albrecht, and Kessler, were convicted on September 16, 1993, but released from prison for health reasons. See Rick Atkinson, "3 Ex-East German Officials Sentenced; Former Top Communists Found Guilty in Deaths of Refugees," *Washington Post*, 17 September 1993; Leon Mangasarian, "East German Leaders Found Guilty of Wall Killings but Set Free," *UPI*, 16 September 1993, available in Lexis, News Library, UPI File. Egon Krenz was put on trial along with five other Politburo members charged with manslaughter for Berlin Wall killings. Krenz, convicted in August 1997, drew a term of six and one-half years. Two other top Politburo members were sentenced to three-year terms. See "Senior East German Officers Jailed for Berlin Wall Killings, *Deutsche Presse Agentur*, 26 March 1998, available in Lexis, News Library. "By 1997, there were 50 trials against some 100 soldiers, military officers and government officers who were charged in connection with shootings on the Berlin Wall. Of those, 55 people have been convicted. Most received either short or suspended prison sentences." Edmund Andrews, "Honecker's Successor Jailed for Wall Killings," *International Herald Tribune*, 26 August 1997, available in Lexis, News Library. For a doctrinal discussion of these cases, see *Germany Yearbook of International Law* 36 (Berlin, 1993): 41. For a journalist's account, see Rosenberg, *Haunted Land*.

74. Judicial proceedings against Jorge R. Videla et al. were originally brought before the Supreme Council of the Armed Forces pursuant to Decree No.158. *Judgment of December* 9, *1985*, secs. 308–314 (Federal Criminal and Correctional Court of Appeals, Federal District of Buenos Aires), as translated and reprinted in Alejandro M. Garro and Henry Dahl, "Legal Accountability for Human Rights Violations in Argentina: One Step Forward and Two Steps Backward," *Human Rights Law Journal* 8 (1987): 417–18. See Paula K. Speck, "The Trial of the Argentine Junta: Responsibilities and Realities," *Inter-American Law Review* 18 (1987): 491.

75. *Judgment of December 30, 1986*, secs. 23–29, 48–49 (Supreme Court of Argentina, Buenos Aires), as translated and reprinted in Garro and Dahl, "Legal Accountability for Human Rights Violations in Argentina," 435–39.

76. For an account of how the military closed ranks under the threat of punishment, see Jaime Malamud-Goti, "Trying Violators of Human Rights: The Dilemma of Transitional Democratic Governments," in *State Crimes: Punishment or Pardon* (Queenstown, Md.: Aspen Institute, 1989), 71–88.

77. See John Merryman, *The Civil Law Tradition* (Stanford: Stanford University Press, 1985).

78. See § 155 (II) StPO (court required to act independently). See *German Code of Criminal Procedure*, vol. 10 (C), "Principles of Proof"; John H. Langbein, *Comparative Criminal Procedure: Germany* (St Paul: West Publishing, 1977).

79. See Sheldon Glueck, *War Criminals: Their Prosecution and Punishment* (New York: Knopf, 1944), 19–36, for an account of the history of the action taken against Ger-

man war criminals under the Treaty of Versailles. See also James F. Willis, *Prologue to Nuremberg: The Politics and Diplomacy of Punishing War Criminals of the First World War* (Westport, Conn.: Greenwood Press, 1982), 116–39, 174–76 (discussing postwar punishment efforts).

80. See Frank M. Buscher, *The U.S. War Crimes Trial Program in Germany, 1946–1955* (New York: Greenwood Publishing Group, 1989), 62–64.

81. See generally Herz, ed., *From Dictatorship to Democracy.*

82. *Amnesty International, Torture in Greece,* 65. Diamandouros, "Regime Change and the Prospects for Democracy in Greece: 1974–1983," 138–64, 161.

83. See "Argentine Seeks Rights-Trial Curb: Alfonsin Urges a Time Limit on Prosecution for Abuses under Military Rule," *New York Times,* 6 December 1986, International section. See also "200 Military Officers Are Pardoned in Argentina," *New York Times,* 8 October 1989, International section, p. 12. On the second round of pardons, see Shirley Christian, "In Echo of the 'Dirty War,' Argentines Fight Pardons," *New York Times,* 28 December 1990, International section, p. A3. See also Americas Watch, *Truth and Justice in Argentina: An Update* (New York: Human Rights Watch, 1991); Carlos Nino, "The Duty to Punish Past Abuses of Human Rights Put into Context: The Case of Argentina," *Yale Law Journal* 100 (1991): 2619.

Recent developments in Argentina challenge this trend. See "President Says He Won't Veto Repeal of Amnesty Laws," *Agence France-Presse,* (Buenos Aires) 26 March 1998; Marcela Valente, "Rights-Argentina: Dissatisfaction with Repeal of Amnesty Laws," *Inter Press Service* (Buenos Aires), 25 March 1998.

84. For a survey of the border guard cases, see Micah Goodman, "After the Wall: The Legal Ramifications of the East German Border Guard Trials in Unified Germany," *Cornell International Law Journal* 29 (1996): 727. See also "Former Albanian President Has Sentence Cut by Three Years," *Agence France-Presse,* 30 November 1994, available in Lexis, News Library, AFP File; Henry Kamm, "President of Albania Rebuffed on Charter," *New York Times,* 1 December 1994, available in Lexis, News Library; "28 Communist Officials Tried for Anticonstitutional Activity," *CTK National News Wire,* 21 September 1994, available in Lexis, News Library, CTK File (sentencing of former Czechoslovakia's Finance Ministers Zak and Ler); "Romanians Protest over Communist Bosses Release," *Reuters World Service,* 21 September 1994, available in Lexis, News Library, Reuters File.

85. See Human Rights Watch Americas, *Unsettled Business: Human Rights in Chile at the Start of the FREI Presidency* (New York: Human Rights Watch, 1994), 1–4.

86. See *Azanian Peoples Organisation (AZAPO) and Others v. President of the Republic of South Africa and Others,* 1996 (8) BCLR 1015 (CC) (upholding Amnesty Act's constitutionality); Lourens du Plessis, "Amnesty and Transition in South Africa," in *Dealing with the Past: Truth and Reconciliation in South Africa,* ed. Alex Boraine et al. (Cape Town: Institute for Democracy in South Africa, 1994).

87. The Tribunal was established for the purpose of "the Prosecution of Persons Responsible for Serious Violations of International Humanitarian Law Committed in the Territory of the Former Yugoslavia since 1991." See *Report of the Secretary-General Pursuant to Paragraph 2 of the U.N. Security Council Resolution* 808, S/25704 (1993).

88. See *International Tribunal for the Prosecution of Persons Responsible for Serious Violations of International Humanitarian Law Committed in the Territory of the Former Yugoslavia since 1991: Rules for Procedure and Evidence,* rule 61, reprinted in *International Legal Materials* 33 (1994): 519. The reference to "super-indictment" is internal to the Tribunal. See Graham Blewitt, deputy prosecutor for Yugoslavia Tribunal, interview with author, Waldorf Astoria Hotel, New York, N.Y., April 7, 1995.

89. See Joel Feinberg, *Doing and Deserving—Essays in the Theory of Responsibility* (Princeton: Princeton University Press, 1970). See also Joel Feinberg, *Rights, Justice, and the Bounds of Liberty* (New York: Oxford University Press, 1984).

90. See *Oxford English Dictionary*, 2d ed., s.v. "prosecution."

91. See Sanford H. Kadish, "Foreword: The Criminal Law and the Luck of the Draw," *Journal of Criminal Law and Criminology* 84 (Winter/Spring 1994): 679, 698.

92. See generally Hart, *Punishment and Responsibility*.

93. For discussion of international criminal justice's relation to the peace in the Balkans conflict context, see Ruti Teitel, "Judgment at the Hague," *East European Constitutional Review* 5, no. 4 (Fall 1996).

94. See Elaine Sciolino, "U.S. Names Figures to Be Prosecuted over War Crimes," *New York Times*, 17 December 1992, International section; Roger Cohen, "U.N. in Bosnia, Black Robes Clash with Blue Hats," *New York Times* 25 April 1995, p. A3.

95. See Jacques Dumas, *Les Sanctions Penales des Crimes Allemands* (Paris: Rousseau et cie, 1916).

96. "The Moscow Declaration on German Atrocities, 1943," reprinted in Falk, Kolko, and Lifton, eds., *Crimes of War*, 73.

97. For an account of the determination to bring charges of aggressive war, see Taylor, *Anatomy of the Nuremberg Trials*, 37–39.

98. See Aristotle, *The Athenian Constitution*, translated with introduction and notes by P.J. Rhodes (Harmondsworth, England: Penguin, 1984), chs. 34–41.1.

99. See José Maria Maravall and Julian Santamaria, "Political Change in Spain and the Prospects for Democracy," in *Transitions from Authoritarian Rule: Southern Europe*, ed. Guillermo O'Donnell et al. (Baltimore: Johns Hopkins University Press, 1991), 71–108. See generally Raymond Carr and Juan Pablo Fusi Aizpurúa, *Spain: Dictatorship to Democracy*, 2d ed. (London: Allen and Unwin, 1981). For a defense of the Spanish amnesty, see Fernando Rodrigo, "The Politics of Reconciliation in Spain's Transition to Democracy" (paper presented at the Conference on Justice in Times of Transition, Salzburg, March 1993).

100. Regarding El Salvador, and Uruguay see note 103. Regarding Haiti, see Le Moniteur, *Journal Officiel de la Republique d'Haiti Order (Arrète) of 2/6/90*, which grants full and total amnesty to those who between September 17, 1988, and February 7, 1990, were involved in crimes and offenses against the national security. Regarding Colombia's amnesties, see Javier Correa, "La Historia de las Amnistías y los Indultos: Volver a Empezar," in *Los Caminos de la Guerra y la Paz*, vol. 1 *La Reinsercíon* (Bogotá: Fondo Editorial Para la Paz, 1990).

101. See Howard W. French, "In Salvador, Amnesty vs. Punishment," *New York Times*, 16 March 1993, International section; Howard W. French, "Offer of Amnesty Removes Obstacle to Accord in Haiti," *New York Times*, 14 April 1993, International section.

102. See "The Deal: Amnesty Law Expected to Clear Junta Very Soon," *New York Times*, 21 Sept. 1994, p. A17.

103. El Salvador (22 March 1993) Legislative Decree No. 486 of 3/22/93 approves the *Law on General Amnesty for Peace Consolidation*. See Todd Howland, "Salvador Peace Starts with Misstep," *Christian Science Monitor*, 7 February 1992. John J. Moore Jr., "Problems with Forgiveness: Granting Amnesty under the Arias Plan in Nicaragua and El Salvador," *Stanford Law Review* 43 (1991): 733. "Ley de Reconciliación Nacional" (*National Reconciliation Law*), Decree No. 145-96 of 23 December 1996, known as the "Ley de Reconciliación Nacional" (*National Reconciliation Law*), reprinted in *Guatemala Constitutional Court Decision on Amnesty, Nos. 8-97 and 20-97*, at 19–20 (7 October 1977), the basic instrument for the reconciliation of persons involved in the internal

armed conflict, provides that all criminal responsibility for political crimes committed in the armed conflict will be extinguished; provides for the extinguishment of responsibilities for other crimes; and does not include genocide, torture, or forced disappearance.

104. See Law No. 15,848, (Uruguay) "Ley de Caducidad de la Pretension Punitiva del Estado (*Law Nullifying the States Claim to Punish Certain Crimes*), Art 1. It is recognized that, as a consequence of the logic of the events stemming from the agreement between the political parties and the armed forces signed in August 1984, and in order to complete the transition to full constitutional order, the state relinquishes the exercise of penal actions with respect to crimes committed until March 1, 1985, by military and police officials either for political reasons or in fulfillment of their functions and in obeying orders from superiors during the de facto period; Americas Watch, *Challenging Impunity: The Ley de Caducidad and the Referendum Campaign in Uruguay* (New York: Human Rights Watch, 1990). See also Shirley Christian, "Uruguay Votes to Retain Amnesty for the Military," *New York Times*, 17 April 1989, International section; Shirley Christian, "In Uruguay, a Vote for Forgiveness," *New York Times*, 18 April 1989, International section, p. A8; Martin Weinstein, *Uruguay-Democracy at the Crossroads* (Boulder: Westview Press, 1984).

105. See the *Due Obedience Law*, Law No. 23,049 (Argentina, 1984). The *Full Stop Law*, Law No. 23,492, was enacted on December 24, 1986, and the *Due Obedience Law*, Law No. 23,521, was enacted on June 8, 1987.

Subsequent to this legislation, by presidential decree, Pardon No. 1002 (October 7, 1989) ordered that any proceedings against persons indicted for human rights violations be discontinued.

106. See generally Jonathan Truman Dorris, *Pardon and Amnesty under Lincoln and Johnson: The Restoration of the Confederates to Their Rights and Privileges, 1861–1898* (Westport, Conn.: Greenwood Press [1953], 1977).

107. See South Africa Interim Const. (1993) *Epilogue on National Unity and Reconciliation*. See § 20(2)(c) of *Promotion of National Unity and Reconciliation Act 34 of 1995*, as amended by *Promotion of National Unity and Reconciliation Act 87 of 1995*. The committee must decide whether a particular offense is associated with an applicable political objective based on whether the offense was advised, planned, directed, ordered, or committed within South Africa between March 1960 and December 1994, by or on behalf of either a publicly known political organization, liberation movement, state agency or member of the security forces, and in light of the specific criteria set forth in the Reconciliation Act. The criteria include an examination of the motive, context, gravity, and objective of the offense, whether the offense was committed under direct order or approval, and whether the offense was committed for either personal gain or out of "personal malice, ill-will or spite directed against the victims." § 20(3)(f)(ii). See generally Allister Sparks, *Tomorrow Is Another Country: The Inside Story of South Africa's Road to Change* (New York: Hill and Wang, 1995).

108. For a leading argument challenging the amnesties accompanying the contemporary wave of transition, see Aryeh Neier, "What Should Be Done about the Guilty?" *New York Review of Books*, 1 February 1990, p. 32.

109. See Stephen Holmes, "Making Sense of Postcommunism" (draft for New York University Program for the Study of Law, Philosophy, and Social Theory), 10–13; Samuel Huntington, *The Third Wave: Democratization in the Late Twentieth Century* (Norman: University of Oklahoma Press, 1991).

110. See Orentlicher, "Settling Accounts," 2537; Naomi Roht-Arriaza, "State Responsibility to Investigate and Prosecute Grave Human Rights Violations in International Law," *California Law Review* 78 (1990): 449.

111. See *Velásquez-Rodríquez Judgment*, Inter-Am. Ct. H.R., Ser. C., No. 4 (1988).

112. See Report No. 28/92, Cases 10.147, 10.181, 10.240, 10.262, 10.309, 10.311, *Argentina's Annual Report of the Inter-American Commission of Human Rights 1992–1993*, at 41b, OAS doc. OES/Ser. 4L/UV/II.83/doc. 14/Corr. 1 (1993). See also Robert Goldman, "Amnesty Laws, International Law, and the American Convention on Human Rights," *The Law Group Docket* 6, no. 1 (1989): at 1.

113. Immanuel Kant, *The Metaphysics of Morals*, trans. Mary Gregor (New York: Cambridge University Press, 1991), 183.

114. See Teitel, "How Are the New Democracies of the Southern Cone Dealing with the Legacy of Past Human Rights Abuses?" There are, however, theorists that ground justifications for pardon policies in retributivist considerations based on lack of desert. See, e.g., Katherine Dean Moore, *Pardons: Justice, Mercy, and the Public Interest* (New York: Oxford University Press, 1989).

115. See John H. Merryman, *The Civil Law Tradition: An Introduction to the Legal Tradition of Western Europe and Latin America* (Stanford: Stanford University Press, 1985); William T. Pizzi, "Understanding Prosecutorial Discretion in the United States: The Limits of Comparative Criminal Procedure as an Instrument of Reform," *Ohio State Law Journal* 54 (1993): 1325.

116. See Moore, *Pardons: Justice, Mercy, and the Public Interest* 79–86; Note, "The Conditional Presidential Pardon," *Stanford Law Review* 28 (1975):149; Daniel T. Kobil, "The Quality of Mercy Strained: Wresting the Pardoning Power from the King," *Texas Law Review* 69 (1991): 569.

117. See Irwin P. Stotzky, ed., *Transition to Democracy in Latin America: The Role of the Judiciary* (Boulder: Westview Press, 1993).

118. See Jeffrie G. Murphy and Jean Hampton, *Forgiveness and Mercy* (Cambridge: Cambridge University Press, 1988), 162–86 (discussing nature and relationship of mercy to justice).

119. For example, the Argentine presidential pardon is justified in the concededly political terms of "social harmony."

120. See A. John Simmons, "Locke and the Right to Punish," *Philosophy and Public Affairs* 20 (1991): 319.

121. See Alexander Hamilton, *The Federalist No. 69*, ed. Jacob E. Cooke (Middletown, Conn.,: Wesleyan University Press) (rationalizing the executive pardon power by comparison with that of the king).

122. *Decision on the Amnesty Law*, Proceedings No. 10-93 (El Salvador, Supreme Court of Justice, 1993).

123. See Law No. 23.040 (December 27, 1983) (revoking de facto Law No. 22.924 as unconstitutional).

124. See Aristotle, *The Athenian Constitution*; Martin Oswald, *From Popular Sovereignty to the Sovereignty of Law: Law, Society, and Politics in Fifth Century Athens* (Berkeley: University of California Press, 1986); Thomas Clark Loening, *The Reconciliation Agreement of 403/402 b.c. in Athens, Its Content and Application* (Stuttgart: Franz Steiner Verlag Wiesbaden, 1987).

125. On the Uruguayan debates over the "Ley de Caducidad," see *Challenging Impunity: The Ley de Caducidad and the Referendum Campaign in Uruguay, An Americas Watch Report* (Americas Watch Committee, 1989), 15–16. In South Africa, the amnesty debates were part of the Parliamentary debates on the adoption of the country's 1993 Constitution. See *Promotion of National Unity and Reconciliation Act 34 of 1995, Juta's Statutes of the Republic of South Africa* vol., 1(1997)

126. See *Bordenkircher v Hayes*, 434 US 357, 364 (1978).

127. For a related point regarding ritual alternation see René Girard, *Violence and the Sacred* (Baltimore: Johns Hopkins University Press, 1977).

128. "Charter of the International Military Tribunal," 8 August 1945, *Treaties and International Agreements Registered or Filed or Reported with the Secretariat of the United Nations* 82 (1945): 279.

129. See Taylor, *Anatomy of the Nuremberg Trials*, 8–20.

130. See generally Egon Schwelb, "Crimes against Humanity," *British Yearbook International* 23 (1946): 178 (tracing development of concept since Hague Convention of 1907). For international discussions regarding offenses against the law of humanity, see Roger S. Clark, "Crimes against Humanity at Nuremberg," in *The Nuremberg Trial and International Law*, ed. George Ginsbergs and V. N. Kudriavtsev (Norwel, Mass.: Kluwer Academic Publishers, 1990), 177–78 (quoting Commission on the Responsibility of the Authors of the War and on Enforcement of Penalties) (report presented to the Preliminary Peace Conference, reprinted in Pamphlet No. 32, Carnegie Endowment for International Peace). See also James Willis, *Prologue to Nuremberg: The Politics and Diplomacy of Prosecuting War Criminals of the First World War* (Westport, Conn.: Greenwood Press, 1982).

131. "European Convention for the Protection of Human Rights and Fundamental Freedoms," 4 November 1950, *Treaties and International Agreements Registered or Filed or Reported with the Secretariat of the United Nations* 312, no. 2889 (1955): Art 7(2).

132. *Government of Israel v Adolf Eichmann*, Judgment of the Supreme Court (1962), secs. 11–12.

133. See *Tadic*, reprinted in *International Legal Materials* 35 (1996): 32 .

134. See *Criminal Code*, R.S.C., ch. c-46, § 6 (1.91) (Canada, 1985), amended by ch. 37, 1987 S.C. 1105.

135. Indeed, this was just the reasoning of the House of Lords. See UK House of Lords *In re Pinochet*, reprinted in *Opinions of the Lords of Appeal for Judgment in the Cause* (January 15, 1999), available at http://www.parliament.the-stationery.off...pa/ld199899/ldjudgmt/jd 990115/pinØ1.htm. There are other prosecutions for crimes under a similar jurisdictional approach. See also "Orden de prisión provisional incondicional de Leopoldo Fortunato Galtieri, Juzgado Número Cinco de la Audiencia Nacional Española" (25 March 1997), available at http://www.derechos.org/nizkor/arg/espana/autogalt.html.

136. On the question of the passage of time and legal responses, see David Matas, *Justice Delayed: Nazi War Criminals in Canada* (Toronto: Summerhill Press 1987); Peter Irons, *Justice at War: The Story of Japanese American Internment Cases* (New York: Oxford University Press, 1983); Harold David Cesarani, *Justice Delayed* (London: Mandarin, 1992); Allan A. Ryan, Jr., *Quiet Neighbors* (San Diego: Harcourt Brace Jovanovich, 1984). See also Ronnie Edelman et al., "Prosecuting World War II Persecutors: Efforts at an Era's End," *Boston College Third World Law Journal* 12 (1991): 199.

137. See *Federal Supreme Court in "Criminal Cases,"* vol. 18, at 37 (Germany,) (interpreting Article 211 of the *Penal Code*, defining murder). The relevant domestic offense under German penal law was murder committed with "base motive." See Robert Monson, "The West German Statute of Limitations on Murder: A Political, Legal, and Historical Explanation," *American Journal of Comparative Law* 30 (1992): 605.

138. "Convention on the Non-Applicability of Statutory Limitations to War Crimes and Crimes against Humanity," *U.N. General Assembly Resolution* 2391 (XXIII), 11 November, 1970.

139. See Law No. 64-1326 of 26 December 1964 (Dalloz, *Code Penal* 767, 1970–1971). See also *Journal Officiel de la Republique Francaise*, 29 December 1964, at 11.788; Pierre Mertens, "L' Imprescriptibilité des crimes de guerre et des crimes contre L'humanité," *Revue de Droit Penal et de Criminologie* 51 (1970): 204.

140. See *Barbie*, 78 ILR 125.

141. Rückerl, *Investigation of Nazi Crimes*, 48.

142. See Martin Abregu, *La Tutela Judicial del Derecho de la Verdad en la Argentina*, 24 Revista IIDH (1996), II, 12–15.

143. United Nations, Economic and Social Council, Commission on Human Rights, Twenty-second Session, *Question of Punishment of War Criminals and of Persons Who Have Committed Crimes against Humanity: Question of the Non-Applicability of Statutory Limitation to War Crimes and Crimes against Humanity*, submitted by the Secretary-General, 1966, p. 84.

144. For an account of Germany's arguments for lifting the statute of limitations on World War II–related murder, see Martin Clausnitzer, "The Statute of Limitations for Murder in the Federal Republic of Germany," *International and Comparative Law Quarterly* 29 (1980): 478; Monson, "The West German Statute of Limitations on Murder, 618–25. See also Jaime Malamud-Goti, "Punishment and a Rights-Based Democracy," *Criminal Justice Ethics* 3 (Summer/Fall 1991). Regarding the role of victims in the pursuit of punishment, see Jeffrie G. Murphy, "Getting Even: The Role of the Victim," in *Crime, Culpability, and Remedy*, ed. Ellen Frankel Paul et al. (Cambridge, Mass.: Blackwell, 1990), 209.

145. See "Questions of Justice," *The All-Party Parliamentary War Crimes Group 1*, Parliamentary Debates, *House of Lords Official Report* 1079 (1990).

146. See *Young v Vuitton*, 481 US 787, 811–12 (1987). There are contemporary countervailing trends; for discussion, see George Fletcher, *With Justice for Some: Victims' Rights in Criminal Trials* (Reading, Mass.: Addison-Wesley., 1995).

147. On victims' moral authority, see Shklar, *Legalism: Law, Morals, and Political Trials*.

148. *Barbie*, 78 ILR at 139–40. See also *Jugement de Maurice Papon* (April 21, 1998) (convicted of crimes against humanity).

149. *Barbie*, 78 ILR at 128.

150. See *Statute of the International Tribunal for the Former Yugoslavia*, at 1173. See also *Tadić*, reprinted in *International Legal Materials* 35 (1996): 32, 48–73.

151. Article 7 of the *Rome Statute of the International Criminal Court* expands the definition of "crimes against humanity":

> [T]he following acts when committed as part of a widespread or systematic attack directed against any civilian population, with knowledge of the attack: (a) Murder; (b) Extermination; (c) Enslavement; (d) Deportation or forcible transfer of population; (e) Imprisonment . . . (f) Torture; (g) Rape, sexual slavery . . . (h) Persecution against any identifiable group or collectivity on political, racial, national, ethnic, cultural, religious, gender . . . grounds . . . (i) Enforced disappearance of persons; (j) The crime of apartheid; and (k) Other inhumane acts of similar character . . .

*Rome Statute of the International Criminal Court*, U.N. Diplomatic Conference of Plenipotentiaries on the Establishment of an International Criminal Court, Art 7, U.N. doc. A/Conf. 183/9, (17 July 1998).

152. A recent American illustration is the third trial in the murder of Medgar Evers. *Mississippi v. Byron De La Beckwith*, 707 S2d 547 (Miss. 1997), cert. denied, 525 vs 880 (1998).

153. See Joel Feinberg, *Doing and Deserving* (Princeton: Princeton University Press, 1970).

154. See Girard, *Violence and the Sacred*.

155. See generally Hart, *Punishment and Responsibility*, 170–73.

*Chapter 3*

1. Alice H. Henkin, "Conference Report," in *State Crimes: Punishment or Pardon*, ed. Alice H. Henkin (Queenstown, Md.: Aspen Institute, 1989), 4–5. There are many advocates for this position in the diplomatic and human rights community. See, e.g., Margaret Popkin and Naomi Roht-Arriaza, "Truth as Justice: Investigatory Commissions in Latin America," *Law and Social Inquiry* 20 (Winter 1995): 79. See also José Zalaquett, "Balancing Ethical Imperatives and Political Constraints: The Dilemma of New Democracies Confronting Past Human Rights Violations," *Hastings Law Journal* 43 (1992): 1425; Timothy Garton Ash, *The File: A Personal History* (New York: Random House, 1997).

2. See R. G. Collingwood, *The Idea of History* (New York: Oxford University Press, 1994).

3. See Peter Novick, *That Noble Dream: The "Objectivity Question" and the American Historical Profession* (Cambridge: Cambridge University Press, 1988). Regarding historical narrative, see Hayden White, *The Content of the Form: Narrative Discourse and Historical Representation* (Baltimore: Johns Hopkins University Press, 1987), 13.

4. See H. G. Gadamer, *Truth and Method* (New York: Crossroad, 1989).

5. For broader discussion of the relation of the role of memory in formation of society, see Friedrich Nietzsche, *On the Genealogy of Morals*, trans. Walter Kaufmann and R. J. Hollingdale (New York: Vintage Books, 1967); Michel Foucault, *Power/Knowledge: Selected Interviews and Other Writings, 1972–1977*, trans. Colin Gordon et al. (New York: Pantheon Books, 1980).

6. See Foucault, *Power/Knowledge*.

7. For the seminal work on the construction of collective memory, see Maurice Halbwachs, *On Collective Memory*, trans. Lewis A. Coser (Chicago: University of Chicago Press, 1992). From a sociological perspective, see Iwona Irwin-Zarecka, *Frames of Remembrance: The Dynamics of Collective Memory* (New Brunswick, N.J.: Transaction Publishers, 1994) (annotated bibliography); Natalie Zeman Davis and Randolph Stern, eds., "Memory and Countermemory," *Representations* 26 (1985):; Jonathan Boyarin, ed., *Remapping Memory: The Politics of Timespace* (Minneapolis: University of Minnesota Press, 1994); Susan A. Crane, "Writing the Individual Back into Collective Memory," *American Historical Review* 20 (1997): 1372. For a historical anthropological perspective, see Gerald Sider and Gavin Smith, eds., *Between History and Histories: The Making of Silences and Commemorations* (Toronto: University of Toronto Press, 1997).

8. For an exploration of this point, see Steven Shapin, *A Social History of Truth* (Chicago: University of Chicago Press, 1994).

9. Foucault, *Power/Knowledge*, 131.

10. For a critique of the uses of criminal prosecution for the purposes of collective memory, see Mark J. Osiel, "Ever Again: Legal Remembrance of Administrative Massacre," *University of Pennsylvania Law Review* 144 (1995): 463.

11. On the role of trials as ceremonies in social memory, see Paul Connerton, *How Societies Remember* (Cambridge: Cambridge University Press, 1989).

12. Compare Mirjan Damaska, "Evidentiary Barriers to Conviction and Two Models of Criminal Procedure: A Comparative Study," *University of Pennsylvania Law Review* 121 (1973): 506, 578–86 (claiming pursuit of truth greater in continental system), with John H. Langbein, "The German Advantage in Civil Procedure," *University of Chicago Law Review* 52 (1985): 823.

13. Michael Walzer, ed., and Marian Rothstein, trans., *Regicide and Revolution: Speeches at the Trial of Louis XVI* (New York: Cambridge University Press, 1974), 129.

14. For exploration of the relationship of criminal procedure to the truth, see note

12 above. For discussion of an "expressive" theory of criminal procedure, see Ruti Teitel, "Persecution and Inquisition: A Case Study," in *Transition to Democracy in Latin America: The Role of the Judiciary*, ed. Irwin P. Stotzky (Boulder: Westview Press, 1993).

15. *In re Winship*, 397 US 358, 364 (1970); see John Calvin Jeffries, Jr., and Paul B. Stephan III, "Defenses, Presumptions, and Burden of Proof in the Criminal Law," *Yale Law Journal* 88 (1979): 1325, 1327.

16. See Norman E. Tutorow, ed., *War Crimes, War Criminals, and War Crimes Trials: An Annotated Bibliography and Source Book* (New York: Greenwood Press, 1986), 18.

17. See Human Rights Watch, *An Americas Watch Report: Truth and Partial Justice in Argentina, an Update* (New York: Human Rights Watch, 1991).

18. See Alex Shoumatoff, *African Madness* (New York: Random House, 1988), 93–127.

19. See Michael R. Marrus, *The Holocaust in History* (Hanover, N.H.: University Press of New England, 1987), 36–51 (historian's account tracing change from intentionalism to functionalism but not linking it to legal developments); Lawrence Douglas, "The Memory of Judgment: The Law, the Holocaust, and Denial," *History and Memory* (Fall-Winter 1996): 100. On change in historical understandings of criminal responsibility, see Raul Hilberg, *Perpetrators, Victims, and Bystanders* (New York: Aaron Asher Books, 1992).

20. See chapter 2 note 44. See also *Public Prosecutor v Menten* (Holland, Proceedings from December 1977–January 1981), translated and reprinted in the *Netherlands Yearbook of International Law*, vol. 12 (Alphen aan den Rijn, Netherlands: Sijthoff and Noordhoff, 1981). For a more in-depth discussion of these trials, see chapter 2 on criminal justice. For an account of these legal developments, see Ronnie Edelman et al., "Prosecuting World War II Persecutors: Efforts at an Era's End," *Boston College Third World Law Journal* 12 (1991): 199.

21. See Robert Gordon, "Undoing Historical Injustice" in *Justice and Injustice in Law and Legal Theory*, ed. Austin Sarat and Thomas R. Kearny (Ann Arbor: University of Michigan Press, 1994).

22. See Hannah Arendt, *Eichmann in Jerusalem: A Report on the Banality of Evil* (New York: Penguin Books, 1964), 135–50.

23. See Alain Finkielkraut, *Remembering in Vain: The Klaus Barbie Trial and Crimes against Humanity*, trans. Roxanne Lapidus with Sima Godfrey (New York: Columbia University Press, 1992). See also Richard J. Golson, ed., *Memory, the Holocaust, and French Justice: The Bousquet and Touvier Affairs* (Hanover, N.H.: University Press of New England, 1996) (for other postwar trials); Guyora Binder, "Representing Nazism: Advocacy and Identity at the Trial of Klaus Barbie," *Yale Law Journal* 98 (1989): 1321.

24. For a detailed description of the disappearances practices, see *Nunca Más: Report of the Argentine National Commission on the Disappeared* (hereafter CONADEP Report), English ed. (New York: Farrar, Straus, Giroux, 1986), 447. The CONADEP Report concluded that many of the bodies had been destroyed to prevent identification.

25. Michel Foucault, *Discipline and Punish: The Birth of the Prison*, trans. Alan Sheridan (New York: Vintage Books, 1979), 25.

26. For an illustrative listing, see Priscilla Hayner, "Fifteen Truth Commissions—1974 to 1994, A Comparative Study," *Human Rights Quarterly* 16 (1994): 597.

27. See Human Rights Watch, *An Americas Watch Report*: 13–17

28. Guatemala's "Commission for the Historical Classification of the Past" was agreed to on June 23, 1997, in Oslo, Norway. See also *Accord on the Establishment of the Commission for Historical Clarification of Human Rights Violations and Acts of Violence*

*Which Have Inflicted Suffering upon the Guatemalan Population* (Guatemala, 1997) Popkin and Roht-Arriaza, "Truth as Justice," 79–116.

29. Decree No. 355 established the Chilean Truth Commission. "Only on the basis of the truth will it be possible to satisfy the basic demands of justice and create indispensable conditions for achieving true national reconciliation" (April 25, 1990). See Jose Zalaquett, Introduction to *Informe de la Comisión Nacional de Verdad y Reconciliacíon (Report of the Chilean National Commission on Truth and Reconciliation)*, trans. Phillip E. Berryman, 2 vols. (Notre Dame: University of Notre Dame Press, 1993), xxiii–xxxiii.

30. See United Nations Observer Mission in El Salvador, *El Salvador Agreements: The Path to Peace* (1992), 16–17 (stating synopsis of agreements reached between government of El Salvador and Frente Farabundo Marti para la Liberacíon Nacional (FMLN) under auspices of Secretary-General of United Nations).

31. See Robert F. Lutz, "Essay: A Piece of the Peace: The Human Rights Accord and the Guatemalan Peace Process," *Southwestern Journal of Trade and Law in the Americas* 2 (1995): 183.

32. See Human Rights Watch, *The Preliminary Report on Disappearance of the National Commissioner for the Protection of Human Rights in Honduras: The Facts Speak for Themselves* (New York: Human Rights Watch, 1994).

33. Order (*Arréte*) of March 28, 1995, created the "Commission Nacional de Verité et de Justice."

34. See Lynn Berat and Yossi Shain, "Retribution or Truth-Telling in South Africa? Legacies of the Transitional Phase," *Law and Social Inquiry* 20 (1995): 163; *Reconciliation through Truth: A Reckoning of Apartheid's Criminal Governance*, ed. Kader Asmal, Louise Asmal, and Ronald Suresh Roberts (New York: St. Martin's, 1997)

35. For a description of the Chad and Uganda commissions, see Jamal Benomar, "Coming to Terms with the Past: How Emerging Democracies Cope with a History of Human Rights Violations" (paper presented at Carter Center of Emory University, Human Rights Program, July 1992), 11–14.

36. See *Promotion of National Unity and Reconciliation Act 34 of 1995, Juta's statutes of the Republic of South Africa*, vol. 1 (1997), 801.

37. See Rigoberta Menchú, *I, Rigoberta Menchú: An Indian Woman in Guatemala*, ed. Elizabeth Burgos-Debrany, trans. Ann Wright (London: Verso, 1984).

38. For an account, see Lawrence Weschler, *A Miracle, A Universe: Settling Accounts with Torturers* (New York: Penguin Books, 1991).

39. See Servicio Paz y Justicia, *Uruguay, Nunca Más: Human Rights Violations, 1972–1985*, trans. Elizabeth Hampsten with an introduction by Lawrence Weschler (Philadelphia: Temple University Press, 1992), xxv.

40. *Nunca Más* is the title of the Argentine report and of the Uruguayan report; *Nunca Mais* (Brazil).

41. For a related idea, see Michel Foucault, *The Birth of the Clinic*, trans. A. M. Sheridan Smith (New York: Vintage Books, 1994).

42. See, e.g., *Report of the Commission on the Truth for El Salvador* (hereafter *El Salvador Truth Commission Report*) (April 1993), 229. See also *CONADEP Report*, 5.

43. On truth in the continental system, see Damaska, "Evidentiary Barriers," 580.

44. See *El Salvador Truth Commission Report*, 24.

45. *CONADEP Report*, 49–51. For an account of a torture session, described in harrowing detail by the victims, see *Uruguay, Nunca Más*, 102–103.

46. For an example, see, Human Rights Watch, *Annual Report* (New York: Human Rights Watch, 1997).

47. Although in South Africa the delegation came from the Parliament, the report would be presented to Nelson Mandela.

48. See *Informe Rettig, Informe de la Comisión Nacional de Verdad y Reconciliación* (February 1991) (hereafter *Rettig Report*), xxxii.

49. See Julia Preston, "2,000 Salvadoreans Helped UN Build Atrocities Case," *Washington Post*, 16 March 1993.

50. Address by President Patricio Aylwin to the Chilean people, transcribed by the British Broadcasting Corporation, March 5, 1991.

51. *El Murano*, 5 March 1991.

52. For a sociological perspective on the significance of apology, see generally Nicholas Tavuchis, *Mea Culpa: A Sociology of Apology and Reconciliation* (Stanford: Stanford University Press, 1991).

53. See CONADEP *Report*, 448–449.

54. See *Rettig Report*, 39–40.

55. CONADEP *Report*, 448.

56. See "Guatemalan Foes Agree to Set up Rights Panel," *New York Times*, 24 June 1994, International section.

57. Guatemala's *"Memory of Silence": Report of the Commission for Historical Clarification* (Conclusions), 1, available at http: hrdata.aaas.org/ceh/report/english/conc.l.html. See the *Report of the Truth and Reconciliation Commission* ("Summary and Guide to Contents") 9–11, available at http://www.truth.org.za/final/execsum.htm. The Commission for Historical Clarification was established through the *Accord of Oslo* on June 23, 1997.

58. *El Salvador Truth Commission Report*, 6–7. See Mark Danner, "The Truth of El Mozote," *New Yorker*, 6 December 1993, pp. 6–7.

59. See *Promotion of National Unity and Reconciliation Act 34 of 1995* (referring to goal of "establishing in as complete a picture as possible . . . the gross violations of human rights . . . including . . . the perspectives of the victims and the motives and perspectives of the persons responsible for the commission of the violations"),. 801; Alex Boraine et al. eds., *Dealing with the Past: Truth and Reconciliation in South Africa* (Cape Town: Idasa, 1994). See also Emily H. McCarthy, "South Africa's Amnesty Process: A Viable Route toward Truth and Reconciliation," *Michigan Journal of Race and Law* 3 (Fall 1997): 183.

60. *Azanian Peoples Organisation (AZAPO) and Others v. President of the Republic of South Africa* 1996 (4) SALR 671, 683–84 (CC).

61. Arendt, *Eichmann in Jerusalem*.

62. See Guatemala's *"Memory of Silence": Report of the Commission for Historical Clarification* ("Conclusions and Recommendations").

63. See *AZAPO* and others, 1996 (4) SA 671 (CC). See "Quien está contra la Nación?" *Madres de la Plaza de Majo*, Jan. 1985, at 11.

64. While most commission reports have confidential annexes, a notable exception was Chad's commission report, which published both the list of names and photos of offenders.

65. Compare Naomi Roht-Arriaza, "State Responsibility to Investigate and Prosecute Human Rights Violations in International Law," *California Law Review* 78 (1990): 449, with José Zalaquett, "Confronting Human Rights Violations Committed by Former Governments: Applicable Principles and Political Constraints," *Hamline Law Review* 13 (1990): 623.

66. See Stephen Holmes, *Passions and Constraint* (Chicago: University of Chicago Press, 1995) (discussing constitutive role of silencing through "gag rules").

67. For a critical analysis of shaming, see James Whitman, "What Is Wrong with Inflicting Shame Sanctions?" *Yale Law Journal* 107 (1998): 1055.

68. *El Salvador Truth Commission Report*, 176.

69. See, e.g., *CONADEP Report*, 386–425. See also *Rettig Report*, 117–29.

70. See Human Rights Watch, *Commission of Inquiry Investigates Causes of Abuses in Uganda* (New York: Human Rights Watch, 1989).

71. See *Informe Sobre Calificación de Victimas de Violaciónes de Derechos Humanos y de la Violencia Politica, Corporación Nacional de Reparación y Reconciliación* (Chile 1996).

72. See, e.g., Jacobo Timerman, *Prisoner without a Name, Cell without a Number* (New York: Knopf, 1981).

73. See, e.g., *Nunca Más*, preamble.

74. See Maurice Halbwachs, *On Collective Memory*, ed. Lewis A. Coser (Chicago: University of Chicago Press, 1992)

75. Václav Havel, "The Power of the Powerless," in *Open Letters: Selected Writings, 1965–1990*, ed. Paul Wilson (New York: Random House, Vintage Books, 1992), 147–48.

76. See Karl Marx and Friedrich Engels, "Manifesto of the Communist Party," in *The Marx-Engels Reader*, 2d ed., ed. Robert C. Tucker (New York: W. W. Norton, 1978).

77. *Webster's New Collegiate Dictionary*, s.v. "archive." For a more extended exegesis on the topic, see Jacques Derrida, *Archive Fever: A Freudian Impression*, trans. Eric Prenaowitz (Chicago: University of Chicago Press, 1996).

78. For an account, see David Remnick, "The Trial of the Old Regime," *New Yorker*, 30 November, 1992, pp. 104–21.

79. Decrees, Nos. 82, 83 24-08 (1991). Regarding the Russian archives, see Vera Tolz, "Access to KGB and CPSU Archives in Russia, Politics," vol. 1, no. 16 (April 17, 1997); N. Ohitin and A. Roginsky, "Remarks on Recent Status of Archives in Russia" in *Truth and Justice: The Delicate Balance* (The Inst. for Constitutional and Legislative Policy C.E.U. 1993).

80. See Jan Obrman, *Laying the Ghosts of the Past* (report on Eastern Europe, no. 24, June 14, 1991).

81. See Tadeusz Olszaski, "Communism's Last Rulers: Fury and Fate," *Warsaw Voice*, 18 November 1992.

82. Jane Perlez, "Hungarian Arrests Set Off Debate: Should '56 Oppressors Be Punished?" *New York Times*, 3 April 1994, International section, p. A14.

83. See "Almost 1,000 killed in Hungarian Uprising: Fact-finding Committee," *Agence France-Presse*, 22 November 1993, available in Lexis, News Library. But the number officially documented is far fewer than the number of people who disappeared—thought to be in the thousands. See Julius Strauss, "Hungary Uprising Killers May Be Tried," *Daily Telegraph*, (Budapest) 2 December 1993; "Almost 1,000 Victims in '56 Mass Shootings," *MTI Hungarian News Agency*, 22 November 1993, available in Lexis, News Library.

84. On May 13, 1992, the German Parliament expressed the mandate of the Eppelmann Commission "to investigate the structure, strategy and instruments of the Communist dictatorship, the question of responsibility for the infringement of human and civil rights." See Stephen Kinzer, "German Panel to Scrutinize East's Rule and Repression," *New York Times*, 30 March 1992, International section, p. A7.

85. See Timothy Garton Ash, *In Europe's Name: Germany and the Divided Continent* (New York: Random House, 1993).

86. See "Czechoslovakia: Former Top Police Officials Jailed," *Reuters*, 30 October 1992, Perlez, "Hungarian Arrests Set Off Debate"; "Former Government Officials Sentenced to Prison Terms," *CTK National News Wire*, 30 October 1992, available in Lexis, News Library, CTK File.

87. Regarding the Czech Republic, see Helsinki Watch Report, *Czechoslovakia:*

*'Decommunization' Measures Violate Freedom of Expression and Due Process Standards* (New York: Human Rights Watch, 1992).

88. See Jon Elster, "Political Justice and Transition to the Rule of Law in East-Central Europe" (presented at conference sponsored by University of Chicago, Center for Constitutionalism in Eastern and Central Europe, unpublished proceedings, Prague, December 13–15, 1991).

For discussion of the debate in the region, see "Truth and Justice, The Delicate Balance: The Documentation of Prior Regimes and Individual Rights," Working Paper No. 1 (Central European University, Institute of Constitutional and Legislative Policy; workshop convened in Budapest on the subject of archives, 1993).

89. See Lung-Chu Chen, *An Introduction to Contemporary International Law* (New Haven: Yale University Press, 1989), 428–29.

90. See Amos Elon, "East Germany: Crime and Punishment," *New York Review of Books,* 14 May 1992; Stephen Kinzer, "East Germans Face Their Accusers," *New York Times Magazine,* 12 April 1992; "Ex-E. German Security Police Moved Over 100,000 Files Abroad," *Reuter Library Report,* 29 April 1991, available in Lexis, News Library—Wires; Richard Meares, "Germany Debates How to Open Pandora's Box of Stasi Files," *Reuters North American Wire,* 22 April 1991, available in Lexis, News Library—Wires.

91. See Joachim Gauck, *Die Stasi-Akten* (Reinbeck bei Hamburg: Rowohlt, 1991).

92. *Brochure of the Federal Commissioner for the Records of the State Security Service of the Former German Democratic Republic on the Task, Structure, and Work of This Authority.* The same language also appears in the preamble of the law on Stasi records. See *Act Regarding the Records of the State Security Service of the Former German Democratic Republic,* December 20, 1991.

93. This has been the subject of substantial journalistic exploration; see, e.g., Jane Kramer, *Letter from Berlin, New Yorker,* 25 November 1991; Jane Kramer, *Letter from Europe, New Yorker,* 25 November 1992; Timothy Garton Ash, *The File: A Personal History* (New York: Random House, 1997).

94. Stasi Files Act, § 1(2).

95. Id, § 1(3).

96. Thus, for example, in Poland, the "right" to obtain information and access to filed documents pertains to "victims," defined as a person "about whom the security services have secretly collected information by purposely gathering data." See *The Polish Access to Files Act of 1998.*

97. *Screening ("Lustration") Law,* Act No. 451/1991 (Czech and Slovak Federal Republic, 1991).

98. Ibid., Arts 4, and 11 (giving Federal Ministry of the Interior control over files and providing for Federal Ministry of the Interior Commission to make findings, respectively).

99. *Constitutional Court Decision on the Screening Law,* Ref. No. Pl. US1/92 (Czech and Slovak Federal Republic, 1992).

100. For a comparative analysis, see Wallach, "Executive Powers of Prior Restraint over Publication of National Security Information: The UK and USA Compared," International and Comparative Law Quarterly 32 (1983): 424.

101. For discussion of the approach of the prior regime, see *Truth and Justice, The Delicate Balance,* 75, 77 (cited in note 79 above).

102. For the balance struck in international law, see *The Johannesburg Principles on National Security, Freedom of Expression and Access to Information* (adopted October 1, 1995), Art 19.

103. See *The Freedom of Information Act, U.S. Code*, vol. 5, sec. 552(b) (1993) (making exceptions for personnel, medical, and law enforcement files that constitute invasion of privacy). See also the *Privacy Act of 1974, U.S. Code*, vol. 5, sec. 552 1993; H. Rpt. 93-1416. See generally Frederick M. Lawrence, "The First Amendment Right to Gather State-Held Information," *Yale Law Journal* 89 (1980): 923. For discussions of the balance in a historical context, see Charles Reich, "The New Property," *Yale Law Journal* 73 (1964) 733.

104. See *Roviaro v United States.*, 353 US 53 (1957).

105. Czech Republic Const, Art 10; Slovak Const, Art 19.

106. Slovenia Const, Art 38.

107. Republic of Hungary Const, Art 59.

108. Republic of Croatia Const, Art 37.

109. Russian Federation Const, Art 24(1).

110. Estonia Const, Art 42.

111. Russian Federation Const, Art 24(2).

112. Slovenia Const, Art 38.

113. Estonia Const, Art 44.

114. Republic of Bulgaria Const, Art 41(2).

115. For an account of the historians' debate, see Charles S. Maier, *The Unmasterable Past: History, Holocaust, and German National Identity* (Cambridge: Harvard University Press, 1988), 9–33. See also Perry Anderson, "On Emplotment: Two Kinds of Ruin," in *Probing the Limits of Representation*, ed. Saul Friedlander (Cambridge: Harvard University Press, 1992).

116. Stephane Courtois, Nicholas Werth, Jean-Louis Panné et al., *Le Livre Noir de Communisme: Crimes, Terreur, Répression* (Paris: Laffont, 1998).

117. Jürgen Habermas, *The New Conservatism: Cultural Criticism and the Historians' Debate*, ed. and trans. Shierry Weber Nicholsen (Cambridge: MIT Press, 1989).

118. See generally Maier, *Unmasterable Past*.

119. See Martin Broszat and Saul Friedlander, "A Controversy about the Historicization of National Socialism," *New German Critique* 44 (1988): 81–126.

120. See Hans Georg Gadamer, "The Historicity of Understanding," in *The Hermeneutic Reader: Texts of the German Tradition from the Enlightenment to the Present*, ed. Kurt Mueller-Vollmer (New York: Continuum Publishing, 1988), 270.

121. See Calvin Sims, "Argentine Tells of Dumping Dirty War Captives in the Sea," *New York Times*, 13 March 1995, International section. For an in-depth study of the "Scilingo Effect," see Marguerite Feitlowitz, *A Lexicon of Terror: Argentina and the Legacies of Torture* (New York: Oxford University Press, 1998).

122. See "Procedure, Practice and Administration" in *Trials of War Criminals before the Nuremberg Military Tribunals*, vol. 15 (Washington, D.C.: Government Printing Office, 1953), 568–70. In U.S. courts, the process is governed by Federal Rule of Evidence 201.

123. See, e.g., *United States v Kowalchuk*, 773 F2d 488 (3d Cir. 1985) ("The horrors of tyranny inflicted upon civilian populations in territories controlled by occupying Nazi forces during World War II are so notorious that no citation is necessary"); *Succession of Steinberg*, 76 S2d 744 (La. Ct. App. 1955) (taking judicial notice of executions in Nazi-dominated Europe).

124. See *German Criminal Code* §§ 130, 131 StGB.

125. Ibid. Art 194, as amended, June 13, 1985. For an analysis of the German legislation, see Eric Stein, "History against Free Speech: The New German Law Against the 'Auschwitz' and Other 'Lies'," *Michigan Law Review* 85 (1986): 277.

126. See *This Week in Germany*, 19 April 1994; reported in NJW (Germany, 1982), at 1803. See also S. J. Roth, "Second Attempt in Germany to Outlaw Denial of the Holocaust," *Patterns of Prejudice* 18 (1985): 46.

127. Ibid.

128. *Statute of 13 July 1990* (France). See also *Licra et autres c. Faurrison*, Tribunal de Grande Instance (8 Juillet, 1981) (Recueil Dalloz, 1982); Roger Errera, "In Defense of Civility: Racial Incitement and Group Libel in French Law," in *Striking a Balance: Hate Speech, Freedom of Expression and Nondiscrimination*, ed. Sandra Coliver, (Human Rights Centre, University London, Art 19 Int'l Center Against Censorship of Essex, 1992) (discussing *Gayssot Law of 13 July 1990* rendering a new offense to contest the existence of crimes against humanity as defined at Nuremberg).

129. *Criminal Code of Canada*, § 181. The most prominent case is *Zundel v The Queen*, 35 DLR (4th) 338, 31 CCC (3d) 97 (Ont. CA.) (1987). For discussion of the Canadian precedents, see "When Academic Freedom and Freedom of Speech Confront Holocaust Denial and Group Libel: Comparative Perspectives," *Boston College Third World Law Journal* 8 (1988): 65.

130. Olivier Biffaud, "M. Le Pen Indesirable Dans Plusieurs Villes," *Le Monde* (Paris), 24 May 1990, available in Lexis; see Susan Anderson, "Chronicle," *New York Times*, 24 May 1990, sec. B, p. 24.

131. Ref. No. VI ZR 140/78 *Entscheidungen des Bundesgerichtshofes in Zivilsachen* (B6H2), 160 et seq *Juristenzeitung* 75 (1979): 811.

132. See *National Institute of Remembrance Act* (Poland 1998). It stipulates punishment for persons publicly denying "Nazi or communist crimes or crimes against humanity."

133. "Universal Declaration of Human Rights," U.N. General Assembly Resolution 217 (III), Art 20, 10 December 1948.

134. "International Convention on the Elimination of All Forms of Racial Discrimination," U.N. General Assembly Resolution 2106 (xx), Art 4, 21 December 1965 (entered into force 2 January 1969).

135. "International Covenant on Civil and Political Rights," U.N. General Assembly Resolution 2200A (xxl), Art 20, 16 December 1966 (entered into force 23 March 1976).

136. *German Criminal Code*, Art 130.

137. *Danish Criminal Code*, § 266(b).

128. *Swedish Penal Code*, Ch. 16(8).

139. *Race Relations Act 1965*, § 6(1).

140. For a review of these statutes, see Anti-Defamation League, *Hate Crimes Laws: A Comprehensive Guide* (New York: Anti-Defamation League, 1997).

141. *Wisconsin v Mitchell*, 508 US 476 (1993) (upholding *Wisconsin Penalty Enhancement Statute*, which provides for enhanced penalties if the person committing the crime "[i]ntentionally selects the person against whom the crime . . . is committed or selects the property that is damaged or otherwise affected by the crime . . . in whole or in part because of the actor's belief or perception regarding the race, religion, color, disability, sexual orientation, national origin or ancestry of that person or the owner or occupant of that property, whether or not the actor's belief or perception was correct"). *Wisconsin Statute* 939.645 (1991–1992).

142. *R. v Keegstra*, 2 WWR 1 (Canada, 1991).

143. Federal Republic of Germany Const. (*Basic Law*), Arts 1,18, 21.

144. See *New York Times v Sullivan*, 376 US 254 (1964) (expanding on central meaning of First Amendment involving a profound national commitment to the principle that debate on public issues "uninhibited, robust, and wide-open) holding the con-

stitution requires a rule prohibiting a public official from recovering damage for a defamatory falsehood relating to his offical conduct, unless there was "actual malice"). For the history, see F. Siebert, *Freedom of the Press in England* (Urbana: University of Illinois Press, 1952), 1476–1776; Philip Hamburger, "The Development of the Law of Seditious Libel and Control of the Press," *Stanford Law Review* 37 (1985): 661; Zechariah Chafee Jr., *Free Speech in the United States* 18 (1941).

145. See Francis Fukuyama, "The End of History?" *National Interest*, no. 16 (Summer 1989): 3–18.

146. See Northrop Frye, *Anatomy of Criticism: Four Essays* (Princeton: Princeton University Press, 1957).

147. See Aristotle, "Poetics," in *The Complete Works of Aristotle*, vol. 2, ed. Jonathan Barnes (Princeton: Princeton University Press, 1984), 2323–24; Timothy J. Reiss, *Tragedy and Truth: Studies in the Development of a Renaissance and Neoclassical Discourse* (New Haven and London: Yale University Press, 1980)

148. *CONADEP Report*, 6.

149. Supreme Decree No. 355, "Creation of the Commission on Truth and Reconciliation," April 25, 1990, reproduced in *Rettig Report*.

150. *El Salvador Truth Commission Report*, 11.

151. *Uruguay, Nunca Más*, vii, x–xi.

152. See René Girard, *The Violence and the Sacred* (Baltimore: John Hopkins University Press, 1972.

153. See generally Saul Friedlander, ed., *Probing the Limits of Representation* (Cambridge: Harvard University Press, 1992.) See, e.g., Elie Wiesel, *Night* Stella Rodway & Francis Mauriac, trans. (Bantam Books, reissued 1982).

154. See Aleksandr Solzhenitsyn, *The Gulag Archipelago: An Experimentation in Literary Investigation* (New York: Harper and Row, 1975). Miguel Bonasso, *Recuerdo de la Muerte* (Buenos Aires: Plancta, 1984). Jacobo Timerman, *Prisoner Without a Name, Cell without a Number* (New York: Knopf, 1981).

155. Czeslaw Milosz, *The Witness of Poetry* (Cambridge, Mass.: Harvard University Press, 1983).

156. Havel, *Power of the Powerless*. Bernhard Schlink, *The Reader*, Trans. Carol Brown Janeway (N.Y.: Vintage Int'l, 1998).

157. See W. Gunther Plaut, ed., "Genesis" in *The Torah: A Modern Commentary* (New York: Union of American Hebrew Congregations, 1981), 32:4–17.

158. "Deliver me, I pray, from the hand of my brother, from the hand of Esau. . . ." Gen. 32:11.

159. See Arnold van Gennep, *The Rites of Passage*, trans. Monika B. Vizedom and Gabrielle L. Caffee (Chicago: University of Chicago Press, 1960).

160. See *The Tempest* 5.1.211–14.

161. See ibid., 3.3.52–77.

162. See ibid., 4.1.

163. Ibid., 5.1. 27–32.

164. See Stanley Cavell, *Disowning Knowledge in Six Plays of Shakespeare* (Cambridge: Harvard University Press, 1987).

165. See Jürgen Habermas, *A Berlin Republic: Writings on Germany*, trans. Steven Rendall (Lincoln: University of Nebraska Press 1997).

166. See Maurice Bloch, *Ritual, History, and Power: Selected Papers in Anthropology* (London: Athlone Press, 1989), 282 (discussing role of ritual in constructing time).

167. See Gordon, "Undoing Historical Injustice."

168. For a thoughtful treatment, see Robert Gordon, "Critical Legal Histories," *Stanford Law Review* 36 (1984): 57.

*Chapter 4*

1. United Nations, Economic and Social Council, 45th Session, *Study Concerning the Right to Restitution, Compensation, and Rehabilitation for Victims of Gross Violations of Human Rights and Fundamental Freedoms: Final Report*, prepared by Theodor Van Boven, 2 July 1993, U.N. doc. E/CN.4/suh.2/1993/8; Theodor Meron, *Human Rights and Humanitarian Norms as Customary Law* (Oxford: Clarendon Press, 1989), 171, n24; 1989, Nigel S. Rodley, *The Treatment of Prisoners Under International Law* (Oxford: Clarendon Press, 1999).

2. W. Gunther Plaut, ed., "Exodus," in *The Torah: A Modern Commentary* (New York: Union of American Hebrew Congregations, 1981), Ibid., 12:35.

3. Ibid., 12:35, 36.

4. Ibid., 3:21–22.

5. See Nehama Leibowitz, *Studies in Shemot: The Book of Exodus*, trans. Aryeh Newman (Jerusalem: World Zionist Organization, Department for Torah Education and Culture in the Diaspora, 1976),185.

6. Germany's obligation to pay for war-related wrongs is set out in the 1907 "Hague Convention IV Respecting the Laws and Customs of War on Land." Article 3 of the convention states: "A belligerent Party which violates the provisions of the said Regulations shall, if the case demands, be liable to pay compensation. It shall be responsible for all acts committed by persons forming part of its armed forces." "Hague Convention Regarding the Laws and Customs of War on Land", Art 3 (entered into force, 26 January 1910), U.S.T.S. 539 (providing for obligation to pay indemnity). See Article 41 of the Hague Convention IV (providing for right to demand indemnity for losses sustained in cases of violation); the Four Geneva Conventions of 12 August 1949 (providing for liability in case of grave breaches). Article 68 of the Geneva Convention relative to the treatment of prisoners of war provides for claims of compensation for prisoners of war. Convention (No. IV) Relative to the Protection of Civilian Persons in Time of War (entered into force 21 October 1950), 6 U.S.T.S. 3114. Protocol I ("Protocol Additional to the Geneva Conventions of 12 August 1949 and Relating To The Protection of Victims of International Armed Conflicts" (entered into force 7 December 1978) provides at Article 91 that parties violating provisions of the convention "shall be liable to pay compensation," *International Law Materials* 16 (1977): 1392. See Hugo Grotius, *Rights of War and Peace: Including the Law of Nature and of Nations* (Winnipeg, Can.: Hyperion Press, 1979), 10. See also Percy Bordwell, *The Law of War between Belligerents: A History and Commentary* (Littleton, Colo.: Fred B. Rothman, 1994).

7. Treaty of Versailles, June 28, 1919, Art 231, part VIII, in *Consolidated Treaty Series*, ed. Clive Parry, vol. 225 (1919).

8. Article 232 provides: "The Allied and Associated Governments recognize that the resources of Germany are not adequate, after taking into account permanant diminutions of such resources which will result from other provisions of the present Treaty, to make complete reparation for all such loss and damage." Ibid.

9. See Federal Republic of Germany, *Restitution*, English ed. (Bonn: Press and Information Office of the Federal Government, June 1988).

10. For an account of the negotiations process, see Nana Sagi, *German Reparations: A History of the Negotiations* (Jerusalem: Magnes Press, Hebrew University, 1980). See also Frederick Honig, "The Reparations Agreement between Israel and the Federal Republic of Germany," *American Journal of International Law* 48 (1954): 564.

11. See generally Federal Republic of Germany, *Restitution*. See also Kurt Schwerin, "German Compensation for Victims of Nazi Persecution," *Northwestern University*

*Law Review* 67 (1972): 479. For a "victimological" approach, see Leslie Sebba, "The Reparations Agreements: A New Perspective," *Annals of the American Academy of Political and Social Science* 450 (1980): 202. For a critical analysis, see Christian Pross, *Paying for the Past: The Struggle over Reparations for Surviving Victims of the Nazi Terror* (Baltimore and London: Johns Hopkins University Press, 1998).

12. Regarding the extension of German compensation to Jewish victims of Nazi persecution in the East, see David Binder, "Jews of Nazi Era Get Claims Details," *New York Times*, 22 December 1992, International section.

13. Ameur Zemmali, "Reparations for Victims of Violations of International Humanitarian Law," in *Seminar on the Right to Restitution, Compensation, and Rehabilitation for Victims of Gross Violations of Human Rights and Fundamental Freedoms* (Maastricht: Netherlands Institute of Human Rights, 1992), 61–75.

14. See generally Sagi, *German Reparations*.

15. *Shilumim* derives from the prophetic tradition. For a discussion of these two concepts and their meaning in the context of the reparations agreement, see Axel Frohn, ed., *Holocaust and Shilumim: The Policy of Wiedergutmachung in the Early 1950s* (Washington, D.C.: German Historical Institute, 1991), 1–5.

16. *Velásquez-Rodríguez Judgment*, Inter-Am. Ct. H.R., Ser. C, No. 4 (1988); *Godinez Judgment*, Inter-Am. Ct. H.R., Ser. C, No. 5 (1989); *Fairen Garbi and Solis Corrales Judgment*, Inter-Am. Ct. H.R. Ser. C, No. 6 (1989). The duty of states to "prevent, investigate and punish" violations appears in the *Velásquez Judgment* at paragraph 166. For a detailed account of these cases written by two of the attorneys in the litigation, see Juan E. Mendez and José Miguel Vivanco, "Disappearances and the Inter-American Court: Reflections on a Litigation Experience," *Hamline Law Review* 13 (1990): 507.

17. Honduras did ultimately assume its reparatory duties. According to Steve Hernandez of Americas Watch (conversation with author, Washington, D.C., July 23, 1997), compensation was awarded in the amount of $300,000 in the *Velásquez-Rodríguez Judgment*, and $250,000 in the *Godinez Judgment*.

18. *Velásquez-Rodríguez Compensation Judgment*, Inter-Am. Ct. H.R., Ser. C, No. 4 (1989), ¶ 46 (see ¶ 39 regarding duty to make moral and material compensation).

19. J. Irizarry & Puente, "The Responsibility of the State as a 'Juristic Person' in Latin America," *Tulane Law Review* 18 (1944): 408, 436 (distinguishing between "material" and "moral" damage). See also H. Street, *Governmental Liability: A Comparative Study* (Cambridge: Cambridge University Press, 1953), 62–63; Linda L. Schlueter and Kenneth R. Redden, *Punitive Damages*, 3d ed. (Charlottesville, Va.: Michie Butterworth, 1990) (analyzing various applications in civil law tradition).

20. *Decision on Full Stop and Due Obedience Laws*, Inter-Am. C.H.R., Report No. 28/92 (Argentina, 1992); *Decision on the Ley de Caducidad*, Inter-Am. C.H.R., Report No. 29/92 (Uruguay, October 2, 1992).

21. The investigatory report is entitled *Informe de la Comicíon Nacional de Verdad y Reconciliacion (Report of the Chilean National Commission for Truth and Reconciliation)*, 2 vols., trans. Phillip E. Berryman (Notre Dame: University of Notre Dame Press, 1993) (hereafter *Chilean Truth and Reconciliation Report*).

For an account of the steps taken by the Aylwin regime, see José Zalaquett, "Balancing Ethical Imperatives and Political Constraints: The Dilemma of New Democracies Confronting Past Human Rights Violations," *Hastings Law Journal* 43 (1992): 1425, 1432–38. See also Jorge Correa, "Dealing with Past Human Rights Violations: The Chilean Case after Dictatorship," *Notre Dame Law Review* 67 (1992): 1455.

22. Address by President Patricio Aylwin to the Chilean people, March 5, 1991,

transcribed by the British Broadcasting Corporation, March 6, 1991. Law No. 19, 123 (Chile, February 8, 1992) provides survivors with a life pension as well as a lump sum, and in kind benefits to health care and education.

23. *Indemnification Law*, No. 24.043 (Argentina, 1991).

24. See *Decision on the Ley de Caducidad* (cited in note 20 above).

25. *Chilean Truth and Reconciliation Report*, 838–40.

26. The term "fair compensation" in the Inter-American Convention on Human Rights, Art 61 (1), is interpreted by the Inter-American Court as compensatory damages. See United Nations, *Study Concerning the Right to Restitution, Compensation, and Rehabilitation for Victims of Gross Violations of Human Rights and Fundamental Freedoms* (cited in note 1 above), at 38.

27. See *El Amparo* case (Reparations), Inter-Am. Ct. H.R. (Ser. C.) ¶ 34 (September 14, 1996), reprinted in the 1996 Annual Report.

28. For a related scholarly discussion of the role of dignity implicated in the punishment/impunity debate, see Jaime Malamud Goti, "Transitional Governments in the Breach: Why Punish State Criminals?" *Human Rights Quarterly* 12, no. 1 (1990): 1–16.

29. See United Nations, *El Salvador Agreements: The Path to Peace, Report of the Commission on Truth for El Salvador*, DPI/1208 (1992).

30. See "Guatemalan Foes Agree to Set up Rights Panel," *New York Times*, 24 June 1994, International section.

31. South African Constitution, Epilogue.

32. See *Azanian Peoples Organisation (AZAPO) and Others v President of the Republic of South Africa and Others*, 1996 (4) SA LR 671 (CC).

33. William Blackstone, "Of Public Wrongs," in *Commentaries on the Laws of England*, vol. 4 (Oxford: Clarendon Press, 1765), 5–6.

34. Jeffrie G. Murphy and Jules L. Coleman, *Philosophy of Law: An Introduction to Jurisprudence* (Boulder: Westview Press, 1990), 114–17, 145, 157—60.

35. See, e.g., *Fédération Nationale de Déportés et Internés Résistants et Patriotes v Barbie*, 78 ILR 125 (Fr., Cass. Crim., 1985).

36. Mary Ann Glendon, M. W. Gordon, and Christopher Osakwe, *Comparative Legal Traditions: Text, Materials, and Cases on the Civil and Common Law Traditions, with Special Reference to French, German, English, and European Law* (St. Paul: West Publishing, 1994), 95–96.

37. *Decision on Full Stop and Due Obedience Laws*, Report No. 28/92, ¶ 32. See *Decision on the "Ley de Caducidad"* (cited in note 20 above), ¶¶ 35, 39.

38. Such purposes are elaborated in the Kantian theory of punishment. See Immanuel Kant, *The Metaphysical Elements of Justice: Part 1 of the Metaphysics of Morals*, trans. J. I. Ladd (Indianapolis: Bobb-Merrill, 1965).

39. For scholarly analyses of the various schemes, see generally "A Forum on Restitution," *East European Constitutional Review* 2 (1993): 30.

40. *Law on Extrajudicial Rehabilitation* ("*Large Restitution Law*") (Czech and Slovak Federal Republic, 1991), reprinted in *Central and Eastern European Legal Texts* (March 1991).

41. *Compensation Laws*, No. 25 (Hungary, 1991).

42. Federal Republic of Germany and Democratic Republic of Germany, "Agreement with Respect to the Unification of Germany," 31 August 1990, BGBI.II, translated and reprinted in *International Legal Materials* 30 (1991): 457 (hereafter "German Unification Treaty"). The principle of "restitution before compensation" appears in Article 41 of the treaty. The details of the scheme appear in Annex III of the treaty, having been part of the Joint Declaration of June 15, 1990, before their incorporation into the treaty.

43. *Land Reform Decision*, Combined Nos. 1 BvR 1170/90, 1174/90, 1175/90, Neue Juristische Wochenschrift 1959 (German Federal Constitutional Court, 1991). See also Keith Highet, George Kahale III, and Charles E. Stewart, "Former German Democratic Republic—Soviet Occupation Expropriations—Constitutionality of German Unification Agreement Clause Providing That Cash Compensation Is Sole Remedy 'Land Reform' Decision," *American Journal of International Law* 85 (1991): 690.

44. *Judgment of July 3, 1991*, No. 28/1991 (IV.3) AB, Magyar Kozlony No. 59/1991 (Hungary, Alkotmánybíróság [Constitutional Court]) (unofficial translation on file with the *Michigan Journal of International Law*). This decision has also been referred to in the literature as "Compensation Case III." For an analysis of the compensation law and the three Constitutional Court decisions resulting in its modification, see Ethan Klingsberg, "Safeguarding the Transition," *East European Constitutional Review* 2, no. 2 (Spring 1993): 44.

45. For a discussion of some of the moral considerations regarding restitution in the region, see Claus Offe, *Varieties of Transition—The East European and East Germany Experience* (Cambridge: MIT Press, 1996).

46. See Vojtech Cepl, "A Note on the Restitution of Property in Post-Communist Czechoslovakia," *Journal of Communist Studies* 7, no. 3 (1991): 368–75.

47. Alberto M. Aronovitz and Miroslaw Wyrzykowski, "The Polish Draft Law on Reprivatization: Some Reflections on Domestic and International Law," *Swiss Review of International and European Law* (1991): 223.

48. For a perceptive analysis of how restitution interest groups have shaped transitional party formation, see Jonathan Stein, "The Radical Czechs: Justice as Politics" (paper presented at Venice Conference on Justice and Transition, convened by the Foundation for a Civil Society, November 1993).

49. Václav Havel, *Open Letters: Selected Writings, 1965–1990*, ed. Paul Wilson (New York: Random House, Vintage Books, 1992).

50. Jon Elster, "On Doing What One Can: An Argument against Post-Communist Restitution and Retribution," *East European Constitutional Review* 1, no. 2 (Summer 1992): 16 (emphasis added).

51. For a good summary, see John Chapman, ed., *Compensatory Justice: Nomos XXXIII* (New York: New York University Press, 1991).

52. See Peter Schuck, "Mass Torts: An Institutional Evolutionist Perspective," *Cornell Law Review* 80 (1995): 941.

53. For the liberal perspective, see Randy E. Barnett, "Compensation and Rights in the Liberal Conception of Justice," in *Nomos XXXIII: Compensatory Justice*, ed. John Chapman (New York: New York University Press, 1991), 311–29.

54. See Schlueter and Redden, *Punitive Damages*. See also B. S. Markesinis, *A Comparative Introduction to the Law of German Torts* (New York: Oxford University Press, 1990).

55. Allen Buchanan, *Marx and Justice: The Radical Critique of Liberalism* (New York: Rowman and Littlefield, 1984), 40–85.

56. See, e.g., *Law on Extrajudicial Rehabilitation* (invoking international law as basis for property rights) (cited note 40 above).

57. See note 40 above.

58. See Steven J. Heyman, "The First Duty of Government: Protection, Liberty, and the Fourteenth Amendment," *Duke Law Journal* 41 (1991): 507.

59. See Lassa Oppenheim, "Peace," vol.1, introduction and pt.1 of *Oppenheim's International Law*, eds. Robert Jennings and Arthur Watts (London: Longman Group, 1992), 234–35.

60. See generally "German Unification Treaty."

61. *Law on Extrajudicial Rehabilitation* (cited in note 40 above), art. 1, para.1.

62. See generally *Land Reform Decision*. See also Offe, *Varieties of Transition*.

63. *Decision of the Czech Constitutional Court*, July 12, 1994.

64. *Judgment of July 3, 1991* (cited in note 44 above), paras. 3.3–4.

65. *Law on Extrajudicial Rehabilitation*, sec. 1, para 1.

66. See US Const., Amend XIV, § 4: "[N]either the United States nor any state shall assume or pay any debt or obligation incurred in aid of insurrection or rebellion against the United States . . . all such debts, obligations and claims shall be held illegal and void."

67. See Nicholas Tavuchis, *Mea Culpa: A Sociology of Apology and Reconciliation* (Stanford: Stanford University Press, 1991).

68. See, e.g., *Legal Rehabilitation Law*, No. 119/1990 (Czech and Slovak Federal Republic, 1990); *Law on Political and Civil Rehabilitation of Oppressed Persons* (Bulgaria, 1991); *Law on Former Victims of Persecution*, No. 7748 (Albania, 1993); *Legislative Decree No. 118* (Romania, 1990); *Law on the Rehabilitation of Victims of Political Repression* (Russia, 1991).

69. See *Russian Press Digest*, 19 August 1992, p. 91. See also *Current Digest of the Post-Soviet Press*, 2 September 1992.

70. See, e.g., *Law on Rehabilitation of Victims of Political Repression* (Russia, 1991), Art 12: "Individuals rehabilitated according to the procedure established by the present law are given back their sociopolitical and civil rights and military and special titles lost because of the repressions, and their orders and medals are also returned to them." Article 15 provides: "Individuals subjected to repressive measures in the form of deprivation of freedom and rehabilitated in keeping with the present law . . . are paid a monetary compensation of 180 rubles for each month of their incarceration . . . ."

71. See "Presidential Decree on Rehabilitation of the Cossacks," British Broadcasting Corporation, June 29, 1992; "Crimean Tatar Village Rehabilitated after 48 Years," British Broadcasting Corporation, November 2, 1992.

72. "Millions of people . . . [were] repressed because of their religious convictions, social, national or other status. . . . The Parliament of Russia expressing its condolences to the victims . . . regards the purges as incompatible with the notion of justice and expresses its resolute will to implement law and civil rights." See note 70 above.

73. For thoughtful analyses, see Jeremy Waldron, "Superseding Historic Injustice," *Ethics* 103 (1992): 4–28 and George Sher, "Ancient Wrongs and Modern Rights," *Philosophy and Public Affairs* 10, no. 1 (1980): 3, 6–7. See also Derek Parfit, *Reasons and Persons* (New York: Oxford University Press, 1989).

74. See Waldron, "Superseding Historic Injustice," 4–28.

75. See John Rawls, *A Theory of Justice* (Cambridge: Harvard University Press, Belknap Press, 1971), 284.

76. For broader discussion of the problems of intergenerational justice, see Brian Barry, *Theories of Justice* (Berkeley: University of California Press, 1989), 189–94.

77. For a general critique of these schemes, see András Sajó, "Preferred Generations: A Paradox of Counter Revolutionary Constitutions," *Cardozo Law Review* 14 (1993): 847.

78. Sagi, *German Reparations*, 62–72 (discussing Chancellor Konrad Adenauer's articulation of justifications for Germany's obligations to make reparations, citing K. Grossman, *Germany's Moral Debt, the German-Israel Agreement*).

79. Sagi, *German Reparations*, 66.

80. See *Chilean Truth and Reconciliation Report*, 13.

81. Commission on Wartime Relocation and Internment of Civilians, *Personal Justice Denied: Report of the Commission on Wartime Relocation and Internment of Civilians* (Washington, D.C.: Commission on Wartime Relocation and Internment of Civilians, 1982), 6–9.

82. *War and National Defense Restitution for World War II Internment of Japanese-Americans and Aleuts,* U.S. *Code,* vol. 50, sec. 1989 (establishing the Civil Liberties Public Education Fund) (1988). For a discussion of the movement for reparations and the implications of the act, see Sarah L. Brew, "Making Amends for History: Legislative Reparations for Japanese Americans and Other Minority Groups," *Law and Inequality* 8.1 (1989): 179. See also Peter Irons, *Justice at War* (Berkeley: University of California Press, 1993).

83. See "First Payments Are Made to Japanese World War II Internees," *New York Times,* 10 October 1990, p. A21 (reparation payments accompanied with letter of apology from President Bush on behalf of nation).

84. See, e.g., Tavuchis, *Mea Culpa.*

85. For a historical account, see Eric Foner, *Reconstruction: America's Unfinished Revolution, 1863–1877* (New York: HarperCollins, 1989). For a thoughtful contemporary analysis, see Jed Rubenfeld, "Affirmative Action," *Yale Law Journal* 107 (1997): 427 (discussing various race-explicit measures adopted in the post–Civil War period, e.g., *Act of July 28, 1866*; *Treaties and Proclamations of the United States of America,* U.S. *Statutes at Large* 14 (1868): 310. See also William Darity, Jr., "Forty Acres and a Mule: Placing a Price Tag on Oppression," in *The Wealth of Races: The Present Value from Past Injustices,* ed. Richard F. America (New York: Greenwood Publishing Group, 1990): 3–13.

86. For an elaboration of the case for reparations to African Americans, see Boris I. Bittker, *The Case for Black Reparations* (New York: Random House 1973); for discussion of the ongoing political debate, see Brent Staples, "Forty Acres and a Mule," *New York Times,* 21 July 1997, Editorial page.

87. For thoughtful analyses, see Michel Rosenfeld, *Affirmative Action and Justice: A Philosophical and Constitutional Inquiry* (New Haven: Yale University Press, 1991); Rubenfeld, "Affirmative Action."

88. For an early version of this view, see *Bakke v Regents of University of California,* 438 US 265, 324 (1978). For a later articulation, see *Richmond v Croson,* 488 US 469 (1989); see also *Adarand Construction, Inc. v. Pena,* 515 US 200 (1995).

89. Kathleen M. Sullivan, "Sins of Discrimination: Last Term's Affirmative Action Cases," *Harvard Law Review* 100 (1986): 78 (arguing that Court's focus on particular wrongdoers prevents it from accepting other justifications for affirmative action programs).

90. See Nell Jessup Newton, "Compensation, Reparations, and Restitution: Indian Property Claims in the United States," *Georgia Law Review* 28 (Winter 1994): 453.

91. Mari J. Matsuda, "Looking to the Bottom: Critical Legal Studies and Reparations," *Harvard Civil Rights–Civil Liberties Law Review* 22 (Spring 1987): 323.

92. *Law on Extrajudicial Rehabilitation,* sec. 3, para. 2.

93. Both the state of Israel and the Claims Conference were such representative bodies and received payments. See Honig, "Reparations Agreement," 567.

94. See *Judiciary Act of 1789,* U.S. *Code,* vol. 28, sec. 1350 (1993).

95. *Filartiga v Pena-Irala,* 630 F2d 876, 890 (2d Cir 1980) (holding act of official torture violates "established norms of the international law of human rights, and hence the law of nations").

96. Ibid., 884–87. See generally Ian Brownlie, *Principles of Public International*

*Law,* 4th ed. (New York: Oxford University Press, 1990) 238–39 (regarding international law on high seas).

97. *Forti v Suarez-Mason,* 672 F Supp 1531 (1987); *Siderman de Blake v Argentina,* 965 F2d 699 (9th Cir 1992).

98. *In re Estate of Ferdinand Marcos,* 25 F3d 1467 (9th Cir 1994).

99. *Kadic v Karadzic; Doe v Karadzic,* 70 F3d 232 (2d Cir 1995).

100. For the debate concerning the status of what this book terms "transitory torts" under customary international law, see Curtis A. Bradley and Jack L. Goldsmith, "Customary International Law as Federal Common Law: A Critique of the Modern Position," *Harvard Law Review* 110 (February 1997): 815 (arguing that international law should not have status of federal common law); Harold Hongju Koh, "Commentary: Is International Law Really State Law?" *Harvard Law Review* 111 (1998): 1824; See also Ryan Goodman and Derek P. Jinks, "Filartiga's Firm Footing: International Human Rights and Federal Common Law," *Fordham Law Review* 66 (1997): 463.

101. See *Argentine Republic v Amerada Hess Shipping Corp.,* 488 US 428 (1989). But see *Siderman de Blake,* 965 F2d 699.

102. *Filartiga,* 630 F2d 876.

103. See *The Foreign Sovereign Immunities Act of 1976, U.S. Code,* vol. 28, secs. 1602–1611 (1994). Occasionally jurisdiction has been found for other offenses, such as disappearances and prolonged arbitrary detention. See *Forti,* 672 F Supp at 1541–42.

104. *Torture Victim Protection Act of 1991, U.S. Code,* vol. 28, sec. 1350 (1993).

105. See *Siderman de Blake,* 965 F2d 699; *In re Estate of Ferdinand Marcos,* 25 F3d 1467. See generally Ralph Steinhardt, "Fulfilling the Promise of Filartiga: Litigating Human Rights Claims against the Estate of Ferdinand Marcos," *Yale Journal of International Law* 20 (1995): 65.

106. On theories of compensatory justice, see Cass Sunstein, "The Limits of Compensatory Justice," in *Nomos XXXIII: Compensatory Justice,* ed. John W. Chapman (New York: New York University Press, 1991), 281.

107. For a discussion of related problems, see Judith Jarvis Thomson, *Rights, Restitution and Risk: Essays in Moral Theory* (Cambridge: Harvard University Press, 1986), 66–77.

108. On the liability of the modern state for wrongdoing, see Peter H. Schuck, *Suing Government: Citizen Remedies for Official Wrongs* (New Haven: Yale University Press, 1983).

## Chapter 5

1. Arthur Koestler, *The Yogi and the Commissar, and Other Essays* (New York: Macmillan, 1945); See Maurice Merleau-Ponty, *Humanism and Terror: An Essay on the Communist Problem* (Boston: Beacon Press, 1969).

2. Carl Schmitt, *The Concept of the Political,* trans. George Schwab (Chicago: University of Chicago Press, 1996), 26.

3. W. Gunther Plaut, ed., "Genesis," in *The Torah: A Modern Commentary* (New York: Union of Hebrew Congregations, 1981), 18:16–19:38

4. Ibid., 18:23–32.

5. See Nehama Leibowitz, *Studies in the Book of Genesis, in the Context of Ancient and Modern Jewish Bible Commentary,* trans. Aryeh Newman (Jerusalem: World Zionist Organization, Department for Torah Education and Culture in the Diaspora, 1976), 185–86.

6. Plaut, ed., "Genesis," 18:20–21.

7. See US Const, Amend XIV, § 4 (stating that "neither the United State nor any State shall assume or pay any debt or obligation incurred in aid of insurrection or rebellion aginst the United States . . . all such debts, obligations and claims shall be held illegal and void").

8. See, e.g., *Texas v White*, 74 US 700 (1868).

9. See Jonathan Truman Dorris, *Pardon and Amnesty under Lincoln and Johnson: The Restoration of the Confederates to Their Rights and Privileges, 1861–1898* (Westport, Conn.: Greenwood Press [1953] 1977).

10. See *White v Hart*, 80 US 646 (1871) (describing operation of Reconstruction Acts requiring rebel states to submit to terms established by Congress in order to be restored to pre-insurrection status).

11. See US Const, Amend XIV, § 3 ("But Congress may, by a vote of two-thirds of each house, remove such disability"). This section took effect in July 1868.

12. See *Oxford English Dictionary*, 2nd ed. (OED), s.v. "purgation: canonical purgation" (i.e., as prescribed by the canon law), the affirmation on oath of his innocence by the accused in a spiritual court, confirmed by the oaths of several of his peers."

13. See US Const, Amend XIV.

14. As provided for in the provision itself, the disqualifications were removed by Congress in 1868. See House Committee on the Judiciary, *Removal of Disabilities Imposed by the Fourteenth Article of the Constitution*, 55th Cong., 2d sess., 1898, H. Rept. 1407.

15. See *Mississippi v Johnson*, 71 US (4 Wall) 475 (1867) (upholding executive branch role in Reconstruction Acts); *Georgia v Stanton*, 73 US (6 Wall) 50 (1868); *Texas v White* 74 US 700 (1868).

16. See *Ex parte McCardle*, 74 US (7 Wall.) 504 (1869).

17. See *Ex parte Milligan*, 71 US (4 Wall.) 2 (1866).

18. See *Ex parte Garland*, 71 US (4 Wall.) 333 (1866).

19. See *Cummings v Missouri*, 71 US (4 Wall.) 277, 279 (1866).

20. Ibid. at 323.

21. On the distinctions between civil and criminal sanctions, see George P. Fletcher, "Punishment and Compensation," *Creighton Law Review* 14 (1981): 691; Maria Foscarinis, "Toward a Constitutional Definition of Punishment," *Columbia Law Review* 80 (1980): 1667. See also *Elfbrandt v Russell*, 384 US 11 (1966); *Kennedy v Mendoza-Martinez*, 372 US 144 (1963); *Wiemann v Updegraff*, 344 US 183 (1952) (striking oath regarding past affiliation with communists).

22. For a critical account of this widely held understanding, see Stanley Kutler, *Judicial Power and Reconstruction Politics* (Chicago: University of Chicago Press, 1968).

23. On this debate, compare Raoul Berger, *Government by Judiciary: The Transformation of the Fourteenth Amendment* (Indianapolis: Liberty Fund, 1977), with Robert J. Kaczorowski, "Revolutionary Constitutionalism in the Era of the Civil War and Reconstruction," *New York University Law Review* 61 (1986): 863.

24. See Norman E. Tutorow, ed., *War Crimes, War Criminals, and the War Crimes Trials: An Annotated Bibliography and Source Book* (New York: Greenwood Press, 1986).

25. See *Act for Liberation from National Socialism and Militarism*, Art 1 (Germany, 1946).

26. See Ingo Müller, *Hitler's Justice: The Courts of the Third Reich* (Cambridge: Harvard University Press, 1991).

27. For an account of the history of the period, see John Herz, ed., *From Dictatorship to Democracy: Coping with the Legacies of Authoritarianism and Totalitarianism* (Westport: Greenwood Press, 1982), 1–38.

28. See John Herz, "The Fiasco of Denazification in Germany," *Political Science Quarterly* 18 (1948): 569.

29. See Müller, *Hitler's Justice*.

30. See e.g., *Ordinance Instituting National Indignity* (France, August 26, 1944) See also *Decree of June 27* (France, 1944); Herbert Lottman, *The Purge: The Purification of French Collaborators after World War II* (New York: William Morrow, 1986), 194–210.

31. See Peter Novick, *The Resistance versus Vichy: The Purge of Collaborators in Liberated France* (New York: Columbia University Press, 1968).

32. See Henry Lloyd Mason, *The Purge of the Dutch Quislings* (The Hague: Nijhoff, 1952), 90.

33. On France, see generally Novick, *Resistance versus Vichy*; Lottman, *The Purge*, 249–63; Tony Judt, *Past Imperfect, French Intellectuals, 1944–1956* (Berkeley: University of California Press, 1992). On Holland, see generally Mason, *Purge of Dutch Quislings*.

34. See Hannah Arendt, *The Origins of Totalitarianism* (New York: Meridian Books, 1958).

35. In France, for example, a selective amnesty law was passed in 1947 and a universal amnesty law in 1951. The law of August 5, 1953 ended the administrative sanctions. See generally Lottman, *The Purge*.

36. Regarding Albania, see Human Rights Watch, *Human Rights in Post Communist Albania* (New York: Human Rights Watch, 1996). Regarding Bulgaria's "Panev" law, see *Democracy and Decommunization: Disqualification Measures in Eastern and Central Europe and the Former Soviet Union*, November 14-15, 1993, pp. 8–9.

37. See *OED.*, s.v. "lustration."

38. *Screening ("Lustration") Law*, Act No. 451/1991 (Czech and Slovak Federal Republic, 1991) enacted by a binational assembly of the Czech and Slovak Federal Republic. Pursuant to section 22, the act enters into effect on the day of its announcement and ceases to have effect on December 31, 1996.

39. There was much criticism of the Lustration Law. See Stephen Engelberg, "The Velvet Revolution Gets Rough," *New York Times Magazine*, 31 May 1992, p. 30; "Prague Approves Purge of Former Communists," *New York Times*, 7 October 1991; Aryeh Neier, "Watching Rights," *The Nation*, 13 January 1992, p. 9; Jeri Laber, "Witch Hunt in Prague," *New York Review of Books*, 23 April 1992, p. 5; "Letters Human Rights in Prague," *New York Review of Books*, 28 May 1992, p. 56; Mary Battiata, "East Europe, Hunts for Reds," *Washington Post*, 28 December 1991; Lawrence Weschler, "The Velvet Purge: The Trials of Jan Kavan," *New Yorker*, 19 October 1992, p. 66; John Tagliabe, "Prague Turns on Those Who Brought the Spring," *New York Times*, 24 February 1992, International section; "The Perils of Lustration," *New York Times*, 7 January 1992, Editorial page. In the Czech English Language Press, see Bill Hungrey, Jr., "Tempest over Lustration," *Prague Post*, 17–23 March 1992.

40. *Specifying Some Further Prerequisites for the Discharge of Some Functions in State Organs and Organizations*, Act No. 451/1991 (Czech and Slovak Federal Republic, 1991) (unofficial translation on file with author).

41. Remarks of Wolfgang Nowak, State Secretary for Education in the East German Land of Saxony, *Rapporteur's Report* (presented to The Foundation for a Civil Society, Venice, Italy, 1993), at 7.

42. Germany's disqualification provisions can be found in the Unification Treaty of August 31, 1990. See Federal Republic of Germany and Democratic Republic of Germany, "Agreement with Respect to the Unification of Germany," 31 August 1990, BGBl.II., translated and reprinted in *International Legal Materials* 30 (1991): 457 (hereafter "Germany Unification Treaty").

43. See *Decision No. 1*, Constitutional Case No. 32 (Hungary, 1993). Decommunization was also justified on the basis of security.

44. *Constitutional Court Decision on the Screening Law*, Ref. No. Pl. US1/92, (Czech and Slovak Federal Republic, 1992).

45. *McAuliffe v City of New Bedford*, 29 NE 517 (Mass. 1892).

46. See *Elfbrandt v Russell*, 384 US 11 (1966). See also *Branti v Finkel*, 445 US 507 (1980) (striking discharge based on party affiliation or support) (striking down condition of state employment on knowing Communist Party membership).

47. See *Elrod v Burns*, 427 US 347 (1976).

48. See *United States v Robel*, 389 US 258, 266 (1967); *Rutan v Republican Party of Illinois*, 497 US 62, 70–71 (1990). See also *Konigsberg v State Bar*, 366 US 36 (1961); *In re Anastapolo*, 366 US 82 (1961).

49. See United Nations, General Assembly, *Universal Declaration of Human Rights*, A/RES/217A(III), 10 December 1948, Art 2.

50. See Art 2(7), "International Covenant on Civil and Political Rights," 6 December 1966, *Treaties and International Agreements Registered or Filed or Reported with the Secretariat of the United Nations* 999, no. 14668 (1976): 171; Art 2(2), "International Covenant on Economic, Social, and Cultural Rights," 16 December 1966, *Treaties and International Agreements Registered or Filed or Reported with the Secretariat of the United Nations* 993, no. 14531 (1976): 3. See also 7(c), "International Covenant on Economic, Social, and Cultural Rights" protecting "equal opportunity" in employment.

51. *Constitutional Court Decision on the Screening Law* (Czech and Slovak Federal Republic, November 26, 1992). See also K. 3/98 *Judgment in the Name of the Republic of Poland Constitutional Court on the Incompatibility of Law of 17.12.97 on amendments of the Law on Judicial System and some other statutes with the Constitution of the Republic of Poland of 02.04.87.* As the court said in the Judgment of 3/98, "[A] transition from an authoritarian state to a democratic state can exceptionally cause solutions which would not be justified under normal circumstances."

52. Later, the Czech law was extended to the year 2000. See Jirina Siklova, "Lustration or the Czech Way of Screening," *East European Constitutional Review* 5, no.1 (Winter 1996): 59. See also "Constitution Watch," *East European Constitutional Review* 4 (Fall 1995): 8–10. Regarding the German understanding, see "German Unification Treaty."

53. See *Constitutional Court Decision on the Screening Law.*

54. See *Act Concerning the Records of the State Security Service of the Former German Democratic Republic* (Germany, 1991) ("Stasi Records Act"). See also "German Unification Treaty."

55. *Judgment by First Senate of Constitutional Court* (Germany, 1995) (author's translation).

56. See Act of 29 April 1985 on the Constitutional Tribunal amended by the Constitutional Tribunal Act of 1 Aug 1997.

57. See "Peace for Affirmative Action" *New York Times,* 21 February 1998, p. A2.

58. For a critical analysis, see Jon Elster, "On Doing What One Can," *East European Constitutional Review* 1 (1992): 15.

59. *Constitutional Court Decision on the Screening Law.*

60. See, e.g., *International Labour Organization Decision on the Screening Law,* GB.252/16/19 (Czech and Slovak Federal Republic, 1992).

61. See *Act on the Illegality of the Communist Regime and Resistance to It*, Act No. 198/1993 (Czech Republic, 1993).

62. *Constitutional Court Decision on the Act on the Illegality of Communist Regime* (Czech Republic, 1993).

63. See generally Dan M. Kahan, "What Do Alternative Sanctions Mean?" *University of Chicago Law Review* 63 (1996): 591.

64. See *Lustration Act 1997* (amended 1998), upheld in Decisions of Oct. 21, 1998, K 24/98, OTK ZV 1998, 507; and *Nov. 10*, 1998, K39/97, OTK ZV 1998, 542.

65. Robert Conquest, *The Great Terror: Stalin's Purge of the Thirties* (New York: Macmillan, 1968).

66. See Victor Turner, *The Ritual Process: Structure and Anti-Structure* (Ithaca: Cornell University Press, 1966); Paul Connerton, *How Societies Remember: Themes in the Social Sciences* (Boston: Cambridge University Press, 1989).

67. Compare Japanese Const, Art 9 (limiting Japanese military to self defense capacity), with Germany's *Basic Law*, Art 115a.

68. See Americas Watch, *Report on Human Rights and U.S. Policy in Latin America, With Friends Like These*, ed. Cynthia Brown (New York: Pantheon Books, 1985).

69. For discussion of some of these regime changes, see *Transitions from Authoritarian Rule: Latin America*, ed. Guillermo O'Donnell et al. (Baltimore: Johns Hopkins University Press, 1986).

70. See Leonard Bird, *Costa Rica: The Unarmed Democracy* (London: Sheppard Press, 1984).

71. See *OED*, s.v. "expurgate."

72. See Lawyers Committee for Human Rights Report, *El Salvador's Negotiated Revolution: Prospects for Legal Reform* (New York: Lawyers Committee for Human Rights, 1993), 50–56.

73. See *OED*, s.v. "purge."

74. See Americas Watch, *El Salvador and Human Rights: The Challenge of Reform* (New York: Human Rights Watch, 1991).

75. For an early expression of this argument, see James Madison, *The Federalist No. 10*, ed. Clinton Rossiter (Middletown, Conn.: Wesleyan University Press, 1961).

76. See Peace Agreement, Annex United Nations Letter dated 27 Jan 1992 from the Permanent Representative of El Salvador to the United Nations addressed to the Secretary General A/46/864 S/23501 (January 30, 1992): 2–3.

77. See Human Rights Watch/Americas National Coalition for Haitian Refugees, *Security Compromised: Recycled Haitian Soldiers on the Front Line*, vol. 7, no. 3 (New York: Human Rights Watch, 1995).

78. Ibid., 1–2, 67.

79. Even by the human rights community. See, e.g. *Human Right Watch World Report 1996* (New York: Human Rights Watch, 1997), 91–93.

80. See *Korematsu v United States*, 323 US 214 (1944).

81. See *Dennis v United States*, 341 US 494 (1951) (upholding prosecution under Smith Act of national leaders of U.S. Communist Party).

82. See Hans Mommsen, *From Weimar to Auschwitz* (Princeton, N.J.: Princeton University Press, 1991). See generally Robert Moss, *The Collapse of Democracy* (London: Abacus, 1977).

83. For the origins of the notion of "militant democracy" in political theory, see Karl Lowenstein, "Militant Democracy and Fundamental Rights," *American Political Science Review* 31 (1937): 417. For the constitutional provisions defining the scope of the vigilant constitutional democracy, the *Basic Law*, Article 21(2) states: "Parties which by reason of their aims or the behavior of their adherents, seek to impair or abolish the free democratic basic order or to endanger the existence of the Federal Republic of Germany shall be unconstitutional."

84. See *Socialist Reich Party Case*, 2 BVerfGE 1 (Germany, 1952); and *Communist Party Case*, 5 BVerfGE 85 (Germany, 1956).

85. Ibid.

86. Constn of the Rep. of Turkey, Art. 69 (amend. 1995); Constn of Portugal, Art. 46 (1992).

87. See, e.g., Republic of Bulgaria Const of July 12, 1991; Republic of Hungary Const, as amended by Act No. 31 of 1989, Art 3(3).

88. See Gordon Wightman, ed., *Party Formation in East-Central Europe: Post-Communist Politics in Czechoslovakia, Hungary, Poland, and Bulgaria:* (Aldershot, England: Edward Elgar, 1995), 205.

89. Excerpt from the Decree of the President of the Russian Federation of August 23, 1991, No. 25, "On Banning the Activity of the Communist Party of the RSFSR" (on file at University of Chicago Center for Constitutionalism in Eastern Europe).

90. See David Remnick, "The Trial of the Old Regime," *New Yorker,* 30 November 1992, p. 104.

91. See Russian Federation Const, Art 165-1, stating that "[t]he Constitutional Court of the Russian Federation will decide the constitutionality of . . . political parties and other public associations."

92. *Communist Party Decision* (on file at University of Chicago Center for Constitutionalism in Eastern Europe.

93. L. Aleksandrova, "Decree of the RSFSR President on the Activities of the CPU and CP RSFSR," *Rossiiskaya Gazeta,* 9 November 1991, p. 2, available in Lexis, World Library, SPD file.

94. See Kelly Couturier, "Turkey Bans Islam-Based Political Party," *Washington Post,* 17 January 1998, p. A20. Regarding the closing down of the "Welfare" Party, see http://www.turkey.org/turkey/politics/p-party.htm.

95. See Michael Walzer, *On Toleration* (New Haven: Yale University Press, 1997). For a related discussion regarding religion, see Ruti Teitel, "A Critique of Religion as Politics in the Public Sphere," *Cornell Law Review* 78 (1993): 747.

96. See John Rawls, "The Law of Peoples," in *On Human Rights: The Oxford Amnesty Lectures, 1993,* ed. Stephen Shute and Susan Hurley (New York: Basic Books, 1993). See also Yael Tamir, *Liberal Nationalism* (Princeton: Princeton University Press, 1993).

97. Plaut, ed., "Exodus," in *The Torah* 18: 22–23.

98. Moses Maimonides, *The Guide of the Perplexed,* trans. Shlomo Pines (Chicago: University of Chicago Press, 1969), 54.

99. Plaut, ed., "Exodus," in *The Torah* 18: 22–33.

100. See US Const, Art II. See also Alexander Hamilton, *The Federalist no, 69,* ed. Jacob E. Cooke (Middletown, Conn.: Wesleyan University Press, 1961) (enunciating differences between proposed executive and the British monarch).

101. See Philippa Fletcher, "Bulgaria: Ex-Communists Win Control over Bulgarian Judiciary," *Reuter News Service,* 15 July 1994, Lexis, Bulgaria Country Files.

102. Indeed, historically, lustration rituals were associated with the census. These rites involving perambulations were part of the inspections of the census. See *OED,* s.v. "Lustration," definitions 3 and 4. See also *OED,* s.v. "lustrum."

103. John Rawls, *A Theory of Justice* (Cambridge: Harvard University Press, Belknap Press, 1971), 284–93.

104. See *OED,* s.v. "ban."

105. For an exploration of this question, see Charles Reich, "The New Property," *Yale Law Journal* 731 (1964): 733.

106. For an argument advocating structural responses, see Robert Gordon, "Undoing Historical Injustice," in *Justice and Injustice in Law and Legal Theory,* ed. Austin Sarat and Thomas R. Kearns. (Ann Arbor: University of Michigan Press, 1996).

## Chapter 6

1. On the contemporary explosion in constitutionmaking, see Julio Faundez, "Constitutionalism: A Timely Revival," in *Constitutionalism and Democracy: Transitions in the Contemporary World*, ed. Douglas Greenberg et al. (New York: Oxford University Press, 1993), 354, 356. See generally Jon Elster and Rune Slagstad, *Constitutionalism and Democracy: Studies in Rationality and Social Change* (New York: Cambridge University Press, 1988) (collecting essays that discuss relation of constitutionalism to democracy).

2. For the realist relation in political theory, see Arend Lijphart, *Democracies: Patterns of Majoritarian and Consensus Government in Twenty-one Countries* (New Haven: Yale University Press, 1984). For an account in a contemporary case study, see Courtney Jung and Ian Shapiro, "South Africa's Negotiated Transition: Democracy, Opposition, and the New Constitutional Order," *Policy and Society* 23 (1995): 269. For a realist account of the American Constitution, see Charles A. Beard, *An Economic Interpretation of the Constitution of the United States* (New York: Macmillan, 1956).

3. Aristotle, *The Politics*, trans. T. A. Sinclair (New York: Penguin Books, 1986). See also Charles H. McIlwain, *Constitutionalism: Ancient and Modern* (Ithaca: Cornell University Press, 1947) (describing ancient conception of constitution); Peter G. Stillman, "Hegel's Idea of Constitutionalism," in *Constitutionalism: The Philosophical Dimension*, ed. Alan S. Rosenbaum (New York: Greenwood Press, 1988).

4. Aristotle, *The Politics*, 198.

5. Ibid., 176.

6. Hannah Arendt, *On Revolution* (New York: Viking Press, 1965), 142. For a good historical account of the development of constitutionalism between the English Civil War and the start of the twentieth century, see M.J.C. Vile, *Constitutionalism and the Separation of Powers* (Oxford: Clarendon Press, 1967).

7. Arendt, *On Revolution*, 143.

8. Id., 232–34.

9. Id., 157.

10. Bruce A. Ackerman, *The Future of Liberal Revolution* (New Haven: Yale University Press, 1992), 57. See generally Michel Rosenfeld, ed., *Constitutionalism, Identity, Difference, and Legitimacy: Theoretical Perspectives* (Durham: Duke University Press, 1994) (analyzing relationship between constitutionalism and group identity).

11. Bruce A. Ackerman, "Constitutional Politics/Constitutional Law," *Yale Law Journal* 99 (1989): 453–547.

12. Ibid., 55.

13. Ibid., 14.

14. See Peter Berkowitz, "Book Review," *Eighteenth Century Studies* 26 (1993): 695 (reviewing Bruce A. Ackerman, *We the People: Foundations* (Cambridge: Harvard University Press, Belknap Press, 1991) (suggesting constitutional ratification elections were marked by low voter turnout).

15. See Bruce A. Ackerman, *The Future of Liberal Revolution*, 193. For a related continental argument, see Ulrich Preuss, *Constitutional Revolution: The Link between Constitutionalism and Progress*, trans. Deborah Lucas Schneider (Atlantic Highlands: Humanities Press, 1995).

16. Compare with John Rawls, *Political Liberalism* (New York: Columbia University Press, 1993), 90–99 (defining "political constructivism").

17. See Aristotle, *The Athenian Constitution*, trans. P. J. Rhodes (New York: Penguin Books, 1984), chs. 29–33.

18. See generally Juan J. Linz and Alfred Stepan, *Problems of Democratic Transi-*

*tion and Consolidation: Southern Europe, South America, and Post-Communist Europe* (Baltimore: Johns Hopkins University Press, 1996) (for an account based on path of transition), 10. See also Guillermo O'Donnell and Philippe C. Schmitter, *Transitions from Authoritarian Rule: Tentative Conclusions about Uncertain Democracies* (Baltimore: Johns Hopkins University Press, 1986).

19. South African Const, ch 15, §251 ("National Unity and Reconciliation"). Other constitutional arrangements reflecting such political compromise are provisions contemplating continuation of the executive power, overseen by a transitional executive council.

20. South African Const, preamble, states: "Whereas it is necessary for such purposes that provision should be made for the promotion of national unity and the restructuring and continued governance of South Africa *while an elected Constitutional Assembly draws up a final Constitution . . .*" (emphasis added).

21. The contemplated second constitution was held invalid by the country's Constitutional Court pursuant to the transitional constitution's animating principles. See *In re Certification of the Constitution of the Republic of South Africa*, 1996 (4) SALR 744 (CC) (S. Afr.). The final constitution was certified shortly before this book went into final form for publication. Compare Germany's Basic Law Art 79(3) (so-called perpetuity clause).

22. Schedule 4 sets forth "Constitutional Principles" not to be altered or contradicted by any subsequent constitution, such as:

> The Constitution shall prohibit racial, gender and all other forms of discrimination and shall promote racial and gender equality and national unity.
>
> . . . .
>
> The legal system shall ensure the equality of all before the law and an equitable legal process. Equality before the law includes laws, programmes or activities that have as their object the amelioration of the conditions of the disadvantaged, including those disadvantaged on the grounds of race, colour or gender.

South African Interim Const, Act 209 of 1993, sched. 4, pts. III and V, reprinted in Dion Basson, *South Africa's Interim Constitution: Text and Notes* (Kenwyn, S. Afr.: Juta and Company, 1994). The way the constitutional consolidation process is expected to work was clarified in the Constitutional Court's decision invalidating a subsequent proposed constitution. See note 21.

23. *See* Andrea Bonime-Blanc, *Spain's Transition to Democracy: The Politics of Constitution-Making* (Boulder: Westview Press, 1987), 31; Jordi Solé Tura, "Iberian Case Study: The Constitutionalism of Democratization," in *Constitutionalism and Democracy: Transitions in the Contemporary World*, ed. Douglas Greenberg et al. (New York: Oxford University Press, 1993), 292–94. See generally O'Donnell and Schmitter, *Transitions: Tentative Conclusions*, 37–72. The subjection of the military to civilian rule is incomplete, however, as the constitution contemplates military power to protect the constitutional order. According to Article 104 of the Spanish Constitution:

> The Security Forces and Corps which are instruments of the Government shall have the mission of protecting the free exercise of rights and liberties and that of guaranteeing the security of citizens. . . . An organic law shall determine the functions, basic principles of action and the Statutes of the Security Forces and Corps.

24. For an account of the transition, see Kenneth Maxwell, "Regime Overthrow and the Prospects for Democratic Transition in Portugal, in Transitions from Authoritarian Rule: Southern Europe, ed. Guillermo O'Donnell et al. (Baltimore: Johns Hopkins University Press, 1986), 108–37. See Tura, "Iberian Case Study," 291–92.

25. For an overview of the transition and an analysis of the 1988 Constitution, see Keith S. Rosenn, "Brazil's New Constitution: An Exercise in Transient Constitutionalism for a Transitional Society," *American Journal of Comparative Law* 38 (1990): 773.

26. For examples of new limits placed on the exercise of states of siege, see Articles 136 and 137 as well as the presidential lawmaking associated with states of emergency. The Constitution of Brazil provides: "Legislative power is exercised by the National Congress. . . ." Brazilian Const, Art 44. Article 62 provides:

> In important and urgent cases, the President of the Republic may adopt provisional measures that have the force of law; however, he must immediately resubmit them to the National Congress which, if it is in recess, shall be convened in special session in order to meet within 5 days . . . .
>
> . . . .
>
> Provisional measures shall lose their effectiveness as of the date of publication if they are not converted into law within 30 days from the date of their publication, and the National Congress shall make provisions to regulate any legal relationship that may stem from such measures.

27. For an example of this argument, see Rosenn, "Brazil's New Constitution," 783.

28. For a brief overview of the negotiations, see "Chile: Chronology 1988–1991," vol. 4 in *Constitutions of the Countries of the World*, ed. Albert P. Blaustein and Gilbert H. Flanz (Dobbs Ferry, N.Y.: Oceana Publications, 1994), 33–36. Article 9 on political parties was amended, as were Articles 95 and 96, which had the effect of weakening the National Security Council.

29. Daniel T. Fox and Anne Stetson, "The 1991 Constitutional Reform: Prospects for Democracy and the Rule of Law in Colombia," *Case Western Reserve Journal of International Law* 24 (1992): 143–44.

30. William C. Banks and Edgar Alvarez, "The New Colombian Constitution: Democratic Victory or Popular Surrender?" *University of Miami Inter-American Law Review* 23 (1991): 55–57. See Fox and Stetson, "The 1991 Constitutional Reform," 142, 145.

31. See Colombian Const, transitory Art 6 (describing National Constituent Assembly), transitory Art 39 (vesting president with "extraordinary powers" to "issue decrees with the force of law" for three months), and transitory Art 30 (concerning amnesties).

32. See Rawls, *Political Liberalism*, 133–72.

33. For a comprehensive account of Japan's constitution-making history, see Kyoko Inoue, *MacArthur's Japanese Constitution: A Linguistic and Cultural Study of Its Making* (Chicago: University of Chicago Press, 1991).

34. For an indictment of "expert" constitutions for their failure to establish authority and stability, see Arendt, *On Revolution*, 144–45.

35. See Japanese Const, Ch III, Art 9. Chapter I of the Japanese Constitution concerns the emperor. Under Article 1, he is made the "symbol of the State." Article 3 states: "The advice and approval of the Cabinet shall be required for all acts of the Emperor in matters of state, and the cabinet shall be responsible therefor." Article 4 states: "The Emperor shall . . . not have powers related to government."

36. For example, Article 14 in Chapter I states: "All of the people are equal under the law and there shall be no discrimination in political, economic or social relations because of race, creed, sex, social status or family origin. . . . Peers and peerage shall not be recognized. . . . No privilege shall accompany any award of honour . . . ."

37. See Ian Buruma, *The Wages of Guilt: Memories of War in Germany and Japan* (New York: Farrar, Straus, Giroux, 1994), 153–76.

38. See generally Norman E. Tutorow, ed., *War Crimes, War Criminals, and War Crimes Trials: An Annotated Bibliography and Source Book* (New York: Greenwood Press, 1986), 257–82 (listing sources on war crimes trials in Asia).

39. See *Basic Law for the Federal Republic of Germany* (1949), translated in Peter H. Merkl, *The Origin of the West German Republic* (New York: Oxford University Press, 1963), app. at 213, p. 319. See also Klaus H. Goetz and Peter J. Cullen, eds., *Constitutional Policy in Unified Germany* (Portland, Ore.: Frank Cass, 1995) (collecting articles on German constitutionalism).

40. See Merkl, *Origin of the West German Republic*, 22–24, 80–89.

41. Chapter V, entitled "The Federal President," consists of eight articles. Article 61 relates to impeachment. *Basic Law of the Federal Republic of Germany*, promulgated by Parliamentary Council, 23 May 1949, reprinted in Flanz, *Constitutions of the World*, vol. 7 (Dobby Ferry, N.Y.: Oceana Publications, 1996).

42. For a historical account, see Frank M. Buscher, *The War Crimes Trial Program in Germany, 1946–1955* (New York: Greenwood Press, 1989), 161.

43. *Basic Law*, Art 3(3). Article 4(1) provides: "Freedom of faith and conscience and freedom of creed in religion and in philosophy of life are inviolable."

44. See Donald P. Kommers, *The Constitutional Jurisprudence of the Federal Republic of Germany*, 2d ed., (Durham: Duke University Press, 1997). For an illustration of this constitutional principle in a decision of the country's Federal Constitutional Court, see *Socialist Reich Party Case*, 2 BVerfGE 1 (Germany 1952), translated in Kommers, *Constitutional Jurisprudence of the Federal Republic of Germany*, 218. See also Donald P. Kommers, "German Constitutionalism: A Prolegomenon," *Emory Law Journal* 40 (1991): 854.

45. Thus, political parties that "by reason of their aims or the conduct of their adherents, seek to impair or do away with the free democratic basic order or threaten the existence of the Federal Republic of Germany, shall be unconstitutional." *Basic Law*, Art 21, § 2. Moreover, individuals forfeit their constitutional rights to expression when there is abuse of the use of speech, press, teaching, and assembly "in order to undermine the free democratic basic order" (Art 18). See prior chapter, "Administrative Justice."

46. See *Basic Law*, Art 74, § 3 (setting forth "eternity" or "perpetuity" clause referring to unamendability of "basic principles" laid down in Articles 1 and 20).

47. See Samuel P. Huntington, *The Third Wave: Democratization in the Late Twentieth Century* (Norman: University of Oklahoma Press, 1979), 23–24. On the East European transitions, see generally Timothy Garton Ash, *The Magic Lantern: The Revolution of '89 Witnessed in Warsaw, Budapest, Berlin, and Prague* (New York: Random House, 1990); Ivo Banac, ed., *Eastern Europe in Revolution* (Ithaca: Cornell University Press, 1992); John Feffer, *Shock Waves: Eastern Europe after the Revolutions* (Boston: South End Press, 1992); and Ken Jowitt, *New World Disorder: The Leninist Distinction* (Berkeley: University of California Press, 1992).

48. Hungary, for example, is still functioning under a much-amended constitution of the Soviet period. See Andrew Arato, "The Constitution-Making Endgame in Hungary," *East European Constitutional Review* 5 (Fall 1996): 31. See generally Péter Paczolay, "The New Hungarian Constitutional State: Challenges and Perspectives," in *Constitution Making in Eastern Europe*, ed. A. E. Dick Howard (Washington, D.C.: Woodrow Wilson Center Press, 1993), 21; Edith Oltay, "Toward the Rule of Law—Hungary," *Radio Free Europe and Radio Liberty Research Report*. (1992): 16. For much of its transition, Poland had been functioning under the so-called Little Constitution, an interim constitution limited to clarifying the structure of the prevailing political system. See Andrzej Rapaczynski, "Constitutional Politics in Poland: A Report on the Constitu-

tional Committee of the Polish Parliament," *University of Chicago Law Review* 58 (1991): 595. It was not until April 1997 that consensus could be gathered on a new constitution. See Andrzej Rzeplinski, "The Polish Bill of Rights and Freedoms: A Case Study of Constitution-Making in Poland," *East European Constitutional Review* 2 (Summer 1993): 26. See also Wiktor Osiatynski, "A Bill of Rights for Poland," *East European Constitutional Review* 1 (Fall 1992): 29. In Russia the struggle over the legitimacy of the country's Soviet-era Parliament and constitution led to a crisis culminating in violent extraconstitutional resolution. See generally Dwight Semler, "The End of the First Russian Republic," *East European Constitutional Review* 3 (Winter 1994): 107; Vera Tolz, "The Moscow Crisis and the Future of Democracy in Russia," *Radio Free Europe and Radio Liberty Research Report.* (1993): 1. In Estonia, 1992 elections were held in accordance with the Communist Constitution of 1938. The September 20, 1992, elections for the president and members of the Parliament were conducted according to the 1938 Constitution. See "Constitution Watch," *East European Constitutional Review* 1 (Fall 1992): 2, 5. In Albania, as of the fall of 1994, a new constitution had not yet been enacted. See "Constitution Watch," *East European Constitutional Review* 3 (Spring 1994): 2. A transitional "Law on Major Constitutional Provisions" remains in force.

49. See generally Paczolay, "New Hungarian Constitutional State," 21; Jon Elster, "Constitutionalism in Eastern Europe: An Introduction," *University of Chicago Law Review* 58 (1991): 447 (presenting account and analysis of transition to constitutional democracies in Eastern Europe). For the majority of states in the former Soviet bloc, the move to a democratically elected regime occurred through roundtable talks between the Communist Party and opposition. See generally Jon Elster, ed., *The Roundtable Talks and the Breakdown of Communism* (Chicago: University of Chicago Press, 1996) (providing comprehensive account of bargaining process enabling transition). In Hungary, the process of concluding the negotiations with a draft constitution took place in a process continually threatened by the possible breakdown of political consensus. As such, the constitutional amending process lacked prolonged deliberation, ending in speedy consideration in the Parliament where the amended document was adopted. See Arato, *Constitution-Making Endgame in Hungary,* 685.

50. See András Sajó, "Preferred Generations: A Paradox of Restoration Constitutions," *Cardozo Law Review* 14 (1993): 853–57. For a discussion regarding the phenomenon of constitutional continuity in East Central Europe, see generally Preuss, *Constitutional Revolution,* and Andrew Arato, "Dilemmas Arising from the Power to Create Constitutions in Eastern Europe," in *Constitutionalism, Identity, Difference, and Legitimacy,* ed. Michel Rosenfeld (Durham: Duke University Press, 1994), 165.

51. Regarding Hungary, see "Constitution Watch: Hungary," *East European Constitutional Review* 5 (Winter 1996): 10; regarding Poland, see "Constitution Watch: Poland," *East European Constitutional Review* 5 (Winter 1996): 16–17.

52. Restoration has certain affinities with the notion of "reactionary" change. See Albert O. Hirschman, *The Rhetoric of Reaction: Perversity, Futility, Jeopardy* (Cambridge: of the Harvard University Press, Belknap Press, 1991), 1–10 (discussing "reactionary" change).

53. See Lloyd Cutler and Herman Schwartz, "Constitutional Reform in Czechoslovakia: E Duobus Unum?" *University of Chicago Law Review* 58 (1991): 531–36; "Constitution Watch: Latvia," *East European Constitutional Review* 2 (Spring 1993): 8–9; "Constitution Watch: Estonia," *East European Constitutional Review* 1 (Spring 1992): 5; Draft of Georgian Const (on file with Center for the Study of Constitutionalism in Eastern and Central Europe, University of Chicago).

54. For a thoughtful account, see Paul W. Kahn, *Legitimacy and History: Self-Government in Constitutional Theory* (New Haven: Yale University Press, 1992), 58–59 (arguing the process of constitutionalism shifted from revolution to maintenance).

55. See Richard B. Bernstein, *Are We to Be a Nation? The Making of the Constitution* (Cambridge: Harvard University Press, 1987), 106. For an argument that continuity between the American Revolution and the U.S. Constitution was part of a single political experience, see David A.J. Richards, "Revolution and Constitutionalism in America," *Cardozo Law Review* 14 (1993): 577–78.

56. For example, the Union assumed the debts of the Confederation. See US Const, Art VI, § 1.

57. For the claim that there are three such constitutive stages, see Ackerman, *We the People: Foundations* (Cambridge: Harvard University Press, Belknap Press, 1991) 40, 58.

58. Compare "James Madison to Thomas Jefferson, 4 February 1790," in *The Mind of the Founder: Sources of the Political Thought of James Madison,* ed. Marvin Meyers, rev. ed. (Hanover, N.H.: University Press of New England, 1981 for Brandeis University Press); 175–79 (expressing skepticism over the desirability of frequent constitutional upheaval and revision), with "Thomas Jefferson to James Madison 30 January, 1787," in *The Portable Thomas Jefferson,* ed. Merrill D. Peterson (Harmondsworth, Eng., and New York: Penguin Books, Viking Portable Library, 1977), 415, 417 (arguing that "a little rebellion now and then is a good thing").

59. See US Const, Art V ("The Congress, whenever two thirds of both houses shall deem it necessary, shall propose Amendments to this Constitution, or, on the Application of the Legislatures of two thirds of the several States, shall call a Convention for proposing Amendments . . ."). On the amendment process, see Sanford Levinson, ed., *Responding to Imperfection: The Theory and Practice of Constitutional Amendment* (Princeton: Princeton University Press, 1995).

60. See Akhil Reed Amar, "Philadelphia Revisited: Amending the Constitution Outside Article V," *University of Chicago Law Review* 55 (1988): 1043 (evaluating whether Article V ought to be regarded as sole source of constitutional change).

61. See US Const, Art I, § 9, cl 1 ("The Migration or Importation of such Persons as any of the States now existing shall think proper to admit, shall not be prohibited by the Congress prior to the Year one thousand eight hundred and eight . . ."). The Constitution also provides for the capture and extradition of fugitive slaves. See US Const, Art IV, § 2, cl 3.

62. See US Const, Art V.

63. See Gordon S. Wood, *The Creation of the American Republic, 1776–1787* (Chapel Hill: University of North Carolina Press, 1969) (discussing impact of years of colonial rule in shaping Union).

64. See James Madison, *The Federalist No. 47,* ed. Clinton Rossiter (Middletown, Conn.: Wesleyan University Press, 1961), 301 ("the accumulation of all powers, legislative, executive, and judiciary, in the same hands, whether of one, a few, or many, and whether hereditary, self-appointed, or elective, may justly be pronounced the very definition of tyranny").

65. At the time of the Articles of Confederation (1791), distrust of centralized power was so powerful that the Continental Congress was impotent to tax and regulate commerce. Article VIII provided:

> [E]xpenses that shall be incurred for the common defense or general welfare, and allowed by the United States in Congress assembled, shall be defrayed out of a common treasury, which shall be supplied by several States, in proportion to the

value of all land within each state. . . . The taxes for paying that proportion shall by laid and levied by the authority and direction of the Legislatures of the several States . . . .

Article IX, in turn, provided:

The United States in Congress assembled, shall have the sole and exclusive right and power of . . . entering into treaties and alliances, provided that no treaty of commerce shall be made whereby the legislative power of the respective States shall be restrained from . . . prohibiting the exportation or importation of any species of goods or commodities whatsoever . . . .

For an argument suggesting a reading of the American Constitution in light of its historical legacy in the Articles of Confederation, though one not explicitly characterized as transitional, see Akhil Reed Amar, "The Bill of Rights as a Constitution," *Yale Law Journal* 100 (1991): 1131.

66. See Daniel A. Farber and Suzanna Sherry, *A History of the American Constitution* (New York: West Publishing, 1990), 80–81.

67. See Karl Loewenstein, "The Presidency Outside the United States: A Study in Comparative Political Institutions," *Journal of Politics* 11(1949): 462.

68. See Alexander Hamilton, *The Federalist No. 69*, ed. Clinton Rossiter (Middletown, Conn.: Wesleyan University Press, 1961), 415–20.

69. See US Const, Art 1, § 9, cl 8 ("No Title of Nobility shall be granted by the United States: And no Person holding any Office or Profit or Trust under them, shall, without the Consent of the Congress, accept of any present, Emolument, Office, or Title, of any kind whatever, from any King, Prince, or foreign State"), Art I, § 10, cl 1 ("No State shall . . . grant any Title of Nobility"); Alexander Hamilton, *The Federalist No. 84*, ed. Clinton Rossiter (Middletown, Conn.: Wesleyan University Press, 1961), 511–14; US Const, Art I, § 2, Art II, § 1, Art III, § I. See also James Madison, *The Federalist Nos. 52, 53*, ed. Clinton Rossiter (Middletown, Conn.: Wesleyan University Press, 1961), 327–32.

70. See US Const, Art I, § 8, cls. 11–16 (granting Congress significant military powers), Amend II ("A well regulated Militia, being necessary to the security of a free state, the right of the people to keep and bear Arms, shall be infringed"), Amend III ("No soldier shall, in times of peace be quartered in any house, without the consent of the Owner, nor in time of war, but in manner to be prescribed by law").

71. See US Const, Amend II; Sanford Levinson, "Comment: The Embarrassing Second Amendment," *Yale Law Journal* 99 (1989): 648 (noting that one foundation of the Second Amendment was "well-justified concern about political corruption and consequent government tyranny").

72. See US Const, Amend XIV, § 4 ("But neither the United States nor any State shall assume or pay any debt or obligation incurred in aid of insurrection or rebellion against the United States . . . but all such debts, obligations and claims shall be held illegal and void").

73. US Const, Amend XIV, §§ 1–2.

74. The Fourteenth Amendment states:

No person shall be a Senator or Representative in Congress, or elector of President and Vice President, or hold any office, civil or military, under the United States, or under any State, who, having previously taken an oath, as a member of Congress, or as an officer of the United States, or as a member of any State legislature, or as an executive or judicial officer of any State, to support the Constitution of the United States, shall have engaged in insurrection or rebellion against the same, or given aid or comfort to the enemies thereof. But Congress may by a vote of two-thirds of each House, remove such disability.

US Const, Amend XIV, § 3. This section took effect in July 1868.

75. *See* Kenneth M. Stampp, *The Era of Reconstruction* (New York: Knopf, 1970), 170.

76. Compare Raoul Berger, *Government by Judiciary: The Transformation of the Fourteenth Amendment* (Cambridge: Harvard University Press, 1977), 167 (arguing that "framers meant to outlaw discrimination only with respect to enumerated privileges" and that Framers did not intend "to open goals beyond those specified in the Civil Rights Act and constitutionalized in the Amendment"), with Robert J. Kaczorowski, "Revolutionary Constitutionalism in the Era of the Civil War and Reconstruction," *New York University Law Review* 61 (1986): 881–903, 910–35 (explaining amendments in context of republican theory of federal citizenship and generic nature of fundamental rights).

77. See generally Berger, *Government by Judiciary* (defending originalism); Robert H. Bork, *The Tempting of America: The Political Seduction of the Law* (New York: Free Press, 1990); Robert H. Bork, "The Constitution, Original Intent, and Economic Rights," *San Diego Law Review* 23 (1986): 823. See also Paul Brest, "The Misconceived Quest for the Original Understanding," *Boston University Law Review* 60 (1980): 204 (criticizing originalism); Henry Monaghan, "Our Perfect Constitution," *New York University Law Review* 56 (1981): 374–87 (criticizing Brest); H. Jefferson Powell, "Rules for Originalists," *Virginia Law Review* 73 (1987): 659 (offering principles for originalist interpretation); Mark V. Tushnet, "Following the Rules Laid Down: A Critique of Interpretivism and Neutral Principles," *Harvard Law Review* 96 (1983): 786–804 (denying possibility of originalism without communitarian underpinnings).

For a thoughtful perspective on originalism that argues for its relevance as a floor, see generally Jed Rubenfeld, "Reading the Constitution as Spoken," *Yale Law Journal* 104 (1995): 1119, which incorporates originalism into a "commitmentarian" interpretative model.

On "fidelity" to the Constitution, see generally Larry Lessig, "Fidelity in Translation," *Texas Law Review* 71 (1993): 1165.

## Chapter 7

1. Compare Samuel P. Huntington, *The Third Wave, Democratization in the Late Twentieth Century* (Norman: University of Oklahoma Press, 1991), 215, with Bruce A. Ackerman, *The Future of Liberal Revolution* (New Haven: Yale University Press, 1992), and Hannah Arendt, *On Revolution* (Westport, Conn.: Greenwood Press, 1963).

2. Ibid.

3. For the definition of transition in political science, see Guillermo O'Donnell and Phillippe C. Schmitter, *Transitions From Authoritarian Rule: Tentative Conclusions About Uncertain Democracies* (Baltimore: Johns Hopkins University Press, 1986), 6.

4. See Thomas S. Kuhn, *The Structure of Scientific Revolutions* (Chicago: University of Chicago Press, 1970), 52–76, 111–134. For a related argument against paradigmatic conceptualization, see Albert Hirschman, "The Search for Paradigms as a Hindrance to Understanding," in *Interpretive Social Science: A Second Look*, ed. Paul Rabinow and William M. Sullivan, (Berleley: University of California Press, 1987).

5. See Lon L. Fuller, *The Morality of Law* (New Haven: Yale University Press, 1964).

6. See H.L.A. Hart, *Punishment and Responsibility: Essays in the Philosophy of Law* (Oxford: Clarendon Press, 1968). See also George Fletcher, *Rethinking Criminal Law* (Boston: Little, Brown, 1978)

7. Regarding South Africa, see Kader Asmal, Louise Asmal, and Ronald Suresh Roberts, *Reconciliation Through Truth: A Reckoning of Apartheid's Criminal Governance* (Cape Town, S. Africa: David Philip Publishers in association with Mayibue Books, University of Western Cape, 1996).

8. For a more extended discussion of this point see chapter 3, "Historical Justice."

9. See *Nunca Más: Report of the Argentine National Commission on the Disappeared*, English ed, (New York: Farrar, Straus, Giroux, 1986) hereafter *Nunca Más*).

10. For the leading such elaboration in ideal theory, *see* John Rawls, *Political Liberalism* (New York: Columbia University Press, 1993).

11. For a broader discussion, see chapter 4, "Reparatory Justice."

12. See chapter 5, "Administrative Justice."

13. See, e.g., Ackerman, *Future of Liberal Revolution*..

14. See *Basic Law for the Federal Republic of Germany*, Art 79 (entrenching core democratic features despite its supposed provisionality).

15. Cf. Carl Schmitt, *The Concept of the Political*, trans. George Schwab (Chicago and London: University of Chicago Press, 1996), 31 n12.

16. See Peter L. Berger and Thomas Luckmann, *The Social Construction of Reality: A Treatise in the Sociology of Knowledge* (New York: Anchor Books, 1966), 86. See also Paul Connerton, *How Societies Remember* (New York: Cambridge University Press 1989). On construction in the law, see Pierre Bourdieu, "The Force of Law: Towards a Sociology of the Juridical Field", *Hastings Law Journal* (1987): 805, 814–40.

17. See Otto Kirchheimer, *Political Justice: The Use of Legal Procedure for Political Ends* (Westport, Conn.: Greenwood Press, 1980)

18. Thus, "prosecution" historically a form of "investigation." See 2d ed. (*Oxford English Dictionary*) s.v. "prosecution," definition 3. The same is true for "lustration," which according to the OED is also historically understood to mean to "view" or to "survey." See OED, s.v., "lustration."

19. On rituals of passage, see Arnold van Gennep, *The Rites of Passage* (Chicago: University of Chicago Press, 1960), originally published as *Les rites de passage* (Paris: E. Nourry, 1909) (for an account of this process in individual development); Victor W. Turner, *The Ritual Process: Structure and Anti-Structure* (London: Routledge, 1969), (discussing concept of "liminality" and its relevance to individual transformation); Nicholas Dirks, "Ritual and Resistance: Subversion as a Social Fact," in *Culture/Power/History: A Reader in Contemporary Theory*, ed. Nicholas Dirks, Geoff Eleyn, and Sherry B. Ortner (Princeton: Princeton University Press, 1944), 488. On ritual generally, see Catherine M. Bell, *Ritual Theory, Ritual Practice* (New York: Oxford University Press, 1992).

20. For related discussion see Murray J. Edelman, *The Symbolic Uses of Politics*, (Urbana: University of Illinois Press, 1964); John Skorupski, *Symbol and Theory: A Philosophical Study of Theories of Religion in Social Anthropology* (Cambridge and New York: Cambridge University Press, 1976),; Dan Sperber, *Rethinking Symbolism* (Cambridge: Cambridge University Press, 1974).

21. See Jürgen Habermas, *The Structural Transformation of the Public Sphere*, trans, Thomas Burger (Cambridge: MIT Press 1989).

22. See David I. Kertzer, *Ritual, Politics, and Power* (New Haven: Yale University Press, 1988). See also *Rites of Power: Symbolism, Ritual, and Politics Since the Middle Ages*, ed. Sean Wilentz (Philadelphia: University of Pennsylvania Press, 1985).

23. On symbolic processes of "evocation," see Sperber, *Rethinking Symbolism,* 143–48.

24. See Edelman, *Symbolic Uses of Politics.*

25. For a discussion of such rites of "institution," see Pierre Bourdieu, *Language and Symbolic Power* (Cambridge: Harvard University Press, 1991).

26. On the "cognitive dimension" see Steven Lukes, "Political Ritual and Social Integration," Sociology 9 (1975): 289. See Skorupski, *Symbol and Theory*; Kertzer, *Ritual Politics, and Power*; Sperber, *Rethinking Symbolism.*

27. See Judith Shklar, *Legalism: Law, Morals, and Political Trials* (Cambridge: Harvard University Press, 1986) (from a political theory perspective); Mary Douglas, *Purity and Danger: An Analysis of The Concepts of Pollution and Taboo* (London and New York: Ark Paperbacks, 1984), 96 (from an anthropological perspective).

28. Pierre Bourdieu, "Symbolic Power," in *Identity and Structure: Issues in the Sociology of Education,* ed. Dennis Gleeson (Driffeld, Eng. Nafferton Books, 1977), 112–19 see Lukes, "Political Ritual," 302–305.

29. See Kirchheimer, *Political Justice,* 430 (contending without law political justice would be "less orderly").

30. See Gunther Teubner, *Law as an Autopoietic System,* (Cambridge, Mass. and Oxford: Blackwell, 1993); Niklas Luhmann, "Law as a Social System," 83 *Northwestern Law Review* 83 (1989); Niklas Luhmann, *Essays on Self-Reference* (New York: Columbia University Press, 1990)

31. See H.L.A. Hart, *The Concept of Law* 2d ed. (Oxford-Clarendon Press 1994).

32. See, e.g., Ackerman, *Future of Liberal Revolution.* For discussion outside of the transitional context see Jeremy Waldron, "Dirty Little Secret," *Columbia Law Review* 98 (1998): 510, 518–22; John Ely , *Democracy and Distrust, A Theory of Judicial Review* (Cambridge and London: Harvard University Press, 1980).

33. A recurring source of such outside norms is international human rights law. See, e.g., *Germany Constitutional Court Decision* (October 24, 1996), BVerfGE, A2.2 BVR 1851/94; 2BvR 1853/94; 2 BvR 1875/94; 2BvR 1852/94, reprinted in *Juristenzeitung,* (1997): 142.

34. For a related point regarding alternation, see Jacques Derrida, "Force of Law: The Mystical Foundation of Authority," *Cardozo Law Review* 11 (1990): 919. On ritual de-differentiation, see René Girard, Violence and the Sacred (Baltimore: Johns Hopkins University Press, 1977), 300–301, 310–341.

35. See, e.g., Timothy Garton Ash, "The Truth about Dictatorship," *New York Review of Books,* 19 February 1998, p. 35; Priscilla Hayner, "Fifteen Truth Commissions 1974–1994: A Comparative Study," *Human Rights Quarterly* 16 (1994): 600.

36. For a penetrating discussion of a related point regarding the relation of truth to political power, see Michel Foucault, *Power/Knowledge: Selected Interviews and Other Writings, 1972–1977,* trans. Colin Gordon et al. (New York: Pantheon Books, 1980), 109–133; Charles Taylor, "Foucault on Freedom and Truth," *Political Theory* 12, no. 2 (1984): 152– 83.

37. See, e.g., *Nunca Más.*

38. See Roberto Mangabeira Unger, *Social Theory: Its Situation and Its Task, A Critical Introduction to Politics, a Work in Constructivist Social Theory* (Cambridge: Cambridge University Press, 1987).

39. See Rawls, *Political Liberalism* (theorizing regarding nontransitional circumstances).

40. See ibid.

41. See, e.g., Ackerman, *Future of Liberal Revolution.*

42. See chapter 6. See also Ruti Teitel, "Post-Communist Constitutionalism: A Transitional Perspective," *Columbia Human Rights Law Review* 26 (1994): 167.

43. See Ruti Teitel, "Human Rights Genealogy," *Fordham Law Review* 66 (1997): 301.

44. On the classical view, see Leo Strauss, *On Tyranny*, ed. Victor Gourevitch and Michael S. Roth, rev. ed. (New York: Free Press 1991).

45. See Schmitt, *The Concept of the Political*, 26–29.

46. This view shares certain affinities with the political theorizing of Jürgen Habermas, Sheldon Wolin, Edmond Cahn, Judith Shklar, and others emphasizing a liberalism situated in legacies of fear and injustice. See Jürgen Habermas, "On the Public Use of History," in *The New Conservatism: Cultural Criticism and the Historians' Debate*, ed. and trans. Shierry Weber Nicholsen (Cambridge: MIT Press, 1989), 229–40; Judith Shklar, "The Liberalism of Fear," *Liberalism and The Moral Life*, ed. Nancy L. Rosenblum (Cambridge: Harvard University Press, 1989), 21; Edmond N. Cahn, *The Sense of Injustice: An Anthropocentric View of Law* (New York: New York University Press, 1949).

47. See Michael Walzer, *Regicide and Revolution*, trans. Marian Rothstein (New York: Columbia University Press, 1974) (discussing the trial of Louis XVI).

48. *See* Louis Henkin, *The Age of Rights* (New York: Columbia University Press, 1990).

49. See *Prosecutor v Tadić*, Case No. IT-94-1-AR72, Decision on the Defense Motion for Interlocutory Appeal on Jurisdiction (Appeals Chambers, *International Criminal Tribunal for the Former Yugoslavia,*

50. For discussion of the effect of globalization on causation and agency, see Samuel Sheffler, "Individual Responsibility in a Global Age," in *Contemporary Political and Social Philosophy*, ed. Ellen Frankel Paul, Fred D. Miller, and Jeffrey Paul (Cambridge: Cambridge University Press, 1995).

51. See, e.g., *Velásquez-Rodríguez Compensation Judgment* Inter-Am. Ct. H.R., Ser. C, No. 4 (1989).

52. On the salience of time, see Jeremy Waldron, "Superseding Historic Injustice," *Ethics* 103 (1992): 4.

53. See generally Ronald Dworkin, *Law's Empire* (Cambridge: Belknap Press, 1986), 168–69.

54. See also Jürgen Habermas, "Kant's Idea of Perpetual Peace with the Benefit of Two Hundred Years' Hindsight," in *Perpetual Peace, Essays on Kant's Cosmopolitan Ideal*, ed. James Bohman and Matthias Lutz-Bachmann (Cambridge and London: MIT Press, 1997).

55. See Theodor Meron, "War Crimes Law Comes of Age," *American Journal Of International Law* 92 (1998); 462; Theodor Meron, *Human Rights and Humanitarian Norms as Customary Law* (Oxford: Clarendon Press; New York: Oxford University Press, 1989), 10–25 discussing convergence in normative definitions). See generally *1998 Yearbook of International Humanitarian Law* (The Hague: T.M.C. Asser Press, 1998–1958).

# Index

LaVergne, TN USA
03 December 2010
207085LV00005B/4/P